D-DAY TO
BERLIN

Also by Andrew Williams

The Battle of the Atlantic

D-DAY TO BERLIN

ANDREW WILLIAMS

Hodder & Stoughton

A CIP catalogue record for this title is
available from the British Library

ISBN 0 340 83396 3

Typeset in Sabon MT by Palimpsest Book Production Ltd,
Polmont, Stirlingshire

Printed and bound by
Clays Ltd, St Ives plc

Hodder Headline's policy is to use papers that are natural, renewable and recyclable
products and made from wood grown in sustainable forests. The logging and
manufacturing processes are expected to conform to the environmental regulations
of the country of origin

Hodder and Stoughton Ltd
A division of Hodder Headline
338 Euston Road
London NW1 3BH

For Chook, Lachlan and Finn

Contents

Author's Note

On a gloriously bright morning last summer I stood on the deck of a Portsmouth car ferry with my kids and a score of other holidaymakers to enjoy our approach to the coast of Normandy. It was a little after six o'clock – the light still gentle enough to throw everything into clear focus. To the west of the port of Ouistreham the sun was rising on a seemingly endless stretch of empty beach. It was a startling and, for me, unexpected view of a strip of coast I had spent the last six weeks studying in books and archive film. I don't know how many of those who stood at the rail beside me were sharing the same thoughts of sixty years ago, a memory perhaps of flickering black-and-white faces, anxious, sick, waiting for a ramp to fall, smoke rising above sand littered with the detritus of war. Later that morning we walked along the shingle bank at Omaha and I tried to explain to my boys why young soldiers from a country 3,000 miles away died at this spot. History can so easily become a catalogue of distant events, as shapeless and strange as the shattered German concrete above Omaha appeared to my children. So few of my generation and the next know what it is to experience war, although they are still fought in our name. 'War? You see sights you never want to see again, sounds you never want to hear,' one of the veterans of Omaha we interviewed recalled. John Burke treated the wounded on the beach on D-Day:

I'm walking somewhere today and I hear the air gushing through telephone wires and it sounds like a mortar – I still cringe up. It's not going to the movies and feeling good about it, walking out and going home and getting dinner. You stay in your hole – all day, all night, rain, snow, cold, people shooting at you. War is fear. There's no place to go. It was the same thing, day after day. You just say to yourself, when is it going to end?

The Second World War was fought for the most part by very young men, in their teens and early twenties, many of whom had never been more than a few miles from home before they joined the army. During the research for this book and the TV series it accompanies, I was struck by how deeply their memories of sixty years ago are etched. Memories of fear, pain and loss painted in intense primary colours. Memories too of an extraordinary comradeship. These vivid recollections are at the heart of this book and the BBC series, and I owe a great debt of gratitude to those who were prepared to share them with me. Many have done so, not from pride or pleasure at the recollection of the past, but as an act of remembrance.

A good deal will be written and broadcast this year to mark the sixtieth anniversary of the D-Day landings. This book and the BBC series it accompanies are an attempt to tell the story of the campaign in north-west Europe beyond the beaches. It is surprising how often people assume that once the Allies were ashore the final defeat of Germany was little more than a formality, but the decisive battles of the campaign were fought in the hedgerows and wheat fields of Normandy. As one senior Allied planner noted before D-Day, 'the crux of the operation is . . . likely to be our ability to drive off the German reserves rather than the initial breaking of the coastal crust'. It is impossible to tell the full story of the campaign in north-west Europe in three one-hour television programmes. This book is able to tackle more, but sadly even here there are gaps, such as the part played by the French Resistance, and men and women on the Home Front. This is primarily the soldier's story. I have tried to strike a balance between the strategic debates that shaped the campaign and the life of those in the field who fought it day after day. I am acutely conscious, of course, that the campaign in the west was fought against the backdrop of the titanic struggle in the east, and that it was the soldiers of the Red Army who claimed the final 'prize' – Berlin.

Of the many people who were involved in the production of the television series on which this book is based I would particularly like to thank my colleagues Rosie Schellenberg, Lucy Heathcoat-Amory, Martina Hall, Adam Levy and Frank Stucke. They played an equal part in the research and the interviews that are at the heart of the series and this book, and I am greatly in their debt. I am also grateful to our series consultant, Jack Livesey of the Imperial War Museum, who read this book in draft form and has been a much-valued critic. In the United States, the historian Patrick O'Donnell was generous with his advice and contacts. The Creative Director of BBC History, Laurence Rees, asked me to make the series, and it has benefited immeasurably from his sure editorial touch. Executive Producer John Farren steered it through the proposal stage, and Penny Heard and Helen Cooper have, with cool efficiency, kept the production on course. I have the unfailing 'eye' of Joanne King to thank for unearthing the marvellous images in the book.

I am very grateful to Rupert Lancaster at Hodder, who commissioned the book and was supportive throughout. He refused to flinch when the deadlines imposed by the broadcasting schedule began to rush towards us. I am also grateful to Hugo Wilkinson for tidying up the notes on sources and Ian Paten, who copy-edited the manuscript and improved it in the process.

Above all I wish to thank my wife, Kate Mavor, and my children, Lachlan and Finn, for their extraordinary patience and support. Too much of the work on the book was crammed into their time, but they were always interested and enthusiastic.

Andrew Williams
February 2004

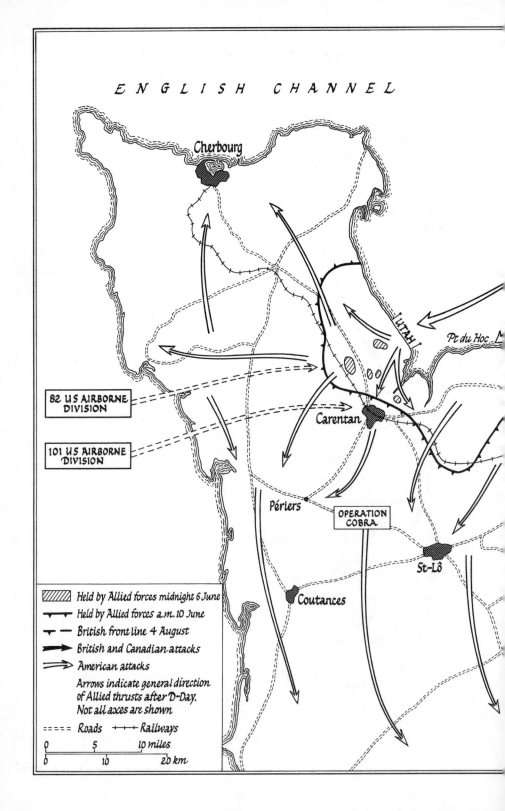

ENGLISH CHANNEL

Cherbourg

Pt du Hoc

UTAH

82 US AIRBORNE
DIVISION

101 US AIRBORNE
DIVISION

Carentan

Périers

OPERATION
COBRA

St-Lô

Coutances

Held by Allied forces midnight 6 June
Held by Allied forces a.m. 10 June
British front line 4 August
British and Canadian attacks
American attacks
Arrows indicate general direction
of Allied thrusts after D-Day.
Not all axes are shown
===== Roads   +-+-+ Railways

0   5   10 miles
0   10   20 km

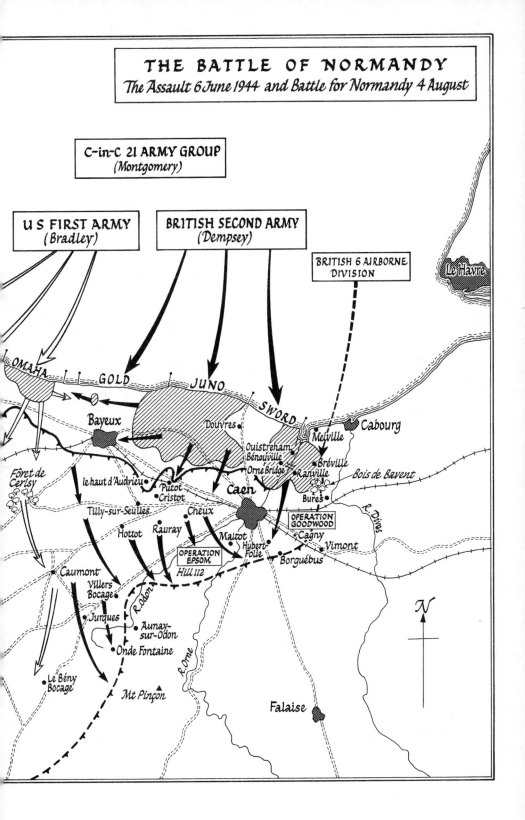

THE BATTLE OF NORMANDY
The Assault 6 June 1944 and Battle for Normandy 4 August

C-in-C 21 ARMY GROUP
(Montgomery)

U S FIRST ARMY
(Bradley)

BRITISH SECOND ARMY
(Dempsey)

BRITISH 6 AIRBORNE
DIVISION

Le Havre

OMAHA

GOLD

JUNO

SWORD

Bayeux

Douvres

Melville

Cabourg

Ouistreham
Bénouville
Orne Bridge

Bréville

Forêt de
Cerisy

le haut d'Audrieu

Putot
Cristot

Ranville

Bois de Bavent

Caen

Bures

Tilly-sur-Seulles

Cheux

Hottot

Rauray

Maltot

OPERATION
GOODWOOD

R. Dives

OPERATION
EPSOM

Hill 112

Hubert
Folie

Cagny

Vimont

Caumont

Villers
Bocage

R. Odon

Borguébus

Jurques

Aunay-
sur-Odon

N

Le Bény
Bocage

Onde Fontaine

Mt Pinçon

R. Orne

Falaise

CHAPTER ONE

'A DARK WALL'

0010 hours, 6 June 1944

S uddenly there was silence. The high-pitched scream of
wind that had held them for an hour stopped with a jerk.
The glider was falling free. It was a little after midnight.
Shoulder to shoulder in the flimsy body of the Horsa were
twenty-eight men of the Oxfordshire and Buckinghamshire Light
Infantry. The bantering and singing that had carried them across
the Channel were over – they were now above the coast of France.
In a matter of minutes Glider 1 would level out at 300 metres
on its final run in to land. Everything depended now on the skill
of the pilots.

Major John Howard reached into the pocket of his battledress
for the red baby shoe he had brought with him for luck – it had
belonged to his two-year-old son, Terry. Howard had suffered
from terrible air sickness during the practice flights, but not on
this one. Adrenalin was pumping now. This was the real thing;
they had spent nearly six months training for this moment.
Howard and his men were going into battle for the first time.
Minutes behind Glider 1 were five more with the rest of D
Company and a detachment of Royal Engineers, a force of 180
men in total. These few were the spearhead of the great Allied
invasion force that in the coming hours would attempt to thrust
its way into Nazi-occupied Europe.

Before take-off Howard had visited his men with encouraging

words, what he called his 'Ham and Jam farewell'. The company was to seize two strategically vital bridges close to the beaches where at dawn British troops would come ashore. The enemy's armoured reserves were expected to rumble westwards down the coast road to challenge the landings – first they would have to cross the River Orne and then the Caen Canal. 'Ham' and 'Jam' would be the code words for the capture of the bridges. 'Your task', Howard's orders helpfully pointed out, '[depends] on surprise, speed and dash for success'. A *'coup de main'* operation, the brigadier had called it; if all went to plan reinforcements from 6th Airborne Division would reach the bridges in the early hours of the morning.

The man entrusted with this most important of tasks was by no means a typical British Army officer. Howard had served in the ranks of the peacetime army and then as a policeman. The war had brought a commission and now, at the age of thirty-one, the command of D Company. He had made the most of it and had forged his men into a formidable unit. Just before take-off one of the company's gliders had been judged to be over-weight and Howard had asked for a volunteer to stay behind – no one had come forward. The men had chosen instead to shed some of their equipment. 'I had a lump in my throat as big as a damn football,' Howard later recalled. 'I was a bit emotional as we took off.' Private Denis Edwards was strapped into Seat 13, just a few feet from his company commander: 'Nothing I had experienced in training could compare with the sheer panic that engulfed me as I sat in the dark glider waiting for take-off and my first trip into battle. I gripped my rifle between my knees so hard that my knuckles must have shown white under the camouflage grease-paint. But at least the weapon stopped my knees knocking together.' As the glider left the ground Edwards's fear turned to exhilaration: 'I felt as if I had had a little too much to drink. I thought to myself, You've had it chum. The die is cast, and there is nothing you can do about it.'

The glider's pitch changed as the pilot began to force its nose up in preparation for landing. The moon was bright enough for Major Howard to judge they were close to their target:

Sitting on my left was Lieutenant Dan Brotheridge, my leading platoon commander, and he undid his safety belt. I held his equipment on one side and his platoon sergeant did the same on the other side and he leaned forward very precariously and opened the door. When Brotheridge slumped back into his seat again I looked forward at the fields of France and it had an amazing tranquillising effect on me. There you had horses and cattle grazing very, very quietly. They were taking no notice at all; it was so quiet it was like being on an exercise in England.

The glider turned sharply to the right and suddenly there below was the Caen Canal.

I looked down and immediately recognised where we were. I'd been studying aerial photographs, the shapes of fields and woods and churches with spires. We'd often practised the drill for landing in those wooden boxes [the gliders] – 'coffins', the men called them. You had to link arms with the man either side of you, put your fingers into a butcher's grip, lift your legs and just pray to God your number wasn't up. There was nothing else you could do. We were all in the hands of those glider pilots. The first thing I remember is this colossal bump.

The glider made contact with the ground, but not for long. 'For about forty to fifty yards we bounced in our wooden seats, as the darkness was filled with a stream of sparks caused by the skids scraping the ground; a sound like a giant sheet being ripped apart, a crash, and my body seemed to be moving in several directions. I was perched at an angle, peering into a misty grey haze,' Private Edwards recalled. 'There was an ominous silence. No one moved. We must all be dead, I thought. To be replaced by the realisation that this was not so, as bodies unstrapped themselves, and the interior of the shattered glider erupted into furious activity.'

The pilots had put them down only yards from their objective. The shadowy outline of steel girders loomed above them –

the bridge. Corporal Bill Gray was one of the first out of the torn and twisted glider: 'Lieutenant Danny Brotheridge leaned over, whipped open the door, and called, "Out Gun Out," and out I went with the Bren. As soon as we were all in position, Brotheridge said, "Come on, lads," and up and off we went, charging like mad up this slope towards the bridge.'

Howard was one of the last to force his way out of the splintered glider. 'I could see the tower of the bridge about fifty yards from where I was standing. The nose of the glider was right through the German wire fence. And above all, and this was the tremendous thing, there was no firing at all. We had really caught old Jerry with his pants down.'

Howard followed the platoon up the track. Just ahead of him there was a flash and a series of thuds — short-fuse grenades. The lead section was attacking the pillbox at the eastern end of the bridge. 'It went up with a hell of a bang and that was the signal to fire,' Howard recalled. 'By this time our men were halfway across the bridge.'

The first German soldier to see the platoon galloping towards him turned and ran. Hard on his heels was Lieutenant Brotheridge. One of the other sentries managed to fire a warning flare before he was cut down by a British machine gun. There was a sharp firefight with the German machine-gun posts at the western end of the bridge. 'It was a tremendous sight to see the tracer bullets firing in all directions,' Major Howard remembered. 'There seemed to be three different colours, red, yellow and white, with the enemy firing at us, and my men firing at them. And while this was happening I suddenly heard two more crashes behind me in the landing zone.' Gliders 2 and 3 had landed just yards from Howard's own. It was then that word reached Howard that Brotheridge had been shot and wounded in the neck at the western end of the bridge. His platoon had pressed forward, machine guns at the hip, and by half past midnight the German defenders had been overcome and the crossing of the canal secured. Lieutenant Brotheridge died half an hour later and was recorded as the first British soldier to lose his life fighting on D-Day. He would be mourned by a wife pregnant with their first child.

The other assault party had landed a few hundred yards along the road and taken the bridge over the River Orne without firing a shot. Only one of D Company's six gliders had gone astray – Howard's second-in-command and a platoon of men had been dumped nearly 15 kilometres away on the wrong river. But Operation Overlord, the assault on Hitler's European fortress, had begun well. Howard gave his wireless operator the order to send out the agreed signal – 'Ham and Jam, Ham and Jam'. D Company had taken its objectives; now it had to hold them.

Leutnant (Lieutenant) Raimund Steiner had deliberately broken orders. The staff at divisional headquarters had instructed all soldiers to sleep in their uniforms with their weapons close at hand. Steiner had changed into his pyjamas. A fine rain had been falling as he had cycled the short distance from the Merville Battery to his command post in the sand dunes. The forecast was bleak enough to convince him that weather and tide would rule out an invasion. It had been an exhausting day. The Allies had bombed the battery on 4 June and the garrison had been busy all day making good the damage. It was a tediously familiar exercise – the battery seemed to be the focus of special attention. A few weeks earlier the Allies had managed a direct hit on one of the reinforced concrete casements. It had barely left a mark, but the force of the explosion had thrown men around the bunker. Steiner had been carried out unconscious and bleeding from his ears and mouth. It had shaken him, but he had continued with his duties – it was a matter of pride. At twenty-three, the diminutive Austrian was already a seasoned campaigner – a veteran of the Russian front who had been severely wounded twice.

The Merville Battery had been built on the east bank of the Orne to defend the river's estuary and the entrance to the adjoining

Caen Canal. It was situated three kilometres from the shore to minimise the risk of enemy bombardment from the sea. Steiner directed his guns from a B-post in the dunes, which commanded a fine view of the estuary and the little port of Ouistreham on the opposite bank of the river. A telephone line had been sunk more than two metres down to ensure a secure link to the guns.

The battery presented a formidable defensive obstacle – Steiner considered it one of the best on the coast. To reach its guns an attacking force would have to pass through a perimeter fence, cross an anti-tank trench and a belt of barbed-wire entanglements, then a minefield and a thicket of wire five metres deep. Beyond all this machine-gun posts guarded the final approach to the concrete casements that housed the guns. The garrison numbered some 130 men from the 716th Artillery Regiment.

Steiner had settled down for what he devoutly hoped would be a quiet night. He had barely had time to change into his pyjamas before he was out of them again. The telephone had rung in his B-post at half past midnight – the battery was once again under attack from the air. Wave after wave of Allied bombers were pounding the fields around the casements and had all but destroyed the nearby village of Gonneville. Steiner's men had sheltered beneath four metres of reinforced concrete and rubble as the storm lashed everything except its intended target – the battery. Not long after the raid the first reports had begun to reach divisional headquarters of enemy air drops to the east of the River Orne.

The telephone had rung in the B-post again at 0430 hours – just before dawn. 'My Battery Officer, Buskotte, rang me; he was in shock,' Steiner recalled. 'A British glider had crashed close to the fourth bunker.' British paratroopers had blown holes in the wire and with reckless courage were crossing the minefield with machine guns blazing. There was fierce close quarters fighting around the battery and the British assault force was pushing on towards the concrete casements. It was difficult making sense of what was happening at the other end of the telephone: 'It was a pitch-black night with drizzle, nobody could tell friend from foe. I told Buskotte to immediately move the rest of the men and the wounded to Casement 1, my command bunker, which was very well fortified and had ventilation tunnels.' Steiner had reported the attack to General Wilhelm Richter of the neighbouring 716th Infantry Division, and support had been promised. But it was soon clear that the British had gained a foothold in the casements. The twenty or so men inside Bunker 1 were struggling to hold on: 'The airborne soldiers had begun working on the bunker. Some of the men inside were gasping for air, some cursing. Buskotte prayed one "Our Father" after the other. "We can't last long, Lieutenant," he told me, "we can barely breathe, the injured are moaning, we have no medicine, the air vents don't work." There were words of goodbye, talk of relatives . . . it was horrible.'

It was a little before half past six in the morning when the telephone rang at the villa in Herrlingen. The man charged with the defence of Nazi-occupied Europe was still in his dressing gown. Field Marshal Erwin Rommel was busy with last-minute preparations for what promised to be a special day. It was Tuesday, 6 June 1944 – his wife Lucie's fiftieth birthday. Rommel had left his headquarters in France two days before with the official intention of seeking an audience with his Führer. Thankfully Hitler was not able to see him until Thursday – that meant the best part of three days away from the war at home in Germany with Lucie. For six relentless months he had thrown himself into the task of improving the four thousand kilometres of coastal defences that made up the 'Atlantic Wall'. He had visited nearly every windswept beach between the Hook of Holland and the French port of Cherbourg. There was no doubting the urgency of the task. The Führer himself had stated, 'if they attack in the West that attack will decide the war'. There was very little reliable intelligence on where the Allies would try to land, but they would certainly come, and soon.

There was much still to be done. On Thursday Rommel would drive the short distance to Hitler's retreat in the Bavarian Alps and tell him so. In particular he would press for two more Panzer divisions and a rocket-launcher brigade to be placed under his command in the Normandy sector. Until then Lucie came first. The house was full of flowers; there were just the presents to arrange on the drawing-room table. Everything would be just so.

It was the housemaid who brought word that the field marshal was wanted on the telephone. The war had found Rommel on his special day. It was his chief of staff: a large number of British and American paratroopers and glider-borne infantry had been dropped in Normandy. No one at headquarters was sure what this meant, but perhaps, yes, it was the prelude to invasion.

There was not a shred of doubt in the mind of Lieutenant Raimund Steiner. From his B-post he could see the dark silhouettes of a vast armada approaching the shore: 'I looked over the sea and, as it got lighter, I could make out what looked like a black wall across the entire width of the sea. A dark wall in which lights flashed from time to time. That was when we realised: now they're coming. Their invasion fleet has arrived. It was so depressing, so hopeless.'

The battle for the Merville Battery was over. The gun casements had fallen and been briefly occupied by the British. The paratroopers had been sent to capture a battery capable of engaging the landing beaches, but for all the concrete and wire defences it housed only vintage 100mm field howitzers. The battery was once again in German hands, but there was little Steiner could do. Only the easternmost end of the landing beaches was in range: 'There were ships of all sizes. I came from the mountains and I had never seen anything like this before – big ships, small ships, cruisers, battleships – and then from the black wall we began to see the muzzle flashes. I thought, We can't do anything against that with our guns.'

Some 50 kilometres along the coast to the west, Gefreiter [Private] Franz Gockel looked out on the same wall of ships and prayed: 'We saw them at dawn, just after first light, an enormous fleet in front of us, erected there as if by ghostly hands. There was hardly a gap in the wall. We thought, we can't fight this, we can only sell our lives as expensively as possible. We had always been told if something happens here you can't retreat, you have to defend yourself to the end.'

It had been a little after 0100 hours when the alarm had sounded in Resistance Nest WN 62. It had dragged Private Gockel back to unwelcome consciousness. He had taken to his bunk at midnight and was due back on duty in under an hour. The alarm had sounded again and again in the last few weeks, and Gockel had dismissed the alert as another exercise to see how quickly the small garrison could respond to the threat of invasion. He had reluctantly swung his legs off the bunk and reached for his boots.

WN 62 overlooked the beach close to the village of Colleville-sur-Mer on the Calvados coast. Work was still taking place on the position. A network of trenches zigzagged its way between machine-gun, flame-thrower and mortar posts and two hastily constructed artillery casements. The casements gaped open to the elements – armoured flaps were yet to be installed in the apertures; until they were, the two 75mm guns they housed would be exposed to whatever the sea could throw at them.

WN 62 was home to fifty men from the 726th Grenadier Regiment, of whom the eighteen-year-old Gockel was the youngest. The sergeant's voice had echoed through the bunker; 'he said it was the highest state of alarm, but we'd heard the same thing so often before at first we thought, Go to hell,' Gockel recalled. 'But a couple of minutes later another non-commissioned officer came running into the bunker and shouted, "Men, this is the real thing, they are on their way."'

Gockel had run an adrenalin-fuelled 300 metres from the main bunker to his machine-gun post. To the relief of all, there had been only dark, empty sea. The platoon had been left to shiver and guess what the morning would bring. Allied bombers had droned back and forth across the Normandy coast all night. The darkness had been punctuated by bright orange flashes as more than a thousand aircraft attacked strongpoints from Caen in the east to the Cotentin peninsula in the west. With first light peace seemed to have returned to the coast. Then, through the dawn mist, Gockel and his comrades had made out the first dark outlines of the approaching invasion fleet – nearly eight thousand ships and landing craft.

The storm broke upon an 80-kilometre stretch of coast. At a little before 0530 hours the first shells came whistling in from the sea. Above the sea barrage some sixteen hundred planes from the United States Eighth and Ninth Air Forces were preparing to renew their assault. Clouds of smoke billowed across the beaches as shells and rockets from more than a hundred Allied warships tore great holes in the ground around Rommel's concrete fortifications. The bombardment seemed to grow in a deadly crescendo as the guns of the invasion fleet were joined by field artillery pieces carried on specially adapted landing craft. The defenders shrank back into their trenches and bunkers – each man fighting his private battle against stomach-twisting fear and the urge to run from the inferno bursting around him.

'We tried to make ourselves as small as possible,' Gockel recalled.

At first the shells whistled overhead. Several large formations of planes flew over us but dropped their bombs inland. But after a while the ships' guns began shelling our position. It was very accurate fire – they could see our position very well. I crouched underneath my heavy machine-gun table – it was made of thick wooden planks, so it gave me some protection against shrapnel – and I prayed out loud as we had all done as a family at home in Hamm during the bombing raids. I prayed to the Virgin Mary, the Mother of God, '*Hilf, Maria, es ist Zeit*' – help me, Mary, my time has come – and I also asked my patron saint, St Francis, for help. My mother had always said in her letters, 'The Lord will protect you.'

The small contingent of German soldiers who were now expected to throw the Allies back from the beaches would scarcely have credited the total confusion with which those charged with decisive leadership at this time had greeted their reports of invasion.

The first vital indication that Allied landings were imminent had come five days before in a BBC broadcast. The German Secret Service, the SD, had managed to identify the coded message the Allies would use to alert the French Resistance – two lines of verse from Paul Verlaine.

> *Les sanglots longs des violins de l'automne*
> *Blessent mon coeur d'une langueur monotone*
>
> The long sobs of the violins of autumn
> Wound my heart with a monotonous languor.

On 1 June a signaller with the 15th Army heard the first line. The signal was broadcast again the next day and then the next. Then on 5 June came the second line. The commander of the 15th Army, General Hans von Salmuth, was immediately notified, and he placed his formations on alert. The intelligence was passed to Rommel's staff at Army Group B Headquarters and to the commander-in-chief of German forces in the west, Field Marshal Gerd von Rundstedt, in Paris. But Rundstedt refused to believe that the Allies would announce the invasion on the BBC – he did nothing. Rommel was with his wife in Herrlingen and was happy to leave the matter to others. On the night of 5 June one of the two armies he commanded was on alert; the other, General Friedrich Dollmann's 7th Army, was not – nor were the vital Panzer reserves on which a successful counter-attack would depend. The Normandy coast was squarely in the 7th Army's sector.

It is richly ironic that Rundstedt and his staff chose to ignore one of the few reliable pieces of intelligence available to them, for much of what they had been told was completely worthless. Above all, a steady flow of intelligence and reconnaissance reports had led all Germany's senior soldiers to believe that the Allies would try to force the Pas de Calais, where the sea crossing was shortest. It was on the Channel coast north of the River Seine that the Atlantic Wall was thickest, and here too in the 15th Army's sector that Rommel's troops were concentrated. The 7th Army was made up of thirteen divisions, seven of which were deployed along the 300-kilometre coastline of Normandy, while the 15th Army could mobilise seventeen. Although Hitler shared the general conviction that the Allies were most likely to land in the Pas de Calais, he had also made a point of drawing the attention of his field marshals to the 'Calvados Coast' and the strategic significance of the port of Cherbourg. Much against his better instincts he had allowed Rundstedt and Rommel to persuade him not to order a general transfer of divisions from 'the main front on the Channel Coast' to Normandy.

Rommel's judgement as to when and where the Allies would land was, he knew well enough, based on the flimsiest of intelligence. 'I know *nothing* for certain about the enemy,' he complained. Uncertainty bedevilled every aspect of the planning for the invasion. At the beginning of June the German army west of the Rhine numbered fifty-eight divisions, nearly one million men, but these units were strung out along a 3,200-kilometre front. The general view had long been that the enemy would try to force the French or Belgian coasts, and yet in the weeks before D-Day intelligence gleaned from Allied signals seemed to indicate plans for a landing at the other end of the Atlantic Wall. Orders for the transfer of five infantry divisions from Norway to France had been immediately rescinded. It was a knee-jerk response to intelligence that was all too soon shown to be totally unreliable. Hitler and his commanders had been badly served in particular by Fremde Heere West (FHW) the intelligence arm of Army High Command (OKH). The FHW was to miss the mark with almost every significant piece of information it offered the High Command.

The Allies had systematically set about constructing a parallel invasion force made up of paper armies, canvas tanks and false wireless signals. The Overlord planners had recognised from the first that it would be impossible to disguise the massive military build-up in Britain, but perhaps the Germans could be hood-winked about when and where the blow would fall. An elabo-rate deception plan, Operation Fortitude, was devised to 'help' the enemy's intelligence officers to the view that the Allies intended to launch a diversionary attack in Norway and then the main assault on the Pas de Calais. The imaginary British 4th Army was created in Scotland with its own staff and radio traffic. The First US Army Group (FUSAG), with a paper strength greater than the American assault force that would eventually carry out the landings, was stationed in and around Dover to threaten the Pas de Calais. German spies turned by the British fed Berlin a steady stream of 'intelligence' on the build-up of men and equipment in the south-east of England. Dummy landing craft floated in the ports of Dover and Ramsgate for the benefit of German air reconnaissance. Hundreds of canvas and inflatable tanks littered the fields of East Anglia. FUSAG was made all the more believable by the inclusion of two real armies in its battle order – the American Third and Canadian First Armies. The crucial role in this extraordinary fiction was given to the man the German High Command considered the best of the Allied commanders – Lieutenant General George S. Patton. He was the perfect choice, for Patton had a gift for making head-lines wherever he went. German intelligence was able to follow his movements in the British papers and through FUSAG wireless traffic. The Fortitude planners left just enough for German intel-ligence to piece together and, gratifyingly for them, the enemy concluded that everything pointed to a main assault near Calais. This was the universal hope of all who served at 'the Wall' in Normandy. 'There was constant talk of invasion in the papers, and among ourselves,' Lieutenant Raimund Steiner remembered. 'People feared it was coming – there was the threat hanging over us. But we were all hoping that it would happen farther north where the coastal positions were ready. We used to tell each other it wouldn't happen here.'

The FHW's assessment that more than one landing should be expected was made all the more plausible by the estimate of Allied strength it offered Hitler and his generals. On the eve of D-Day it was considered likely that seventy-nine British and American divisions could be assembled for the invasion; in fact there were only forty-seven. Rundstedt expected as many as twenty divisions to be landed in the 'first wave' – the Allies were hoping to manage six.

If the Allies were to be beaten a strong and timely counter-attack would have to be launched at once – that much was known by every soldier on the Atlantic Wall. But the High Command's uncertainty as to Allied intentions was matched by crippling indecision about how best to meet this challenge when it came. The two field marshals charged with the defence of the invasion coast had been unable to agree on the positioning of the vital mobile reserve upon which hope of a successful counter-attack rested. Officially Rundstedt presided in the west and Rommel was responsible for one of the two army groups under his command. In practice Rommel reported directly to Hitler. From the first Rommel had held that the enemy would have to be defeated on or as near to the landing beaches as possible. The coastal defences were to be as formidable as time and *matériel* would allow.

Rommel had thrown himself into the task with all the restless energy characteristic of the man. Private Franz Gockel was impressed with how quickly improvements were made after the field marshal's visit to his resistance nest in January 1944: 'We felt honoured that the famous "desert fox" had come to visit us,' Gockel recalled.

But we heard from our CO later that Rommel had been angry about the totally inadequate fortifications on our part of the coast. He told the officers present that our bay was similar to the Bay of Salerno in Italy and the Americans had landed in Salerno in September 1943. He said that something must be done quickly and within a few days the builders were there. And after a few weeks it really looked different.

Underwater obstacles were laid to trap landing craft, beach defences to hold tanks and advancing infantry, and in a death zone up to eight kilometres inland field upon field of stakes – 'Rommel's Asparagus' – to deter glider-borne landings. Rommel ordered 50 million mines for the Atlantic Wall, although by June his men had managed to sow just a tenth of that number. 'The wooden stakes were hidden by the sea at high tide – we had been told that if they come, they will certainly come at high tide,' Gockel recalled.

The field marshal who had made his reputation as a master of Panzer warfare – the lightning tank thrust – had vigorously pressed the case for what amounted to a static defence. His driving energy had transformed preparations for the invasion, and in places the Atlantic Wall presented a formidable obstacle. But for the most part it represented only a thin defensive crust – one that would be all too easily breached by a determined and well-equipped enemy. Nor were the soldiers who manned the resistance nests and bunkers of the wall of the best quality. For most of the war the Western Front had been welcomed as a quiet, generally relaxed posting – suitable for the old and very young, or those recuperating from wounds received on the Eastern Front. One veteran of the war in Russia was disgusted with the lack of discipline he found on the coast. Lieutenant Raimund Steiner arrived in Normandy on Christmas Day 1943 and was posted at first to Colleville-sur-Mer:

When I got there, there was nobody in the battery. After a long wait, I found a guard and asked him: 'Where is the CO, where is everyone else?' The guard replied: 'They are all on holiday with their girl-friends.' They called a trip to the town 'a holiday'. This was completely strange to me. Up to that point I had served in an Alpine unit and we had always had tough discipline. I was told the CO was with his girlfriend in Riva-Bella and he wouldn't be back for a few days. I thought, this is impossible. I couldn't imagine that this was the German army. I sat down in the mess and thought about what I should do. It didn't take long for the door to open and in walked a pretty blonde in a fur coat. Fur coats had not been seen for a long time in the Third Reich and now, all of a sudden, as if from a different time, a pretty girl in furs. And she told me straight away: 'You must be Lieutenant Steiner!' I was flabbergasted – she had walked into the officers' mess as if she lived there and she knew who I was. And then she said: 'You are going to a bunker near La Brèche – that will be your next post.'

Discipline was still slack in some units five months later. Steiner was ordered to the Merville Battery at the end of May as a replacement for the previous commander, who had been killed in an air raid. 'He had liked to live well and had commandeered a chateau,' Steiner recalled. 'It was only on the morning after the raid and with a lot of effort that we were able to dig his body and his girlfriend's out of the rubble.'

The Reich had begun to scrape the bottom of the manpower barrel, and the average age of those serving in many of the coastal units was thirty-seven. Rommel had pushed tirelessly for more and better troops but his divisions were still under strength, and in some cases reluctant Russians, Poles and Georgians had been press-ganged into green-grey to help make up numbers. A detachment of Poles was sent to Private Franz Gockel's resistance nest: 'They spoke very broken German and some had no German at all. We called them "*Beute Deutsches*" [looted Germans].'

For all his passionate advocacy of strong fixed defences, Rommel expected the enemy to struggle ashore somewhere and in strength. It was above all vital that armoured reserves, Panzer and Panzer grenadier units, were thrown into a counter-attack before the Allies were established beyond the beaches. In Rommel's judgement the mobile reserves on which a successful defence depended needed to be deployed near the coast to ensure they were immediately available to his army commanders. His experience in North Africa and again in Italy only the year before had taught him that Allied aircraft would make the movement of armoured formations a hazardous business. If the Panzer reserves were too far from the beaches they would play no part in the crucial first hours of the invasion. 'Rommel says mobile operations with armoured formations are a thing of the past,' the chief of operations at Armed Forces High Command (OKW), General Alfred Jodl, recorded in his notes in April.

Germany's most senior field marshal, Gerd von Rundstedt, was of an altogether different view. The Grand Old Man of the German army was at sixty-eight a tough veteran of both field and conference chamber, but, as one senior British intelligence officer later observed, 'by this time Rundstedt's arteries were hardening'. He was tired, disillusioned and altogether pessimistic about Germany's future. 'To me things look black,' he had openly admitted to Rommel. Hitler had sacked him twice and then just as suddenly reinstated him – he remained in post, a great weather-beaten rock, comfortingly familiar and seemingly immovable.

Most of the Panzer forces in France were controlled by Panzer Group West, and its commander, General Leo Geyr von Schweppenburg, reported directly to Rundstedt. It was the fixed view of both men that Rommel's insistence on a shoreline defence flew in the face of all military experience. The Allies would certainly be able to fight their way ashore. 'The Atlantic Wall was anything but a wall,' Rundstedt would later remark, 'it was just a bit of cheap bluff.' Rundstedt, Geyr von Schweppenburg and everyone on the staff of OB West in Paris accepted the need for a strong counter-punch, but no one was sure where this would have to be delivered. If the Panzer reserves were spread thinly along the coast the counter-attack would fail to carry the necessary weight. The Allies could also rely on overwhelming naval fire power to help counter advancing armour. The only hope of success, both men argued, rested in concentrating the Panzer reserves away from the coast on ground suitable for armoured warfare – then, perhaps, the enemy could be decisively defeated.

Sharp words had been exchanged between Geyr von Schweppenburg and Rommel. 'I am an experienced tank commander,' Rommel tartly told Geyr von Schweppenburg. 'You and I do not see eye to eye on anything. I refuse to work with you any more.' The matter was finally decided by Hitler, who opted for a solution guaranteed to satisfy nobody. Neither Rundstedt nor Rommel would control the reserves – they were to be directed by Hitler himself. A reserve of four armoured divisions under his ultimate control would be held back from the coast – these would form part of Geyr von Schweppenburg's Panzer Group West. The remaining three divisions were placed under Rommel's operational control – just one, the 21st Panzer, was assigned to the Normandy front. It was an unholy compromise that served only to weaken further what was already a fragile defence. Rundstedt no longer had any reserves under his personal control. 'It was dictated from above,' he later complained, 'practically the disposition of every man was fixed for me.' Hitler had chosen to secure a direct role for himself in the forthcoming battle and in doing so had undermined the authority of his commander-in-chief in the west. Rundstedt had never been able to direct the air or naval forces stationed in France – now he had lost what little authority he had over the army. 'The organisation and chain of command of the major commands in the West was somewhere between confusion and chaos,' Rommel's chief of staff, General Hans Speidel, later observed.

By the spring of 1944 Field Marshal Rommel was quite sure the war could not be won by Germany. In the east, the Red Army was pressing relentlessly forward in a series of cripplingly costly engagements that were draining the Reich of men and *matériel*, while at home the Allied air forces were gradually reducing the country's cities to rubble. Total defeat might yet be avoided if the Allies were prevented from opening a second front in north-west Europe. British and American forces were already fighting in Italy, but Rommel believed they could be contained there for a while at least. Germany needed the time and the men to dig in on the Reich's border in the east. Above all it needed a nego-tiated peace. There were other fears too – ones the field marshal was prepared to discuss that spring only with those closest to him. 'I know my father hoped that, if the Germans could stall the invasion, the chance of a negotiated peace would increase,' his son Manfred recalled. 'He was particularly keen to get condi-tions for Germany because it had become more widely known in his circles that atrocities had been committed in the name of Germany. He was generally very afraid of what the Allies, the Americans, French and British, would do in the case of victory.'

Everything now rested on defeating the invasion. Rommel's mood swung between cautious optimism and black pessimism. In January 1944 he had written to his wife, Lucie, 'I believe we'll be able to beat off the assault,' and then again in May, 'I'm convinced that the enemy will have a rough time of it when he attacks, and ultimately achieve no success.' But to old comrades from the desert he painted an altogether less rosy picture – it had become a question simply of doing one's 'duty'.

Rolf Munninger had served as a *Gefechtsschreiber* or 'battle writer' on Rommel's staff in North Africa, with special respon-sibility for drawing up and distributing the orders of the day. The field marshal liked to have familiar faces around him and the twenty-three-year-old Munninger – a fellow Swabian – had rejoined his staff at La Roche Guyon. 'Rommel realised of course that he had to radiate optimism with the troops during his front line visits,' Munninger recalled. 'He was a split man – in front of the men he presented the attitude "we can do this", but in his heart he felt the exact opposite.' In Hitler's immediate circle this general pessimism was known as Rommel's '*Afrikanische*

Krankheit' – his African sickness – and those joining the field marshal were warned to be on their guard against it. He was no longer the brashly confident Panzer commander who three years before had trounced the Allies in North Africa.

The available intelligence had pointed to an invasion in the spring and throughout April and May there had been a noticeable increase in Allied bombing operations in France. But by June the threat seemed to have receded a little. Rundstedt expressed the view that the raids were evidence of an 'advanced state of readiness' on the part of the Allies, but that there was no 'immediate prospect of the invasion'. On 4 June the German meteorological service had advised that bad weather in the Channel would rule out the possibility for several days to come. Rommel had felt sufficiently confident to return home for Lucie's birthday. In his absence a general insouciance seemed to settle on the German 7th Army in Normandy.

The failure to respond to the first reports of Allied airborne operations on D-Day with clear, decisive leadership was to prove little short of disastrous. Finding those with power to command was no easy matter on the night of 5/6 June. Field Marshal Rommel – the commander of Army Group B – was in bed with his wife in southern Germany, some nine hundred kilometres away. The commander of the nearest armoured reserve – the 21st Panzer Division – was in bed with somebody else's wife, or so it was assumed, for no one could find him. General Dollmann and the staff of the 7th Army were at a *'Kriegspiel'* or war game in Rennes. General Hans Speidel, Rommel's chief of staff, had used the field marshal's absence to invite a group of anti-Hitler conspirators to join him for drinks at La Roche Guyon. It was only at 6 a.m. that Rundstedt's staff requested the release of the critical armoured reserves; by then the first Allied landing craft had begun struggling towards the Normandy beaches. Only Hitler could give permission for the deployment of the reserves and nobody wanted to wake him. In mitigation, the German army could point to the total failure in those first critical hours of both the navy and air force – they had failed to detect the approach of the largest invasion fleet ever assembled.

From his command post, platoon leader Feldwebel Pieh could see the landing craft edging closer to the beach in front of WN 62. The commander of the 726th had rung from Port en Bessin to impress on him the need for his men to hold their fire until the enemy was almost on the beach. Franz Gockel stood by his old Polish-made machine gun and waited:

The naval guns opened up again and the targets this time were the defensive stakes in the beach – the 'Rommel Spargel'. After a time they aimed towards our positions again. The whole sea looked like a wall of fire. By then the tide was at its lowest and we could see that more and more landing craft were approaching. We had always been told that they would only come at high tide and now here they were at low tide.

The Americans were knee deep in the sea when the order to fire was at last given.

In the ships and landing craft of the invasion fleet thousands of Allied soldiers were preparing for the moment – 'H hour' – when a ramp would drop and the order would be given to run at a hidden enemy. 'What a gigantic effort each man now has to make to face up to something like this,' wrote Captain Alastair Bannerman of the 2nd Battalion, the Royal Warwickshire Regiment, on the eve of D-Day. 'Men who may have had only little of life, men with little education and little knowledge and no philosophical supports, men with ailing, estranged or poor or needy families, men who have never been loved, men who had never had high ambitions or wanted a new world order. Yet we're all here, we're all going, as ordered, willingly into battle.'

The thirty-year-old Bannerman had been obliged for more than two years to suspend normal family life and his profession – he was a successful actor – and train for this day. 'I pray for courage because I know that I am not a fighter,' he confided in a letter to his wife, Elizabeth. 'Now is not the time to doubt; let us follow our ideals and do everything to finish our task and to purify the air again so that humanity can breathe freely and rebuild.'

Many of the 'hostilities only' men who were crammed shoulder to shoulder in the landing craft that day felt the same way. 'I had little time to think much about it, but in all our minds was the thought, would this be the last time we would see England?' Lieutenant Kingston Adams of A Company, the 2nd Warwicks, had confided to his diary the evening before. The twenty-two-year-old Adams had joined the army from Oxford University, where he had been studying law: 'I still couldn't believe we were going into action at last, would be shot at, mortared, and would have every weapon the Germans possessed thrown at us to drive us away from their shores. Yet there was not one of us who was not proud to think he would be amongst the first to land on one of the greatest expeditions ever known in history.'

The 2nd Battalion, the Royal Warwickshire Regiment, was to come ashore with the rest of the British 3rd Division on the beach at Ouistreham in what had been designated 'Sword' sector. This was the most easterly of five landing beaches. The Canadian 3rd Division was to land a little farther up the coast on 'Juno' and the British 50th at 'Gold'. In the west the American 1st and 29th Divisions were to come ashore at 'Omaha' and the 4th on 'Utah' beach. The first wave would be preceded on the British and Canadian beaches by assault teams of combat engineers and specially adapted tanks that were to clear a path through Rommel's obstacles for the attacking infantry.

Talk of an Allied invasion of occupied Europe had begun within weeks of the American entry into the war in December 1941 – serious planning for Overlord only the year before. At first the British were full of misgivings: 'my dear friend, this is much the greatest thing we have ever attempted,' Prime Minister Winston

Churchill wrote to President Roosevelt. And so it would prove. The British had been unceremoniously thrown out of France in 1940 by the most formidable army in the world. An amphibious assault on Fortress Europe was fraught with problems.

To force their way back, the Allies would need to enjoy total domination of air and sea. Above all it was essential that the time and exact location of the landings should be hidden from the enemy – a seemingly impossible task given the scale of the Allied preparations in the weeks before D-Day. Once ashore they would need to be able to supply and reinforce the armies for a break-out from the bridgehead. Concrete harbours – Mulberries – were to be floated across the Channel and sunk off the beaches, and two oil pipelines were planned so fuel could be pumped directly from England. The Germans could be expected to throw their best divisions at the beachhead. As one senior Allied planner put it: 'The crux of the operation is . . . likely to be our ability to drive off the German reserves rather than the initial breaking of the coastal crust.'

A new urgency had been given to the invasion plans with the appointment of a Supreme Allied Commander – General Dwight D. Eisenhower. The Americans had insisted on an American. The big, fifty-three-year-old Kansan had enjoyed a meteoric rise from colonel to general in three years, but had barely heard a shot fired in anger. He had looked across the battlefield of Wadi Akarit in North Africa the year before and with typical candour admitted to his companion, 'Say, Broadie, that's the first time I've seen a dead body!' There were plenty of critical voices – not all of them British – who questioned the wisdom of such an appointment. But for all his lack of experience in the field, Eisenhower had already demonstrated a light touch in the conference chamber. His good-humoured patience and generosity of spirit would be tested to the full, not least by the man appointed to command the Allied armies on the ground – General Bernard Law Montgomery. 'Nice chap Ike, no soldier,' Montgomery had observed when he had first met Eisenhower in North Africa.

'Monty' took pride in being every inch the professional soldier.
He was three years older than Eisenhower and had held almost
every senior position in the British army – he had seen a good
many bodies. Before his appointment to the command of the
8th Army in 1942 there had been very few victories to celebrate.
The hero of 'Alamein' had turned the tide in North Africa and
in doing so had won enormous popularity among his soldiers
and the British public alike. He was supremely confident in his
own judgement, his own fitness to command. His extraordinary
self-belief helped inspire the trust of subordinates, but with his
peers he often appeared arrogant and intolerant. Even those who
admired Monty found it difficult to like him. But Montgomery
was the natural choice as Allied land commander. He had
stamped his mark on the plans for Overlord before his appointment had been officially announced. Churchill had first shown
him plans for the invasion on New Year's Eve. He had spent the
night studying them and in the morning confidently pronounced
them to be seriously flawed. Instead of a landing by three assault
divisions, he argued, the Allies would have to put five ashore on
a much broader front, and this was the plan agreed upon three
weeks later.

The initial assault by five divisions would be on the coast
between the River Orne and the Cotentin peninsula. Once
ashore, the immediate objective was to secure a large lodgement,
including the port of Cherbourg in the west and the city of Caen
in the east. Into this the Allies would pour four armies – thirty-
seven divisions – in preparation for a break-out across France.
If everything went to plan, Monty expected the Allied armies to
be on the River Seine within three months – D + 90 days. It was
an ambitious target – success would depend on 'the violence of
our assault' and on the great weight of supporting fire from the
sea and air, he told Allied commanders in May. The Germans
would do their level best to 'Dunkirk' the Allies in the first few
days – to press them back into the sea as they had in 1940.
Monty's old adversary from the desert – Field Marshal Rommel

– had 'made a world of difference' since his appointment, and his reserves included some of the finest Panzer divisions in the German army. Monty was able to number them all with certainty in the days before D-Day. The Allies had thoroughly penetrated the German Enigma codes and the Overlord planners had benefited from a steady stream of reliable intelligence gleaned from their signals traffic. This 'Ultra' intelligence also gave them an insight into the fierce strategic debate in the German army on the best plan to counter the invasion. Monty knew Rommel had been able to deploy only one Panzer division at the coast – he knew too that the Allies' Fortitude deception plan had succeeded brilliantly in deflecting attention to the Pas de Calais. The initiative lay squarely with the Allies, and Monty was supremely confident of success.

The attack would be launched at low tide so the assault troops could negotiate the enemy's beach defences. The date finally settled on was dawn on 5 June. In the last tense days before D-Day the whole of southern England was smothered by a thick blanket of security. Allied soldiers were confined to camp, sailors to their ships, a 16-kilometre exclusion zone was established along the south and east coast of England, and all transatlantic telephone and cable links were cut. For all the careful security measures, it was impossible to stifle the sense of tense anticipation felt by soldiers and civilians alike.

Major Peter Martin, a company commander with the 2nd Battalion, the Cheshire Regiment, recalled the last tense days in England:

We marched from our camp in Nightingale Wood, just outside Southampton, down to the docks on 3 June. We were due to embark that day and sail the next evening ready for D-Day on the 5th. We'd done two full dress rehearsals of the embarkation procedure and on each of them the townspeople of Southampton had turned out and had some fun at our expense – joking comments like 'Don't get your feet wet, lads' and that sort of thing. But on this particular day, when we were doing it for real, there was absolute dead silence. The crowds were there but not a word was said. And we got down to the docks in Southampton and boarded our LCI [Landing Craft Infantry]. The next morning, 4 June, we were visited down on the docks by Winston Churchill accompanied by Field Marshal Smuts. And I can remember seeing them leaning over the dockside looking very sort of morosely down the Solent, as if they expected awful things to happen. It was their sombreness I remember. And then on 4 June we suddenly got the word that D-Day was postponed because of bad weather. These LCIs were by no means comfortable, they carried about 250 soldiers, all cramped below decks in hammocks. We got the soldiers off on to the dockside and played football and I think the NAAFI [Army canteen] came down and opened up and everyone was in very good form, very cheerful. I can remember there was a launch going round Southampton harbour with a couple of very attractive Wrens on board distributing mail and that caused great cheers from the troops.

The weather had intervened on the eve of departure. The conditions were critical. Success depended on air support and steady seas, and the forecast was altogether gloomy – the weather on 5 June would be overcast and stormy, with low cloud and Force 5 winds. Eisenhower had been left with no choice but to postpone D-Day. Ships already at sea had to be recalled and the soldiers of the Allied Expeditionary Force were obliged to spend an uncomfortable and uncertain day at anchor. The 2nd Battalion, the Warwicks, was held at Newhaven. 'We all lie now side by side in the quiet harbour and nobody knows what is going on,' Captain Bannerman wrote to his wife.

We had a visit from our battalion commander, who was in good form, and we were able to recognise our friends on boats moored in the vicinity. On the jeep of Sergeant Matthews in which I am going to land, the whole Section has painted the names of their girls with a Cupid's heart in chalk. So in order not to be left out I have added your name as well to the gallery and it now stands between the Doris of Lance Corporal Baker and the Vera of Sgt Matthews: Elizabeth

Aear [Bannerman]. I know two officers very well whose wives expect a baby today and I can understand their feelings.

'More letters were written and weapons cleaned,' Lieutenant Adams of A Company, the 2nd Warwicks, wrote in his diary.

The evening was spent in a wonderful singsong between members of the various boats in the harbour. The BBC had erected a mike and was broadcasting from one of the LCIs and various people started singing. This led to competition from the other boats and soon the whole harbour was ringing with songs. Laid down my bed on the upper deck tonight and just got settled down when a Scotch mist came down.

On the evening of 4 June Eisenhower and his most senior commanders had met at Southwick House near Portsmouth – the new advanced headquarters for Overlord – to consider the forecast. The senior meteorologist had found what appeared to be a window in the weather for 6 June with 'more favourable' cloud and wind conditions. Montgomery was emphatic – 'Go.' The Allied airmen were hesitant. It was the voice of Admiral Sir Bertram Ramsey, the commander of the great naval task force, that was to prove decisive – if D-Day were to go ahead on 6 June 'a provisional warning' would need to be given within the hour. The final decision was Eisenhower's to make – the navy was instructed to put to sea. A final, irrevocable decision was made at 4.30 the next morning. The forecast was more certain – winds along the assault coast would not exceed Force 3 and the cloud would be high enough for air operations. 'OK, let's go,' Eisenhower told his senior commanders. D-Day would be 6 June.

'What a sight it was when we got out into the Channel! Hundreds of ships of all sizes, all setting out together,' Lieutenant Adams wrote in his diary on 5 June. It is difficult to over-estimate the size of the task the British and American navies faced. Nearly eight thousand ships and craft had set out from the British coast to pre-arranged assembly points in the Channel. From there they were funnelled into ten lanes swept free of mines – a fast and a slow passage for each of the five assault forces. All this was to be achieved in the utmost secrecy and in variable weather conditions. These soon began to take their toll on the men. 'We are thrown to and fro and the waves break with a tremendous roar and a cloud of foam, and the deck is swamped with water,' Captain Alastair Bannerman wrote in the diary he was keeping for his wife. 'I felt extremely excited about this gigantic adventure. As I also felt a little seasick I took a pill which worked miracles!' Not everyone was as lucky. 'The officers were in a cabin but my platoon was down in the bowels of the ship and the atmosphere was awful,' Lieutenant Kingston Adams on A Company's transport, LCI 315, later recalled.

The ship was rocking and rolling and a good number of them were very ill. Some people were being sick in our cabin too, and I had to go into the engine room to get some sleep. I went up on deck to take the air a few times and it was an amazing sight – a huge armada. Overhead there were hundreds of aircraft darting in and out to protect us – but there was no sign of the enemy at all.

Adams and the other officers of A Company were finally told their destination at a little after midnight: 'The Company commander, Harry Illing, called an "O" group meeting [orders meeting for officers and NCOs] on the LCI and issued us with our maps. We had eighteen of them and it was an awful business getting them all into our map cases. It was then that we were told our destination was part of the Normandy coast north of Caen – the village of Lion-sur-Mer.'

'Hitherto we had studied maps with spurious names, so that we should not know the actual places where we were going to land,' Captain Illing later recalled. 'Here at last we saw our destination with its proper name – Lion-sur-Mer. We could see on our photos the landmark we would aim for, a "gable-end house". Would it still be standing?'

Bannerman had been obliged to brief his platoon through a megaphone: 'I had to cling to the railing to hold my papers and to prevent the megaphone from being blown out of my hand by the wind,' he wrote to his wife. 'What a painful discipline of body and mind this all is but it is certainly worth the trouble to bring back peace and goodwill to this earth.'

Not everyone was quite as dewy eyed. 'Some of the men were looking towards D-Day with a certain amount of foreboding,' Major Peter Martin of the 2nd Battalion, the Cheshire Regiment, recalled. The battalion had been rescued from the beaches at Dunkirk four years earlier, and as part of the 50th Division had fought with distinction in North Africa and Italy. The 50th was going to lead the line again, and some of the old sweats wanted to know why. The division's officers had been called together in the days before D-Day for a briefing. Martin remembered the divisional commander telling them all that it had been a 'toss-up' between the 50th and the 51st Highland Division:

He said, 'I'm delighted to say that we won and that we will have the honour of leading the assault on the beaches,' at which there was a great moan all round the cinema. I think we reckoned that by that time we'd done our stuff. What were all these divisions back in England doing? Why didn't they have the 'honour' of leading the attack? I can remember talking it over with a fellow company commander and reckoning that our chances of getting across the beach alive were going to be pretty small. Every day during the preparation period we were given aerial photographs and maps marked up with the latest German defences – new minefields, new underwater obstacles. It really did look extremely dangerous.

It was strangely heartening to learn that after a successful assault on the beach A Company was expected to join a 32-kilometre armoured push inland. 'That made me realise that the great man "Monty" obviously didn't believe that the beaches were going to be as dangerous as we'd thought. I can remember briefing my soldiers on the plan and the sort of happy smiles that came over their faces when I told them about this strike inland at the end of D-Day.'

Martin was woken in the early hours of 6 June by the smashing of crockery in the ship's galley. Cold soya was served for breakfast; 'a peculiarly revolting sort of ersatz sausage that was just about edible when heated but the galley's rings weren't working and we had to have it cold'. It was too much for even the hardest of stomachs. 'Dawn came – few had had much sleep – even fewer managed to eat breakfast – some looked very ill in spite of seasick pills, boiled sweets and cups of tea,' Captain Illing recalled. 'Went down to the platoon's quarters and the smell made me sick at once and I raced upstairs just in time,' Lieutenant Adams of A Company wrote in his diary later. 'Tried to get each man to eat something but it was the devil's own game – poor chaps.'

The first sight of the French coast was greeted in silence by the men in Trooper Austin Baker's transport. The 4th/7th Royal Dragoon Guards were to give armoured support to the first assault wave on Gold – they would be among the first British tanks ashore on D-Day. Baker was the wireless operator in C Squadron's armoured recovery vehicle (ARV). It was a far cry from the library in Bedford where the twenty-year-old Baker had worked until his call-up:

There were several cruisers firing broadside after broadside. We passed within a couple of hundred yards of one, the *HMS Belfast* – the noise of her guns was ear-splitting. There was a battleship firing in the distance – the *Rodney*, so the skipper announced over the loud-hailer on the bridge . . . There were destroyers right in close to the beach, firing like mad. They must have been almost aground. Rocket ships – landing craft carrying batteries of rocket guns – added to the general din. Smoke hung over everything and we could see the flashes of exploding shells on land. About half a mile from the beach a navy motor boat drifted past with a dead sailor lying across the foredeck. I'd never seen anybody dead before.

We were still two or three hundred yards offshore when a big spout of water shot up near our starboard side, followed by another in almost the same place. 'We are now being shelled,' the skipper said dramatically. It was very novel and unpleasant.

The British sector covered a 40-kilometre stretch of the coast, but less than eight kilometres of this was to be attacked in the initial phase. The landings on Gold, Juno and Sword were to take place almost simultaneously – once the beaches had been secured, the three divisions were expected to push rapidly inland. The Allies hoped that by the end of D-Day the bridgehead would stretch from Port-en-Bessin in the west to the Orne in the east and would include the city of Caen.

The assault teams from the 50th Division began to land at Gold at a little after 7.30 in the morning. Major R. J. L. Jackson of the 6th Battalion, the Green Howards, landed at the eastern end of the beach near the village of La Rivière:

The beach was completely deserted as we approached and I remember being puzzled by the comparative silence. Of course the Allied bombardment was landing far ahead and we could see some of the big shells passing over us, but the absence of any fire directed at us was strange. Our biggest fear concerned the first few seconds when the landing-craft doors were opened and we presented a tight, congested target for any machine-gunners. Because of this we lost a sergeant, who jumped too soon into the sea when we hit a false bottom. The water was some eight feet deep, but he thought we had struck the beach. He was carrying so much equipment that he sank straight away and was drowned.

Ironically his fears were without foundation. When we landed the doors opened, we jumped out, but there were no bullets. The beach was apparently still deserted. The water was only about a foot deep and I quickly advanced up the beach, flanked by a radio operator and a regimental policeman carrying a sten gun. At every step we expected to be fired at, but were not. The lack of opposition became eerie. Then after about 200 yards, we must have reached a German fixed line. Suddenly they threw everything at us. The mortars took us first and I was hit badly in the leg. My radio operator and policeman were both killed outright by the same explosion.

The radio still worked and Jackson was able to help direct those advancing behind him for a while.

'The doors of the craft opened, the ramp went down . . . this was it,' twenty-two-year-old Private Francis Williams of the 6th Green Howards recalled.

Sergeant William Hill – nicknamed Rufty – my best mate, was first to go, followed by two privates whose names I can't recall. That was the last I saw of them. The landing craft had not run aground and they were sucked under, the three of them drowning . . . He had got out of Dunkirk a few years earlier, had been through all the battles in the Western desert and Sicily, now he was dead without even getting ashore.

The landing craft carrying twenty-four-year-old Sergeant Reg Webb of the 141 Royal Armoured Corps (The Buffs) also came ashore at La Rivière: 'Just before we got in a shell hit the bridge of the LCT [Landing Craft Transport] but we still came in exactly on the right spot, the ramp went down, the petty officer checked the depth of the water and we were told we were OK – it was less than six feet deep. He was a liar, it was over six feet, I'm sure.' First off the landing craft was a small machine-gun carrier – it sank without trace. It was followed by a Sherman flail – a mine clearer – then Webb's own flame-throwing tank or 'Crocodile'. 'As I went down the ramp I hit one of these mines on a pole – the blast didn't do any real damage and we managed to follow the flail tank ashore, but then he was hit.' 'On our left a flail tank went forward and blew up,' Francis Williams remembered. 'One of its wheels rolled right along the beach and just missed one of our sergeants, who was lying on the sand with a wound in his leg and half his jaw blown away.' 'It was absolute chaos. Shells were dropping on the beach and you could hear machine-gun bullets pinging off this and that,' Reg Webb remembered. 'It was no good going ahead so I decided to go along to the right. I couldn't. There was so much debris – landing craft with infantry coming ashore, and a lot of wounded and dead too.'

As Webb tried to make his way back through the surf the Crocodile fell into a huge bomb crater: 'The tank nosedived and the engine flooded and that was that. The best thing we could do was to bail out.'

Francis Williams recalled:

Just 50 or 60 yards in front of me a Spandau [German machine gun] was firing to our right . . . I jumped up and ran at the machine-gun post, firing short bursts from the hip. I was on them before they knew what was happening. I shot two of the occupants and, shouting '*Hande hoch!*', the other six gave themselves up. I ran them towards the track with their hands on their head . . . before I left them I noticed one of them had a sort of band around the bottom of his sleeve and on it were the words Afrika Korps. I said to him, 'You Rommel's man?' He said, '*Ja.*' Pointing to my Africa Star [medal ribbon], I said, 'Me Eighth Army.' It was a bit like Tarzan and Jane. I shook his hand and went back to what was left of 17 Platoon.

'Our landing craft made a false approach and was swung round by the current and we found ourselves in amongst the infantry who were wading ashore. They were up to their waists in water holding rifles above their heads,' Trooper Austin Baker of the 4th/7th Royal Dragoon Guards recalled.

When we went in the next time they lowered the ramp on top of a mine that was attached to one of the beach stakes. There was a tremendous explosion and I was thrown against the rim of the tank's hatch and broke a tooth on it and, well, this made the whole thing seem a bit more real. The ramp went down and the first scout car down it was hit by a shell and the driver was injured. But then next thing we knew we were going up the beach. There were hordes of men and machines all over the beach and a lot of explosions. Before we were off the beach I saw two lorries turn over in the waves. I remember thinking this doesn't look very promising, but in a very short time we were off the beach.

Baker's tank pressed on beyond La Rivière to the village of Ver-sur-Mer:

We went straight through the village and out the other end. Quite suddenly, I realised that all the other vehicles had disappeared and we were quite alone, charging up a quiet country lane by ourselves. I knew this was wrong, because I had seen the orchard where we were to rendezvous on the map, and knew it was at the edge of the village . . . I told Dabby [the tank's commander] this, and had a bit of an argument before I managed to convince him. We turned round in a field about half a mile up the lane.

By the time Major Peter Martin of the 2nd Cheshires landed with the second wave, the eastern end of Gold beach had been secured. Major Martin's landing was not without incident, however:

The brigadier had ordained that we would land wearing gas-proof trousers, sort of mackintosh-type trousers which fastened round the waist and came over the boots so that we would be entirely dry when we landed. As I came down the ramp from the landing craft I stumbled over an underwater obstacle and went flat on my face. There was air inside my trousers and it rushed to the top of the water – my front end was laden down with equipment and tin hat and that was under water. So I had a slightly nasty moment – it was the most dangerous thing to happen to me on the landing. I was pulled up by my batman and was I indignant about it!

The scene on the beach was of apparent chaos – there were tanks burning, bodies all over the place and it looked an absolute disaster, but in fact everything by that time had quietened down and we weren't under fire of any sort. We filed off the beach, past one or two rather disgruntled-looking Frenchmen, who quite naturally were very shocked by the noise and kerfuffle and also the fact that their homes were being destroyed and their animals killed and so on, so there wasn't the enthusiastic welcome we'd envisaged there might be.

The fiercest fighting was at the western end of Gold, near the village of Le Hamel, where the first assault wave was held up for a time by a more than usually determined defence. But by late morning the 50th Division had begun to press inland towards Bayeux. Nearly three kilometres to the east of La Rivière, the Canadian 3rd Division had begun to land on Juno. The first assault teams had been late closing the shore and a turning tide had swept their landing craft among the beach obstacles. Of the 306 landing craft used by the division ninety were lost or damaged that morning. Miraculously the navy managed to land the assault brigades with very few casualties. The port of Courseulles was particularly well defended and the Canadians were obliged to fight their way street by street through the town – it was not finally cleared until the afternoon. This did not hold up the advance, and by late morning the 'follow-up' brigades had begun to land and press on towards Caen. A good number of bicycles were carried down the ramps in the wake of the armour – and some did prove of use in the dash for roads and villages.

The last of the beaches allotted to the British 21st Army Group was Sword – some five kilometres farther up the coast from Juno. The enemy's main fortified positions here were in the small seaside village of Lion-sur-Mer and the port of Ouistreham. Between the two the Germans had also built a strongpoint at La Brèche with concrete casements for artillery pieces and heavy mortars. The 3rd Division's assault followed much the same pattern – an intense suppressing barrage by destroyers and other supporting craft, followed by the launch of the amphibious or Duplex drive (DD) tanks. These had been fitted with a propeller and canvas screens for flotation so they could 'swim' ashore. The wind was driving the sea onshore and the landing crafts were obliged to run the gauntlet of beach defences here too. Casualties were at first high. There was particularly fierce fighting at La Brèche – it was three hours before its guns were finally silenced.

The officers and men of A Company, the 2nd Warwicks, had

watched as units of the 8th Brigade had closed the beach for the initial assault. 'At 7.30 a.m. – "H" hour – we were almost motionless and the ship too far out to hear what sort of reception the 8th Brigade was getting,' Lieutenant Adams wrote in his diary. The Warwicks were to land at 9.30 a.m. with the 'follow-up' brigade and push on across the beach to the city of Caen. 'Kits were put on, guns checked over, all was ready and the men moved forward to their action stations. Occasionally a whining sound would swish over the ship, our first experience of an angry missile,' Captain Harry Illing recalled later. Through his field glasses Illing could see the 'gable-end house' in Lion-sur-Mer which was the company's marker.

Adams wrote an account of Landing Craft 315's final approach in his diary later that day:

We put on our mackintosh waders over all our equipment, but Harry decided to leave them behind after all, so we proceeded to struggle out of them again. We were going full speed for the shore now, and through our binoculars could see what was left of our objectives after the terrific hammering of the RAF. All the men were fully dressed and waiting in the correct order below decks ready to come up. I went down and wished them all good luck.

'We were very keyed-up – unnaturally calm, with thumping chests and a deep sinking feeling in our stomachs,' Illing remembered. 'At last we touched the beach.' The company waded waist deep through the water to the shore – Adams was over six feet tall, but it was a lot harder for the shorter men: 'Though the beach was meant to be clear there were still a few snipers blazing away. One in particular I remember firing away from the top of a ruined house – we took shelter behind a Sherman tank which had been knocked out and in the next moment the house which was firing blew up with a round from an Oerlikon [anti-aircraft gun].' The company picked its way through the wrecked vehicles, beach obstacles and bodies and reached Lion-sur-Mer without serious casualties.

By late morning high winds had driven the tide up the beach, pressing the 3rd Division's vehicles into a thin strip of foreshore. Captain Alastair Bannerman was to land with the 2nd Battalion's Bren gun carriers and artillery:

When we came in close we could see that the beach was completely chock-a-block with vehicles. We had to steer over to the east and to look round for a bit . . . The waves were running high, but our water-proofed carriers made it safely. There were no ready-made beach exits anywhere but finally I got hold of a bulldozer which brought our gun and carrier up a dune and then we had to wait and actually queue up to move inland. The houses along the coast were only shells and it was a terrible experience when I saw for the first time dead bodies, first a German soldier and afterwards quite a few of our own soldiers. I can never forget all this or somehow forgive. Finally, we could move on and arrived at the end of a lane at a crossroad where I met the CO. He looked pale and a little shaken but was sitting quite cold-bloodedly upon a bicycle. He told me that the battalion would be moving up there and would join me.

A member of the Free French Resistance was waiting in Lion-sur-Mer to guide Harry Illing and his men to their first objective – the cemetery:

'Mine, mine,' he shouted, pointing to our intended route across the fields. We ploughed on with mine detectors to the fore, but no mine exploded, and soon we reached the cemetery and started digging in. It all seemed very easy – only a few chaps had been hurt. There was plenty of fire about, but we hadn't been badly shot up. It seemed peaceful enough at the cemetery for about ten minutes, and then we began to realise there really were some enemy. First snipers started and then fairly heavy machine-gun fire came down.

The company found itself pinned down around the cemetery – only some of the men had managed to dig slit trenches for cover. Lieutenant Adams found a little shelter behind the trunk of a tree:

The platoon was round me in trenches . . . unfortunately C Company got a lot of casualties as they had not dug in – what a lesson! Private Cross was our only casualty, with a bullet in his wrist. He was standing a yard from me when they had first opened up. Poor old Dicky Pratt was hit in both legs – our first officer casualty. Harry got orders to me to withdraw into the cemetery, but the only entrance was well and truly covered by the Boche, so we put down a smoke-screen and section by section raced for the open gap. Luckily we managed it.

The company's sniper team was sent forward and managed to find one German in a tree and another in bushes, but time could not be spared to engage the rest. 'The first day's objective was Caen and we were told that by hook or by crook we had to get there,' Adams recalled. This was the first action A Company had experienced and a dozen men had been wounded at the cemetery. It was, Illing wrote later, an 'aperitif for battle'.

The road to Caen would take the 2nd Royal Warwicks through the village of Bénouville later that day and past the canal bridge that had been taken in the early hours by Major Howard and his men. At daybreak Howard had heard the intense naval bombardment of the coast and said a little prayer of thanks: 'We thought of those poor devils coming in by sea . . . and we were damn glad we were where we were.' Throughout the night paratroopers from the 6th Airborne had straggled in from the surrounding countryside and had taken up positions around Bénouville. The Germans had made a number of attempts to retake the bridges but these had been easily beaten off. The 6th Airborne had established a first-aid post in a café at the western end of what has been known since the end of the war as 'Pegasus' Bridge (after the symbol of the winged horse used by the Airborne). The battle for the bridge had driven the café proprietor, Georges Gondrée, and his family into the cellar, but at dawn there had been a knock at the door. Gondrée had tentatively opened it to be confronted by two men in battledress and camouflage paint – were they British soldiers or German? 'For a moment there was silence,' he later recalled, 'then one soldier turned to the other and said, "It's alright chum." At last I knew they were English and burst into tears.' Gondrée went out into his back garden with a spade – four years earlier he had hidden a hundred bottles of champagne. Liberation seemed to have come at last – this was the time to celebrate.

CHAPTER TWO

·

OMAHA

Lieutenant Commander Harry Butcher had crunched down the cinder path to Eisenhower's 'circus caravan' in his slippers at a little before seven o'clock on the morning of D-Day. He could see the Supreme Commander's silhouette through the window – he was sitting up in bed with a book in hand, his customary Western. Eisenhower had greeted his friend with a grin, reached for his first cigarette and then listened carefully to the sketchy reports from Normandy. The airborne landings had been a success and casualties were light, Butcher told him, but there was nothing concrete as yet from Utah and Omaha, where 'H' hour was an hour earlier than on the British beaches. Butcher 'skedaddled' back to his tent to wash and dress and then joined Ike at the office caravan. Eisenhower had established his 'circus' close to the advanced command centre of the Supreme Headquarters Allied Expeditionary Force [SHAEF] at Southwick House near Portsmouth. The morning papers were full of the fall of Rome to the Allies – there was no mention of D-Day. Eisenhower drafted a brief message to Washington – everything appeared to be going according to plan, although there was no news from the American beaches. Breakfast, and lots of strong coffee were followed by more reports and visits from senior SHAEF staff. There was nothing to do but wait. By 10 a.m. it was clear the British had succeeded in forcing their way ashore, but there was still no definite news from Utah and Omaha. The silence was becoming deafening.

* * *

From the deck of the cruiser *USS Augusta* General Omar Bradley could see little more than the pall of thin grey smoke that hung above the beach at Omaha. It was four hours after the start of the operation when he received his first official report from the commander of his V Corps. It was terse and totally inconclusive: 'obstacles mined, progress slow'. But unofficial reports had begun to trickle in within an hour of the first assault – the Germans were pouring heavy fire on to the beach, the amphibious or DD tanks had sunk, there were heavy casualties. At least the operation at Utah beach appeared to be going well. The *Augusta* was just 15 kilometres from the Omaha beach but the commander of the US First Army had no more power to direct events from her deck than Eisenhower did from his headquarters in England. 'We fought off our fears,' he wrote later, 'attributing the delay to a jam-up in communications.'

Bradley's makeshift command post was a 20-by-10-foot steel cabin that had been bolted to the deck of the *Augusta*. The cabin was full of clerks and Bradley's personal staff – among them his friend and aide, Major Chester Hansen, who recalled: 'There was great apprehension aboard the *Augusta* – the resistance was so much more severe than we had anticipated.' Debate around the plotting table was punctuated by the boom of the *Augusta*'s guns. Bradley tried to hide his concern, but the twenty-seven-year-old Hansen knew the general well – he had served with him for two years, in North Africa and in Sicily. 'We had planned this thing for so long, we thought we had covered everything that had to be covered; in fact, we found it difficult to understand how things could go wrong.'

The landings on Omaha were to be carried out by the 1st and 29th Divisions of V Corps, supported by two special forces battalions – the 2nd and 5th Rangers. From the first it had been recognised that this stretch of coast would pose particular problems for an attacking force. The beach was overlooked at all points by steep bluffs, and it was on these that a careful enemy had sited his strongpoints. The beach itself was fringed by either a sharp shingle bank or a low sea wall. Four 'draws' or ravines wound their way up to the fields above, and these offered the only route off the beach for armour. Those charged with drawing up the plans for the assault had done nothing to make V Corps' task easier. The lowering position for the transports was 18 kilometres from the coast — six kilometres farther out than those chosen by the British. Instead of a two-hour bombardment the Americans had elected for a short, sharp forty minutes. The specially adapted armoured vehicles that were to prove so effective in clearing obstacles from the British beaches had been rejected by the US First Army. When the infantry reached the beach it was expected to launch an old-fashioned frontal assault. This approach was to be cruelly exposed by the weight of fire the Germans were able to pour on to the beach from the bluffs. Allied intelligence had failed to pick up a new and more formidable enemy in the villages and strongpoints beyond Omaha — the 716th Division had been reinforced by the veteran 352nd Infantry Division.

As 'H' hour approached the tidal current and a brisk northwesterly wind had combined to produce a dangerously high sea. The long journey to the shore began in darkness — the first to attempt it were the DD tanks. Of the thirty-two launched at sea, twenty-seven were lost — swamped by the swell. Bradley had looked out across the dark channel in some trepidation: 'the decision as to whether those tanks would swim or be carted ashore could not be made aboard the *Augusta*,' he later wrote, 'it fell to the commanders of those tank detachments. By now Overload had run beyond the reach of its admirals and generals.'

Lieutenant Sidney Salomon had no illusions about the task he faced on D-Day — the Rangers had spent six months training for this operation, storming beaches and cliff faces all over Britain. It had finally been officially confirmed that the 2nd Battalion would be at the forefront of the invasion two weeks before. The thirty-one-year-old Salomon was one of the army's brightest —

a graduate of New York University, he had volunteered for service when America joined the war and had won promotion from private to lieutenant in just nine months. C Company was to land and attack German positions close to the village of Vierville and then press on to the coastal road. Salomon had already decided that he would be the first down the ramp. It would be a race for terra firma. The Rangers had struggled into their landing craft in the dark: 'We didn't have any idea how far out we were,' Salomon recalled later. Those who had been able to manage breakfast struggled to hold it down.

Shells from American and British warships began whistling over the landing craft and the shore was soon shrouded in smoke. Corporal Tom Herring of C Company, the 5th Ranger Battalion, was enjoying the spectacle: 'We were standing up in the landing craft looking over the sides watching the navy ships fire and the other landing craft. You could see the shells hit the shore.' Private Ellis Reed of D Company, the 5th Ranger Battalion, was altogether less sanguine. In keeping with the best traditions of Nelson, the British sailors on the transport ship had shared their rum ration with D Company – the benefit was short lived: 'I was carrying three Bangalore torpedoes [large explosive charges for blowing holes in wire], a rifle, two bandoliers of ammunition, four hand grenades and two rifle grenades and some demolition charges on my back – a hundred and forty pounds,' Reed recalls. 'I was only nineteen years old and kind of apprehensive. I was saying to myself, "Am I gonna get this right, am I gonna do it right, am I?" I didn't know if I was going to be good enough.'

The German soldiers in Resistance Nest 62 had watched the approach of the assault force with growing apprehension. 'Landing craft making for the beach to our left off Vierville,' Corporal Hein Severloh shouted to the men in his bunker. 'Are they mad? They're going to sail right under our guns,' Sergeant Krone observed. Private Franz Gockel waited patiently as the first wave of American infantry jumped from their landing craft and pushed towards the beach: 'They were about three hundred metres away. Only then did we start to defend ourselves.' Gockel and his comrades unleashed a torrent of artillery and machine-gun fire on to the beach. 'Of this first wave most fell and did not rise again. From the next wave and then the next there were whole rows of attackers who fell and did not get up. They lay sometimes in groups as they had jumped from the landing craft. I asked myself, why do they keep on coming? They can see how many of their comrades lie dead on the beach.' The first men ashore sought what little cover they could find behind the splintered remains of Rommel's beach obstacles. 'After a while they were also able to shelter behind the damaged landing craft, but there wasn't much cover,' Gockel remembered. 'My only thought was, how can I save my own life? It was a question of defence – what can I do to hold them back? Of course, I thought, thank God they can't reach me. I was glad that the first and second waves didn't manage to get up on to the beach.' Gockel watched as the tide turned and the dead began to drift towards the shore, 'just like large pieces of flotsam'.

'I didn't have the slightest idea how deep it would be, but I'm six foot one and the sea was up to my chest and it took me a while to find my feet,' Lieutenant Sid Salomon recalled. The men of C Company, the 2nd Rangers, were among the first to land at the western end of Omaha, near the Vierville draw. Sergeant Oliver Reed was the second man off Salomon's landing craft – he was hit as he plunged into the sea. 'I reached over and grabbed him by the jacket and pulled him out from under the ramp, otherwise he'd have been steamrollered by the landing craft,' Salomon recalled. Machine-gun bullets were striking the water around the transport as the rest of the platoon followed their Lieutenant.

I pulled Reed out of the surf and maybe twenty yards up to the beach and I said, 'OK, Sergeant, this is as far as I can take you now. I'll get the first-aid man over to you, I've got to go in with the rest of the platoon and complete our mission.' So I dropped him there and just then a mortar shell landed behind me, killed or wounded almost all my mortar section and knocked me flat on my face and I thought, what the hell, I must be dead. All of a sudden sand was kicking up in my face and I said to myself, 'Ah, it's the German, he's shooting at me, he's trying to get my range, this is no place to be lying down.'

Salomon jumped up and ran hard for the cover of the cliff. He looked back on a scene of fear and death: 'Bodies lay still . . . trickles of blood reddening the sand. Some of the wounded were crawling as best they could, some with a look of despair and bewilderment on their tortured and panic-racked faces. Others tried to get back on their feet, only to be hit again by enemy fire.' More than half of C Company had been killed or wounded in the short distance between the landing craft and the cliff – thirty-seven out of sixty-eight Rangers.

The 5th Rangers managed to avoid the worst of the enemy's fire by landing to the east of the Vierville draw. Private John Burke was a twenty-one-year-old medic with A Company:

The first real sense of someone trying to get me was when a shell landed in the water and the concussion hit me and flipped me over. I came back up and started going in and I was sort of foggy at that point. Then I have a vivid recollection of machine-gun bullets hitting the water in front of me and saying to myself, 'My God, how close can it get?' And the next thing a bunch of us got to the beach and there were guys falling and somebody was yelling, 'Keep going, keep going, don't stop, don't stop.'

Around the 5th Rangers were the shell-shocked, disorganised remnants of the 116th Regiment – the first unit on the beach. Private Burke remembers looking back from the cover of the sea wall:

There was smoke all over the beach, guys dropping. There were guys lying on the beach – dead. Shells were hitting it and machine-gun fire ripping across it. Guys screaming out commands to others: 'Get over here, sniper up there.' I remember a tank running up and down the beach and it ran over some guys that were dead and it was firing up into the hill. A landing craft off to our right got a dead hit as the ramp went down. I heard this tremendous screech and looked across – it had hit the ramp as they were unloading these guys. Just blew that sucker right out of the water. Hell of a sight, awful.

The medics did what they could but it was almost impossible to reach men still in the field of fire. Private Burke remembered treating his first wounded man on the edge of the beach – a comrade from A Company:

He had a gaping chest wound. He was lying there – ashen in colour. I said to myself: 'My God, I don't know what I can do for this guy,' and I knew him very well. He was gasping and asking: 'Water, give me some water.' I said, 'I can't give you any water, but we're going to take care of you, going to get you back, just lie there.' All the time I was trying to do something for him, he was moving around in great pain. I shot him with morphine in the thigh and he kind of quietened down a little bit and then I poured sulphur in the wound and packed it with a compress and tied it across his chest. I remember trying to write on this little blue card with a string on it – it was something we were supposed to do, but I was having a tough time writing. I wrote his name down, pulled out his dog tag so they could see it and put down what I had done on the card and then I moved on. I had to leave him for the stretcher-bearers, if there were any prepared to pick him up.

The situation was still critical at the eastern end, where the veteran 1st Division was attacking the beach in front of Colleville-sur-Mer. Allied destroyers kept up a steady, accurate barrage of German positions on the buffs, and there was some sporadic mortar fire from below, but the defenders held firm. In Resistance Nest 62, Private Franz Gockel's machine gun had been silenced by a mortar round that had burst close to his bunker, peppering the barrel with shrapnel. Gockel had picked up his rifle and begun to choose his targets with care:

A large troop transport appeared in front of our position. A comrade of mine crawled over to the remains of my bunker and shouted, 'Franz, it's our turn now, we're for it.' He had a rifle too. I aimed to the left and he took a position on the right. When the troop transport reached us we could see that both sides of the gangway were full of Allied soldiers. We managed to delay the landing of this boat for perhaps ten or fifteen minutes with our rifles. There was a lot of chaos on the gangways, some of the Americans wanted to disembark, others tried to get back in, some tried to jump over the side into the water. After a little while the boat cast off again and stood out to sea looking for somewhere quieter to land.

For a time there was a lull in the fighting in front of WN 62 and the young and naively hopeful were prepared to believe the Allies had given up. 'But not long after that the first tanks arrived from the west,' Gockel recalled.

They drove along a narrow path towards the shingle bank at the edge of the beach – there was a gap there between WN 62 and WN 61. The tanks were hoping to break out through this breach. The comrade who had joined me aimed his mortar at the breach in the embankment and managed to cripple the first tank. The other tank tried to squeeze past but my comrade hit this one too and it burst into flames. Both tanks now blocked the gap in the shingle and the route off the beach. The rest of the tanks drove up and down nervously looking for another way off, but there wasn't one near us.

On the *Augusta*, a very anxious Bradley still had only the haziest sense of the situation ashore. It seemed horribly close to chaos. The beach was choked with landing craft and fresh combat troops were struggling to land. The men who had managed to make the shore were pinned down by machine-gun and artillery fire. As the tide began to turn the beach became narrower – the 'draws' needed to be captured or the traffic pressing for a route away from the mayhem would prevent follow-up waves landing. Bradley decided to send his aide, Major Chester Hansen, to the beach in a torpedo boat to report on the situation: 'It was a mess, there were landing craft clanking against one another in the surf, lots of dead, lots of noise,' Hansen recalled. It was impossible for Hansen to establish who was in command and what progress was being made by the men ashore.

Hansen had no way of knowing it but slowly the course of the battle had begun to turn. It was, as the historian Max Hastings has observed, the courage and leadership of a few individual soldiers which was to prove decisive at Omaha. At the western end of the beach the remnants of C Company, the 2nd Rangers, had taken only moments to collect themselves at the base of the cliff. More than half the company had been lost on the beach, but the CO and two of his lieutenants had made it. It was clear to Captain Ralph Goranson that he could not count on what was left of the men from the adjoining 116th Regiment for support and C Company would not be able to force the Vierville draw on its own. There was only one way to escape from the bottom of the cliff, and that was to climb it. Along the length and breadth of the beach men were cowering behind what cover they could find, but C Company was experiencing a combat high, and in spite of its losses Goranson and his men were hell bent on completing their mission. 'This was what I was supposed to do and I was well trained and confident in what I was doing,' Lieutenant Sid Salomon recalled.

Salomon had been wounded by the mortar round that had killed many of his men on the beach. The company medic picked a number of shrapnel fragments from his back: '"That's all I can do now, Lieutenant," he told me. I put my shirt and my jacket back on, and said, "OK, let's go up."' The cliff presented a sheer 30-metre wall down which the enemy could roll its concussion grenades, but Goranson's men found a crevice that offered some cover and two of the company's best climbers were chosen to attempt the ascent. Using their bayonets as pitons for footholds, the men scrambled to the top, followed by the rest of the company. 'We lay flat and kept low and I looked around to see what the hell was out in front of us,' Salomon remembered. Only nine of the thirty-seven men Salomon had led from the landing craft had made it up the cliff; the rest were dead or wounded. Set back from the edge of the cliff was a farmhouse, and behind this a network of German trenches and strongpoints. Captain Goranson had decided that the company would force its way along the high ground towards the Vierville draw, but first the farmhouse and cliff-top defences would have to be cleared. Salomon watched from the edge of the cliff as an assault team led by Lieutenant Bill Moody attacked and captured the farmhouse:

We were flat on our stomachs there, and I peeked out over this shell hole and I saw what looked like a trench about twenty-five yards ahead. Just then Bill Moody jumped into the shell hole alongside me. And I said, 'Bill, I just saw a trench ahead.' He leaned up on his elbows and peeked over. It was just a couple of seconds, a glance, but then I felt Bill fall against my right shoulder. I turned and looked. He'd been killed instantly – shot through the forehead.

Salomon took over the command of the assault team: 'I grabbed one of the men: "Otto, follow me." And we jumped ahead and ran the twenty-five yards into the trench, and cleaned it out.' Salomon pressed on towards a mortar position and attacked it with phosphorus grenades, before moving on to another trench:

Just as we came around a bend in the trench a German soldier came from the opposite direction. He was more surprised than I was. I grabbed him. Otto, the private with me, said, 'Let me finish him, Lieutenant.' I said, 'No, maybe we can get some information from him. Let's send him down to see the company commander. Take him back to the top of the cliff and just give him a nudge down.' Well, he got down there with just a little bit of a nudge and he was a big help.

C Company was the first assault unit to reach the high ground at Omaha. From it Salomon could look down on the beach: 'I thought, oh, it's a failure, it's going to be a long swim back to England.'

But almost imperceptibly order was being forged from the chaos. Pockets of infantry were beginning to establish themselves ashore throughout the Omaha sector.

To the west, Companies D, E and F of the 2nd Rangers had landed beneath the high cliffs of the Pointe du Hoc. This had long been earmarked as a key objective on D-Day. The six-gun battery that commanded the point was thought to threaten the approaches to both Omaha and Utah. The Rangers scaled the heights under fire and then pressed forward through a blasted landscape, pockmarked by the Allied bombardment, towards the concrete gun casements. After a bitter and confused battle, they succeeded in securing the position, only to find that the 155mm guns that had threatened to dominate the coast had been removed inland. They were eventually found in an orchard close to the coast road and destroyed. Half the Ranger force had been wounded or killed in the action, but the Pointe du Hoc was in Allied hands.

The commanding presence of one man helped to bring order and hope to the western half of Omaha beach. Brigadier General Norman Cota, the assistant commander of the 29th Division, had landed with men from the 116th Regiment that morning. The fifty-one-year-old brigadier enjoyed a well-deserved reputation as a tough, no-nonsense soldier – from the first he had questioned the wisdom of the attack planned for Omaha. The remnants of the first assault wave had been pinned down on the beach for an hour when Cota landed. Hundreds of men were huddled in the lee of the sea wall. Behind them lay the dead and the dying. The main attack had stalled. It was clear to Cota that it would be impossible to force the draw in front of Vierville – the best chance of capturing it would be from the inland side, and that meant climbing the bluffs.

Careless of the risk he ran, Cota clambered up on to the sea wall and urged his shell-shocked men to do the same. He passed

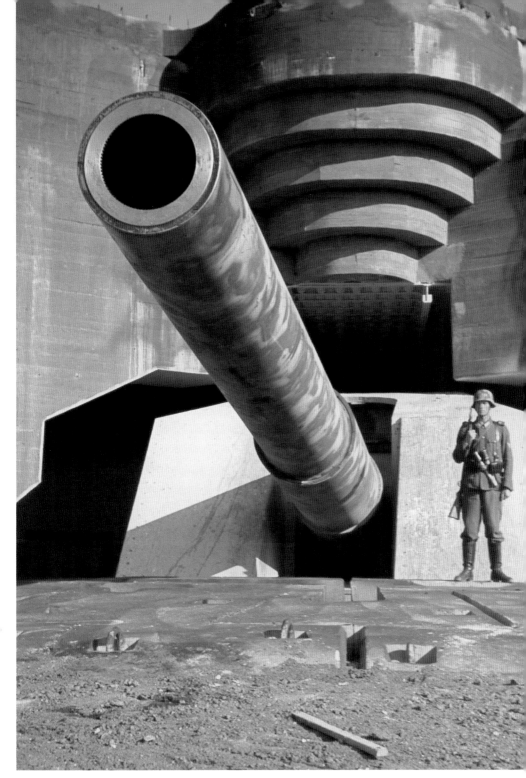

1. The Atlantic Wall the Propaganda Ministry presented to the Home Front. A German soldier with the 406mm cannon of the Lindemann Battery near Calais. It was powerful enough to reach the English coast. The invasion was expected at Calais and the defences here at least were formidable.

2. Field Marshal Rommel injected a new sense of urgency into preparations for the invasion in the spring of 1944, but German defences along the Normandy coast were a long way from completion on D-Day.

3. Artillery pieces like this were used to devastating effect by the battery at Resistance Nest 62 on Omaha Beach.

4. The seizure of the port of Cherbourg was one of the key Overlord objectives. Hitler wanted it to be defended to the last bullet.

5. The soldiers in the strongpoints along the Normandy coast were generally of poor quality. Rommel relied on his armoured reserves to repel the invasion.

6. Soldiers from 4 Commando wade ashore with bicycles at Sword on D-Day. They were given the task of seizing the nearby town of Ouistreham.

7. Rangers shelter from intense enemy fire on Omaha Beach.

8. A wounded GI is treated beneath the cliff at Colleville on Omaha Beach. The first assault wave was hit by a barrage of artillery and machine-gun fire.

9. A motley group of prisoners rounded up at Omaha on D-Day.

10. The Commander-in-Chief in the West, Field Marshal Gerd von Rundstedt – the grand old man of the German army. He was pessimistic about the chances of holding the Allies in Normandy.

11. Germany's celebrity field marshal – 'The Desert Fox' – Erwin Rommel. His experience in Africa had taught him to fear Allied air power.

12. Allied Supreme Commander General Dwight D. Eisenhower [right] is visited by General Omar Bradley of US First Army [centre] on 7 June. Both men were still anxious about the small beach-head at Omaha.

13. General Montgomery in characteristic dress and pose with Winston Churchill and Field Marshal Sir Alan Brooke on 12 June 1944. They are standing in front of the caravans Monty used as his forward headquarters throughout the war.

14. Trooper Austin Baker of the 4th/7th Royal Dragoon Guards.

15. Major Peter Martin of the 2nd Battalion, The Cheshires – a veteran of Dunkirk, North Africa and D-Day.

16. Private Franz Gockel of the 726 Grenadier Regiment was wounded while resisting the American assault at Omaha.

17. Rolf Munninger served on Rommel's staff in North Africa and in France. He was with Army Group B Headquarters from D-Day to the fall of the Reich.

up and down the line, encouraging the frightened and beleaguered GIs out and up towards the bluffs.

Private Ellis Reed of D Company was at the sea wall when
Cota reached the 5th Rangers: 'He came to our place and said
to our CO, "Colonel Schneider, I want the Rangers to lead the
way."'

Reed had lugged his Bangalore torpedoes off the landing craft
and across the beach – the time to use them had come:

Beyond the wall was a road and across it a barbed-wire entanglement – both were covered by artillery and machine-gun fire. When
my lieutenant gave the signal I climbed up the wall and crawled across
the road. When we got to the barbed-wire entanglement, I hollered,
'Fire in the hole,' and me and my buddy fired. The Bangalores had
a five-second fuse. The explosion did enough to blow a hole in the
wire – we got up and ran through it.

The rest of Lieutenant Francis Dawson's platoon was hard on
his heels, followed by the 5th Rangers Headquarters Company
and stragglers from the 29th Division. Dawson's platoon pressed
on through a minefield and up the bluff. In places the scrub and
grass were on fire, covering the slopes with a thick blanket of
smoke, and many of the Rangers resorted to the gas masks they
carried in their kit. Bill Reed recalled:

There was machine-gun fire from our right flank. Lieutenant Dawson
said, 'Reed, give them one of your rifle grenades.' I fired but it didn't
go off, it was a dud, so my impatient lieutenant got up with his sub-
machine gun and ran right at it. They put their hands up at once.
He said, 'Reed, take those people down to the beach.' I thought, OK,
I've got to get them down. But another company was coming up to
my right and they didn't know that these Germans had surrendered
and they cut them all down in front of me. When you're nineteen
years old and you see blood splatter all over the place it kind of gets
you a little shook. It was probably a big old accident, but it did
happen.

Most Germans who surrendered were marched into captivity but a handful were shot in the heat of the battle. Corporal Tom Herring of C Company, the 5th Rangers, recalled:

The Channel was behind us and the Germans were in front of us, so when a German surrendered there was nothing to do but kill him because you had no place to send him and you couldn't trust him. So there were a lot of Germans who surrendered on the beaches that were killed for just that purpose. People can call it inhuman, but it was a matter of survival for us.

By late morning the 5th Rangers and men from the 116th were on top of the bluffs. The battle had moved to the fields and hedgerows beyond – the German strongpoint at Vierville was outflanked and the village finally fell to the Americans. The battleship *USS Texas* began shelling the concrete obstacles at the bottom of the all-important 'draw' from the beach: 'the concussion from the bursts of these guns seemed to make the pavement of the street in Vierville actually rise beneath our feet in a bucking sensation', Brigadier Cota's aide later recorded. But the *Texas'* shells failed to force a significant breach – it was the indefatigable Brigadier Cota who finally managed to clear the draw. He found a bulldozer loaded with high explosives that had been dumped on the beach. 'Who drives this thing?' he asked a group of soldiers sheltering behind the sea wall. No one answered. 'They need TNT down at the exit,' he told them. 'Hasn't anyone got guts enough to drive it down?' At last a young, red-headed soldier volunteered. The engineers managed to blow a hole in the sea wall but it was some time before the rubble and mines were finally cleared.

At the eastern end of Omaha beach the defenders in WN 62 were still holding their ground. By midday Corporal Hein Severloh had fired 12,000 rounds from his machine gun and all he had left to fire were night tracer bullets. It had been eighteen hours since most of the men in the resistance nest had eaten. In a brief lull in the fighting, Private Franz Gockel was sent in search of food. He stopped short of the main bunker at a machine-gun post held by two men from his regiment – the 726th Grenadiers: 'They were trying to hold the Americans approaching from the west. I told them to cover my back while I ran into the bunker. I managed to get some bread and milk I had collected from a farmer the night before. I also managed to get my soldier's pay-book, a rosary and a medallion that my father had kept in the First World War.' Gockel ran back from the bunker and jumped into the machine-gun post: 'I sat in the trench with my two comrades and ate the bread and drank the cold milk – in fact I drank it too quickly. I had to drop my trousers and run behind a bank where I couldn't be seen from the seaward side. I managed to get there OK.' Gockel was less fortunate on his way back to his machine-gun post: 'As I carefully lifted my head over the edge of the bank to talk to my mates, I was hit in my left hand. The impact sent me tumbling back down the bank. I didn't see those two comrades again. I found them later in the war cemetery at Colleville.'

Gockel made his way to a nearby mortar post where his hand was bandaged by a medical orderly: 'To cheer me up the medic said: "This is a good wound, you're going home. We don't know if we will ever get out of here."' Gockel made his way to the company's headquarters bunker in Colleville: 'When I entered HQ I heard our CO, who'd been wounded too, say, "I've just come from WN 62, there is nobody there alive."' Not long afterwards American soldiers were reported to have taken the church-yard at Colleville, just 60 metres from the company command post. Units from the 1st Division had outflanked German strong-points on the bluffs and had fought their way through to the outskirts of the village. Gockel was one of the lucky few to escape that day: 'My only concern was to get back to a hospital in Germany and to my family.'

At one point that morning Bradley had considered abandoning Omaha and transferring the follow-up troops to Utah or a British beach. News of the progress made up and along the bluffs was slow to reach the *Augusta*. It was not until 1.30 in the afternoon that V Corps reported the advance up the heights above the beach. By then the landings at Omaha were badly behind schedule. The beach was littered with wrecked tanks and landing craft – everywhere the dead lay sprawled across the shingle like so much grim flotsam. In the first hours after dawn a German officer in command of one of the strongpoints at the western end of the beach had felt confident enough to report that the invasion had been stopped. The fire from German strongpoints had inflicted heavy losses, he explained, and a great many tanks and other vehicles were burning on the beach. A similar report was sent to Army Group B at 1 p.m. – 'Landing near Vierville as good as repulsed'. The Americans had captured the village three hours earlier. For a short time it had appeared a close-run thing – the presence of the veteran 352nd Infantry Division had made it much tougher than the Allied planners had expected. More than two thousand men had been killed or wounded on the beach and it had taken the determined leadership of men like Brigadier Cota to push the assault forward. But in the end the German line had proved a thin one. The combined navies had kept up a continuous and accurate bombardment of the strongpoints above the beach. Without reserves or air support to call on, the defenders had faced what they had known to be a hopeless task.

The assault on the most westerly of the Allied beaches – Utah – was an altogether different affair. VII Corps, commanded by the edgy, able General J. Lawton Collins – 'Lightning Joe' – had come ashore on the Cotentin peninsula. The lowering positions were again more than 10 miles from the shore but the 4th Division had been fortunate to reach the beach in the lee of the land. A strong current had swept the first assault wave a mile south of the designated landing points but this had proved a remarkable stroke of luck, for the beach obstacles and defensive positions here proved much less formidable than those farther to the north. The first units ashore met only light resistance and within an hour the beach was cleared. By ten o'clock six battalions of infantry had landed and were pushing inland.

Remarkably, it was only at ten o'clock that Field Marshal Rommel decided the situation in Normandy was serious enough to require his personal attention. By then the BBC had broadcast an official confirmation: 'Under the command of General Eisenhower, Allied naval forces supported by strong air forces began landing Allied armies this morning on the coast of France.' It was to take Rommel nearly twelve hours to drive from Herrlingen back to his headquarters in France. He had argued passionately that the Allies needed to be fought and held close to the beaches, and yet in the first crucial hours he was beyond the reach of his commanders in the field.

No one had dared to wake the Führer. He had talked and watched films with his mistress, Eva Braun, well into the small hours and surfaced only at ten o'clock. Hitler greeted the news with surprising equanimity. 'As long as they were in Britain we couldn't get at them,' he told his generals. 'Now we have them where we can destroy them.' The reports from Normandy were not judged serious enough to require a change to the Führer's official programme, and later that morning he was driven from the Berghof to Klessheim Castle to meet the new Hungarian prime minister. It was here, in a room beside the entrance hall, that he was given his first full briefing. It was to be, in the words of one staff officer present, a 'performance'. Hitler studied the map of France intently and then 'chuckled in a carefree manner'. Turning to the assembled staff, he declared in an unusually broad Austrian accent, 'So, we're off.' General orders were then issued for determined counter-attacks against the Allied landings.

The Führer's confidence was sorely misplaced. There were no serious counter-attacks that morning and only a rather half-hearted effort in the afternoon of D-Day. The muddled chain of command and the absence of so many senior officers had led to a general paralysis throughout the 7th Army sector. The failure to release armoured reserves for a major counter-attack was critical, and responsibility for this rested with Hitler himself. The Fortitude planners had succeeded beyond their wildest hopes. Hitler and the generals of the Armed Forces High Command (OKW) were not yet convinced that this was the main attack. It had become the gospel at OKW that there would first be a diversionary operation to deflect attention from the real Allied invasion force – remarkably this view was to persist for many weeks to come. No serious effort was made to consult the soldiers called upon to throw back the Allied 'diversionary' force. Staff at the headquarters of the 84th Corps in St-Lô had identified soldiers from three Allied airborne divisions and from the US 1st and 4th Divisions. The Canadian 3rd Division had landed as well as the British 50th and 7th Armoured Divisions. 'All that's missing is the 51st Highland and 1st Armoured Divisions and we'll have Montgomery's entire 8th Army from Africa at our throats!' one senior staff officer observed. 'If this isn't the invasion, what are they going to come with?'

The reserve formation closest to the coast was the 21st Panzer Division. Most of its armour was stationed to the south-east of Caen, but four grenadier battalions straddled the River Orne between the city and the sea – within easy striking distance of Sword Beach. The 21st Panzer had served with distinction in North Africa and a cadre of its officers and senior NCOs had been extricated before the final defeat to form the core of a new, reconstituted division. It was to the 21st Panzer that the infantry at the coast had looked in the early hours of D-Day. General Richter of the 716th Division had twice appealed for assistance to counter the British airborne landings to the east of the Orne, but to no avail. His frustration was shared by many of the 21st Panzer's senior officers. It was clear to the commander of the 125th Panzer Grenadier Regiment, Major Hans von Luck, that a large Allied operation was under way, perhaps the invasion itself. He had called out his regiment at 0130 hours, but his men had been kept waiting by their armoured vehicles for more than five hours. Luck's regiment was within striking distance of the bridges over the Orne and Caen Canal, and would certainly have been capable of dislodging Major Howard's *coup de main* force. But it was the 21st Panzer's misfortune to be commanded by a man without real combat experience who had that night put 'procedure' first. General Edgar Feuchtinger had sought authority to order his division into action from Army Group B. It had been withheld. Rommel was in Germany and his new chief of staff, General Speidel, was no more willing to act on his own initiative than Feuchtinger. The 21st Panzer Division had been obliged to wait until 6.30 a.m. – then, unable to bear the inaction a moment longer, its commander had finally ordered a limited attack on the British 6th Airborne. By the time the 21st Panzer received its first operational order from a higher command, the Allies were well on their way to establishing themselves ashore. During the course of the morning the division's tanks rumbled across the Orne at Caen. Once established to the west of the river, a battle group of ninety tanks with two battalions of infantry attacked north-ward towards the coast.

The 21st Panzer could not hope to roll back the Allied invasion on its own – that required a much more substantial armoured force. The Panzer reserves best placed to offer support were in the 15th Army sector – the 12th SS Panzer and Panzer Lehr Divisions. Both were formidable units, but both were under the direct control of Hitler. The Panzer Lehr Division had been placed on alert in the early hours of the 6th by Field Marshal von Rundstedt, and preparations for a dash to the coast were well under way. The Panzer Lehr's commander, General Fritz Bayerlein, had anticipated a difficult journey. Bayerlein had been Rommel's chief of staff in North Africa and as such had witnessed the extraordinary destructive power of the Allied air forces. He had done what he could to prepare his division to meet this threat: 'I increased flak armament, although I didn't get all the anti-aircraft guns I wanted,' he told his interrogators after the war. 'I placed every emphasis on camouflage against air attack. We trained to move at night, and dispersed in small attachments in woods and villages.' In Bayerlein's opinion the army was dominated by senior officers who had cut their teeth on the Eastern Front, where the threat from the air was significantly less. The Inspector General of the German Armed Forces had told Bayerlein that his division was capable of driving the Allies back into the sea on its own: 'Your goal is not the coast, it is the sea.' It was not meant as a jest. The Panzer Lehr had been established only the year before and was the best equipped German armoured division in the west – boasting 150 tanks and 600 tracked vehicles. Its fighting strength comprised 14,600 officers and men, most of whom were veterans drawn from the military schools or 'Lehr'.

'We were absolutely convinced, without a doubt, that we could push any attacker back into the sea,' Hauptmann (Captain) Helmut Ritgen of II Battalion, the 130th Panzer Lehr Regiment, recalled. 'This was not a question of optimism at all. Until that time we had always felt ourselves to be more capable than all our enemies.' The twenty-eight-year-old Ritgen had fought in France before – he had played his part in the humiliation of the British at Dunkirk in 1940. Since then he had commanded a company of tanks in the hard proving ground of the Eastern Front. 'Today the invasion has been launched!' he wrote to his wife with relish on the morning of the 6th. Ritgen had expected the Atlantic Wall to be breached but the Panzer Lehr would be there to throw the Allies back – just as long as the Luftwaffe was able to support the ground forces.

But Rundstedt's orders to the Panzer Lehr and 12th SS Panzer had been countermanded by the High Command (OKW), and their tanks were left slowly overheating for the best part of the day. Hitler finally released both divisions in the afternoon – too late for them to play any part on D-Day. The 12th SS could not arrive in the Caen area before the morning of the 7th, while the

Panzer Lehr was 160 kilometres from the coast and would play no part until the 8th.

'I was told to begin moving north that afternoon at five o'clock,' Bayerlein later recalled. 'My request for a delay until twilight was refused. We moved as ordered, and immediately came under air attack.' Captain Ritgen was acting commander of his battalion that day: 'Needless to say we were spotted by reconnaissance planes and before long we were under attack from fighter bombers. Tanks started to explode into flames and so did our fuel tankers. It was not a pretty sight.'

The Panzer Lehr had lost as many as thirty tanks by nightfall – Bayerlein only narrowly escaped death when he was strafed near Alençon. The Luftwaffe had all but abandoned the skies above Normandy to the Allies.

At a little before 5 p.m. on D-Day Field Marshal Rommel had broken his journey at Reims to telephone his headquarters. His chief of staff, General Speidel, gave him the latest grim reports from the coast – the Allies ashore at five different points and pressing inland towards Caen and Bayeux, large numbers of American paratroopers in the Cotentin peninsula and British Airborne to the north of Caen. 'How far has our own counterattack progressed?' Rommel asked. Not far was the reply. 'Attack at once,' Rommel barked back – the 21st Panzer Division, at least, should press on to the coast.

Feuchtinger had been attempting to do just that. Even as Rommel was issuing his orders from the road, a battle group of forty tanks from the 21st Panzer was engaging the vanguard of the British advance. The battle group had been surprised by the 2nd King's Own Shropshire Light Infantry, which had pushed forward from Sword to a position just three miles from the city of Caen itself. In the engagement that followed, the Shropshires, supported by tanks from the Staffordshire Yeomanry, destroyed thirteen of Feuchtinger's tanks – another six were lost to Allied aircraft as the battle group pulled back towards the city. A small force of German tanks was able to find a gap in the Allied line and advance through it to the coast near Lion-sur-Mer. Once there Feuchtinger lost his nerve and ordered a withdrawal – everywhere the Allies were advancing and his men risked being isolated and destroyed. By nightfall the 21st Panzer had lost at least fifty tanks, more than a third of its battle order, but had precious little to show for it.

During the course of the day the Allied expeditionary force had pushed on from the beaches in an effort to establish the largest possible bridgehead by nightfall. Beyond the coast the advancing troops had to pass through what the German newsreels had christened the 'death zone' – a belt of defended country up to 10 kilometres deep. Along the British 2nd Army's front – Sword, Juno and Gold – this zone was defended by thirteen battalions of German infantry with 260 field guns – including more than thirty self-propelled 88mms. Many of the British armoured units were to encounter this most formidable of anti-tank weapons for the first time as they pressed forward from the beaches.

The tanks of the 4th/7th Royal Dragoon Guards had been among the first ashore on Gold. Casualties on the beach had been light and the 4th/7th had begun to push on through the coastal zone. As far as Trooper Austin Baker of C Squadron was concerned, 'Everything seemed to have gone with a swing.' A troop leader and a sergeant had been killed by snipers during fighting in La Rivière and another officer wounded by shellfire, but that was better than most in the squadron had dared hope. But the news from the regiment's A and B Squadrons was not as good. Baker recalled:

Two chaps from B Squadron arrived at our harbour – a corporal driver and his co-driver from one of Lieutenant Charlton's crew. They had gone over a rise and spotted a Jerry SP [self-propelled gun] down the road ahead of them. They had fired and missed, and the next moment the Jerry had got them through the turret twice, killing the operator and wounding the commander and gunner. They had baled out and the two from the turret had disappeared somewhere (they got back, we found out later, but Charlton lost a leg). The corporal and his mate had walked all the way back to us, a distance of several miles. They were very much shaken up.

Later that evening there was worse news from A Squadron. 'They had reached a place called Fresnay-le-Crotteur, quite a long way inland, and they had had four tanks knocked out by two 88s,' Baker recorded. 'It was the first time that we really knew the Sherman tank was very vulnerable indeed – we hadn't realised that one shot from an 88mm anti-tank gun could send the whole thing up in flames and that anyone inside who wasn't dead had about five seconds to get out of it.'

A Squadron had pressed on through what appeared to be peaceful countryside and was just south of the village of Creully, some six kilometres from the coast, when it was attacked. The squadron commander was Captain Alastair Morrison:

The leading tank stopped and a great plume of flame came out of its turret. One person jumped out, landed on the ground, and then a great black column of smoke climbed up about 200 feet in the air. While I was watching it another tank stopped and exactly the same thing happened. We had no idea until then that a Sherman could blow up in this way.

Six men were killed and ten more injured.

It had been a nasty shock but by evening A Squadron had almost reached the Caen–Bayeux road some eight kilometres inland. Resistance had been patchy throughout the 50th Division's sector. Major Peter Martin's company of 2nd Cheshires had advanced without difficulty: 'The only Germans we encountered were going in the same direction as us, after leaving the beaches in a rush,' he recalled. 'I remember relieving one German officer of a Luger pistol and a rather nice pair of binoculars. There was no hostile action at all. We were supposed to get up to the line of the Caen–Bayeux main road and we got within about a thousand yards of it and then we were told to stop.' There was no apparent reason for the hold-up so Martin decided to carry out his own recce along the main road:

I said to my driver, 'Shall we go and liberate Bayeux?' and he said, 'What a good idea, sir.' At this time I imagined that 56th Brigade on the right flank must have got into the town of Bayeux, so I wasn't being all that gallant. We cruised down the road towards Bayeux and when we got just into the outskirts a French civilian standing on the corner of the road whistled and said, 'Boche, Boche,' so we stopped and did a rapid about-turn and went back towards Caen.

Martin and his driver were forced to scramble into a ditch when an American fighter plane took them for Germans. The jeep lost a wheel in the attack: 'We did the quickest wheel change ever done outside a grand prix and went and rejoined the company.' Martin's company dug in for the night just 900 metres back from their D-Day objective. 'As a mechanised [machine gun] company we had compo rations with us, not the ordinary twenty-four-hour ration packs which the rest of the unfortunate infantry had, so we had steak and kidney pie and treacle tarts and somebody went and milked a cow and we had hot chocolate and bedded down where we were for the night. It was just beginning to rain.' Just four years before, the twenty-four-year-old Martin had been rescued from the beach at Dunkirk: 'I think most of us felt pretty ashamed – it was not the proudest moment of British military history. So we felt a sense of triumph to be back in France and firmly established on French soil again, and the fact that we were still alive after all our forebodings, I think it filled us all with a sense of euphoria as well.'

The 50th Division had not managed to capture Bayeux, the ambitious objective it had been set for D-Day, but it was firmly established in the countryside to the north of the town and had linked up with the Canadians advancing from Juno. After a slow start the 3rd Canadian Division had advanced rapidly through broad cornfields towards the Bayeux–Caen road. At one point two tank troops had penetrated as far as Carpiquet on the western outskirts of Caen – the day's final objective. They had been forced to withdraw for lack of infantry support, but by nightfall the Canadian bridgehead extended up to eight kilometres inland. To the east the British 3rd Division had advanced to within five kilometres of Caen before being forced to consolidate for the night. The 185th Brigade was to have led the division into the city. The Shropshires had pressed on gamely with the support of just one squadron of tanks, but the main body of the brigade – the 2nd Royal Warwickshire and 1st Royal Norfolk Regiments – had become caught up in a series of small actions to secure the bridgehead.

The city of Caen was one of Montgomery's key objectives and the failure to seize it on D-Day was to haunt the Allies for weeks to come. Monty had made it 'the hinge' of his plan for the break-out from the beachhead – the right of the Allied line was to 'pivot' on Caen. All the more remarkable, then, that the effort to capture it before the enemy's reserves had reached the new front had proved so half hearted. As historians have been quick to point out, far too much was expected of the British 3rd Division on D-Day. Monty had known full well that a veteran Panzer division was stationed close to the city and that two more of Germany's finest were within striking distance. The 21st Panzer was firmly established to the north and west of the city by the late afternoon, and the first units of the 12th SS Panzer Division began to arrive at its outskirts the following morning. Was it realistic to expect a brigade to sweep a Panzer division aside and march into a city of 50,000 people – one, moreover, the Germans were determined to hold? The men of the British 185th Brigade had been tossed around their landing craft for many sleepless hours before they had launched their amphibious assault on Sword – Caen was one step too far.

At the other end of the new Allied bridgehead the US 4th Division's assault on Utah was close to being an unqualified success. In just fifteen hours 20,000 men and 1,700 vehicles had come ashore and the first links had been made with positions seized in the Cotentin by the American 82nd and 101st Airborne Divisions in the early hours of D-Day. Less than two hundred men had lost their lives in the initial assault. The following morning the US 4th would begin the struggle for control of the peninsula and the deep-water port of Cherbourg.

It was still a very different story at Omaha. The Americans were ashore but only just. The bridgehead here was at no point more than three kilometres deep. The enemy had been able to shell the beach for most of the day. It had been a tough experience for the infantry in particular – they had been obliged to fight without proper armoured support. A large number of tanks had been lost in the approach to the beach, and very few artillery pieces had been landed during the course of the afternoon. But the American 1st and 29th Divisions were digging in ashore, and after what had been a tempestuous morning that in itself was cause enough to be thankful.

At ten o'clock that night General Montgomery boarded the destroyer *HMS Faulkenor* at Portsmouth and set sail for France fifteen minutes later. His aide-de-camp was a twenty-four-year-old captain in the 12th Royal Lancers – Johnny Henderson had been with Monty since the desert. That night he was struck by how matter-of-fact the General seemed about what was little short of a triumph: 'He was just calm, amazingly calm. He said wake me at six o'clock in the morning and give me the news of the battle.' It was typical 'Monty', but his staff could not hide their 'considerable excitement'.

D-Day was an overwhelming success – more than 156,000 Allied soldiers had landed in France. Fewer than 10,000 men had been killed or wounded in the assault on the beaches – the Overlord planners had expected many more. The Atlantic Wall had crumbled. It was just the beginning – Monty knew his old adversary, Field Marshal Rommel, would do everything in his power to snuff out the bridgehead before it could be firmly established. Some of the German army's finest Panzer divisions were already approaching the coast – the battle to come would be decisive, not just for the combatants, but for the occupied peoples of Europe. But after D-Day the Allies were in a better position to resist the German counter-attack than many at SHAEF had dared to hope.

Rommel's staff car finally swept up to the steps of the ancient chateau of La Roche Guyon at ten o'clock that night. It had been a fraught journey. The field marshal was tense with anxiety and had repeatedly leaned forward to urge his driver to make better speed. Beside him in the back of the Horch was his adjutant, Captain Helmut Lang: 'I remember him punching one gloved fist into another as he said, "You see, Lang, I was right all the time. I should have had the Panzer Lehr and the 12th SS under my command near the beaches."' At one point during the journey Lang remembered Rommel saying, 'If Montgomery only knew the mess we are in he'd have no worries tonight.' There was already an air of desperation at Army Group B headquarters. As the field marshal's car pulled up, Lang jumped out and ran into the chateau. He was instantly conscious of loud music echoing down the hall. It was coming from the office of Rommel's chief of staff, General Speidel. Lang later recalled:

It sounded like the strains of a Wagnerian opera. Speidel came out and was walking forward to meet Rommel. I said to him, in a sort of surprised way, 'General, the invasion, it's begun, and you're able to listen to Wagner.' He just said, 'My dear Lang, do you honestly believe that my listening to Wagner will make any difference whatsoever to the course of the invasion?' Speidel greeted Rommel and the two men went into his office. I was very depressed by what was happening because everyone knew by then that the landings had been a success.

'Sir, do you think we'll be able to manage it, hold them back?' Lang asked Field Marshal Rommel later that night. Every

German soldier in France was asking the same question. 'Lang, I hope we can,' Rommel replied. 'I have always succeeded up to now.'

CHAPTER THREE

HARD LESSONS

It was with a feeling of weary relief that Captain Alastair Bannerman greeted the dawn. He had spent a short, cold night in a ditch, huddled for warmth with his dispatch rider beneath a large gas cape. 'I have had time to wash and write and breakfast,' Bannerman noted in the diary he was keeping for his wife, Elizabeth. 'This is our big day. We have to attack the hill beyond this village.'

The men of the 2nd Warwicks had been creeping along the road to Caen in the dark when the order to dig in finally reached them. The battalion had been expected to push on to Caen on D-Day, but instead it had become embroiled in the fighting to secure the bridgehead over the River Orne. Progress had been slow – the roads crammed with columns of troops and armour. Precious time was wasted clearing the village of Bénouville, although there had been welcome and unexpected support from a small armada of gliders: 'A whole regiment of airborne troops were arriving,' Bannerman noted, 'one swarm after the other of these aeroplanes and gliders came over from England, the gliders turning and crashing through the anti-landing poles. They really looked magnificent landing all round us and soon men, guns and jeeps were unloaded.'

'What a cheerful sight it was to us, who had been on the move all day,' Lieutenant Kingston Adams of A Company logged in his diary. It was Adams's company which had been ordered to storm Bénouville. It had not been a textbook engagement –

'rather a shambles', he noted. Fortunately the Germans had offered little in the way of organised resistance. A few men were lost to snipers – among them Adams's nineteen-year-old batman: 'He was on the other side of the road from me at the time, and was shot in the head and died very quickly, which was merciful. He was a grand lad and I was awfully sad to lose him – poor chap.'

By the time A Company had cleared the ruined and burning village it was evening and the men were, Adams observed, 'tired and rather moody'. The battalion had assembled on the road to Caen in the dark:

We passed a burning British tank which lit up the place for yards around. We were warned it was full of high-explosive ammo and might blow up any minute, but nothing happened, and I remember thinking what a trifling worry it was, compared to all the others that we had gone through that day, and yet how scared we would have probably been had we passed the same thing on an exercise in England.

Adams's platoon had spent a broken night in a wood on the outskirts of Blainville: 'I got no sleep during the night but had one spell of rest while Sergeant Day took over and it was then that I began to feel terribly tired.' At about four in the morning a German soldier had stumbled into the platoon's picket – 'a huge sullen arrogant brute', Adams logged in his diary. 'I sent him along to Company HQ and settled the section down again as they had all been rather excited at taking their first prisoner.'

A short time later Adams was summoned to company head-quarters for an 'O' Group meeting so orders for D + 1 could be issued. The 3rd Division's first objective was the high ground to the north of Caen, from where they were to press on to the city itself. Once again the 185th Brigade was entrusted with the task – this time with the 2nd Warwicks in the van. The rising ground on the road to Caen was crowned by woodland – beyond it lay the village of Lebisey. The Shropshires had reached the wood by dusk on D-Day but had found it strongly held by soldiers from the 21st Panzer Division. This piece of intelligence seems to have been omitted from the briefing the officers of the 2nd Warwicks were given the following morning. 'It was thought that the wood was unlikely to be held in much strength, if at all,' A Company's commander, Captain Harry Illing, later wrote. The battalion had left one rifle company with the airborne troops at the bridges over the Orne and the Caen Canal – the remaining three would begin advancing from the start line at a little before nine o'clock. No reconnaissance had been carried out on the woods during the night and the attack was to be made without close armoured support. There was, however, the promise of support from one of the navy's cruisers and from artillery in the field.

The 2nd Warwicks had been scooped from the beach at Dunkirk and was officially a regular unit, but there were few in its ranks four years on with real combat experience. The regulars numbered less than fifty. Harry Illing had worked for a bank before the war and was one of those who joined the battalion after Dunkirk. One of the regiment's old regulars was by then the Allied Land Forces Commander – General Montgomery. Monty had maintained a keen interest in his old regiment: 'He visited us on the eve of D-Day – he knew a lot of the officers by name,' Lieutenant Adams recalled. Alastair Bannerman's father had served in the regiment with Monty during the First World War. 'I think he was always regarded by the soldiers as one of them,' Illing recalled. The Royal Warwicks could be sure their progress would be carefully watched at 21st Army Group Headquarters.

The battalion had begun to move up to the start line for the attack in the dark. 'It was an awful effort getting the platoon to move,' Adams logged in his diary. 'I would have given anything for a good wash and shave and to get my boots off.' It was soon clear that the plan of attack was seriously flawed. The start line was a stream halfway between Blainville and the wood. 'It wasn't secured,' Captain Illing remembered. 'It was an elementary error.' The battalion would have to fight its way to the stream.

Illing climbed a water tower on the edge of the village but was unable to see the stream: 'I decided to go forward in my armoured carrier with my platoon commanders to recce and give out orders, and for my company to follow on as quickly as possible under the company's second-in-command. Soon after I had started off my carrier got fairly peppered by fire and it was clear to me that there were plenty of enemy still about.'

Lieutenant Adams was a member of the 'O' group: 'The start line was a little strip of wood bordered by a largish stream. You could see the top of Lebisey Wood five to six hundred yards away up the convex slope of a wheat field.'

Captain Bannerman carried out his own recce to see whether the support company's anti-tank guns would be able to cross the stream: 'I found myself rather eerily in a vast wheat field and as I went farther forward on foot I felt extraordinarily vulnerable and expected every moment to meet a German,' he later recalled. 'I decided the valley was impossible for carriers [Bren gun carriers] and guns and returned to report to my CO.' Lieutenant Colonel Herdon was a worried man. The supporting fire from a cruiser offshore had been cancelled and no contact could be made with the field artillery. It looked as if the lead companies would be dependent on their own mortars for close support.

From the start line Captain Illing could see B Company on his right advancing slowly across a wheat field towards the objective. Illing had expected the attack to begin with an artillery barrage – was A Company to advance or not? It was impossible to reach Lieutenant Colonel Herdon on the radio. 'No covering fire. Harry did not know whether he was coming or going, I felt very sorry for him,' Adams later recalled. Illing decided not to wait any longer – A Company swung into position and began to press forward. Bannerman watched them advance towards the top of the ridge: 'I could see the small brown figures climbing on the open slope steadily and bravely. It was all rather touching and hopeful. The CO [Lieutenant Colonel Herdon] was walking about the skyline in a way that seemed to ask for trouble but he appeared quite unconcerned and ignored the mortar fire which kept dropping sporadically round us.'

Lieutenant Adams's platoon was one of the two leading A Company's advance: 'We started to move up the convex slope, through very tall corn – over the heads of some of the chaps. It gave cover but it wasn't comfortable to struggle through with heavy packs. It went well until we reached the top of the ridge. We were within two hundred yards of the wood when all hell broke loose.' During the night the wood and village had been occupied by a battalion of grenadiers from the 21st Panzer Division. It had dug in and waited.

Adams recalled:

We did our best to get into the wood – two sections of my platoon moved up, covered by the other two – leapfrogging. I did not have a sense of the casualties we were taking, but I think I lost three or four men approaching the wood. You could hear shouts and screams but you couldn't do much about it. They were spraying heavy machine-gun fire at us. They couldn't see us clearly. I had been told to get into the wood and that is what I tried to do. The enemy fire seemed to get stronger as we got closer.

The lead platoons found it difficult to push on beyond the fringes of the wood. 'One complete platoon on the right got into the wood and charged an enemy group,' Illing recalled later. 'The platoon commander got within ten yards, only to be shot dead. Virtually his entire platoon became casualties.' At first Lieutenant Adams was able to maintain contact with his men: 'We tried to move forward and find a gap, putting down smoke grenades and what machine-gun fire we could muster, but we struggled to make any progress. After we'd failed to get through to the second thickness of the wood, we tried to get orders from Company HQ. Harry said, "Get down and take what cover you can."'

The battalion CO, Lieutenant Colonel Herdon, went forward

to see what was happening, but he was cut down by machine-gun fire. Three companies were pinned down along the perimeter of the wood. The situation improved a little with the arrival of the fourth company, which attacked the north-east corner of the wood and for a time seemed to win a foothold inside it. The battalion was in desperate need of artillery and armoured support. Its carriers and anti-tank guns had been sent round to the right flank of the attack and were waiting near the village of Biéville for orders. As Captain Bannerman, the commander of the anti-tank platoon, recalled later, the orders that were eventually given were to prove nothing short of disastrous:

Suddenly the brigadier dashed up in a flap and jumped out with his red tabs blazing. He told me the battalion had captured the hill and I was to proceed on down the road and join them as there were Jerry tanks about. I saluted and called my chaps and told them to follow me about 100 yards between each carrier and gun and off we started down the road. We had gone for about half a mile when all hell let loose. The noise was fantastic, cracking and humming past us. Luckily the banks were high and I suppose we were too low for them. Somehow we weren't hit and we pressed on up the hill. We couldn't turn round and anyhow I felt to stop was fatal, so we accelerated madly and fired our Bren and our three Stens at either side of the road as we passed. Suddenly there appeared a low bridge, a mass of rubble and broken houses that had been the village of Lebisey. Worse still was the sight of scurrying Germans in their sickening greenish-grey, darting behind the houses as we careered forlornly into the middle of them.

Bannerman's carrier 'bucketed' on, passed a German tank and out the other end of the village. By this time it was on its own – the other five in the platoon had been knocked out. There was no point in pressing on farther so Bannerman gave the order 'action rear' and his men unhitched the gun and took aim at the tank they had just passed. 'We hit and holed it,' Bannerman recalled. 'Suddenly there was this almighty crash – a shell had hit our carrier, knocking us sideways. We scrambled away – I knew we had no hope, so I said, "Everyone for himself, good luck," and off we went.'

The battalion struggled on into the afternoon under intense fire. 'It was getting heavier and heavier,' Adams recalled. 'One of my sections entered a clearing in the wood and was making some progress and I moved up to join them. As I was doing that I felt something hit me – it burst and I was covered in smoke. I felt my right thigh burning – phosphorus. I had been hit by a smoke grenade. I tried to strip off my burning trousers but my right hand began to burn – the skin peeled off like a glove.' Adams was also shot in the left hand: 'The smoke may have saved my life because I was only hit the once.' Through the trees it was possible to see flashes of grey-green uniform and hear orders shouted in German. Lieutenant Adams sank behind a tree trunk and after a time began to drift in and out of consciousness. He was later found and carried back down the wheat field to the stream that had been the start line for the attack: 'A corporal took charge of me – he saw I was burned and said, "Let's put him in the water." The phosphorus had spread across my thighs and would have carried on burning.' It was the start of a long and painful journey back to England, where he was to spend eleven months at a special burns unit. A third of his platoon was listed as casualties.

It did not take the Germans long to find Captain Bannerman's party: 'The wheat was only too revealing as we crushed it flat, and soon I could hear shouts approaching.' Bannerman pulled the pin out of a grenade and peered over the wheat:

To my despair and horror I saw a German pointing a Schmeizer [machine gun] at me and shouting and jerking his gun to tell me to get up. I saw just behind him three of my chaps with their hands up and a tracked vehicle covering us all. I still held the pinless grenade, and tried vainly to wedge it in the hard earth. But the handle started to spring away and I had to grab it again. So I stood up with the grenade in my right hand and my arms above my head. I couldn't throw it as I would have killed my own men, besides suffering certain death myself, so I pointed to it with my left hand and said, 'Grenade' rather feebly. The German bellowed again, so I chucked it hard over my shoulder behind me and it went off a few yards away in the wheat.

Alastair Bannerman and his men were marched into the wood – prisoners of the 125th Panzer Grenadier Regiment: 'They seemed vastly amused by the sight of us in our camouflaged steel helmets and all our khaki palaver. Remarkably efficient and cool, they looked.' Later that day Bannerman was forced to take refuge from the artillery support the Warwicks had been waiting so long to receive:

Everyone tensed and crouched as the sound of an express train approached, tore over our heads with a monstrous clap and exploded with a roar in the wheat field. The Germans at last showed a little concern and donned steel helmets. We were given long-handled shovels and told to dig, which we did enthusiastically. I realised that at last it was the naval fire support from *HMS Warspite*'s 16-inch guns ranging on this wood. Fortunately the trains continued to hurtle over us into the wheat field.

The Englishmen found themselves side by side with their German captors – Bannerman was sharing a slit trench with an amiable corporal: 'He insisted on showing me photos of his girlfriend in Hamburg, and I politely returned the gesture by showing him my wife and children. The whole irony of the situation seemed quite extraordinary. War seemed so unnecessary when ordinary men of each side could still be human and friendly. I hadn't met any Nazis then.'

By late afternoon German tanks had managed to work their way behind the 2nd Warwicks and were firing into the battalion's rear. The 1st Battalion of the Royal Norfolk Regiment was thrown into the attack on the right, but was soon pinned down by the same intense fire. Captain Illing had been wounded in both shoulders at the edge of the wood. He had carried on fighting with the company until his wounds forced him back down the hill to the stream: 'I was able to totter back down, but when I got there I found the position was under fire from German tanks who had forced their way round. A good number of wounded were lying around.' Illing managed to organise their evacuation to the village of Blainville.

The Warwicks had fought all day for a foothold in the wood – by evening they were forced to relinquish it. 'So in the blackness of the night,' Illing recalled, 'carrying our wounded with us, we walked back along the route we had come the previous night.' Illing was awarded the Military Cross for the leadership he had shown in the battle – it had been only his second day in the field and by an extraordinary coincidence his twenty-fourth birthday.

The Battle of Lebisey had been lost and with it the immediate prospect of capturing Caen. There were some hard lessons to be learned. The attack had begun to unravel from the first. Very little in the way of reconnaissance had been carried out and too few troops were committed to an initial advance that was unsupported by artillery or armour. The men had fought bravely but it was their first real experience of a major engagement; in Illing's judgement, 'there was the doctrine of "getting on", "taking risks" and "staking a claim". There was a real determination to succeed or die in the attempt.' The 2nd Warwicks had been badly mauled. Many of its senior officers had been killed, captured or wounded – among them its popular and respected colonel. After its poor showing on D-Day, the 21st Panzer Division had demonstrated that it was still a formidable unit. 'They sat on their backsides at the top of the hill, no doubt gloating – "we have seen that lot off",' Illing observed. In the end the 3rd Division had made it easy for them. The 185th Brigade had been committed to the attack in dribs and drabs – a battalion of the Shropshires on D-Day, the 2nd Warwicks on the morning of D + 1 and the 1st Norfolks in the afternoon. The commander of the 185th Brigade was quietly shipped back to England – another casualty of what had been a disastrously planned action.

Great store had been set by the capture of Caen – the 2nd Army's plan on the eve of D-Day had described it as 'vital' to future operations. The city was less than 80 kilometres from the Seine, 200 from Paris. The open and gently rolling country-side beyond it was ideal for tank warfare. Montgomery expected the best of the German divisions to be drawn to this, the extreme eastern edge of the Allied bridgehead. If all went to plan, they would batter away in the east, allowing the Americans in the west to take Cherbourg and then, in General Bradley's words, 'pivot on the British position like a windlass in the direction of Paris'. Monty had outlined his plans for the campaign to a gath-ering of the great and good three weeks before D-Day. The King, the Prime Minister, Eisenhower and several hundred senior offi-cers listened to a detailed explanation of operations up to D + 90. It had been a masterly performance. Monty had repeatedly emphasised the need for the British and Canadians to 'contain the maximum enemy forces facing the eastern flank of the bridge-head', so the Americans could swing towards Paris and the Seine. But first it was essential to win a 'good lodgement' – to 'peg out claims well inland'. Bradley remembered talk of Allied tanks penetrating well beyond Caen: 'Pointing toward Falaise, he [Montgomery] talked of breaking his tanks free on D-Day "to knock about a bit down there".' Falaise was 50 kilometres by road from the nearest of the beaches – Caen a mere ten. But at corps level it had been recognised that Caen was still a very ambitious objective. Order No. 1 of the 2nd Army's plan for D-Day had stated 'I Corps will capture Caen'. But the orders issued by I Corps to the 3rd Division had already anticipated failure. If the enemy proved too strong, 'further direct frontal assaults which may prove costly will not be undertaken without refer-ence to I Corps'. The 3rd Division would be expected to 'contain' the enemy in Caen while heavy air raids reduced the city to rubble and ensured that its retention by the enemy would be 'a costly business'. This is the approach the Allies were eventually to adopt.

The postmaster in the Dorset village where the Bannerman family lived had rung to tell Elizabeth that a telegram had arrived: 'He said, "Mrs Bannerman, I couldn't, I just could not send you a telegram." At that of course my heart sank right down. He said: "I had to ring up and tell you myself that I have now been informed that your husband is missing."'

Captain Alastair Bannerman was still very much alive and had become one of the first Allied soldiers to reach Caen. On D + 2 he was marched past his burnt-out armoured carrier and down the road to the city. On the outskirts Bannerman encountered a very different sort of German soldier to the corporal he had shared a trench with: 'We came on this very unpleasant, vicious-looking lot of young men, I have to say, teenagers, they looked almost, the Hitler Jugend SS Panzer Division, lined up, ready to support the 21st, and they sort of spat at us and called us names and mocked and all the rest of it, and I thought, well, thank God I wasn't captured by them.' Bannerman passed on into Caen, where the results of the first Allied air bombardments were all too obvious: 'The city was unbelievably devastated and very few French were to be seen. We approached the centre past ruined churches and shells of houses.' The prisoners had half a hope that the Allies would capture the city before they were shipped to Germany. It was not to be. But in Bannerman's first camp the British prisoners were given a chance to send a message to their families – some dismissed the offer as German propaganda, but Bannerman accepted: 'I said, "If my wife can't listen to a German radio without becoming a Nazi at this stage of the war, heaven help us."' A crofter in the north of Scotland picked up the German radio broadcast and sent word to Elizabeth Bannerman. Her husband had sent a simple message: 'I am alive, darling, I love you.' 'That was the end of my agony. I was one of the lucky ones,' Elizabeth Bannermann recalled later.

Little news of the 2nd Warwick's action reached its old CO

General Montgomery, on D + 1. The Ground Forces Commander spent 7 June at sea, shuttling from one shipboard conference to another. His aide-de-camp, Captain Johnny Henderson, had woken Monty as bidden at six o'clock that morning with the news that the captain of their destroyer was lost:

I had gone up on deck at about five o'clock and said to the captain, 'Where are we?' And he said, 'I wish to hell we knew, we lost the swept channel two hours ago.' And so I went and told him [Montgomery] and he came up to the bridge shortly afterwards as bright as anything, saying, 'Lost? Are we lost?' He thought it was quite funny. Shortly afterwards a battleship was sighted, and luckily it turned out to be an American one.

The *Faulkenor* had been swept down to the Cotentin peninsula. Once her position had been established, Monty sought out Bradley aboard the *Augusta* for a briefing on the American beaches – 'good at Utah but very bad at Omaha', he noted. He was anxious to impress upon Bradley the importance of linking up the beach-heads before Rommel could concentrate his forces against any one in particular. Later that morning Monty sent a summary of the situation to his chief of staff at 21st Army Group in England: 'Appears likely the 21st Panzer Division intends to hold Caen,' he observed, but the 2nd Army was to 'proceed relentlessly with the original plan' – the capture of Caen and Bayeux. It was essential to keep the pressure up throughout the emerging bridgehead. Montgomery expected Rommel to commit his reserves at the earliest possible opportunity; 'he is best at the spoiling attack; his forte is disruption; he is too impulsive for the set-piece battle,' he had told Allied generals in May.

It was not until the early hours of D + 1 that the first units of the 12th SS Panzer Division began to pass through Caen. The first of its senior officers to reach the new front was Obersturmbannführer [Colonel] Kurt Meyer – the commander of the 25th Panzer Grenadier Regiment. On his way through the city Meyer had met General Feuchtinger of the 21st Panzer to discuss plans for a counter-attack the following morning. Feuchtinger had counselled patience; in his judgement it was better to wait and launch an attack with three Panzer divisions and the Panzer Lehr was not expected before 8 June. But as Monty had predicted, Rommel was determined to attack at the earliest possible opportunity and Feuchtinger had been overruled. The two Panzer divisions had been instructed to 'drive the enemy back into the sea'. Meyer at least was confident his division would do just that – the English 'kleine fische' (little fish) would, he assured Feuchtinger, be thrown back.

The 12th SS Panzer Division had been created to, in the words of its Führer, 'strike wonder into the enemy'. Its soldiers were drawn exclusively from the ranks of the Hitler Jugend (Hitler Youth) – 20,000 fanatical teenagers, the 'best' of Nazi youth, well trained and superbly equipped. Special emphasis had been placed on close combat training and the use of camouflage – both skills that would prove of special value in the close country of Normandy. Less useful would be the weekly ideological sessions the division's soldiers were obliged to attend on themes like 'Germany's demand for living space', and 'the enemies of Germany are the enemies of Europe'. It was these young, ideologically committed soldiers that Alastair Bannerman was unfortunate to encounter when he was marched into Caen on the morning of D + 2.

A hard core of experienced SS officers had been drawn from other divisions to lead Hitler's young 'warriors' – among them Kurt 'Panzer' Meyer. The British interrogation report written after his capture describes Meyer as 'the personification of National Socialism. His mind, paralysed by propaganda, is quite unable to even consider any other point of view.' There might be some who would 'drag the Führer's name in the dust', Meyer told his interrogators, but the men of the 12th SS 'would always maintain their faith in what he had taught them'. He was five foot ten inches tall, broad shouldered and thickset – those who met him were invariably struck by his 'grey-blue eyes', and his unnerving tendency to fix people with a distant, unblinking stare. Meyer's former commanding officer in the 1st SS (Leibstandarte Adolf Hitler) Division described him as a 'passionate soldier' – he was also a ruthless and resourceful one. Meyer had marched into Poland in 1939, France the following year, and had been in the van when the Germans advanced into Russia. Within a few days of arriving in Normandy he was to take command of the 12th SS Panzer – at thirty-three, the youngest divisional general in the German army.

The first of the division's Panzer grenadiers had begun to take up positions to the west of Caen at dawn on D + 1, but it was not until midday that sufficient tanks had been assembled to launch an attack. Kurt Meyer had established a forward control post in the precincts of the Ardennes Abbey, a little to the north west of the city. From one of the church's corner turrets he was able to gaze across the chequerboard of carefully cultivated fields and farming villages to the coast itself. Silver barrage balloons floated above the landing beaches – an altogether unnecessary precaution as the Luftwaffe was conspicuously absent from the skies above the battlefield. Through his field glasses Meyer could also see enemy tanks pushing towards the Caen–Bayeux road and the airfield at Carpiquet beyond. Rommel's counter-attack was in danger of being trumped by the Allied advance. Meyer's men were in well-camouflaged positions. He waited until the Canadian armoured units were almost upon his tanks and artillery before he gave the order to fire. In the engagement that followed the 27th Canadian Armoured Regiment was badly mauled and forced to fall back on the village of Buron. Towards evening soldiers from the 12th SS managed to capture the villages too, only to find themselves caught in a ferocious artillery barrage, the like of which Meyer had not experienced before. It was, the division's operation's officer, Major Hubert Meyer, wrote later, 'a lesson in what was to be our fate in the coming weeks'. The great 16-inch guns of the battleship *HMS Rodney* bombarded the German front line for two hours; 'the whistling of the approaching heavy shells and the explosions as they struck had a devastating effect,' Hubert Meyer recalled. By nightfall the shattered village of Buron was empty – a no man's land between the German and Canadian positions.

The Canadians suffered more than three hundred casualties in the fighting and lost twenty-one tanks – a further seven had been severely damaged. They had been caught off guard and thrown back three kilometres – forced to relinquish the north-west approaches to Caen. 'These events,' the official Canadian history states, 'helped to ensure that Caen would remain in German hands and the eastern flank of the Allied bridgehead would be much more constricted than had been planned.' But it was a costly encounter for the SS too, with three hundred listed as dead or missing. The division was a long way from carrying out the orders it had been given by Rommel. Meyer had been offered very little support from the 21st Panzer on his right – Feuchtinger had been thrown on to the defensive by the 2nd Warwick's assault on Lebisey Wood. It had been a baptism of fire for the Hitler Jugend.

Lessons should have been learned. Time was critical. Rommel had always held that the Allies had to be dislodged in the first few days, before they managed to consolidate their position in the bridgehead. Fresh orders were issued for a counter-attack on the morning of 8 June – an armoured thrust by three divisions to be directed by I SS Panzer Corps. But the only division in any sort of position to carry out these orders was the 12th SS – the 21st Panzer was holding the line to the north of Caen and the Panzer Lehr was just beginning to reach the front. Armour advancing close to the bridgehead was under constant threat from the air. Allied fighter-bombers swept the skies unchallenged, and it was almost impossible for more than a handful of tanks to move by day without being attacked. Air attacks were also disrupting German communications – by 8 June I SS Panzer Corps had only four working radio sets out of twenty, not enough for the close direction of an attack by three divisions.

The 12th SS Panzer Division went into action again on D + 2 but was unable to make significant progress against a determined Canadian defence. The fighting was frantic and at times merciless. Shortly before nightfall a battle group of Panther tanks, led by the indomitable Meyer in a motorcycle sidecar, attempted to push forward along the Caen–Bayeux road. On the outskirts of Bretteville the Panthers were met by a stiff barrage of anti-tank fire. A confused battle raged through the night. Parachute flares lit the sky as the Canadians sought to track the German tanks. At one point a Panther forced its way through to the battalion headquarters of the Regina Rifles in the centre of the village. It was summarily dispatched by a PIAT anti-tank weapon. In the confusion of gunfire and burning buildings, some of the attackers became dangerously isolated. A group of seven Germans fought their way through to the church, where they sent out a pre-arranged signal for the Panthers to follow. None made it through and the men were left behind when the battle group pulled back. Meyer himself was lucky to escape with his life when his motorcycle was hit and burst into flames. Further efforts to break through the Canadian line on 9 and 10 June also ended in failure. The 12th SS had been defeated by the determined resistance of a well-equipped adversary.

The author of the official Canadian history put it succinctly: 'The German operations at this stage leave the impression of rather hasty and ineffective improvisation. The attacks were pressed with courage and determination but with no particular tactical skill.' They had been ill conceived and, once launched, badly commanded – too much had been left to the judgement of relatively junior officers.

The Hitler Youth division had fought with uncommon ferocity – with the sort of callous disregard for humanity that characterised Waffen SS operations on the Eastern Front. On the morning of 8 June seven Canadian prisoners had been brought to Kurt Meyer's command post at the Ardennes Abbey. 'Why do you bring prisoners to the rear?' Meyer asked his men. 'They only eat our rations.' One by one the Canadians were taken into the abbey garden, where they were shot in the back of the head. An eyewitness told Allied investigators after the war that the men knew what was about to happen to them, for the shots and an occasional scream could be clearly heard by those in the abbey precincts. The 12th SS are thought to have murdered at least 130 Canadians in Normandy, the majority in the first days of the battle. In an effort to hide the crime, bodies were sometimes dragged on to roads to be crushed by passing tanks. It was a thankfully rare occurrence, but prisoners were shot by the soldiers of both sides in Normandy.

Rommel had thrown his Panzer reserves into the attack as soon as they arrived on the battlefield. But they had been committed piecemeal, without the strength to seriously trouble the Allied bridgehead. As one senior Panzer commander put it later, 'the fist was unclenched just as it was ready to strike'. Once the reserves were drawn into the line it was difficult to extricate them again for a concerted push. There was a good deal of concern at High Command (OKW) that the opportunity to force a decision near the beaches was slipping through Rommel's hands. The field marshal needed to draw on all the reserves he could, but he was remarkably reluctant to use units from the other army under his command. Rommel was still waiting for the 'real' invasion to take place. It is hard to credit now, but on the evening of the 8th he telephoned the chief of the operations staff at OKW, General Jodl, to argue against the transfer of divisions from the 15th Army to Normandy. Authority for such a transfer rested in the hands of Hitler. The Allied deception plan, Fortitude, was proving more successful than its architects could have dared imagine. But there would be another counter-attack, Rommel reassured Jodl, a powerful armoured thrust towards Bayeux to split the British and American forces. It would be directed by the commander of Panzer Group West, General Geyr von Schweppenburg, and would involve elements of the 12th SS and 21st Panzer Divisions, but the great weight of the attack would be carried by the Panzer Lehr.

The Panzer Lehr had, in the words of its commander, 'enforced camouflage discipline with a will' throughout its long journey to the front. But by the time General Bayerlein's division had reached its positions, it had already lost eighty-five half-tracks (armoured vehicles) and some 130 lorries, including forty tankers. The Panzer Lehr had been forced to push on to the new front by day: 'My men were calling the main road a *Jabo Rennstrecke* – a fighter-bomber racecourse,' Bayerlein recalled later.

Unteroffizier (Sergeant) Otto Henning was a 'tank leader' with the 2nd Company of Armoured Reconnaissance Battalion 130: 'Large numbers of fighter planes were in the air and we were forced at times to move literally from tree to tree to seek as much shelter as we could find. The moment these bombers noticed us an attack would begin.' Henning's unit had made all speed to the coast to reconnoitre the positions the division were to occupy: 'My eyes became so infected from the dust and dirt the chains of our tanks threw up that I couldn't see the map on my knees. We had been assigned a target area but, because of the strict radio silence we had to maintain, to avoid giving away our positions to the enemy, we really didn't have any idea what we were supposed to do once we reached our sector.'

The twenty-year-old Henning was one of Rommel's desert veterans and he had seen a good deal of action already.

We were ordered to probe until we encountered resistance. We drove up to the British and American tank positions to observe their armoured columns. We did not see any German troops. You can imagine the effect on our morale. On one occasion the enemy opened fire and our column was forced to stop. I was ordered with another Sergeant – Kobs was his name – to accompany our lieutenant on a foot patrol. We could already see enemy troops crossing the street behind us to cut off our retreat. We carefully moved forward, keeping out of sight behind a hedge, but then our lieutenant noticed a British soldier not even two metres away, standing there looking towards our tanks. Our lieutenant took my machine gun and shot him. Then of course there was a massive firefight. I threw myself down and, being an old soldier, I realised that I had to keep my nerve and stay on the ground absolutely still. If I panicked and tried to run away, that would be the end. After the first frantic shooting subsided a little, I looked up and noticed that the lieutenant was no longer with us. Kobs was beside me and we slowly crawled away from our position back to our tanks. The street behind us had been blocked, and when the first of our Puma armoured vehicles tried to break through it was destroyed. My driver braked hard and we slipped round the crippled Puma. My comrades saw a jet of flame jump from close to my vehicle and they thought I'd also been hit. But we'd made it. Our remaining vehicles managed to shoot their way through the roadblock and break out. We assumed our comrades in the first Puma had burned to death.

Captain Helmut Ritgen was still full of optimism when his column arrived on the evening of 7 June. Ritgen had been the acting commander of II Battalion, the 130th Panzer Lehr Regiment, during the march: 'We reached our positions in the evening, battered but not defeated. It had been a difficult journey but we were completely convinced that we were able to push our enemies back into the sea.' His optimism began to fade as the seriousness of the situation the division faced began to dawn on him: 'Enemy aircraft had effectively destroyed radio communications – it meant the division's staff officers were completely in the dark regarding our own position for at least twenty-four hours. We were given orders to take Bayeux on 9 June – nobody knew that Bayeux had already fallen.'

The attack the Panzer Lehr was preparing to make with the 12th SS and 21st Panzer was changed just hours before the tanks were expected to roll across the start line. Field Marshal Rommel visited the division on the evening of the 8th and personally informed Bayerlein that Bayeux was in British hands. The town had fallen to the veteran 50th Division. 'The British 50th, Bayerlein, our special friends from Africa,' Rommel had told his old chief of staff. The Panzer Lehr would have to move westward to new positions near Tilly-sur-Seulles in readiness to attack the following morning. The division's tanks had trundled into new positions that night. At one point, as Sergeant Otto Henning recalled, they heard a welcome and unusual sound: 'There were three planes overhead and we realised they were Junkers 88, I recognised the sound the engines made from Africa. These planes came under anti-aircraft fire from the coast and it was practically impossible for any plane to pierce that wall of fire. The planes realised they would not reach the ships, so they dropped their bombs on us instead!'

The division's push on the morning of 9 June was to have been made by two battle groups, but one of these was diverted to Tilly to hold an Allied attack. The tanks of Helmut Ritgen's battalion led the attack under their commander, Colonel Prince Wilhelm Schönburg-Waldenburg, who had rejoined his men the evening before. 'Group Schönburg' pressed northward between the British and American sectors and by the afternoon had advanced to within five kilometres of Bayeux. Just as it looked as if a German counter-attack might at last come to something, Prince Schönburg-Waldenburg received an order that left all the battalion's officers furious and confused. Later that day Captain Ritgen spoke to his commander: 'He said, "Suddenly we received the order 'stop attack and return to original positions'. We just couldn't understand it – someone has led us up the garden path."' The only classic German Panzer attack the division was to make in Normandy was over almost as soon as it had begun. As Group Schönburg had advanced northward, a strong Allied tank force had forced its way through a gap in the German line to the east beyond Tilly. There were no reserves to throw against it – Group Schönburg was recalled to stiffen the line.

The Panzer Lehr Division had been thrown on to the defensive by the British 50th Division, which had pushed on from Bayeux and was trying to force a way through to the high ground above the village of Villers-Bocage. The 8th Armoured Brigade had managed to establish a foothold on a hill south of the village of Le Haut d'Audrieu – Point 103. Major Peter Martin's machine gun company was part of the small force of tanks and field guns that was holding the hill on the 9th:

At first light German tanks approached from the south, engaged the forward tanks of the Sherwood Rangers, knocking out some. The remainder withdrew to the reverse slope of Point 103, leaving my two platoons completely isolated. The enemy tanks stood off about 120 yards away, hull down, and shelled our bank with high explosive. These burst in the trees above the platoon positions, raining shrapnel down on the gun positions, causing casualties. On several occasions, when the German tanks cruised too far forward, with turrets open, our machine gunners fired at them to make them close down. The situation was precarious, because if the enemy put in a determined attack from the south, he would be right on top of us before encountering our tanks or anti-tank guns. So we were very cheered when soon after midday recce parties from the 1st Dorsets arrived to say that Audrieu was being cleared, and the battalion would soon come to join us. They also said the 8th DLI [Durham Light Infantry] was to come under the command of 8th Armoured Brigade, and was to capture St-Pierre. At about that time, one of my platoons came up on the wireless and asked for help with evacuating a seriously wounded corporal. The only way was by jeep over an open field being shelled like fury. I thought I'd better drive the jeep myself. I told my driver to get out. To my disappointment, instead of saying, 'No, sir. I will go,' he said, 'Right, sir,' and got out.

I drove the jeep to a gap in the hedge of the field where the shells were bursting. I remember saying, 'Oh God, please stop the shells. If you stop them, I'll be good for always.' They stopped. I got the corporal out. Many times during the war one promised one would be a better person if one was allowed to survive. The promises did not last all that long.

The Panzer Lehr Division had been reduced to 'firefighting' the Allied advance. On the evening of the 9th, Ritgen led his battalion's supply vehicles up the line. He found Prince Schönburg-Waldenburg lying on the engine compartment of his command tank. The thirty-one-year-old prince was a holder of the Knight's Cross – the Reich's most prestigious decoration – a veteran of the fighting in Poland, France and Russia. He had experienced setbacks on the battlefield many times, but this was somehow different. 'He called to me,' Ritgen recalled.

He was deeply depressed . . . underneath the swelling and receding thunder and lightning of the powerful artillery in the north, we spoke of God and the world, about our present situation, which, in the light of the already evident enemy superiority, there was little we could do about, and how completely different from the Eastern Front the war would become out here. The Prinz had lost his usual composure and confidence and I could find no words to comfort him.

The Panzer Lehr renewed its attack on Point 103 the following day, and for a time German and British tanks fought it out in the village of St-Pierre on the right bank of the River Seulles. Major Peter Martin's company was holding its position on the hill:

At dusk, enemy tanks closed in on Point 103. Shermans were blazing everywhere. Going to the brigadier's tank, I was hailed by the CO of the 24th Lancers, sitting on the ground, with his arm in a sling. He handed me a rifle, saying, 'Put a round in the breech, at least I'll take one of them with me,' I thought, Good God, it's as bad as that, is it? Shortly after, all firing ceased. It was the final attempt by the enemy, before pulling out and leaving St-Pierre.

On 10 June Rommel braved the roads and drove to the headquarters of Panzer Group West, which had established itself in an orchard in the village of Le Caine, 32 kilometres to the south of Caen. He found General Geyr von Schweppenburg to be very much of his own mind – there were more Panzer reserve units on their way to Normandy but for the time being plans for a further major push would have to be shelved. Nothing was being done to counter the constant threat from the air, Geyr von Schweppenburg complained; the supply situation was critical, with the Panzer divisions reporting a shortage of fuel and ammunition. Orders would be sent out the following day placing the Panzer Lehr and the other divisions on the defensive – this would merely serve to confirm the existing state of affairs. To grimly underscore Geyr von Schweppenburg's point an Allied fighter-bomber attacked his headquarters just an hour after the field marshal's visit. Almost all the group's staff officers were killed in the attack. It had been no chance strike – the group's signals had betrayed its position to the Allied code-breakers.

Rommel had a long, sobering drive back to La Roche Guyon. That night he wrote at length to the OKW with a special request that 'the Führer be informed' of his assessment. It was clear, he pointed out, that Montgomery was intent on forcing the battle around Caen in preparation 'for a powerful attack later into the interior of France'. He was also intent on capturing the port of Cherbourg. Army Group B was establishing a defensive line along the Allied bridgehead until armoured divisions could be replaced by infantry reserves; only then would it be possible to consider a major counter-attack. Endless formations of fighter-bombers, the heavy naval barrage the Allies could summon up at will – these were preventing even minor formations moving freely about the battlefield. There was, Rommel insisted, a real danger of the battle becoming a *Materialschlacht* in which the sheer weight of firepower would be decisive in determining victory or defeat. 'The material equipment of the Americans, with numerous new weapons and war material, is far and away superior to that of our divisions,' he noted in his report. There was already an air of quiet desperation at the headquarters of Army Group B. 'The long husbanded strength of two world powers is now coming into action,' Rommel confided to his wife Lucie. 'It will all be decided very quickly. We are doing what we can. I often think of you at home, with heartfelt wishes and the hope that everything can still be guided to a tolerable end.'

The battle around Tilly rolled on into 11 June. The 901st Panzer Grenadier Lehr Regiment was under heavy attack to the east of the town and had requested support from the Panzer Battalion 'Schönburg'. Captain Helmut Ritgen drove forward that afternoon with supplies for the battalion's Panzers. The prince had been summoned to a conference with the colonel commanding the 901st:

Before my arrival a bomb had slammed into his command post. It was a miracle that none of the company commanders were wounded. Only the prince's old valet, Corporal Füssel, was killed. A little later the prince returned with an order to attack and eliminate the enemy penetration. He was very shaken by his valet's death. He said that he had lost his best friend. Füssel had been with him 25 years. Moreover, his heart was not in the attack that had been ordered. He judged the ground to be totally unsuitable for armour.

Ritgen later recalled the prince's words to him as he left: 'He said to me, "Who knows if we'll all die!"'

It was late that evening when Ritgen heard what had happened to his friend. The battalion's tanks had rattled forward towards two woods at the foot of Hill 103 – between them was a gap just 300 metres wide, and it was this bottleneck between the trees that the British artillery chose to attack. Prince Schönburg-Waldenburg's command tank managed to reach the crest of Hill 103 but almost immediately it was hit on the turret by an armour-piercing shell. The prince and his communications officer were killed.

That night Ritgen took command of the battalion: 'How often I had silently longed for this position, but not under these tragic and horrible circumstances. The death of the prince touched me deeply, but not only me. Almost all the members of the battalion felt as I did.' The following evening the bodies of the prince and his men were buried together in a nearby village churchyard. Helmut Ritgen took the service – the divisional chaplains were too busy with the wounded: 'The prince could not be buried until it was dark because of the air threat. I made a short speech, then we lowered our fallen leader into his grave, beside his valet and communications officer, and said the Lord's Prayer together.' It all passed off to the strange, distant swoosh and crump of naval shells falling on the German positions at nearby Villers-Bocage.

CHAPTER FOUR

CAEN IS THE KEY

———————

It was a cardinal rule of General Bernard Law Montgomery's to exude competence and confidence at all times – anything less was plain 'bad generalship'. There was good cause for satisfaction. He had received a stirring welcome from the soldiers of the British army when he landed on 8 June. 'Tired and weary faces lighted up, soldiers waved from all directions,' his aide-de-camp, Captain Johnny Henderson, noted in his diary. After Africa and El Alamein, after Italy, the funny little man in the tank beret and grey jersey seemed to be a sort of talisman of success, and Monty revelled in it: 'He'd been told, "You mustn't make yourself too conspicuous or you'll be in danger." And he said, "No, no, I want to be seen,"' Henderson recalled.

'He was a showman and it went down well with the troops, they were deeply impressed by this little chap,' another officer on Monty's personal staff recalled. But Monty also seemed to care about the ordinary soldier. He would make a point of stopping his jeep to hand out cigarettes – Henderson fed him box after box: 'He liked to hand them out to troops wherever he went. He'd stop and say, "I think you want some of these, don't use them myself you know." It gave him just a chance to talk to them and he'd often tell them what was happening, he liked to bring them into the picture.'

There was a good deal of confidence in the ranks that Monty would be a careful and a lucky general. Lives would not be thrown away in pointless, costly engagements. Monty had promised as much only hours after setting foot ashore: 'The Germans are doing everything they can to hold on to Caen,' he explained in a letter to the War Office. 'I have decided not to have a lot of casualties by butting up against the place; so I have ordered Second Army to keep up a good pressure at Caen, and to make its main effort towards Villers-Bocage and Evrecy and thence south-east towards Falaise.'

The plan drawn up by General Miles Dempsey's staff at 2nd Army headquarters was altogether more ambitious. It proposed attacks in the east and west of the British sector to envelop Caen. The advance to Villers-Bocage in the west would be made by the 7th Armoured – 'the Desert Rats' – the one to the east by the 51st Highland Division. They were desert veterans – Monty's 'best batsmen', respected and trusted by their old commander. Monty's chief of staff was instructed to keep the Supreme Commander in the picture and Eisenhower was reported to be 'buoyed up' by a plan that promised to squeeze the German Panzer divisions into an Allied pocket.

On 12 June Monty briefed the Prime Minister – the first of a number of important 'sightseers' to the new front. Churchill was met on the beach by a 'smiling and confident' Monty, who drove him to the advanced headquarters he had established in the grounds of a chateau. 'We lunched in a tent looking towards the enemy,' Churchill recalled later. 'The General was in the highest spirits.'

Monty's tactical headquarters (TAC HQ) was a surprisingly small establishment even by the standards of the day. The largest single element was the signals section with wireless and teleprinter links to the main headquarters of 21st Army Group. This was set apart from the nucleus of the camp – the caravans used by the land commander himself. There were three of these – the first a personal office, the second a spartan bedroom, fitted rather like a ship's cabin, and the third, and most important, Monty's map caravan.

'He had the map lorry especially made before we went to

Europe,' Henderson recalled. 'The big map covered almost one side of it and we marked this up every day.' On it Monty could see at a glance Allied and German dispositions in Normandy and beyond. He had taken a leaf from the Duke of Wellington's book and established a small team of liaison officers whose particular task was to keep 'the chief' in touch with the front. Major Carol Mather had served on Monty's staff in North Africa, but had left to join the SAS – he rejoined as a liaison officer just before D-Day:

We usually worked with the same divisions and corps, though if there was a major attack somewhere then obviously we would all concentrate on that. At six o'clock every evening we would go into his caravan, mark up his map, and he'd come in about a quarter of an hour later and we'd each in turn say our bits about where we'd been, what we'd seen, what his divisional and corps commanders said about the situation, what their plans were.

There were usually six liaison officers on the TAC HQ staff – 'young officers of character, initiative and courage; they had seen much fighting,' Monty was to write in his memoirs. 'I selected each personally, and my standard was high.' The 'chief' was a stickler for detail: 'He wanted to be involved in every appointment down to the colonel of regiments,' Henderson recalled. Just two days before Churchill's visit, Monty had found time to approve a replacement for his old regiment, the 2nd Warwicks, which had lost its CO in its attempt on Caen. The staff at 21st Army Group were instructed to 'Send him over at once' – the commander-in-chief wanted to meet the new man.

It was to the map caravan that Monty steered Churchill on 12 June. After six days the Allies had managed to establish a continuous bridgehead 80 kilometres long. The US First Army was tightening its grip on the Cotentin – its VII Corps had captured the town of Carentan and was preparing to isolate Cherbourg in a drive across the neck of the peninsula. V Corps, which had struggled so hard to establish itself on Omaha, was now pushing south to Caumont. The Allies were capitalising on German mistakes. They had done just what Monty expected and committed most of their Panzer reserves to the defence of Caen. This, Monty explained to his guest, presented an opportunity for a decisive blow – a pincer movement to encircle and trap Rommel's Panzer divisions in the Caen area. The 51st Highland Division had already passed into the airborne bridgehead east of the Orne and was striking towards to the south-east of the city. At the same time the 7th Armoured was pushing south through the 50th Division in front of Tilly and would then turn to the east.

Churchill went home satisfied. He wrote with enthusiasm to the Soviet leader, Joseph Stalin: 'We hope to encircle Caen, and perhaps to make a capture there of prisoners.' He was wise enough, however, to dampen expectations of a rapid break-through: 'I should think it quite likely that we should work up to a battle of about a million a side, lasting through June and July.' In the event the great envelopment was to fall well short of his and Monty's expectations.

While Churchill was watching Monty's great sweeps of confi-dence across the maps in his TAC HQ caravan, the men who were to carry out his ambitious pincer movement were pushing up to their start line. It was not until late that afternoon that the order was finally given for the tanks of the 7th Armoured Division to roll forward towards Villers-Bocage. Its orders had changed that morning. The division had been engaged to the right of the 50th in the countryside about Tilly, but it had struggled to make real progress against formidable resistance from the Panzer Lehr. On the morning of 12 June a decrypted enemy signal revealed that more German Panzer reserves were expected to be deployed near Villers-Bocage – the 7th Armoured would need to make good speed if the plan was to have any hope of success. General Miles Dempsey decided to move the 7th Armoured a little to the west towards what reconnaissance suggested was a weak point in the German line. The division was instructed to press through this 'with real drive' – then there was 'a chance' it would be able to fight its way through 'before the front congeals'.

The tanks of the 4th County of London Yeomanry (the Sharpshooters) had been chosen to lead the advance. Orders to disengage from the battle around Tilly had arrived early in the afternoon and the regiment had been obliged to swing smartly to the west in preparation for the new thrust. Some tough lessons had been learned in front of Tilly. There was a general consensus that Normandy was no place for a tank. The battlefield across the bridgehead varied markedly. At the eastern end of the British sector the countryside rolled gently southward, a patchwork of cornfields and copses, of grey stone villages and towns. A number of steep-sided river valleys presented particular difficulties for attacking armour. The ground was no better to the south of Caen, where the steep slopes of the *Suisse Normandie* (Swiss Normandy) formed a natural defensive barrier. But the countryside the Sharpshooters were to attack through was classic Norman 'bocage' – close country of densely packed fields and orchards, bounded everywhere by sunken lanes and ancient hedges, growing from root-tangled rocky banks. This 'hedgerow country' dominated the battlefield in the west of the bridgehead. Major Peter Martin of the 2nd Cheshires was to spend many weeks fighting through it: 'The visibility was no more than about fifty yards from one hedgerow to the next. Wonderful defensive country. It was terrible for tanks, because to get over the banks and hedges they had to either blast their way through or expose their bellies as they tried to climb them. The Germans were in their element.'

The SHAEF planners had appreciated some of the difficulties the terrain presented and advised that 'the tactics to be employed in fighting through bocage country should be given considerable study'. But as the historian Max Hastings has pointed out, this recommendation was not pursued with anything like the necessary vigour. The 7th Armoured Division had carried out its training in the large, open fields of East Anglia. It was all very different from the desert where the division had made its name.

Lieutenant John Cloudsley-Thompson was one of the 4th County of London Yeomanry's (CLY) North Africa veterans. The twenty-three-year-old lieutenant was rather an unlikely tank commander – he was obliged to squeeze six feet two inches of lanky frame into the turret of his Cromwell. He counted himself 'lucky' to be in Normandy. A severe leg injury picked up in the Western Desert had almost ruled him out, and he had managed to secure his place in a landing craft only by 'wangling' a medical 'upgrade'. The 'bocage problem' became apparent to Cloudsley-Thompson on D + 3 when the division was moved up in support of the advance on Tilly: 'There were a lot of snipers and it was very close country. You had to use earphones when you were commanding the tank because you had to have your head out. Well, the trouble with the Cromwell was that if you were wearing these earphones you couldn't wear a tin hat, it wouldn't fit over. We had to wear our berets.' A succession of tank commanders were picked off by a shot to the head. British artillery also claimed two of the 4th CLY's tank commanders in the first days. Communications on the battlefield were difficult at the best of times, but it was harder still in the bocage, where it was often impossible to see farther than the next hedge. On 10 June A Squadron had come under 'friendly fire' from the 8th Armoured Brigade. 'It was three-quarters of an hour before we could get a message through telling them to stop,' Cloudsley-Thompson recalled. 'In the meantime one of my best sergeants had his head shot off.' Above all the initiative rested with a well-concealed and skilful enemy. A whole troop had been lost to a German Panther tank – Cloudsley-Thompson had followed the engagement on his headphones: 'We sat in the field while C Squadron skirmished in front. They lost a troop which, temporarily under the command of infantry, was sent down a narrow lane. It was a fatal place to go, as there was no room to manoeuvre, and every tank was knocked out. I saw these tanks a few weeks later. The body of a driver, his legs burned to nothing, was still in one: and there were graves by all the others.'

It was ambush country and Allied tanks were proving no match for their German counterparts. Cloudsley-Thompson recalled:

Our feeling was, why have we got such terrible tanks? We had these Crusaders in the desert and then, for Normandy, Cromwells. In the meantime, there'd been Centaurs, Covenanters, and these had been condemned as being useless for anything but training. The Cromwell tank was no better than the Crusader of three years before. The armour plating was absolutely vertical so that shots didn't glance off. And the thing that worried me most of all was that if you traversed the tank's turret more than about 30 degrees either way, the driver couldn't bale out. It's very inhibiting in a war when you're being shot at and you're constantly having to remember, 'Can the driver bale out?'

The other Allied battle tanker – the Sherman – shared many of the same faults. Trooper Austin Baker of the 4th/7th Royal Dragoon Guards became very familiar with its shortcomings in his first few days in the bridgehead. Baker was the wireless operator in the regiment's armoured recovery vehicle – also a Sherman:

We were meant to be a sort of battlefield AA [Automobile Association], helping damaged tanks. But our main job turned out to be collecting lengths of track from knocked-out tanks so they could be welded on to existing tanks as extra armour. It was quickly realised something had to be done, and if you draped the whole front of the tank with track, there was a better chance of resisting projectiles, although they still went through pretty easily.

German tanks boasted better armour and better guns. The Sherman's 75mm gun was no match for the German Tiger and Panther tanks. A small number of Shermans had been fitted with the 17-pounder anti-tank gun, and these 'Fireflies' proved comparable to the German 88mm. But there were only a handful of these in each armoured regiment – five out of sixty-one tanks in the 4th/7th Royal Dragoon Guards. Baker saw plenty of evidence in those first days of the devastating power of the German 88mm: 'A high-explosive shell would not affect a Sherman unless it was very large but our armour wasn't thick enough to keep any sort of armour-piercing shot out. This was more like solid shot – it punctures its way through and as it does so carries with it a trail of molten armour. It not only kills anyone in its way but the red-hot shot sets fire to the vapour inside and then the ammunition.' The Cromwell was no better. 'We had a hundred and ten gallons of petrol on board,' Cloudsley-Thompson recalled. 'They talked about the Shermans being Ronsons [a type of cigarette lighter]. Well, the Cromwells could burn pretty quickly if they were hit.' Baker had lost his best friend, Wally Walters, on D + 2:

A brewed-up tank is always a grim sight – the outside is usually a dull, dirty, rust colour, and inside it is a blackened shambles. There is a queer indescribable smell. The bottom of Jonah's tank had been blown right out, and we could peer inside from underneath. There was no trace of anybody in the turret, but some stuff in the driving seat that must have been Walker. There was a body on the ground by the left-hand track. Somebody had thrown a groundsheet over it, but we lifted it off. It was probably Brigham Young, but it was impossible to recognise him – he was burned quite black all over, and only parts of his anklets remained of his clothes. Nobody ever found any sign of Wally.

It was with great care that the 4th CLY began its advance on 12 June. Cloudsley-Thompson was the leader of the Regimental Headquarters Troop:

All went well as far as Livry, when the advance guard bumped into an enemy force and lost one tank; the Motor Company of the Rifle

Brigade had to be called up to help clear the village. From a hill farther back I watched the tanks of the leading squadron of my regiment fan out in a cornfield and saw the tracer of their machine guns firing at the German infantry . . . that night we leaguered several miles farther inland than any other of the allied forces.

The reconnaissance units had been out that evening trying to get the measure of the gap in the German line. They found the edge of the Panzer Lehr line a little under three kilometres to the east – to the west there appeared to be open country between 7th Armoured and the advancing American V Corps. The night was broken by the distant rumble of artillery fire to the west, but there was no other sign of the enemy. It was after midnight by the time the last units of the division had pulled off the road to set up camp – four hours later they were on the move again. It was a slow, cautious advance with the main column crammed on to one narrow road. A good deal of effort was required to prevent the tanks bunching together – a huddle of stationary armour presented a broad and tempting target for a German 88mm. It was quiet, but nobody expected that to last long. By the early hours of 13 June the division had pushed well into the enemy's position. Lieutenant Cloudsley-Thompson's Headquarters Troop was near the head of the column:

The countryside was pleasant and the French peasants greeted us with delight, giving us butter, cider and throwing flowers at our tanks. We heard a rumour from the local people that there were some German tanks stranded at Tracy-Bocage through lack of petrol. There was still no opposition however, and we hoped to seize the high ground beyond Villers-Bocage before the enemy could forestall us. On the way into the town, the tank in front of mine spotted a German armoured car, about three hundred yards away to the left. He called up and told me, so I traversed the gun ready to fire through a gap in the hedge, but by the time I got there it had gone. Villers-Bocage is a fair sized country town; there was no sign of the enemy as we drove straight along the main street. The Brigadier and the

Colonel went forward in their scout cars to join the leading troops and we were ordered to close up as much as possible.

It was just after nine o'clock in the morning. The tanks of A Squadron had already pushed on through the town and were beginning to occupy the high ground to the east of Villers. That day's objective was within grasp. But the regiment was advancing in the dark – very little reconnaissance had been carried out. Its colonel – Viscount Cranley – was uneasy, but his orders were to press on without delay. Cranley had good cause for concern. The Reich's leading tank ace, Obersturmführer (Lieutenant) Michael Wittmann, was following the British advance from a concealed position close to the road out of town. He watched, no doubt in astonishment, as soldiers from A Company of the 1st Rifle Brigade drew up less than a kilometre away, jumped out of their armoured vehicles and began to brew up a cup of tea. Wittmann had arrived on the outskirts of the town the evening before with an advance party of six Tiger tanks from 2nd Company, the 101st Heavy SS-Panzer Battalion. The tanks had spent five exhausting days on the road, travelling at night to avoid the Allied fighter-bombers. The morning of 13 June had been set aside for general maintenance to the tanks – then Wittmann's men had picked out the advancing column of British armour. The Obersturmführer had more than a hundred 'kills' to his name. At Wittmann's throat hung the much coveted Knights Cross with Oak Leaves, a mark of the Führer's 'appreciation of your heroic actions in the battle for the future of our people'.

Lieutenant Cloudsley-Thompson and the rest of the Regimental Headquarters [RHQ] Troop were waiting for orders at the top of the main street through Villers-Bocage:

There was the colonel's tank with Arthur Carr, the second-in-command, in it and then my tank. Behind me was the adjutant's tank – he had gone forward, but Pat Dyas, the assistant adjutant, was in it and behind him was the regimental sergeant major's tank. Then

B Squadron and C Squadron in the rear. Suddenly there was an explosion in front and the reconnaissance tank about a hundred yards
ahead of Arthur Carr's blew up. Every RHQ tank began to reverse,
but one of the faults of the Cromwell was that its maximum speed
in reverse gear was about two miles per hour. The brigadier, who
had been discussing the situation with the colonel, ran across the
road, jumped into his scout car and drove back past us, followed by
another scout car. While I was still reversing, Arthur Carr's tank
exploded and there were clouds and clouds of smoke. And then an
armour piercing shell whizzed between my head and the wireless
operator who was looking out next to me on my right. It was so
close that even though I was wearing headphones I was deafened in
my right ear for at least twenty-four hours afterwards – I don't think
it can have missed me by more than half an inch. It was so vicious,
a supersonic shell passing so close, and this was the first time, I think,
I'd ever been frightened, really, really frightened, in my life. After
that, I tended to feel that nothing could ever miss me again.

I felt sure there must be a hidden anti-tank gun firing down the
road, so I told the driver: 'Left stick' and we backed through a hedge
between two houses. Pat the adjutant reversed his tank alongside
mine. He was bleeding from the forehead. He told me later that a
burst of Spandau machine-gun fire from one of the first-floor
windows of the houses had just missed his head and chipped fragments of steel from the turret of his tank, some of which had cut
him. By this time all the tanks immediately in front seemed to be on
fire. Through the smoke loomed the gigantic form of a Tiger. It
cannot have been more than 35 yards away, yet our 75mm shots just
bounced off its massive armour. I fired the two-inch bomb thrower,
but the smoke bomb passed clean over it. The Tiger traversed its big
88mm gun very slightly. Wham! We were hit.

My troop sergeant in the hull machine-gun position was leaning
over to the driver saying, 'Can you see what's happening?' And so it
just missed his head. I know it went between my legs, because I could
sort of feel a tingling from it. It landed up in the engine and a sheet
of flame came over the tank, I had my head out and I saw it coming.

I said to the crew, 'Bale out,' and we all baled out and nobody was killed or even hurt, that's incredible. You haven't got long because if the petrol's going like that, a hundred gallons, it makes a terrific flame and sets fire to the ammunition, then the whole thing explodes.

Cloudsley-Thompson and his crew sought what little cover there was in a nearby garden and the lone Tiger tank passed on into the town leaving a trail of choking black smoke in its wake. In the turret – hatch open slightly to help sight the next target – sat Obersturmführer Wittmann.

'A dreadful noise was going on in the town so I decided to go back beside a wall at the rear of the houses and try to reach B Squadron,' Cloudsley-Thompson recalled. Along the main street he could see the assistant adjutant, Captain Pat Dyas, trailing back on foot. He had pursued the Tiger and had managed to hit it, but to no effect. Wittmann had summarily dispatched Dyas's Cromwell with a round through the turret. In the course of his foray into Villers, Wittmann accounted for eleven tanks, nine armoured half-tracks, four Bren carriers and two anti-tank guns. It had taken just ten minutes. The Tiger was finally silenced by a brave but lucky shot from a six-pounder anti-tank gun which struck its running gear. Wittmann and his crew escaped through the town and back towards the headquarters of the nearby Panzer Lehr Division in Orbois, some five kilometres away. 'The enemy was thrown into total confusion,' Wittmann told a radio inter-viewer later that day. No one from the Sharpshooters would have disputed this verdict.

The rest of Wittmann's small party played their part. The other four serviceable Tigers had kept up the pressure on A Squadron and what was left of the Rifle Brigade Company. Although the squadron could still muster nine tanks – two of which were Fireflies – Colonel Cranley directed his men to take up defensive positions around the high ground outside the town – Point 213 – and wait for a relieving force. The tanks of B and C Squadrons in the town had listened in disbelief to the reports from the head of the column. Was it possible that a lone Tiger could inflict such devastating losses? The tall column of smoke to the east suggested it could and that more of the same was to come. The commander of B Squadron, Major Ibby Aird, began preparing for the defence of the town. Until infantry support reached him, nothing could be done for the remaining tanks of A Squadron.

Meanwhile Wittmann had made his report to the Panzer Lehr and a column of the division's tanks was rumbling towards Villers-Bocage. It was led by the acting commander of II Battalion, the 130th Panzer Lehr Regiment – Helmut Ritgen: 'I received orders to advance to the area north of Villers with every available Panzer – about fifteen – in order to prevent the strike in the division's flank that we had feared.' The Panzer Lehr could also count on the support of ten Tigers from Wittmann's battalion, and from the 2nd Panzer Division, which was pressing up from the south. 'All the northern exits from the town had to be blocked and a counter-attack prepared,' Ritgen recalled. 'I met General Bayerlein, who was waiting for me north of the village of Villy. It was from him I learned of Wittmann's successful attack.' By early afternoon Point 213 was again in German hands. The remnants of A Squadron had waited too long – an attempt at the eleventh hour to force a way back to the town had failed almost as soon as it began. With A Squadron in the bag the German armour turned towards the town.

The tanks of B and C Squadrons had taken up careful defensive positions in the streets and main square. They were supported by soldiers from the 1st/7th Queens Regiment armed with anti-tank guns and the PIAT shoulder-launched weapon. Before long the heavy trundle of Tiger tracks could be clearly heard at the top of the main street. German infantry followed in their wake. This time the British were prepared. Trooper Harold Currie of B Squadron was a wireless operator with No. 4 Troop – one of the new boys who had joined the regiment since the desert campaign: 'We became aware that German tanks were spreading out around us. My tank was overlooking one of the main streets from the square and we had our gun trained on this. And while we were sitting there we heard the rumble of a Tiger tank coming down the street.' The troop commander, Lieutenant Bill Cotton, had arranged his men around the main square – a Firefly at the eastern end and the two Cromwells near the town hall. A six-pounder manned by men from the 1st/7th Queens was positioned in a side street behind the Cromwells. The crews were told to cut their engines and listen – where was the enemy approaching from? Cotton had decided to direct his troop from the ground, armed only with an umbrella. He had given up the unequal struggle with his own tank – it mounted a 95mm howitzer, of little use against German armour.

The first Tiger to enter the square was dispatched by the six-pounder – the rest beat a hasty retreat. The Germans began to search for another approach. 'You could follow the battle elsewhere in the town on the headset,' Currie recalled. 'You would hear, "There's a tank coming up towards me now and I'm trying to manoeuvre myself to fire at it from the side," and then suddenly you heard a loud explosion.' Three more tanks were destroyed in adjoining streets by the 1st/7th Queens. Another Tiger was eventually spotted approaching the square by a side street – the Firefly managed to fire two rounds at it through the windows of a corner shop and one hit and damaged the tank's mantle. The German tank commander decided to rush forward in an effort to escape the ambush but was stopped by a shell from Trooper Currie's tank: 'As soon as the 88-millimetre gun came into view we fired. We must have killed the driver, because the tank went out of control and hit a shop just round the corner.' The nineteen-year-old Currie was unable to suppress his excitement and curiosity: 'I did a silly thing, actually. I got out of our tank and went down from the square into the street where the Tiger had been destroyed to look at it.' He returned safely with a souvenir – a much-prized German Luger pistol.

The British fought in streets drenched by heavy rain to hold an enemy growing by the hour in strength. By the late afternoon German infantry units had succeeded in infiltrating the British line and the headquarters of the Queen's Battalion was under heavy fire. The Germans had abandoned attempts to force their armour through and had begun to shell the western edge of the town. The commander of the 7th Armoured Division decided to order a general withdrawal from the town – by nightfall the shattered streets of Villers were German once again. The 7th Armoured withdrew to high ground at nearby Tracy-Bocage – this was, General Erskine told his division, 'to be held at all cost'.

Lieutenant Cloudsley-Thompson and his crew knew they were on their own when British shells began to fall around them. They had been forced to take cover in the cellar of a house at the eastern end of the town: 'Machine guns rattled all round and shells were bursting near by so I decided that we had better wait for darkness before trying to rejoin the regiment. In the afternoon a Tiger tank drew up outside the window and began firing. We could hear the unmistakable crackle of ammunition exploding in burning tanks and feared they must be British Cromwells.'

At a little after midnight Cloudsley-Thompson and his men crept up the steps from the cellar and round the side of the house. A flickering light from buildings burning in the near distance threatened to betray their presence and they were forced to crawl into a nearby field: 'I said, "I'm going to go in front to see if I can find where the Germans are." I crawled round the field and came to a dugout and there were Germans in it. I could tell, because it was warm and I could smell people and they didn't smell like English people. I remember my father – who had fought in the Great War – saying, "You can always tell a German trench from a British trench because they have different smells."' Cloudsley-Thompson skirted the dugout and pushed on into the town, but was forced back to his cellar by another

British artillery barrage. The following night they tried again and this time managed to circle the town and strike out across country. At dawn, thirsty and exhausted, Cloudsley-Thompson and his men approached a village:

We could hear half-tracks starting up. I thought they were probably American, so I sent the crew over the road one by one, then I went last. I was halfway across when a German with a rifle came round the corner on a bicycle. He shouted, '*Hande Hoch!*' I guessed that was 'hands up'. But I thought, well, if I mistook them for Americans, perhaps he mistakes me for something – I hadn't got a hat on, I had a beret. So I didn't do anything and then he said it again, so I grunted a bit and hoped to mislead him. Then he said it a third time, so I put my hands up. He beckoned me towards him and stepped back, and his rifle, which had been pointing at my stomach, swung off, and the moment that happened, I jumped sideways through the hedge and called my crew. They were creeping up the hedge to shoot him through it. I said, 'Come on,' and we climbed over a wall and ran across a farmyard, through a field, a small wood and into another field. I saw three French nuns picking flowers – '*Où sont les Boches?*' I panted. And this frightened them very much, and the youngest said, 'Everywhere.' I said, 'Well, where can we hide?' and she said, 'What about that wood?' I didn't think that was very much help.

After another close call with a German armoured car, the little party decided to take shelter in a wood until nightfall. 'It was only 8 a.m. but we lay there until 11.30 p.m., scarcely daring to move. We were too cold, wet and miserable to sleep.' That night they retraced their steps to the village. It was full of German tanks and armoured cars and it was only with great patience and good fortune that they managed to find a way through it. After another day spent waiting in a ditch and then a third night on the run Cloudsley-Thompson had almost come to the end of his tether: 'My leg had been packing up, the one that was wounded in the desert, and I'd been crawling bits of the time, rather than walking.' He knew they were close to the British line because shells were dropping in the fields near by. Then a voice came booming from a hole in a hedge, '*Hande hoch!*' This is a bit much, I thought. The crew scattered and I took out my pistol and said, "Are you English or German?" And the sentry said, "We're English."'

Cloudsley-Thompson had spent four days in hiding or on the run from the enemy. In that time the 7th Armoured Division's attack had collapsed and with it the pincer move on Caen. After the war General Bayerlein told his interrogators that 'two companies of Panzer IVs and one company of Tigers from the Panzer Lehr annihilated a combat command of the 7th British Armoured Division . . . here the long gun came into its own'. This statement is wrong on almost all counts. The action at Villers-Bocage did prove conclusively, if proof were needed, that the Cromwell and Sherman were no match for 54 tons of Tiger. But although it had been a devastating attack, the 4th County of London Yeomanry had not been 'annihilated', as Bayerlein later claimed. The hardest blow had fallen on A Squadron – eleven out of fourteen Cromwells and its four Fireflies were destroyed. The Regimental Headquarters and Recce Troops lost another seven tanks between them. For all that, B and C Squadrons, with support from the 1st/7th Queens, had given an excellent account of themselves in the town. At least five Tigers were destroyed and an unknown number of Panzer IVs. It is impossible, however, to dispute the nerve and resourcefulness of Obersturmführer Michael Wittmann. His final remarkable tally is thought to have been twelve tanks, thirteen troop carriers and two anti-tank guns – destroyed in just ten minutes. His attack had brought the 7th Armoured's advance to a crunching halt.

By the afternoon of the 13th the Panzer Lehr and the 2nd Panzer had begun to squeeze the wedge the British had thrust into the German line. The following day the 50th Division attacked at Tilly 11 kilometres to the north but failed to break through, leaving the 7th Armoured Division's narrow salient dangerously exposed to counter-attack. On the evening of the 14th the Germans launched a wholehearted assault on the 7th Armoured's forward positions at Tracy-Bocage. The attack was broken only by a massive bombardment from 160 British and American guns of every calibre. At a little after midnight on the 14th, the 7th Armoured Division began to withdraw from Tracy – a position it was to 'hold at all cost'. It had been a less than glorious episode. Blame would later fall in equal measure on both the divisional commander, General Erskine, and General Bucknall at XXX Corps. Dempsey was furious – the attack had not been pressed home with sufficient vigour; heads would roll: 'My feeling that Bucknall and Erskine would have to go started with that failure,' he wrote later. 'Early on the morning of 12 June I went down to see Erskine – gave him his orders and told him to get moving . . . If he had carried out my orders he would not have been kicked out of Villers-Bocage but by this time the 7th Armoured Division was living on its reputation and the whole handling of that battle was a disgrace.' Harsh words, but the failure to exploit this last gap in the defences around Caen before the front hardened was, in the judgement of the American historian Carlo D'Este, 'to prove one of the costliest Allied mistakes' of the campaign.

The other arm of the pincer had fared no better. The attack by the 51st Highland Division across the Orne had petered out after three days. The performance of Monty's 8th Army veterans was less than impressive. Questions have often been raised about the wisdom of throwing veteran units like the 51st, 50th and 7th Armoured into Normandy. There is little doubt that some of the men in these divisions felt that after Africa and Italy they had done more than their fair share of fighting. Lieutenant Edwin Bramall had joined the 2nd King's Royal Rifle Corps just before D-Day – a new boy in a unit of veterans:

They'd been through the battles since Alamein onwards and they'd given their all. Many who'd served had been killed. Some of them had been promoted. And those that were left were tired, and so I don't think they were all that enthusiastic about taking more risks than was absolutely necessary. I remember one old sweat coming up to me and saying: 'Don't you worry, sir, you'll be all right, we'll look after you.' But you realised, actually it was your job to look after them and they did need somebody to look after them and encourage them and put some enthusiasm into them.

The twenty-one-year-old lieutenant would in due course become a field marshal and Britain's most senior professional soldier. Casting his mind back to those first days in Normandy, he remembered noting that experienced formations were markedly more cautious than the 'fresh ones' from England which were 'raring to go'.

A highly respected New Zealand veteran of the desert campaign, Brigadier James Hargest, landed with the 50th and observed it in action throughout the Battle of Normandy. He noted that the division 'fights well' but casualties had been heavy in the first ten days – over three thousand men. The number of officers lost in the bocage country seemed particularly high: 'The men lie down in such country and are only urged forward by the personal example of their officers . . . the division is tired and whenever men get into shelter they want to sleep. They cannot be alert while in this condition.' The ordinary Tommy was in Hargest's view sometimes short on initiative: 'I notice that as soon as men lose their officers in the thick undergrowth they lose heart. Today I met several Bren gun sections coming back and in reply to my enquiries, "Why?" they said the fire was heavy and they had got out of touch. It did not occur to them to go on. Result: great loss of firepower.' It was not a question of courage but a lack of independence. Although these observations were made regarding the 50th Division, they held true for most of the British formations fighting in Normandy.

Of particular interest in light of the failure at Villers-Bocage are the brigadier's observations on the use the 7th Armoured made of its tanks. Hargest had joined the division on D + 5 – the day before the advance on Villers. It had met with little organised resistance and yet a promising advance had ground to a halt for lack of infantry support. So much was obvious to the 'tank officers', but Hargest was given short shrift when he attempted to press their case with the division's commander: 'Infantry was necessary to consolidate immediately and to mop up,' he told Major General Erskine. 'As it was the enemy lay down and peppered the rear after the tanks had passed.' But as far as Erskine was concerned, the speed of the advance was 'too hot' for infantry. The march to Villers-Bocage demonstrated this to be a dangerously short-sighted view. Hargest did not mince his words – his analysis of the 7th Armoured was damning: 'My conclusion is that our tanks are badly led and fought. Only our superior numbers and our magnificent artillery support keeps them in the field at all. They violate most of the elementary principles of war. They bunch up – they are the reverse of aggressive – they are not possessed of the will to attack the enemy.' As if to rub further salt into the wound, Hargest contrasted British efforts with the American armoured force advancing to the west – it had 'reached Caumont twenty-four hours ahead of the 7th, stayed there and still holds it'.

Monty had no patience with the failure of his veteran divisions, and in the days to come the commanders of both the 7th and the 51st would find themselves on the boat home. Nor was he happy with the reports he was receiving from some units of a 'Tiger fever' among the men. In the weeks before D-Day he had gone out of his way to praise publicly 'the quality of our arms' – the overwhelming material and technical superiority the Allies enjoyed made victory nothing short of a certainty. On the day after the battle in Villers-Bocage he wrote to his chief of staff at 21st Army Group's main HQ in England urging him to do all he could to stamp on criticism of British armour: 'Any suggestion that we have been taken by surprise at the performance of

British and American tanks vis-à-vis German tanks is complete nonsense.' If these reports trickled down to the troops, 'they may have a very great effect upon their fighting'. In particular, Monty noted 'a danger of the troops developing a "Tiger" and "Panther" complex – when every tank becomes one of these types'. The vast majority of German tanks at this time were in fact Panzer IVs, an altogether less formidable weapon than the Tiger or Panther.

If Monty was disappointed with the outcome of his pincer attack he went out of his way not to show it. In a letter to the War Office in London on the 14th he declared himself to be 'very happy about the situation'. The sudden appearance of the 2nd Panzer Division in the area of Caumont–Villers-Bocage had forced him to 'think again', but 'So long as Rommel uses his strategic reserves to plug holes – that is good.' He was firmly of the view that pressure by the British in the east would enable the Americans in the west to take Cherbourg, then break out and force the issue. This was the plan he had outlined to Allied commanders in May, and he had restated it repeatedly since. General Bradley acknowledged as much in his account of the campaign: 'The British and Canadians were to decoy the enemy reserves and draw them to their front on the extreme eastern edge of the Allied beachhead. Thus while Monty taunted the enemy at Caen, we were to make our break on the long round-about road toward Paris.' It was not a role that was likely to add lustre to the reputation of British arms – Bradley described it as a 'sacrificial' part.

The Supreme Allied Commander took an altogether less generous view. 'Ike was anxious that the Germans be kept off balance and that our drive never stop,' his aide Harry Butcher noted on 15 June; 'Ike also said that yesterday we had made no gains, which he didn't like.' The euphoria felt in the first days after the landings was wearing thin. Progress seemed much slower when the battles were fought only in armchairs or in front of wall plots. Eisenhower was impatient to climb down from his 'lofty perch' and direct the campaign in person – torn between the need to delegate and his own natural desire to play a more hands-on part. Senior courtiers at SHAEF were beginning to whisper against Monty – the Allied airmen were particularly critical. 'The only thing necessary to move forward is sufficient guts on the part of the ground commanders,' an American Air Force general told Eisenhower. Monty made little effort to put his Supreme Commander's mind at rest. His stubborn refusal to ever admit to Eisenhower that there had been a setback served only to undermine confidence in his judgement. Nor was it always clear what Monty's exact intentions were. On the one hand he was planning an American break-out in the west, on the other a pincer move to envelop the German Panzer reserves at Caen. After the war Monty would write that Caen was only important as a magnet for Rommel's best divisions, and yet at the time he was quite determined to take the city. 'Once we get Caen . . . we will be very well placed to develop the operations as originally planned,' Monty wrote on the 13th, and then again on the 18th: 'Once we capture Caen and Cherbourg and all face in the same direction, the enemy's problem becomes enormous.'

To that end planning began for a second 'pincer' attack on Caen from east and west. In the end it was decided that the bridgehead to the east of Caen was too small for an attack by an entire armoured and infantry corps; the new operation – Epsom – would be concentrated in the west of the British sector. On 19 June Monty wrote a chipper letter to the War Office promising 'a blitz attack supported by all available air power'. The task was given to VIII Corps under Monty's friend, the desert veteran Lieutenant General Sir Richard O'Connor. His entire corps – the 15th Scottish, 11th Armoured and 43rd Wessex divisions – was to advance on a six-kilometre front, force crossings of the Odon and Orne and then establish itself on the high ground north-east of Bretteville-sur-Laize. The build-up of forces on both sides was such that all hope of a breakthrough by a single division had been abandoned – the British would attack with 60,000 men and 600 tanks. But it promised to be a tough task. The battle would be fought in difficult country – 'its broken contours and abundance of cover' made it, the British Official History notes, 'almost ideal for defence'. The ground had been held for almost three weeks by the 12th SS Panzer, elements of the 21st Panzer and Panzer Lehr, and they had prepared their defensive line well. Infantry positions had been strengthened with minefields and wire and between sixty and eighty 88mm guns sited in the hedgerows and woods along the front.

Allied preparations were set back by a howling gale that broke on the Normandy coast in the early hours of the 19th. For three unrelenting days high winds and seas pounded the breakwaters the Allies had built off the beaches – the worst June storm in forty years. The invasion coast was strewn with the wreckage of landing craft – hundreds of vessels of all types were damaged or destroyed. Thirty thousand Allied troops had come ashore in the three days before the storm, with 6,000 vehicles and 25,000 tons of supplies – in its wake the build-up was cut by more than half.

The offensive finally began on 25 June with a preliminary attack by the 49th Division and 8th Armoured Brigade, which was designed to cover the right flank of the main thrust. It would be renewed again the following day – the first of Operation Epsom proper. Trooper Austin Baker of the 4th/7th Royal Dragoon Guards took part in the attack. By this time he had transferred from the C Squadron armoured recovery vehicle to a tank:

The regiment was to be under the command of a newly arrived division – the 49th (West Riding). It was beginning to get light when we arrived at the start point for the attack – a damp, misty, cheerless morning. The tanks were parked in a sort of depression in the ground, sheltered by a high bank. Some infantry carriers were there too. It all seemed very quiet. A message came over the wireless telling us that we could dismount for half an hour and get breakfast. We were unlucky in our crew, because we couldn't get the petrol cooker working and so we couldn't have any tea, which was the chief thing we wanted. Mr Lilly's [troop leader Lieutenant Lilly] tank was next to ours and I remember how furious he was when he came back from a troop leaders' conference and found that his crew had not cooked anything, but had finished off the last tins of self-heating soup. Lilly was pretty rude to Lance Corporal Fairman, his driver. Fairman was going to be dead within an hour.

I must admit that at the time I had very little idea of what the plan of attack was, but it was soon obvious even to me that something had gone wrong. As usual in the bocage, visibility was limited to one field. We moved along a hedge, with the infantry walking alongside, and we had gone no more than a few yards when machine-gun tracers started whistling through the hedge – and they were red British tracers at that! The firing ceased after a minute or two and we carried on. We turned left through a gap in the hedge and bumped down a bank into the next field. It was a largish field with a wood running about half the length of the far hedge. The field sloped downhill away from us, but beyond the far gap the ground rose again.

Well, 4th Troop bowled off merrily down the field, with Lilly leading followed by Harris [troop sergeant] and then by ourselves. None of the tanks fired, but the infantry charged towards the wood with their Sten guns blazing away. Nobody fired back, and I was beginning to think this was going to be a quiet affair. I was very much mistaken. I couldn't see 1st Troop, but I think they must have been moving down on our right. Anyway, Second Lieutenant Thompson came over the air with a message that made my stomach turn over. His tank had pushed through a hedge and been knocked out by a Jerry tank just across the field. None of the crew had been hurt and, amazingly enough, they had stayed in and knocked out the Jerry before baling out. I guessed that there would be other Jerry tanks about and there were.

We reached the far hedge and halted for a moment, then Lilly pushed on through the gap into the next field. He trundled off across the field, swinging his turret to the left and firing at something behind the wood. Harris was halfway through the gap and we were just about to follow him. Suddenly Freddie Haigh [the commander of Baker's tank] yelled, 'Reverse!' Harris was coming back through the gap and beyond him I could see smoke beginning to drift up from Lilly's turret. I had a glimpse of two figures leaping off it. We reversed in a hurry. A mortar bomb went off right in front of Harris. I lost sight of Lilly's tank for a moment, and when I looked again flames were shooting up from it. We moved round to the left and parked under cover of the hedge near the left-hand corner of the field. And there we stayed! The whole squadron was now in the field, with the tanks scattered around by the hedges. We soon discovered from the wireless that we were in a trap. There appeared to be Tigers and Panthers all around us – there were about six on the ground ahead, four in the edge of the wood just across the field to our left, and possibly others.

In our tank we sat without saying much, listening intently to what was going on over the wireless. I was eating boiled sweets by the dozen and the others were smoking furiously. I don't know how long we'd been sitting there when the tank behind us was hit. The infantry was pinned down by Spandau [machine-gun] fire and there was a fair amount of mortaring. Looking over towards the other side of the field I was amazed to see one of the tanks beginning to brew up. Somebody severely burned scrambled down the front and dashed away up the field. The tank had been in the same position for a long time and I had naturally supposed it to have been out of sight of Jerry. We found out from wireless reports that it was Sergeant Andy Roger's tank from 1st Troop. We watched as the ammunition inside began to blow up and flames and black smoke poured upwards. Eric Santer and Cooper had baled out safely, but Sid Francis had been killed and Andy, having been carried away delirious with one leg sliced off, died shortly after.

Suddenly Sergeant Harris started on a little offensive action. He changed places with Freddie for a few hectic minutes. There was a gap in the hedge a few yards behind us, and Harris said, 'We're going to reverse into the gap and fire some HE into the hedge across the next field. I think there's an anti-tank gun there.'

I loaded the 75mm with an HE round. This was the first time either of us had fired a shot at the enemy. We loosed off eleven rounds, dropping them in a line all along the hedge. I was loading as fast as I could, but it wasn't fast enough for Harris, who kept shouting for more speed. 'Now give them a belt of Browning!' he said. I think he was enjoying himself really. He was an impressive-looking bloke with a bristling waxed moustache and there was a mad gleam in his eye. We sprayed the hedge from end to end with Browning bullets. 'Driver, forward!' said Harris, and we moved back behind cover. I have no idea why we were not knocked out.

By late afternoon it was clear the situation was hopeless. The infantry had taken a lot of casualties and six of the squadron's tanks had been destroyed. 'A message came over the air to Knocker [Major Bell, squadron leader] from the CO, saying that "Big Sunray" [the brigadier] was very anxious to organise a Tiger hunt and we were to withdraw immediately and be ready to take part in it. Of course, the last thing we wanted to do by then was to get involved in a Tiger hunt, but we were all in favour of withdrawal if that could be managed.'

The squadron was to withdraw under the cover of a smoke-screen. As Baker's tank approached the gap in the hedge the branches in the tree above snapped and splintered under enemy fire. 'There was quite a steep bank up to the next field and going up it Tom stalled the engine, so that we slid backwards and stopped right in the gap. For a moment that seemed like an hour I felt that every 88mm gunner in the German army had his sights dead on our turret, but if they had they didn't fire.'

The 4th/7th had advanced one field, only to be pinned down at the edge of the next for the rest of the day. Progress was better elsewhere.

Operation Epsom began on the following day – 26 June – with a ferocious barrage from 700 artillery and naval guns. It was a grim, overcast day and low cloud ruled out any hope of air support. A soaking mist hung over the cornfields as the first of the 15th Scottish Division began to push forward behind the barrage. Initially progress was good, but as the artillery moved forward the German defenders emerged from their foxholes and dugouts and a ferocious close-quarters battle ensued. The villages of Mauvieu, Cheux and Le Haut du Bosq were taken only after hand-to-hand fighting. The 2nd Glasgow Highlanders were under constant shellfire in Cheux, and the village was reduced street by street to rubble. The battalion lost twelve officers and 200 men during the course of the day. Lieutenant Edwin Bramall of the 2nd King's Royal Rifle Corps had watched them advance through the corn:

The 15th Scottish Division attacked behind an enormous artillery barrage as it was done in the First World War. There was an opportunity of rushing these cornfields and getting down and coming up somewhere else and doing what the army later called pepper-potting. But the initial attack on Epsom was unimaginative. It was what you might call a partridge drive with artillery going down in front and the infantry getting as near as they could and then rushing the first objective and then hoping the artillery would lift on to the next objective and then doing the same again.

It was not the way the German army liked to go about things. 'The English should have made better use of the ground,' one SS officer later observed. 'They should have kept their heads down, moving in short bursts. Taking cover again, then firing from a prone position or from their knees. But not standing up in the open, so we could identify their officers.'

At a little after midday the 11th Armoured Brigade was ordered to press on through the infantry to the crossings over the Odon. But the division was stopped just south of Cheux by a determined defence. In an effort to hold the line, the new commander of the 12th SS Panzer Division, Brigadeführer Kurt Meyer, threw his last reserves into the battle, including the reconnaissance company of his old regiment – men he knew well. Meyer watched as the company attempted to hold the British armoured column: 'The sporadic German artillery fire is incapable of stemming the enemy attack. The British tanks continue to wreak havoc. For the first time I feel a burning emptiness in my heart, and I curse the murder. For what I am now witnessing is no longer war, but naked murder. I know every one of these young grenadiers. The oldest among them is barely eighteen . . . Tears run down my face and I begin to hate this war.' But by evening Meyer's young grenadiers had done enough to halt the British advance. The attack petered out in a blinding downpour – it had punched a hole three kilometres deep in the German line but was short of the Odon. The key high ground between the British line and the river was still in German hands. At Rommel's headquarters the Army Group B diarist recorded it as a 'complete defensive success', but for the 12th SS Panzer it had been the worst day in the field so far. The division had lost more than 700 dead and wounded.

That night O'Connor moved the 43rd Wessex Division up in support – many of those in its ranks were going into battle for the first time: 'As we moved into Cheux there was a big six-ton truck parked up in a farmyard and in the high cab there was a chap over the steering wheel with the top of his head sheared off – he was from the 15th Scottish – and I looked at him and I thought, well, I won't have to check his breathing,' Private Bill Edwards recalled. Edwards was serving as a stretcher-bearer with the 1st Battalion, the Worcestershire Regiment. He had lied about his age to enlist – he was still only seventeen. 'He was the first casualty I saw and I suppose it was an odd reaction, a sort of defence mechanism. I didn't like what I saw but I knew I wouldn't have to do anything about it.' Edwards squelched up the line past a young lieutenant in the 6th King's Own Scottish Borderers: 'Back through the melancholy rain-swept night we trudged,' Robert Woollcombe later wrote.

I was placed in charge of a burial party. All Highlanders, the dead were scattered along the hedges round the field. The complete course of a platoon attack could be traced in detail. The platoon commander, a lieutenant, looking faintly surprised, a slight twist to his neck and not a mark but for some congealed stains where his battle-dress covered his kidneys. In a breast pocket a slab of chocolate as I had in mine, and a snapshot of his wedding a month earlier. Here, a corporal huddled over his sten gun, taken completely unawares . . . A corporal from 'C' Company was among the burial party. 'I know him! He was in my ward in hospital last Christmas – that bloke!'

It was becoming a bloody infantry slog:

> New men, new weapons, bear the brunt
> New slogans guild the ancient game
> The infantry are still in front
> And mud and dust are much the same.
> (A. P. Herbert)

On the morning of the 27th just 600 men from the 2nd Argyll and Sutherland Highlanders surprised the enemy and seized two bridges over the Odon – over them poured the tanks of the 11th Armoured Division. They pushed on to the slopes of a long low ridge to the south-east – Hill 112. Over the next few days the battle would be concentrated around and on this hill as the Germans made repeated efforts to push the British back over the Odon. The small bridgehead across the river was hemmed on three sides by high ground from which fire could be directed on to the beleaguered British van. By the end of June the first units from II SS Panzer Corps were arriving on the battlefield from the Russian front – the formidable veterans of the 9th and 10th SS Panzer Divisions. Units from six German armoured divisions were already in the line, including the first soldiers from the 1st SS Panzer Division – Leibstandarte Adolf Hitler. General O'Connor decided a further advance to the River Orne would not be possible until the British salient was secure. By 29 June it was eight kilometres deep but less than three kilometres wide, and there was good evidence to suggest that the II Panzer Corps was preparing to launch a major counter-attack.

On 29 June the 43rd Wessex Division was ordered to clear the villages on the eastern flank of the new salient. Private Bill Edwards's battalion, the 1st Worcesters, attacked the village of Mouen:

We had to make our way across cornfields towards the village. I was with the leading rifle company on that. The stretcher-bearers were allocated two to a company. Our job was first recovery – as casualties fell you would move to them and do what you could. It was a firm principle in the infantry that no rifleman stopped if the companion next to him was wounded or dropped. He must keep on going. Somebody would just take the wounded man's rifle – the bayonet would be fixed – and drive it into the ground so you could see the butt and you knew where he was. When we got through the corn to the railway line we started meeting real opposition. The commander of C Company was wounded in the neck – my first real casualty, and it happened to be the company commander. I can recall holding him there while my colleague put the field dressing on round his neck. And me, a very young private. This man was nearly God to me – he was a major and the company commander – and there I was, seventeen years of age, telling him he'd be OK, that it wasn't serious, he'd be back in Blighty in no time, lucky dog.

We had small capsules of morphine like a small toothpaste tube with a little needle on the end. You found the vein if you could, otherwise you just pushed it in and squeezed and that was one milligram of morphine. You were supposed to mark the wounded man's forehead with a number – one or two doses. You could never find the indelible pencil you were issued with, so more often than not you marked him with blood – just an M on the forehead.

The wounded were taken to a regimental first-aid post and then to one of the bridgehead's casualty clearing stations. By the third day of the Epsom operation VIII Corps had taken 4,000 casualties – 2,300 from the 15th Scottish and 1,200 from the 11th Armoured and the 43rd Wessex Divisions.

'They were usually on a stretcher when they were brought into the reception area, which was a tent, and we sorted them out there – they went to either the surgeon or the physician, depending on their wounds,' Private William Wood recalled. The nineteen-year-old Wood was serving with the army's dental corps at the 32nd Casualty Clearing Station (CCS).

The reception area was usually quite silent. There were some who didn't know what they were doing, they did moan but it was very quiet really, and with our patients, very few of them were unconscious. Usually a bullet or shrapnel had gone straight through, taken part of the face away, but that numbed the man because most of the nerve centres were injured or taken away and so they were quite conscious when we came to treat them.

Our area was the face, the upper and the lower jaw – the medics didn't touch that area, they coped with the eyes but not the face. My officer was a dental surgeon. We just stabilised – there wasn't a lot we could do. We had to make sure they weren't bleeding too profusely, and that they didn't lose anything. Nothing was to be taken away from that area because the men needed all they could get for reconstruction later. The tongue was one of our biggest problems. We made headsets with a face bar and we sutured the tongue on to the face bar, made sure that it could not drop down into the throat on the way back to the base hospital or the beachhead.

The staff at the 32nd Casualty Clearing Station – had been the first to take the wounded after D-Day. There were five surgeons, an X-ray and blood transfusion unit, a staff a hundred strong, but no beds. As soon as a wounded man was stabilised he was sent back to a field hospital or the beach for evacuation. The medical staff liked things to be 'tidy', and when a lot of wounded came through in a short time it was anything but – then men would have to queue for theatre. At such times the exhausted staff were offered tablets to keep them awake and working: 'The abdominal wounds were the worst, I think. Our facial ones were quite hard. Making sure they weren't losing too much blood, that was our biggest problem there. It was a matter of preparing them so they could be evacuated without any more loss of life,' Wood recalled.

There was no time to befriend the wounded, and nursing staff were never told if patients lived or died, but it was not easy to forget the faces of the young men who passed through: 'Many of the men we dealt with couldn't talk,' Wood recalled. 'But they could look, and we'd to be very careful we didn't show any reaction at all. There were no mirrors there so we knew that they wouldn't know just how bad they were, but of course they were anxious. We did not explain what was wrong with them, we'd sort of generalise if they were conscious enough to notice.' The 32nd CCS also had its own mortuary man.

The Germans obligingly chose to launch their counter-attack on a bright, clear summer's day – 30 June. Allied fighter-bombers were out hunting in strength from first light. The tanks of II SS Panzer Corps were attacked again and again as they pushed forward towards the start line. Their advance also came under fire from the field artillery of three British corps. So relentless was the bombardment that the commander of II SS Panzer Corps, General Paul Hausser, was forced to postpone his attack until the afternoon: 'The murderous fire from naval guns in the Channel and the terrible British artillery destroyed the bulk of our attacking force in its assembly area,' he told his interrogators at the end of the war. 'The few tanks that did manage to go forward were easily stopped by the British anti-tank guns.' The comparative ease with which the Germans were held led Generals Dempsey and O'Connor to believe that the attack had been only a preliminary skirmish and a heavier blow was yet to fall. At half past eight that evening Operation Epsom was called off. It was cruelly ironic, for earlier that day the 11th Armoured Division had managed to fight its way to the summit of Hill 112. A few hours later it was rolling back over ground it had cost many lives to take. All armour was withdrawn to the north bank of the Odon and only an infantry bridgehead was left on the south side of the river.

At SHAEF it was judged to have been little short of a defeat. It had certainly not been 'the blitz attack' Monty had led everyone to expect. He had sent a rash signal to Eisenhower on the eve of the Epsom battle promising to 'continue the battle on the eastern flank till one of us cracks and it will NOT be us.' But in the same message he had restated the main purpose of the attack: 'If we can pull the enemy on to Second Army it will make it easier for [US] First Army when it attacks southwards.' In this respect Operation Epsom was certainly successful. By the end of June there were substantial formations from eight different Panzer divisions in the line around Caen – some of the best units the German army could muster. There were no Panzer divisions in the Cotentin peninsula, although by this time the number of British and American soldiers in the field was almost equal. While the British were battering away at Caen the US First Army had dashed across the neck of the Cotentin peninsula, isolating the German defenders to the north. The fiery, capable commander of VII Corps, General Joe Lawton, had then swung his three divisions northward towards the port of Cherbourg. The final assault had begun on 22 June with a devastating bombardment from the air. One by one the network of forts and strongpoints that dominated the city fell to the American advance, and after five days of close fighting the Germans were forced to surrender. Hitler had expected the garrison to hold out for months – he had issued a personal order to it to fight to the death: 'it is your duty to defend the last bunker and leave the enemy not a harbour but a field of ruins'. The garrison had carried out at least one of its orders – German engineers had systematically reduced the port facilities to rubble. By the time it was capable of playing a significant part in Allied planning, the fighting in Normandy was over. There was nevertheless something to celebrate, and a good deal of booze was 'liberated' from the city for just that purpose – the readily available tipple was the local apple brandy, Calvados. 'Some of the American correspondents called it "the breakfast of champions",' Andy Rooney recalled. Rooney was a twenty-three-year-old New Yorker, on assignment with the US Army's newspaper, *Stars and Stripes*: 'There was this cave outside Cherbourg – there were even railroad tracks that went into it – and it was the storage area for German officers' liquor, and they had the best wines in France, Scotch and every conceivable liquor. And the correspondents pretty much helped themselves to anything they wanted.'

As Rooney passed through the shattered towns and villages of the Cotentin he witnessed a good deal of looting – not all of it of alcohol: 'It's a funny thing, but in a war it's hard to get a sense of property, you don't have any feeling that anybody owns anything. People would leave these grand homes empty and their things and they didn't seem to belong to anybody. They did, of course, but you ignore it in a war, and the newspaper people were no better than the soldiers about taking anything they saw around.'

During the short siege of Cherbourg, Bradley and Collins had shared a wry joke at the expense of the Allied Land Forces Commander: 'He [Bradley] told me with a chuckle: "Joe, you will love this. Monty has just announced, 'Caen is the key to Cherbourg'." I said: "Brad, let's wire him to send us the key." In the interest of Allied amity we did not do it.' It was typically undiplomatic of Monty to say it, but it was true nonetheless. The Americans faced poorer-quality troops, who were outnumbered and outgunned. Allied estimates in the first week of July suggested the Americans enjoyed a three-to-one superiority in infantry over the Germans in the west and could deploy eight times the number of tanks.

It had taken longer than Monty had hoped to capture Cherbourg, but by the end of June the US First Army was preparing to push south at last. On the 30th – the day the German counter-attack at Epsom was 'seen off' – Monty summoned Bradley and Dempsey to TAC HQ to discuss future operations. 'General Montgomery was very crisp, very peppery, spoke in staccato tones,' Bradley's aide, Major Chester Hansen, remembered. 'He used to scare me to death. He dominated much of the conversation. We were a little deferential to Monty at the beginning, because he had come in there with such a reputation. But General Bradley and he got along famously, no problems. Monty was, of course, the senior commander at that time and he understood us and our capabilities and we treated him with great respect.' Monty had drawn up a directive for the meeting – a copy was sent to Eisenhower. In it he promised to proceed 'relentlessly with our plans' to 'hold the maximum number of enemy divisions in our eastern flank between Caen and Villers-Bocage and to swing the [American] western or right flank southwards and eastwards in a wide sweep so as to threaten the line of withdrawal of such enemy divisions to the south of Paris.' A strong force in the Le Mans –Alençon area would, Monty noted, threaten to trap German forces west of the River Seine. As Monty's biographer Nigel Hamilton points out, this was in essence the plan Bradley would carry out a little more than three weeks later. After the war Monty's part in shaping what would become Operation Cobra was forgotten or ignored in the scramble for credit. It became an entirely American plan – the author held to be General Bradley alone. But the outline of a plan for 'break-out' was drawn on the 30th by Monty – another plank in the 'broad policy' he had first formulated before D-Day. 'We have been successful in this policy,' Monty concluded in his directive. His Supreme Commander was not convinced.

An anxious Eisenhower had followed the course of the battle around Caen with growing dismay. The Supreme Commander's mood had not been improved by a number of broken nights. The first of Hitler's 'wonder weapons' had begun to fall on London. The V-1 flying bombs were passing uncomfortably close to Ike's 'cottage' on the outskirts of south London. 'Around 1 a.m. I was awakened by the siren and went to Ike's room where I found him still reading,' Harry Butcher noted in his diary for 17 June. 'He said he preferred staying in his room rather than shuttling back and forth to the shelter all night.' In the end 'a bursting diver' had forced Eisenhower to take refuge – he woke the following morning with a splitting headache. Nerves at SHAEF were frayed: 'Most of the people I know are semi-dazed from loss of sleep and have the jitters,' Butcher logged on the 20th. It was one more reason for pressing for a quick victory. Eisenhower had too much time to brood. Some of those around him were beginning to whisper the word 'stalemate'. General George Patton – tired of commanding a paper army in Britain – was champing at the bit for a real one in France. Monty was failing to gain his objectives around Caen, he told the British military writer Basil Liddell-Hart – thank God for the Americans at Cherbourg. 'It struck me as curious that he should express such slighting comparisons between the American and British effort to anyone with whom he had quite a short acquaintance,' Liddell-Hart noted in his diary.

There would be much debate after the war about Monty's intentions at Caen. That Eisenhower knew and had discussed the strategy many times is not in doubt. 'A firm left' to hold the enemy and a swinging right to advance – 'Eisenhower, Montgomery, and I had agreed to the plan without a moment's dissension,' Bradley wrote in his memoirs. Yet there was still a good deal of confusion at SHAEF. Eisenhower's chief of staff later claimed that Ike 'made up his mind' to break out on the American front when it became clear the 'advance was not going to take place as originally planned on the east flank'. This was, of course, Monty's plan. A break-out at Caen had never been discussed – except in the press. Eisenhower's judgement was clouded by loose talk. Some of the blame rested with those around him at SHAEF, but a good deal rested with Monty himself.

Bradley gives full credit to Monty for 'brilliantly' succeeding in his 'diversionary mission', but points out that he made the mistake of overemphasising the importance of his thrust and of the city of Caen:

Had he limited himself simply to the containment without making Caen a symbol of it, he would have been credited with success instead of being charged, as he was, with failure at Caen. For Monty's success should have been measured in the panzer divisions the enemy rushed against him while Collins sped on toward Cherbourg. Instead, the Allied newspaper readers clamoured for a place name called Caen which Monty had once promised but failed to win for them.

Monty would claim after the war that everything had gone to plan – that was arrant nonsense. But enough was going to plan. It was impossible, of course, to explain this to the press without making a present of it to the enemy.

Eisenhower had very little appreciation of how fragile the German position was in Normandy. Fresh Panzer reserves were being thrown into the line as soon as they arrived at the front. Armoured divisions were being wasted in a static defence better suited to infantry. The remorseless Allied bombardment from air, sea and land was inflicting heavy losses that could not be replaced – more than 80,000 casualties by the end of June. The leaders of the German armies in the west were almost powerless to do anything about the situation. Field Marshal von Rundstedt had requested permission for an immediate 'evacuation of the Caen bridgehead' to positions beyond the range of the Allied naval guns. A report written by the commander of Panzer Group West, Geyr von Schweppenburg, was also sent to the OKW: 'A clear-cut choice must be made between the inevitable patchwork of a rigid defence, which leaves the initiative to the enemy, and flexible tactics which give us the initiative sometimes at least . . . an elastic conduct of operations is the better course.' This advice was roundly rejected. Hitler refused to countenance any sort of strategic withdrawal. 'I could have stood on my head,' Rundstedt later observed, 'but I would still not have been able to budge a division if Hitler disagreed with my judgement.'

Rommel and Rundstedt met Hitler on the last day of the Epsom offensive, the 29th, to press their case in person. They had agreed to pull no punches and the meeting was a stormy one. Rommel was invited to speak first: '*Mein Führer*, I think it is high time that I – on behalf of the German people to whom I am also answerable – tell you the situation in the west. I should like to begin with our political situation. The entire world stands arrayed against Germany and this balance of strength . . .' Hitler interrupted him with a sharp 'The Field Marshal will restrict himself to the military situation'. Rommel was obliged to do just that for a time, but at the end of his report he turned again to the crisis Germany was facing: 'I must speak bluntly, I cannot leave here without speaking on the subject of Germany.' Hitler refused to listen to more. 'Field Marshal, I think you had better leave the room.' It was to be their last meeting. Rundstedt had put it bluntly to Hitler's chief of staff on the telephone when Cherbourg fell. 'What shall we do?' Field Marshal Keitel had asked. 'What shall you do? Make peace, you idiots! What else can you do?' was Rundstedt's reply. Defeatist talk was not to be tolerated, and within days of his meeting with Hitler the old field marshal had gone.

Monty had a sense of how tightly drawn the enemy's line had become and was able to communicate some of this to Eisenhower in person on 2 July when the Supreme Commander visited TAC HQ. Bradley and his ADC were of the party: 'Got to Monty's as spoonily clad guards officers were returning from chapel with prayer books and bibles in their hands. Very proper,' Chester

Hansen recorded in his diary. 'Attitude of ease and comfort in their headquarters. It was Sunday . . . Monty not there originally, arrives, downy, corduroys and sweater with black beret . . . Trees green in the valley, tiny church visible on opposite hill to the west and we could hear the ringing of bells mingled with the thunder of cannon down on 1st Division Front.' Monty led Ike to his map lorry, where he briefed him on the battle. Another counter-attack had been beaten off the day before, he reported, and on the morrow – 3 July – the American VII and VIII Corps would begin their push south towards Coutances and St-Lô. It was vital they press forward before the enemy switched more mobile reserves to the west – there would be a fresh attempt on Caen to keep the Panzer divisions busy in the British sector. Eisenhower left reassured by Monty's ever confident demeanour – there was something to tell the great press posse that had accompanied him to France. But the headlines were depressingly familiar two days later when he returned to England. The American push south had begun to stall in the bocage. Some at SHAEF were quick to blame Monty for the failure to make 'gains' – Eisenhower himself was 'fed up with Monty's lack of drive'. It was a criticism that would have amazed the soldiers of the British 2nd Army as they prepared to launch yet another push on Caen.

This time Monty proposed using the enormous weight of Allied firepower to 'write down' the enemy before an advance on the city. On the night of 7 July more than 450 heavy bombers attacked the northern outskirts. There were no public air-raid shelters in the city. An eighteen-year-old student and French Resistance worker, André Heintz, was among those who sought refuge in the ancient abbey of St Etienne:

There were more than a thousand people in the church, and altogether, with the abbey buildings next door and the improvised hospital behind, there must have been 10,000 refugees hiding and surviving in it. The lucky ones that could rescue a mattress brought it into the church. Straw was brought later on so that everybody could sleep in the church. They trusted those walls which are so thick, more than six feet thick, and also the heavy pillars, and there was some sort of superstition attached to it because they knew that William the Conqueror was buried there and they thought the British would never dare destroy the grave of one of their kings.

As many as 6,000 French people may have been killed in the bombing. To BBC war correspondent Frank Gillard it looked like a city that had been 'murdered': 'My own feeling about the bombing was that it was really unnecessary,' he later observed. 'I felt that it was an act of sheer frustration on the part of the higher command. That there we had been for weeks hammering away on the outskirts and failing to penetrate the defences and we had this great air weapon which could in the last resort be used.'

After two days of intense fighting in the rubble-choked streets, British and Canadian soldiers finally reached the centre of the city. There the advance stopped. The Germans had blown the bridges over the Orne. After more than a month of fighting the British had taken the objective Monty had set for D-Day. The city was in ruins but its people cheered: 'The reception which its citizens have given to us has been moving in the extreme,' Gillard told the audience back home. 'Not a word of reproach; not a word of self-pity.'

There were no flags of celebration at SHAEF. Eisenhower had written to Monty urging him to 'use all possible energy in a determined effort to prevent a stalemate'. The advance in front of Caen 'has been slow and laborious' – the situation called for 'a major full-dress attack on the left supported by everything we could bring to bear'. The American press was impatient; so too were senior administration figures in Washington. Churchill was grumbling about the lack of progress and Monty's critics at SHAEF were urging his replacement. Monty stood his ground: 'My dear Ike, I am, myself, quite happy with the situation. I have been working throughout on a very definite plan, and I now begin to see daylight.' But another fortnight would pass before the critics were silenced.

CHAPTER FIVE

THE BATTLEFIELD

B y the end of June more than a million men were living, fighting and dying in the close hedges and orchards of the Normandy countryside. The battle drifted through shattered villages and fields of crushed wheat – gains were measured in metres and what was lost today was often taken again tomorrow. Montgomery confidently assured Eisenhower that there was one thing of which he could be quite certain – 'there will be no stalemate'. Eisenhower felt his patience and trust were being tested to the full, but he at least could question Monty, badger him and perhaps replace him. For the fighting men it was, as always, a leap of faith. That faith was beginning to wear a little thin. Major Peter Martin was a veteran of Dunkirk and the desert – his machine-gun company had landed with the 50th Division on D-Day:

We, of course, the poor wretched people on the ground, had no idea of the great Monty plan and we went through a phase when it all seemed totally pointless. Every day a battalion from each brigade would launch an attack to capture another couple of hedgerows. They would probably lose something like two to three hundred men in the process. Up with the rations the next day would come another two hundred men to fill the gap. And then another battalion the following day would do a similar attack. And the casualties were enormous. It all seemed to us on the ground totally pointless. Why did we have to expend all these lives capturing the hedgerow in front?

Wasn't there some better way of doing it? I've got some letters I wrote home to my mother and early in July I wrote to her and said, 'We don't think much of your friend Betty's husband.' Betty was the wife of the senior operations staff officer of 50th Div. and therefore in our minds he was responsible for a lot of the senseless battling that was going on, and I went on to say, 'and we think even less of his boss,' who was of course the divisional commander. And that's the only time I think during the war, the whole war, when I was ever critical of higher command.

Major Martin was attached to the brigadier's tactical head-quarters, and he often accompanied him on visits to other units: 'I saw more of the brigade than many more senior officers. I could see the effect of casualties on battalions. By the end of June, 50 Div. had lost – killed, wounded and missing – over three hundred officers and three thousand soldiers.'

Even those new to battle became cynical about talk of 'one last push' before the breakthrough. Lieutenant Edwin Bramall's battalion, the 2nd King's Royal Rifle Corps, was also part of the 50th:

Was it all going according to plan? Our commander-in-chief, Field Marshal Montgomery, was very insistent that before every battle, Epsom was one of them, we were told what was going to happen. Of course, often what we were told was really quite optimistic. On the first day of Epsom we were going to get across this river, go on to that river, and so on. And, of course, after a time, when these things didn't work out quite according to plan, you got a bit sceptical.

But the disappointments and setbacks did remarkably little to shake the ordinary British soldier's confidence in Monty, and those with doubts often kept them hidden: 'I was always defending him in my letters home to my mother,' Major Peter Martin recalled.

I said to her, 'I expect you're all worried about the slow rate of progress out here, but I can tell you that this is all part of Monty's preparation and when Monty prepares something it'll be something very good to follow and no doubt when his push starts we shall be in Paris within a week.' And I was always writing sort of pro-Monty statements and saying that the delays were due to bad weather. So I think it would be fair to say that all of us in the army out there in Normandy would have defended Monty absolutely heart and soul against public criticism – but we didn't necessarily feel that way towards him ourselves.

While the casualties seemed high to the men in the line – 24,698 British and Canadian soldiers by 30 June – they were lower than had been allowed for by the Overlord planners. By contrast the US First Army had taken 37,034 killed, wounded and missing – this against lighter enemy forces. Senior American commanders would later cite this as evidence of a greater determination to get the job done quickly. Eisenhower's aide, Harry Butcher, put it like this in his diary on 24 July:

Ike wanted to have a word with Monty's chief of staff, General de Guingand. The words lasted for an hour. Meanwhile, friends at Naval Headquarters said they felt that Monty, his British Army commander, Dempsey, the British corps commanders, and even those of the divisions are so conscious of Britain's ebbing manpower that they hesitate to commit an attack where a division may be lost. To replace the division is practically impossible.

In other words, the British were not pressing home the attack for fear of too many casualties.

It is undeniably true that Monty and his commanders believed in an economy of effort, the careful nurturing of men and machines. At the beginning of July the British and American armies in Normandy were of equal strength – the equivalent of fifteen or sixteen divisions apiece. But the Americans had nine in England and many more back home preparing for the journey across the Atlantic. The British and Canadians could muster only another six, and it was not certain they would be able to maintain more than the existing force in the field. The historian Max Hastings quotes Monty's head of intelligence: 'We always said: Waste all the ammunition you like, but not lives.' Some British units and their commanders were reluctant to push too hard. In July Monty was obliged to report to the Chief of the Imperial General Staff: '51 Division is at present not (repeat not) battle worthy. It does not fight with determination and has failed in every operation it has been given to do. It cannot (cannot) fight the German successfully. I consider the divisional commander is to blame and I am removing him from command.' Nor was Monty any happier with the leadership of the Canadian 3rd Division, where there were 'signs' of a lack of 'calm, balanced judgement and firm command'. Heads were to roll at divisional level and below. But this was by no means just a 'British problem'. Bradley was exasperated with the performance of his 90th Division and its commander was given his marching orders. 'We're going to make that division go,' Bradley told his replacement, 'if we've got to can every senior officer in it.'

But the mismatch in British and American casualty figures in the first three weeks of Overlord also reflects the general lack of combat experience in the US First Army. Infantry divisions seem to have been less well prepared for bocage fighting, and shortly after D-Day Bradley was obliged to order special 'in theatre' training. Lieutenant Sid Salomon of the 2nd Rangers had fought his way up the bluffs at Omaha to find himself in totally unfamiliar country: 'We were told about hedgerows but we didn't have the slightest idea what it meant. What's a hedgerow? I have a hedgerow in my back yard, but it's not like the Normandy ones. It has taken three hundred years to grow – you had to be very careful. You could walk alongside a hedgerow and you couldn't be seen on the other side. The Germans were on one side, we were on the other.' The two divisions that had landed at Omaha, the 1st and 29th, had suffered heavy casualties, and the fresh faces brought in to make up the numbers were altogether less well trained. As the fighting in the bridgehead dragged on into July, this became a problem for all front-line units.

Major Martin of the 2nd Cheshires noted a change in the quality of the rifle companies he found himself supporting in the line:

Reinforcements came up every night to plug the holes before the next day's attack. The individual soldiers were super as they always had been, the courage was still there, but the skills were going, and it showed. If our own artillery or mortar fire failed to dislodge the enemy, our infantry seemed to become at a loss about what to do; instead of using fire and movement to get forward, they stopped. Untrained or semi-skilled three-inch mortar men would fire their mortars from underneath trees, killing themselves with their own bombs exploding in the branches above.

Replacements were often thrust into the line with very little time to prepare for what – no matter how good the training – was still a shocking, foreign experience: 'For the new arrivals, it's very frightening when you've never been in action before,' Peter Martin recalled.

There's the fear of not knowing how you're going to behave. Are you going to be able to take it? I mean, I've seen people who had never heard a shot fired in anger who disintegrated at the first round of shellfire somewhere near them; there are others who are brand new to the battle who are foolhardy in the extreme, perhaps without even realising they are being foolhardy. I can remember my very first time in action in Belgium in 1940 – I was walking down a street with my company commander when a couple of shells fell on the roadway about fifty yards behind us. There was a perfectly good ditch beside me which I longed to dive into but my company commander went walking slowly on down the road and I knew I couldn't do it, I had to go with him. Years afterwards he said to me, 'Do you remember that occasion when we were under fire? I can tell you now that I was just longing to jump in that ditch, but because you weren't showing any sign of fear I had to go on.' Since then, of course, I've had no inhibitions about jumping straight in the nearest hole. That was inexperience.

Stretcher-bearer Bill Edwards of the 1st Worcesters watched the fresh faces come and go: 'Someone would come into the battalion one morning and disappear that evening. Nobody knew him and after a while nobody could ever recall him being there. And for relatives it can be quite upsetting. They say, "Well, we know he was in your battalion, why doesn't anybody know him?" It was because they would come up and then they were gone again. That was not at all unusual.' The casualties in infantry battalions were the highest, with some rifle companies turning over 100 per cent of their total strength in the first three weeks of the campaign.

Monty's pre D-Day estimates had forecast that by 1 July the bridgehead would extend from St-Malo in the west to Lisieux in the east – well beyond Villers-Bocage and Caen. The actual ground taken amounted to no more than a fifth of this – the Allied armies were roped into a small bridgehead by a deter-mined enemy who was proving a master of the battlefield and of the bocage in particular. 'Wonderful defensive country,' Major Peter Martin recalled. 'The visibility was not more than about fifty yards from one hedgerow to the next. The Germans, who had always been very fine soldiers, were in their element.' It was not the war of movement Sergeant Otto Henning of the Panzer Lehr Reconnaissance Battalion 130 had expected to fight: 'We carefully hid our tanks behind these "bocage" hedges and the Allied tanks had to manoeuvre around us. We would clear some of the vegetation to create a free line of fire and then we dug holes beneath our tank so that we could crawl beneath them for shelter from grenade attack. Sometimes we spent whole days there just crouching beneath our tanks.' To move from a camouflaged posi-tion risked an instant Allied response. 'The Allies had excellent radio detection equipment,' Captain Helmut Ritgen of the II Battalion, the 130th Panzer Lehr Regiment, recalled. 'Any engine noise, any general noise and almost any movement triggered instant enemy fire. We in the tanks were not that bothered but tanks cannot fight without infantry and Panzer grenadiers risked being hacked to pieces.'

The enemy always seemed to be less than a field away in Normandy. Peter Martin remembered: 'If you're in open country the chances of the enemy creeping up on you are pretty small, but once you're in that very thick country there's the constant tension of knowing that they're very close to you and that they can be on you at the drop of a hat.'

'The Germans were very good at infiltrating our lines,' Lieutenant Edwin Bramall of the 2nd King's Royal Rifle Corps (KRRC) recalled. 'They would hold a false front – very lightly held, and that took a lot of the main artillery fire. Then when you thought, well, we're through this now, you find you're coming on to the second line of defence and even the third line of defence.' Pockets of German resistance would remain behind the Allied advance – ready to counter-attack. In July a special report by the Panzer Lehr Division's operations officers fell into British hands. It made for sober reading. It demonstrated not only how thoroughly the Panzer Lehr prepared its defensive line, but also how painfully predictable the attacks launched against it often proved to be. The report covers the first two weeks in the field: 'In this period the division has beaten off eleven full-scale attacks and fifteen smaller attacks and has made nine attacks and fourteen local counter-attacks.' The Panzer Lehr operations staff noted that in that time the British attacked only after the German line had received a thorough soaking from the artillery – a barrage of anything up to three hours: 'Immediately after the barrage the enemy attacks. The enemy tanks get into position in front of our weapons pits and shoot up our troops in their positions with machine-gun and tank-gun fire. The enemy infantry breaks in under this covering fire.' To resist this type of attack, it concluded, the main line of resistance is to be 'occupied only thinly', and behind every sector a local reserve of infantry and tanks should be held in readiness: 'It is best to attack the English, who are very sensitive to close combat and flank attack, at their weakest moment – that is, when they have to fight without their artillery.' The main line of German resistance was to be disguised by 'active patrolling' and careful camouflage discipline. 'Let the enemy tanks approach and attack them at the closest possible range. If they cannot be destroyed let them carry on. Try and destroy them in the rear areas, thus separating the infantry from the tanks . . . The fighting morale of the English infantry is not very great. They rely largely on the "arty" [artillery] and air force.' The report notes, 'the enemy is extraordinarily nervous of close combat. Whenever the enemy infantry is energetically engaged, they mostly retreat or surrender.'

Damning stuff, but there was some truth in it. Hans Bernhard was a Hauptsturmführer (captain) on the staff of the 1st SS Panzer Division (Leibstandarte Adolf Hitler). The twenty-four-year-old Bernhard had joined the division in 1940 and had campaigned in Greece and Russia, where he had been wounded four times. 'I had the impression that the enemy was proceeding with too much hesitance,' Bernhard recalled. 'Without wanting to appear arrogant, we would have done it totally differently. They waited for artillery and tanks to destroy us.' Brigadier James Hargest had noted the tendency in units of the British 50th Division. He observed: 'The old trouble of not relying on their own weapons is prevalent among infantry here. They call for supporting fire always and often when held up whereas they might well get on alone.' Veterans of the Russian front were struck by the difference between the Soviet soldier and his British counterpart. 'The Russians would hold their ground and preferred to be killed rather than give up territory,' Major Ritgen of the 130th Panzer Lehr Regiment recalled. 'If one was able to counter-attack before the British settled into new positions they abandoned all their gains and one could recapture them. But of course this could not be accomplished without losses, which we couldn't easily replace.'

Only a fraction of the 80,000 German casualties taken in June were replaced. The Panzer Lehr Division had lost fifty tanks, eighty half-tracks and 3,500 men in three weeks of fighting – it received no new tanks and only half the new recruits it needed, and the battering continued.

It was often the constant attention of Allied aircraft which most troubled the German soldier. Gefreiter (Private) Robert Vogt was serving in a field replacement battalion in the 352nd – the infantry division that had made it so difficult for the Americans at Omaha. The twenty-year-old Vogt was marched from pillar to post in the first days of the battle – wherever there was a gap in the line that needed to be filled: 'We constantly had to run for cover. The enemy's planes ruled the air absolutely from morning till night. They would drop down to perhaps fifty meters and open fire. We threw ourselves behind bushes and trees and tried to press ourselves as closely to the trunk as possible.'

Sergeant Otto Henning of the Panzer Lehr was caught taking photographs of the British tanks wrecked in the fighting in Villers-Bocage:

I looked up. I noticed a number of fighter planes coming out of the sun towards us. I just had time enough to shout 'Low-flying planes', to run across the street and to throw myself into a ditch just as the bombs began to drop. I really thought, this is the end; I saw the planes regrouping and I recognised them as Lightnings – nine of them. The Lightning was a relatively quiet plane and at times one couldn't hear its approach, particularly when our tanks were on the move. The planes turned for another run and strafed us with their on-board cannons. I threw myself into another bomb crater and I truly believed that my end had come. This attack gave me such a shock that I put my camera away for good – it was just too dangerous.

The artillery dominated the battlefield on both sides of the line. It seemed impossible to escape even for a moment. 'It was terribly noisy because the bridgehead was small,' Lieutenant Bramall of the 2nd KRRC recalled.

Your field guns were firing probably from just behind you. The Germans had these awful things called *Nebelwerfer* – 'Moaning Minnies' – they were multi-barrelled mortars, and as it was in the air you heard this moaning sound – a distinct moaning sound. And you looked around for the nearest trench or ditch and got into it before this great cluster of bombs landed – it covered about the size of a football field. If you were above ground you'd be in trouble. Once we were shelled by a German 240mm, which made a noise exactly like the District Line coming into Sloane Square station in London. There was an awful lot of noise and terrible destruction. Many of the villages were completely obliterated.

Every soldier understood the importance of 'digging in' as soon as a position was reached. A big hole in the ground was generally the best protection from mortar and shell. Private Frank Porter of the 4th Dorsets spent almost as much time holding a spade as his rifle: 'We all became soil mechanics. You could tell instantly what was going to be a hard dig and what was going to be a soft dig. You were paired – one would dig while the other kept guard. And that's where the pair of you lived for however long you were there – you ate your food there, you slept there and you became really, really close.' Digging in became something of a science. Both sides quickly learned that shells had a nasty habit of bursting in the hedges and trees. Shrapnel splinters would be sent spinning down to punish those who had dug in the wrong place. 'I purloined a number of railway sleepers which were carried on the armoured carriers,' Peter Martin of the 2nd Cheshires recalled. 'Once the hole was dug and the machine gun in position, these were put overhead to cover it.'

On one occasion Sergeant Reg Webb of the 141st Royal

Armoured Corps (The Buffs) found shelter in an old German trench: 'It wasn't a quick job to dig a decent slit trench. At night-time, if you found a slit trench looking nice and dry, you got in it. One or two of us found this German trench and I for one got some sleep. But next morning I found a German jackboot with half a leg in it, in the slit trench beside me. Not good for the stomach.'

Tank crews could generally count on the cover of their vehicle. Many chose to dig their trench and then drive the tank over the top of it. The practice had been discouraged at first because it was feared the tanks would slowly sink into the ground in wet weather and crush the sleeping men beneath, but most crews – Allied and German – felt they ran a much greater risk of being killed by shellfire. 'We lived in the ground like foxes, under our Panzers which were surrounded by earthern walls to protect us from shell fragments,' Captain Ritgen of the Panzer Lehr recalled. 'Our command post was also set up under our Panzer, along with a shelter and sleeping area for my crew. A little room was left so visitors could conduct business.'

It was important not to invite enemy fire. In high summer the narrow lanes and tracks were covered in a thick grey film of dust. Roadside notices urged tank drivers to keep their speed down – 'Dust means Death'. Private Bill Edwards of the 1st Worcesters recalled: 'The artillery spotters on the other side would see the clouds of dust and they knew somebody was on the move. They'd bring mortar fire to bear on that area and you never seemed to be out of range of artillery or mortar fire. It was constant even in the rest areas. You began to understand the noises around you – "this one's going over my head". Self-preservation is a very, very good teacher.'

Captain Ritgen was an 'old front soldier' who had been ducking shells since 1939: 'Believe it or not, one can get used to it. I can remember one incident when I was caught out in the open. I was on my way to an officers' meeting and I jumped and threw myself down, straight into two cowpats. Afterwards I got up and carried on to the meeting. My fellow officers moved quite markedly away from me because I smelled so sweet.'

Sometimes there was nowhere to jump. Not long after the Epsom offensive, Lieutenant Edwin Bramall's company of the 2nd KRRC was caught on a hillside near the village of Maltot:

The company commander called an O group – it consisted of myself, another platoon commander, the company commander, the sergeant-major, the signaller and the driver. Suddenly observed fire was brought down on us. We obviously tried to take what cover we could. Shells started firing fierce and fast. Bertie Jackson [the other platoon commander] and I got under a half-track. I remember Bertie saying: 'Do you think we've had it?' And I said, and I don't remember being in a panic: 'It rather looks that way.' Then suddenly there was this frightful crash and a shell came right through the vehicle and burst underneath it. There was dust everywhere and when I sort of pulled myself together and tried to see if I was all in one piece, I found that Bertie, who'd been lying right beside me, was dead, and he was not only dead but pitch black from head to foot, because he'd taken the full force of the blast. The company commander was also dead – the signaller, the driver and the sergeant-major were dead. They were all dead except me. Anyhow, I got out from underneath and there was still this shelling going on and the vehicles were on fire, and then I discovered that I'd been hit down the left-hand side too.

Bramall was evacuated to England for treatment, but was back with his battalion for the last days of the battle in Normandy.

The grim struggle on the battlefield was made all the more relentless by the long summer days. There never seemed to be time for sleep. The officers were often busiest. Major Martin's machine-gun company was in the line from D-Day until 15 August – nine weeks without relief:

The hours of darkness were very limited. You were attacking up until eleven o'clock at night. Then you had to feed the soldiers, get them a hot meal and go round all the positions to see that the chaps were all right. You also had to plan the attack you were going to support the next day and have your platoon commanders in to give them their orders. At some point along the way your batman would thrust a plate of food in your face. By about two o'clock in the morning you were wrapped up in your blanket and sleeping. By three o'clock you were up and standing to for the next day. It was incredibly tiring, very, very tiring.

There were times when the soldiers of both sides were too exhausted to care about the risks they ran. Captain Helmut Ritgen of the Panzer Lehr remembered: 'The correct procedures become second nature, but of course, if you have not slept for forty-eight hours, you just drop down without much thought about camouflage or even the necessity to dig a hole for protection.'

'If you are tired and don't have anything urgent to do you sleep – on the floor, in the forest, in a field or in a trench, wherever you can, and you keep your uniform on,' Captain Hans Bernhard of the 1st SS recalled. 'We wore the same uniform and underwear for four weeks.' Otto Henning of the Panzer Lehr remembered going for many days without a proper wash: 'Human beings get used to anything and I cannot say that we were particularly depressed because we could not wash properly or shave; we got used to it.'

Food was a different matter altogether. Food was, as always, important for morale, but there was often precious little of it on the German side of the lines. Supply lines were under constant attack from the air – a round trip that should have taken no more than two nights often took up to five. Robert Vogt of the 352nd Infantry Division recalled: 'There were days when we had nothing at all and then we might receive a little bread, perhaps some soup. The next day the field kitchens were hit and again nothing.' To avoid going without the Panzer Lehr Division set up its own farms just behind the front where cattle were driven from the land to be milked or slaughtered. 'The dry summer weather and the constant strain on the nerves made you very thirsty,' Helmut Ritgen recalled. 'We drank large quantities of cider, Calvados, wine and cognac, without becoming drunk. To relax ourselves we smoked cigarettes.' There were some who tried to make a point of not caring – Hans Bernhard of the 1st SS Panzer (Leibstandarte Adolf Hitler) for one: 'Sometimes we had nothing to eat, but then it is all about sticking it out. If you have everything, ammunition, air force, artillery, supplies, cigarettes, then it is easy to wage war. We cursed and were annoyed, but it didn't break our fighting spirit.'

It was a very different story in the Allied armies – the armoured brigades were the luckiest. 'We had these seven-man compo boxes in our vehicles and they were excellent. Absolutely excellent,' Edwin Bramall of the 2nd KRRC recalled. 'You probably wouldn't have got the quality today. I mean, the steak and kidney pudding, the rice and the steamed pudding were very good. Nothing wrong with the rations. But of course when you're busy and you're a bit frightened you don't actually need an awful lot.' The rations available to the American troops became legendary. A GI required 30 pounds of supplies to sustain him in the field, a Tommy some 20 pounds – their German enemy was often obliged to make do with just four pounds. It seemed to Otto Henning of the Panzer Lehr that the Allies had an endless supply of everything: 'The German situation was somewhat different and we made jokes that we had to fetch our shells by bicycle or perhaps in a rucksack. We were under orders to permanently save ammunition and were permitted perhaps three shots a day. We were constantly under fire but only returned it when we were in direct contact with the enemy.' On one occasion Captain Ritgen's tanks were stationary for four days, their fuel tanks empty: 'The tank crews were still in them, equally motionless. They ended up with terribly swollen arms and legs. We had to call a doctor to get some of them out of the tanks.'

It broke all the principles of armoured warfare – Ritgen's Panzers found themselves acting as tank destroyers, providing

18. Hitler with his armaments minister, Albert Speer [extreme left], and staff at a weapons demonstration near Freilassing in Bavaria in 1944. Hitler became increasingly involved in the direction of his armies in the west.

19. Field Marshal Günther von Kluge succeeded Rundstedt and Rommel. He took his own life in August to avoid public disgrace.

20. Obersturmführer Michael Wittmann, Germany's leading tank ace and the 'hero' of the action at Villers-Bocage on 13 June 1944.

21. A veteran of the Russian Front, Hauptsturmführer Hans Bernard was on the staff of 1st SS Panzer (Leibstandarte Adolf Hitler) in Normandy.

22. Major Chester Hansen [right] with General Omar Bradley. Hansen served as Bradley's aide-de-camp in Sicily, North Africa and throughout the campaign in north west Europe.

23. The bodies of American soldiers killed in the first ten days of fighting are prepared for burial in Normandy.

24. Derby Day in the bridgehead. Corporal Day has set up his board and is taking bets for the race. The result was heard on the radio. British operations in Normandy were given the names of famous racecourses.

25. British infantry and armour press through the chest-high corn near Tilly-sur-Seulles in the summer of 1944.

26. Sherman tanks push on down a typical hedge-lined lane in the Normandy bocage in July 1944.

27. Caen is plastered by 450 heavy bombers on 7 July 1944 as a prelude to the British and Canadian assault on the city. The rubble was finally captured after a month of fighting.

28. The Germans clung tenaciously to Caen and the city was devastated in fighting which claimed the lives of many of its citizens.

29. Dust means death. German artillery took its range from the dust thrown up by traffic. This tank is pressing forward to the start line on 18 July – the first day of Operation Goodwood.

30. A Bren gun carrier passes a troop of German prisoners at dawn on 30 July 1944, as it makes its way towards the British front near Caumont.

31. Canadian and British soldiers on the road from Caen watch the bombardment as the Germans are slowly squeezed into the Falaise pocket.

firepower and protection. Single tanks were posted in camouflaged positions at the front with light infantry support. These
were usually enough to alert companies in the rear of an Allied
attack, and when the Germans had enough ammunition their
weapons proved to be extremely effective. 'You used to hear one
of three things being shouted in Normandy,' Edwin Bramall
recalled.

'Tiger', when somebody had come across a Tiger tank. 'Panzerfaust',
which was the hand-held anti-tank weapon that the Germans had –
very effective against anything but the heaviest armour. And 'Sniper'.
Sniper was often a rather inflated title. It just meant that as we moved
forward from the bridgehead the Germans who'd been holding the
front line very lightly were left behind and popped up to make a
nuisance of themselves.

The Panzerfaust proved an ideal anti-tank weapon in the bocage,
where it was possible for German infantry to approach Allied
tanks under close cover. The British equivalent – the PIAT – was
altogether less impressive. Awkward to carry, cock and fire, it
was of limited value against heavier German armour. 'Our
soldiers used to say if all else fails, we can Pee-at them,' Edwin
Bramall recalled. The German MG 42 or Spandau could rattle
through 1,200 rounds a minute – the British Bren gun just 500.
A small group of Panzer grenadiers, supported by two or more
MG 42s, could present a formidable wall of fire to advancing
Allied infantry. In the 88mm the Germans possessed the most
effective anti-tank gun of the war. Major Martin first met the
88mm in the desert: 'You only had to mention to a tank
commander, "There's an eighty-eight out there somewhere" and
you would put the fear of God into him.'

But the British had weapons that were to prove of great use
in the bocage too. One in particular enjoyed a fearsome reputation – the Crocodile. It was one of the British army's 'funnies'
– a Churchill tank that had been especially adapted to fire a jet
of flame at enemy strongpoints. An armour-plated pipe ran from

the tank to a trailer loaded with 400 gallons of sticky jellied petrol and high-pressure nitrogen bottles. Sergeant Reg Webb of the 141st Regiment, Royal Armoured Corps (The Buffs), was the commander of a Crocodile:

You'd have a meeting with the infantry and you'd get some information, perhaps a sketch of the area you were going to attack – a suggestion that it would be a good idea if you flamed that hedgerow or barn. The maximum range, depending on the weather, particularly the wind, was about 120 yards. If you came up against a German strongpoint, you could fire two or three blasts at it without igniting it, and then you could send another shot in to ignite it and of course the whole lot would go up. It was very powerful. One of the dreadful things was that it was sticky – you couldn't brush it off, it would stick to you. If there was a machine-gun nest you could use the tank's machine gun, the cannon or the flame-thrower. And the flame-thrower was a nice, quick short-range weapon. It didn't need pinpoint accuracy because it spread a bit as you fired.

The commander would give the order 'Flame gun, fire!' and a jet of flame would leap from the front of the tank with a roar. Everything in its path would be carpeted in burning fuel. One Crocodile commander with The Buffs later recalled pouring flame on to hedges until 'the fire rose in one fierce, red wall'. The gun would splutter and hiss like 'an empty soda-water siphon' when it was time for a new bottle. It was a formidable weapon. 'It was horrible to use and the result was horrible,' Webb recalled. 'You got the horrifying picture of somebody alight running away. But do as you would be done by. If you didn't hit him, he might have a Panzerfaust and that was you finished.'

Crocodile crews rarely saw their handiwork; when they did it was a distressing sight. Lieutenant Andrew Wilson, who served as a troop leader with The Buffs, described one such occasion: 'There were bodies which seemed to have been blown back by the force of the flame and lay in naked, blackened heaps. Others were caught in twisted poses, as if the flame had frozen them. Their clothes had burned away. Only their helmets and boots remained, ridiculous and horrible.' The bodies had a profound effect on Wilson. They seemed to present him with a choice – protest at the inhumanity of his weapon and the war or fight on and do 'everything more thoroughly and conscientiously than ever before, so there was no time to think'. He chose to fight on.

The dead enemy was often passed unnoticed, but the face of one German soldier has always remained with the historian General Sir David Fraser. Fraser served as a twenty-three-year-old tank commander with the 2nd Battalion, (Armoured), the Grenadier Guards:

He was completely unmarked . . . he was wearing a camouflage-type smock – I think this was a Parachute Division, excellent troops. He was very young and very dark; black haired, swarthy, giving a southern European or possibly southern Russian impression. A handsome lad, his brown eyes were open and slightly bloodshot, the only physical thing amiss. His expression was determined and a little angry. His Spandau machine gun was beside him. I do not know why of all the enemy soldiers I saw dead his face comes most vividly to me. A friend of mine has told me that on every day of Remembrance he says a prayer 'for all the men I killed'. This is absolutely right. In most wars one is closer in spirit to the enemy than to non-combatants on one's own side.

The smell of death hung everywhere that summer: 'This awful stench of battle – Normandy was wonderful pastoral country and there were lots of cattle and horses killed,' Lieutenant Edwin Bramall recalled. 'So quite apart from the human casualties there were these dead horses, dead cattle lying around. It was June – hot weather, and after a day or so they began to stink to high heaven.' Lieutenant John Cloudsley-Thompson of the 4th County of London Yeomanry also remembered the overpowering stench from the battlefield: 'It smelled absolutely awful.

Most of the people were in sort of shallow graves. The horses and cows were lying everywhere, blown up with gas so they looked like stuffed toys, with their legs in the air.'

The battlefield was shaped by the overwhelming material superiority of the Allies on the one hand and by Hitler's determination to hang on to every foot of Norman soil on the other. German soldiers like Robert Vogt of the 352nd Infantry Division envied their enemy's capacity – the determination to rely on 'metal not flesh':

They would move forward to the nearest hedge and when we noticed them we would use our machine gun once or twice and then there was silence. A few moments later one would hear plop, plop, plop and the grenades would come in our direction, then there would be heavy artillery and perhaps tanks. We had the impression that the American commanders were very protective towards their men. This was possible because they had so much material. If you sit in your hole with an MG 42 and you see a tank in front of you with its massive 5cm or 6cm cannon and others opening fire on to the positions of your comrades you have only one choice – retreat. Everything else would be insanity. The Americans protected their soldiers and our commanders couldn't because they didn't have the war *matériel*. This was depressing. But you said to yourself, 'Something will happen, new weapons will arrive – these setbacks are only temporary.'

Captain Hans Bernhard of the 1st SS Panzer put it like this: 'They didn't have to work as hard as us, and what was at stake for them? We were fighting for our Fatherland – we had to sacrifice men because we had no *matériel*.' A report compiled by the 2nd Panzer Division's staff on the first weeks in Normandy observed that 'the Allies are waging war regardless of expense'.

That the Allies were struggling to make headway is above all a tribute to the quality of the German soldier. The historian Carlo D'Este observed, 'The most consistent mistake made by the Allied commanders in North West Europe was a failure to realise – despite repeated examples – the will and tenacity of the German Army to resist against overwhelming odds and in the most appalling conditions.' An operational policy paper drawn up by the British I Corps in July sheepishly pointed to the overwhelming superiority it had enjoyed on its front at Caen in the weeks before the city finally fell. It noted that the six British divisions to the west of the Orne were opposed by just four, all of which were well below 'establishment'. The Germans held the 'active' front with just four battalions and a regiment of tanks – I Corps was attacking with twelve battalions and three tank regiments.

It was the Allies' great misfortune, of course, to be confronted by some of the most formidable divisions in the German army – tough, determined SS units. The soldiers in these divisions considered themselves to be a cut above, not just the Allies, but their comrades in the regular army. Captain Hans Bernard of the 1st SS Panzer commented: 'Our will to fight, our moral will to fight, seemed bigger, and in general our successes were bigger.' The most celebrated of the Waffen SS divisions in Normandy was the 1st – it carried the name of the Führer himself; the Leibstandarte Adolf Hitler had once acted as his 'household guard'. Recruitment into its ranks was based on rigid physical and racial rules. 'There was a certain selection in terms of health, constitution, attitude – that was crucial,' Bernhard recalled. The soldiers of the division were to demonstrate '*Härte*' – toughness, a determination to do one's duty no matter what the cost, a willingness to go to the limits of physical and mental endurance. Hans Bernhard recalled: 'They knew they could make higher demands on us, we were tougher – they knew we were reliable. I was really proud to join them because it was already a famous division at the time. It was simple – you saw yourself as a member of an elite.' Men like Bernhard made formidable opponents; there was a hard ideological core to their soldiering – an unquestioning dedication to *Volk*, Führer and Fatherland.

The German soldier was often prepared to hold the line when reason and casualties might have suggested all was lost. Improvised groups or 'Kampfgruppen' were formed from units torn apart by the battle – a company of SS Panzer grenadiers, a handful of tanks from a regular unit, men from an anti-aircraft battery – pulled into action together. These ad hoc battle groups played a significant part in holding Allied attacks when all else had failed. It was only possible because the German soldier was generally better trained and more disciplined than his Allied counterpart. In an analysis of the fighting, Helmut Ritgen of the Panzer Lehr later pointed to the difference in battlefield command between the sides: 'British fighting principles were too rigid and systematic,' he concluded. 'They allowed the junior commanders too little initiative.' Small, effective Kampfgruppen were possible in the German army because officers, NCOs and the men themselves were encouraged to show initiative. The operations officers at the 2nd Panzer Division noted that 'attacks prepared "according to the book" have little chance of succeeding'. Large concentrations of infantry invited attention from enemy aircraft; 'better results have been obtained by . . . assault detachments' that penetrated Allied lines noiselessly. In assault detachments, the leadership of NCOs was often decisive – 'only an energetic commander will get his men to go forward'. There was often precious little direction from corps and divisional staff – radio communication with soldiers in the line was at best difficult, at times quite impossible. It was a problem Hans Bernhard experienced on the staff of the 1st SS Panzer:

We often didn't know who was doing what and where. 'What is Geyer doing? What is Müller doing? Where are they now? How many men do they have left, how much fuel, how much ammunition?' We didn't know because it changed on a daily basis. Leadership had practically become impossible. The units had to fight through by themselves. But they were used to taking decisions somewhat independently, not just following orders. As Frederick the Great once said to an officer, 'I didn't turn you into an officer so you would only follow orders.'

Nor was leadership in the field left just to junior officers – special emphasis was also placed on the role of the *Unteroffizier*.

Private Robert Vogt of the 352nd Infantry Division was a member of a small battle group holding the line in the American sector near the town of St-Lô. On 16 June his unit was attacked by a large body of American tanks:

There had been infantry skirmishes beforehand. Anyway, they carried on firing and I said to my machine gunner: 'Something is not right here, stop shooting,' and then suddenly the hedge closest to us parted, it was about 150 metres away, and a tank appeared and then another tank and another and another. They rolled forwards very slowly and then stopped perhaps 20 or 30 metres away, in front of the hedge, and opened fire.

Vogt and his machine gunner pulled back: 'We were lucky in the mêlée, but I could see comrades who had been hit and one NCO who I knew well was lying there with his entrails hanging out.' Vogt and his comrades took up a new position in a semicircle around an 88mm anti-tank gun set back a little in the cover of a wood:

We were ordered to hold the position and that is what we did. I had moved perhaps 200 metres in front of the flak gun. The American tanks rolled cautiously into the wood. One tank turned and I saw it coming straight towards me. I got a case of 'tank shock' and did something I shouldn't have – I jumped up and tried to run back. I felt a sudden blow to my knee as if someone had used a sledge-hammer on me and I went down. Then, despite the pain, I started to crawl towards the German line.

Vogt had to make his way through the curtain of fire put up by his comrades. His unit, under the direction of junior NCOs, had pulled back from its 'false front' and was engaging a superior force with the aid of one anti-tank gun. Vogt play no further part in the engagement – 'For you the war is over,' he was told at the field hospital. It was not over, but by the time he was fit to fight again the battlefield had moved to Germany.

In the first week of July a report landed on Monty's desk that made for disturbing reading. It was from the colonel commanding the 6th Battalion, the Duke of Wellington's Regiment (DWR), stating that the '6DWR is not fit to take its place in the line'. Lieutenant Colonel Turner had joined the battalion on the first day of the Epsom offensive – by the end of it he had concluded that if it was not possible to withdraw the 6th DWR then it should be disbanded. 'Being a regular officer I realise the seriousness of this request and its effect on my career,' Turner states in his report. 'On the other hand I have the lives of the new officer personnel to consider. Three days running a Major has been killed or seriously wounded because I have ordered him to help me to "in effect" stop them [the men] from running during mortar concentrations.' Turner claimed that he had twice had to draw his revolver on retreating men. This breakdown in discipline was above all caused by a lack of leadership. In fourteen days of fighting the battalion had lost twenty-three officers, including all the company commanders. One company had lost every officer and another all but one. 'NCO leadership is weak in most cases and the newly drafted officers are in consequence having to expose themselves unduly to try and get anything done.'

The 6th DWR had taken a mauling in its first engagement on 17–18 June and had not recovered. Captain John Allan was the commander of the battalion's support company – the Bren carriers, six-pounder anti-tank guns and three-inch mortars. The twenty-five-year-old Yorkshireman had joined the regiment as a territorial soldier before the war: 'We were looking forward to going into action. After all, we'd been kicking our heels for four years, and felt rather that other people had been doing the important stuff and we hadn't.' On 17 June the battalion was ordered to attack Le Parc de Boislande – a chateau in thickly wooded parkland on a ridge not far from Tilly-sur-Seulles. Very little was known about the objective – the 6th DWR was told to expect 'local troops' of generally low quality. The battalion had advanced up the slope behind a creeping barrage with tanks in support, its leading companies making good progress in the face of intense mortar and machine-gun fire. It took just two hours to clear the chateau and surrounding woodland. 'We were absolutely over the moon,' Allan recalled. 'We thought, here's our first success. It was a very good feeling.' It was not without price. Casualties had been high – nine officers and 150 men. The 6th DWR dug in round the chateau. 'In the absence of any move by the brigadier to send forward some support on our flanks we were in a very exposed position, two thousand yards forward of our own troops and open to attack from three sides,' Allan noted later. The following day there was a counter-attack by a large force of German infantry and tanks, supported by heavy mortar and artillery fire. The lead companies were quickly overrun. Captain Allan was behind the front line with his support company: 'We saw our troops, running back through the woods in some disarray, which was a terrible shock. We tried to stop them, but they were obviously not ready to listen, they were on their way, and were being shelled at the same time.' Allan and his men joined the general rout: 'Orders were given to abandon the position and this we did, in some chaos and with more heavy losses.' The battalion retreated over the ground it had taken at such cost the day before. Over the next few days reinforcements arrived in dribs and drabs but morale seemed to have been broken. 'It was a very, very unhappy, a very depressing time,' Allan recalled. 'We were ashamed. We had reinforcements, about a hundred and eighty, but no NCOs or officers. So we simply dug holes for ourselves and went into a defensive position until it was decided what to do with us.' More than half the battalion had become casualties. In his report, its new CO, Lieutenant

Colonel Turner, judged those that were left to be 'jumpy' under shellfire. There had been five cases of self-inflicted wounds in three days and

each time men are killed or wounded a number of men become casualties through shell shock or hysteria. In addition to genuine hysteria a large number of men have left their posts after shelling on one pretext or another and gone to the rear until sent back by the Medical Officer or myself. The new drafts have been affected, and three young soldiers became casualties with hysteria after hearing our own guns.

Monty was not impressed. He sent Turner's report to his friend, the Secretary of State for War, Sir James Grigg, with this tart observation: 'I consider the CO displays a defeatist mentality and is not a "proper chap".' But Monty followed Colonel Turner's advice – the loss of 'key personnel' meant the battalion was unable to 'assimilate the reinforcements'. The 6th DWR was sent back to England and broken up. Allan joined the 2nd Royal Warwicks in Normandy and fought on with distinction. This sort of collapse in morale and discipline was exceptional, but it does serve to highlight the dependence on 'key personnel' – in particular the officers and NCOs – in what had been a generally well-trained and capable battalion.

Traditional German military virtues certainly played their part in shoring up the defence – it was the duty of a soldier to fight whether or not victory was possible. Many if not most soldiers had been confident of 'Dunkirking' the Allies – by July that optimism had all but evaporated. During the course of the battle in Normandy, Hans Bernhard of the 1st SS Panzer visited his old regimental commander:

He commanded a higher artillery unit behind the front by then. After he had given me the compulsory cognac and a fine cigar, he said, 'Bernhard, we are losing the war.' I told him that we shouldn't think about that, we had to defend ourselves whether we were or not, and to give of our best. What we believed or didn't believe was not important. It was impossible to win with enemies in the east and in the west. But as officers we were there to defend and that is what we were doing. Duty, honour, obedience, comrades and nothing else.

Even less ideologically committed soldiers like Otto Henning of the Panzer Lehr talked the same way: 'We knew that this war could not be won. There was one comrade in our unit who had been a Nazi Party member for a long time and he helped us to keep our morale up. He told us that new weapons were on the way – we didn't really believe him. Still, we were soldiers and had to do our duty until the end.' Robert Vogt of the 352nd had more faith in the new weapons the propaganda ministry promised the German people: 'We hoped that when the new weapons hit the enemy life would be a little easier for us – that the *matériel* imbalance would be addressed.' The first of them, the V-1 flying bomb, had already begun to drop on London: 'Of course we were happy to hear it,' Helmut Ritgen of the Panzer Lehr recalled. 'Why should only our major cities become dust and ashes? We only wished that we had received the news earlier.' Ritgen had taken 'the ruins express' on the way to the front five months before – it had taken him through the shattered cities of the Ruhr. It left him with the conviction that there was no alternative to fighting on – the Allies were insisting on 'unconditional surrender' and seemed prepared to go to any lengths to secure it: 'We felt we were in a fortress, the fortress of Greater Germany, and we thought, as long as the Russian front in the east holds, we have to hold in the west in order to protect our families.'

'We soldiers were there for our homeland,' Robert Vogt recalled.

This was clear to us, we did not discuss it – this feeling of love for the Fatherland was as natural to us as drawing breath. This helped us to endure and, to be honest, we also felt quite brave. I was afraid, I would like to state that – who wasn't afraid! A man who says he's never been afraid is a man who has never been at the front. But I always had the feeling – 'I will be able to overcome this.'

Above all, it was comradeship which sustained the men on both sides. Trooper Austin Baker of the 4th/7th Royal Dragoon Guards recalled:

You have at the back of your mind a lot of apprehension but in the intervals between the fighting it was all quite jolly, you know. I mean, a lot of jokes and having a good time, listening to the American Forces Network around a radio in the field, that sort of thing. There wasn't a sort of total gloom over everything. It's surprising how cheerful you can be in extraordinary circumstances. And I never thought it would be me who would be hit, but I suppose everyone's telling themselves that. By the end of Normandy one member of the squadron in four had been killed and another one in four had been wounded. You got rather used to men being killed, in a way. I don't mean you felt heartless about it, but you just expected it.

Soldiers became 'detached' – death lost its strangeness. Major Martin of the 2nd Cheshires recalled: 'We were supporting an attack by the Essex Regiment and I was talking to the second-in-command of the battalion when he suddenly dropped dead beside me with a bullet through his head. That sort of thing could happen.'

There was always a steady drip, drip of casualties. Bill Edwards of the 1st Worcesters was more aware of it than most – he was a stretcher-bearer:

I didn't get used to it in the sense that I became indifferent. But you don't think, oh my God, this poor chap's got a wife and children and all the rest of it. It just doesn't occur to you. You have a casualty there, he has to be treated to the best of your ability – it's a sort of detachment. You did get to a point where you thought, well, maybe this is the last morning I shall be here, but if it happens I hope it's quick, I hope it's complete and there's not a long period of pain and agony. Then you just got on with your day and at the end of it you'd think, well, I've made it through.

Night-time was the time I didn't like much. You would get the call 'Stretcher-bearer' in the dark, under bombardment, and you'd look at your mate and it was obvious the thought crossing between you – 'Do we go? We're safer here than we would be out there.' But you do go because you know you have to, the call's there. And then you find the casualty and he's in a hole so you don't know how badly he's wounded, where he's wounded. Getting him out of the slit trench was difficult and you didn't know what extra damage you might be doing. There was a lot of noise crashing around you – you were doing something that was physically and emotionally difficult. But you got on with it. And then you go back to your own hole in the ground and the shakes would start and you'd think, thank God Almighty, I don't want to do that again. And you'd look at your mate and you'd say, 'Shall we hear the next one or shall we block our ears?' But you do hear the next one. But a lot of chaps really couldn't cope with it – it just overwhelmed them. I think it was because they didn't have this ability to shut it out of their minds.

It was a protective shell. The American medic Private John Burke of the 5th Rangers sheltered within it: 'War does things to you, makes you so hard you feel you lose your emotions. I'd see guys with their legs blown off or chest wounds, head wounds, my brother getting killed – and I've said to myself, why didn't I cry? I don't know what happens to you, it just drains you of emotions.'

But some men were worn down by the constant stress of being close to death. Major Martin's company had fought in the desert, it had landed in Sicily and it was still in the line nine weeks after D-Day. After a time Martin began to notice worrying signs of battle fatigue: 'Lord Moran wrote in *Anatomy of Courage* that everyone has a bank balance of courage which is irreplaceable and there comes a time when you have spent it and can take no more. I can remember a young corporal of mine who was a super chap suddenly collapsing, just bursting into tears. He was unable to move.'

'After six weeks we had a few cases of self-inflicted wounds.

Someone shot himself in the leg in the hope that he would be sent home,' Captain Helmut Ritgen of the Panzer Lehr recalled. 'But overall the strong bonds of comradeship held us. No one spoke of military virtues, we lived them. No one spoke of trust in God, one either had it or not. Those who did had some support to overcome the anxiety and horror of war.'

CHAPTER SIX

BREAK-OUT

B y dawn the tanks of the 11th Armoured Division were over the River Orne and pushing up to the start line. Behind them two more armoured divisions – the Guards and the 7th – were moving steadily eastward through the bridgehead. Monty's great armoured 'showdown', Operation Goodwood, was under way.

'The early morning of 18 July was exquisite – it was exciting, a great adventure – it was our first movement into battle,' Lieutenant David Fraser recalled. The Guards Armoured had landed at the end of June, too late to play a part in Epsom or the capture of Caen – Goodwood was to be its first major commitment. Monty hoped that the three armoured divisions of VIII Corps would be able to force their way through 'into the open country' astride the Caen–Falaise road. The attack was to begin with the largest air bombardment in support of ground forces yet launched – more than a thousand aircraft would drop 6,000 tons of high explosive and fragmentation bombs from low attitude. The first faint hum was heard at a little before dawn; it grew to a steady roar and the sky to the north of Caen was soon full of aircraft. As they passed over the waiting tanks, a supporting barrage from 400 guns opened up on the woods and villages to the south and east of the city where enemy forces were concentrated. 'It was a magnificent, awe-inspiring sight,' Fraser recalled, 'a sustained roar of bursting bombs. It must have been perfectly terrifying for the defenders and the inhabitants of

Caen.' From the bridgehead the tank crews watched a pall of thick smoke and dust rise over the wooded high ground to the south. As the aircraft turned for home the tempo of the artillery barrage became more insistent. 'We thought this was going to be a big break-out,' Fraser recalled.

General Adair [the divisional commander] had spoken to most of the officers of the Guards Armoured Division in an orchard the day before and very clearly and graphically described how he saw the battle going. He had an enormous map on which he pointed out various places and I remember him saying that the army commander who had seen him that morning had emphasised one or two points – and he pointed to the little town of Vimont and said that General Montgomery had been perfectly clear we must get Vimont – Vimont was a sort of hinge.

Vimont was 16 kilometres from the British front line. The officers of 7th Armoured had been told the same thing: 'We definitely thought this was going to be the break-out,' Lieutenant John Cloudsley-Thompson recalled. Cloudsley-Thompson had taken over a troop in B Squadron, the 4th County of London Yeomanry, after the battle for Villers-Bocage.

Eisenhower was also sure that this was Monty's intention. It was to be an enormous effort with aircraft, artillery and 750 tanks; Monty had promised him that the 'whole Eastern flank will burst into flames'. 'I would not be at all surprised to see you gaining a victory that will make some of the "old classics" look like a skirmish between patrols,' Ike had replied. The Supreme Commander was confident that Bradley could be counted on 'to keep his troops fighting like the very devil, twenty-four hours a day, to provide the opportunity your armoured corps will need'. Generous words of encouragement, but they should perhaps have rung alarm bells at TAC HQ. Nothing had changed. Monty's plan remained the same. Great things were planned, an advance of 16 kilometres or more, but the real object was, in the words of Monty's military assistant, 'to muck up and write off enemy troops'. Lieutenant Colonel Kit Dawnay had been packed off to London on 14 July with instructions to explain the objectives to the Director of Military Operations at the War Office: 'All the activities on the eastern flank are designed to help the [American] forces in the west while ensuring that a firm bastion is kept in the east. At the same time all is ready to take advantage of any situation which gives reason to think that the enemy is disintegrating.' Operation Goodwood was not conceived as the final break-out.

The attempt to press forward on the American front in preparation for the long hoped-for break-out had stalled before the town of St-Lô. At a meeting of the army commanders on 10 July Bradley had admitted that progress in the west was painfully slow – 'take all the time you need', Monty had told him, with more magnanimity than he must have felt. Goodwood was to have been followed two days later by the break-out battle – Operation Cobra. In principle the strategy remained unchanged. The directive that emerged from the meeting on the 10th made that clear; the strategy 'is to draw the main enemy forces in the battle on our eastern flank, and to fight them there, so that our affairs on the western flank may proceed the easier'. Eisenhower was sent a copy of this and was briefed by Monty's chief of staff, and yet he clearly expected much more than the directive promised. 'All senior airmen are in full accord,' Eisenhower telegraphed Monty on the 14th – the operation would be a 'brilliant stroke, which will knock loose our present shackles'. 'The senior airmen' were perhaps the key to the misunderstanding, chief among them Eisenhower's deputy, Air Chief Marshal Sir Arthur Tedder. An 'airman' with precious little experience of the battlefield, Tedder nevertheless considered himself quite qualified to pronounce on Monty's strategy – his views were almost wholly negative. By July he was urging Eisenhower to bully Monty into a break-out on the eastern flank – Monty's directive of 10 July restating his intention to do exactly the opposite was judged by Tedder to be 'most unsatisfactory'. Time, Tedder argued, was slipping through Monty's fingers – 'few weeks of summer remained – our urgent need was to get across the Seine', he later wrote. To win the support of Tedder and the other 'senior airmen' Monty may have felt it necessary 'to overstate the aims of the operation'. That at least was the view of his loyal army commander, General Dempsey. That there was a mismatch in hopes and expectations is clear. Eisenhower's chief champion, Stephen Ambrose, believed that 'the main reason Montgomery so egregiously exaggerated the aim of Goodwood was his real-isation that the pressure on Eisenhower to dismiss him was mounting. Gossips at SHAEF were speculating on "who would succeed Monty if sacked".' But there is little evidence to suggest that Monty allowed himself to be flustered by 'gossips at SHAEF'. It is altogether easier to understand the optimistic talk of a breakthrough at divisional and battalion briefings. If the Germans were to be convinced that Goodwood was the main thrust, the ordinary British soldier would have to be too.

The 11th Armoured Division was to lead the way down a narrow corridor blasted through the enemy's defences by the air bombardment. It was to drive on south-west towards Bourguébus ridge; the Guards would follow behind and swing south-east towards Vimont, allowing the 7th Armoured the centre ground due south. The ground was well suited for armour – broad wheat fields rolled gently up to the higher, wooded ground to the south. The field pattern was broken by little stone villages and copses – two long railway embankments also offered the Germans strong defensive positions. The armoured advance was to be supported on its left and right flanks by British and Canadian infantry.

The 11th Armoured's tanks trundled forward behind a creeping barrage at a little before 8 a.m. and at first met with little resistance. A steady stream of dazed and wounded Germans were led back down the corridor to the British start line past Lieutenant David Fraser's tank: 'They had been completely shat-tered by the weight of our air attack.' 'Messages and reports over the wireless indicated that the 11th Armoured were doing quite well,' Lieutenant Cloudsley-Thompson recalled. 'Guns were firing on all sides and long columns of prisoners marched past. There was an unpleasant smell of corpses and in the distance we could hear the moaning of the German six-barrelled mortars or "*Nebelwerfers*".' By nine o'clock the lead tanks had passed beyond the range of the supporting artillery and were breaking towards the second of the two railway embankments that cut across the battlefield – the air bombardment seemed to have done its job. 'Nothing could live under it,' Monty noted in his diary. He was wrong.

The Germans had been expecting the attack. It was impossible to hide the build-up of three armoured divisions in such a small bridgehead. Rommel had prepared a formidable defensive shield 15 kilometres in depth: a thinly held line to cover the initial artillery and air barrage, then beyond this, in the scattered hamlets and copses, tanks, infantry and anti-tank guns. The battlefield was overlooked by a line of nearly eighty tank-busting 88s – carefully sited on the edge of the Bourguébus ridge. These were supported by a large body of infantry and tank reserves. Goodwood would be the climax of the grim attritional struggle around Caen.

By the beginning of July the Germans were outnumbered four to one in tanks and two to one in infantry in the British sector – in the American sector it was eight to one and three to two. Slowly men and machines were being ground down by the overwhelming *matériel* superiority of the Allies. 'The morale of the troops is good,' the chief of staff at Panzer Group West told Rommel, 'but one can't beat the *matériel* of the enemy with courage alone'. There were reserves, but Fortitude was still playing its part – six weeks on, a good part of the 15th Army remained idle in the Pas de Calais. The German army in Normandy was wasting away. The new commander-in-chief in the west, Rundstedt's replacement, was Field Marshal Günther von Kluge – a tough veteran of the Eastern Front. He had been instructed to shake things up in Normandy – to bring Rommel to heel. 'Our command at Army Group B was considered defeatist and rebellious as well as pessimistic,' Rommel's *Gefechtsschreiber* (battle writer), Rolf Munninger, recalled. 'We didn't have a good image with the High Command [OKW]. It had been like that for months – it is of course terrible if the army that is supposed to repel the invasion is from the beginning considered not quite dependable.' It had not taken Kluge long to grasp the reality of the brutal *Materialschlacht* his soldiers were fighting. Rolf Munninger recalled: 'When he came to view the front-line troops he could not fail to notice the same pessimism which had invaded us. We all knew that with our resources, and one must not forget we were in the fifth year of war, we could not succeed. Kluge realised the same and that an Allied breakthrough was eventually inevitable.' Just two days before the Goodwood offensive Rommel had written what he called his 'ultimatum'. He had warned that the decisive point of the battle had been reached – the enemy would soon break through. By the middle of July the army had lost 117,000 men but had received only 10,000 replacements – 'the troops are fighting heroically everywhere, but the unequal struggle is nearing its end. It is in my opinion necessary to draw the proper conclusion from the situation.' Field Marshal von Kluge had done just that, and had agreed to forward Rommel's remarks to Hitler with a covering letter in which he stated that 'the Field Marshal was unfortunately right'. Kluge's smart volte-face, executed in just two weeks, should have been proof enough of the critical situation in the west, but the observations of both field marshals were lost in the welter of recrimination and fear that was about to engulf the German Wehrmacht.

The storm of Allied bombs and shells that broke around the German defenders on 18 July was the heaviest they had ever encountered. Lieutenant Hans Krebs of the 16th Luftwaffe Field Division described it like this: 'There were waves and waves of bombers coming forward like a dark cloud, it was a terrible roaring, you couldn't hear anything but these bombers, and then you see a steel helmet with the head of a soldier in it. It's burst and it's rolling to the side. It was a terrible sight, you know, a terrible sight.' For Werner Kortenhaus, a tank commander in the 22nd Panzer Regiment of the 21st Panzer Division, it was the most terrifying hour of his life: 'It was a bomb carpet, ploughing up the ground. Among the thunder of the explosions we could hear the wounded scream and the insane howling of men who had been driven mad.' The Germans had cowered in their tanks and slit trenches as the inferno burst around them – there were many casualties, but many survived too. It was an echo of the monstrous bombardments on the Western Front nearly thirty years before, and again the Allies had expected too much. The Germans began to crawl out of the ground to take up station on the guns that remained. Major Hans von Luck was in charge of a battle group drawn from the 21st Panzer and the 16th Luftwaffe Field Division. He had returned from leave in Paris at a little after nine o'clock that morning to be greeted by the deadly chaos of the Allied bombardment. No radio contact could be made with his units so he climbed into the turret of his Panzer IV tank and set off down the Vimont–Caen road:

I approached the village of Cagny which lay exactly in the middle of my sector and was not occupied by us. The eastern part as far as the church was undamaged; the western part had been flattened. When I came to the western edge of the village, I saw to my dismay about twenty-five to thirty British tanks, which had already passed southward over the main road to Caen . . . where my number 1 Battalion ought to be, or had been, in combat positions. The whole area was dotted with British tanks, which were slowly rolling south against no opposition.

At Cagny church Luck found four 88mm guns pointing skyward:

I ran over to the commandant of this battery, he was a young captain, and I said, 'Do you know what's happening there?' He said, 'No.' I said, 'You've already been passed by British tanks.' And I said, 'You must go and fight them.' He said, 'No, I'm Luftwaffe, my job is to fight the bombers, your job is to fight the tanks down there.' So I took my pistol and said, 'You will be a dead man immediately or get a prestigious decoration.' He decided he would go for the decoration. So I put his four guns in a big apple orchard and said, 'Come on, file up your guns and get them from the flank.' Within minutes they had killed sixteen tanks.

The lead elements of the 11th Armoured were across the second railway embankment and making for the ridge when they were met by the withering fire from the 88mm guns. 'You could see many of our tanks burning, the leading tanks had caught it pretty badly,' Lieutenant David Fraser recalled. Fraser was commanding his battalion's Headquarters Troop: 'Enemy fire appeared to come from hedges, farmhouses, woods, anything which they had found possible to convert into defensive positions – isolated strongpoints – it was sporadic, but it was very good. One was conscious of our tanks being hit and bursting into flames – like a match being struck.'

Fraser could see shells flash past but the sound was eerily muffled: 'I was surprised at the absence of noise on the battlefield. We had radio sets, and our earphones blanked out almost all noise except the signals that were coming through. One was aware of the explosions from the German fire – you could see the earth being kicked up by shells but it didn't deafen you and that was for me rather a relief.'

Farther down the line the 7th Armoured was struggling to play a part in the battle. 'At first it was just a huge traffic jam moving rather slowly,' Lieutenant Cloudsley-Thompson remembered.

After a while we advanced towards Colombelles, the industrial area of Caen. Huge fires were burning as a result of the morning's bombardment and the sinister factory chimneys and columns of black smoke were tinged by the setting sun. We took up battle positions. My troop was on the right front overlooking the remains of a small copse which had been heavily shelled. We watched some Sherman tanks firing into the factory buildings on our right until they were counter-attacked and forced to withdraw.

By late afternoon it was clear to those in the field that the 'show-down' was not going according to plan.

Seduced by the initial advance, Monty had sent a signal to the Chief of the Imperial General Staff, Field Marshal Sir Alan Brooke, suggesting just the opposite: 'Operations this morning a total success. The effect of the air bombing was decisive and the spectacle terrific.' The Guards were in Vimont, he reported, the 11th Armoured had reached the area near Tilly la Campagne, and the 7th Armoured was moving on La Hogue. The truth was very different. The battered 11th Armoured Division was still short of Tilly, the Guards were five kilometres from Vimont, and the 7th Armoured six from La Hogue. But Monty's rose-tinted appreciation of the battle so far was the one given to the press: 'Early this morning British and Canadian troops of 2nd Army attacked and broke through into the area east of Orne and south-east of Caen . . .' Expectations were unnecessarily raised. Progress had indeed been made. By the end of the day the bridge-head across the Orne had been extended 10 kilometres to the south, the whole of Caen and its suburbs were in British hands, and a foothold had been won on the slopes of the Bourguébus ridge. But this was not the break-out and the cost was punishing – 1,500 men and 200 tanks had been lost. On the eve of battle the commander of the 11th Armoured, General 'Pip' Roberts, had warned against an armoured thrust without infantry support – his concerns were brushed aside and there had been too few soldiers in armoured vehicles to mop up the German anti-tank nests. But it was a long catalogue of failure. The attack had been expected, the defences carefully prepared, and when the British armour had finally cut loose into open country it had been met by the 88mm.

The 7th Armoured Division had barely put in an appearance

on the battlefield. It had lost only six tanks on the first day. Progress was still slow on the morning of the second. The 4th County of London Yeomanry trundled down the swept corridor towards the new front. Lieutenant John Cloudsley-Thompson recalled:

We were held up all day by the Guards Armoured Division who were massed thickly in front because their leading troops were held up at Cagny and there was insufficient space for them to deploy. During the afternoon a most unfortunate accident occurred. One of our 17-pounder Sherman [Firefly] drivers was climbing out of his tank when a burst was fired from the turret machine gun and several bullets went through his body. We did what we could, but loops of intestine were coming out through his ghastly wounds and he looked very white. An ambulance drove up and he was lifted gently on to a stretcher and taken away. I remember that he smiled and wished us 'good luck' as he left.

It was not until the evening that the tanks of the 4th CLY were able to move beyond the second railway embankment and through the Guards. 'We advanced across an open stretch of corn and were shelled heavily and accurately as we did so,' John Cloudsley-Thompson remembered. 'We were being overlooked by the church tower in the village of Ifs on our right and called for artillery support. Within a couple of minutes the 25-pounders of 'K' Battery, 5th Royal Horse Artillery, had blown the church down.' At dusk Cloudsley-Thompson's troop led B Squadron up towards a hedge on the skyline:

It was rather frightening. Cornfields sloped gently for nearly a mile up to the hedge, there were seven Cromwells burning quite fiercely – they were from the 11th Armoured Division, who had gone in first of all. I thought, there's an 88mm behind that hedge, and that's what's knocked those tanks out, so I was going forward very cautiously. I put my tank forward and then called up the other two Cromwells and made them go ahead, then I called the Sherman Firefly with the 17-pounder – and we zigzagged up like that. I heard the colonel saying on the wireless, 'Can't you get him to hurry up,' and the leader of B Squadron saying, 'No, he's doing very well from what I see, we don't want to hurry up any more than this.' Anyway, we got up to the hedge before it got dark, and I saw the white tracer of a German anti-tank gun firing beyond it. I put down some high-explosive shells around it and it didn't fire again. A couple of infantry patrols were sent up to liaise with me, and they said they'd make my tank their headquarters for the night. They were crawling about very quietly – they were very frightened. At about 3.30 a.m. there was suddenly a colossal bang and one patrol had thrown a grenade at the other – and wounded one man quite badly. We thought for a time that it was this anti-tank gun that we'd seen. In the morning, two men from my troop corporal's tank came up and said: 'We've just had as much as we can stand, and we'd rather have a court martial than go on any more,' because it was so frightening. I knew they'd baled out about twelve times before – they'd been in the regiment since the beginning. I said to them, 'I think everybody would, but we haven't got the opportunity so we've got to go on.' And we did.

Cloudsley-Thompson's 3 Troop was still leading the right of his squadron on the morning of the 20th. It came under constant heavy mortar and shellfire as it pressed on southward across the slopes of the Verrières ridge. A report of approaching enemy tanks drove the 4th CLY to seek cover in a wood: 'The shelling continued and several tanks were hit,' Cloudsley-Thompson recalled. 'The explosions were deafeningly close and although the air reeked of cordite and petrol we thought it wiser to close the turret flaps in case a shell should fall inside. The sun shone warmly and I could barely keep awake.' After an hour the order was given to withdraw – a Canadian attack was expected and the presence of two troops of tanks in the wood was upsetting their artillery plan. Cloudsley-Thompson's squadron had advanced farther than any other unit in the Goodwood operation:

I had an uneasy feeling as we left the wood and I told my driver to speed up. It was just as well, for German tanks had arrived on the skyline at the other side of the wood and almost immediately we came under fire from them. We sped down the hollow and across the road. My tank nearly crashed into another Cromwell which was also closed up . . . Having put a couple of miles between ourselves and the enemy, we halted. All the Fireflies, of which we had four per squadron, lined up along a hedge in front and fired together. The range was 2,000 yards, yet the first shot 'brewed up' one of the German tanks and the other five were knocked out before they could shoot back. It was a most heartening sight. If only our Cromwell tanks had had 17-pounders instead of 75mm guns we might have met the enemy on less unequal terms.

Not long afterwards the sun left the battlefield and it began to pour with rain – Goodwood was over. Slit trenches were soon full of water, the tracks were torn up and no wheeled vehicles could move. Armoured fighting was impossible. 'We sat in holes under our tanks, shivering,' Cloudsley-Thompson recalled. 'Shells came over every few minutes, and it was not safe to go out.'

There was not much to cheer on the battlefield. Nothing substantial had been achieved in the two days of fighting that had followed the initial attack. 'We thought it was a dismal failure – we were all very depressed,' Cloudsley-Thompson recalled.

The battle had cost the British 400 tanks – almost 40 per cent of its armoured strength in Normandy. The 4th CLY was pulled back a short time after the close to the ruined village of Ifs, and among the rubble Cloudsley-Thompson found a poignant reminder of the legacy of suffering the fighting would leave: 'I picked up the torn fragments of a photograph. On the back was written: "To my darling husband whom I love more than anything in life. May God spare him for me." But there was a grave in the ditch outside.'

Yet for all the cost in tanks and men Goodwood was a success of sorts. It had been Monty's avowed intention to keep Rommel's Panzer divisions fighting in the east in preparation for the break-out in the west, and that much of the plan had gone well. To meet the challenge at Caen two armoured divisions transferred to the American sector were recalled. The Germans had lost fewer tanks, but they could not afford to lose any. Since D-Day they had lost 2,117 but had received only seventeen replacements. The Allies were able to call on an apparently endless supply – within two days the armoured divisions that had borne the brunt of the Goodwood fighting had made good their tank losses. Replacing the crews was altogether harder. By late July the Germans could muster only 850 tanks – the Allies 4,500. The *Materialschlacht* was almost over. Kluge acknowledged as much on the day after the end of the battle. In a letter to Hitler he warned that 'the moment has drawn near when this front, already so heavily strained, will break'. The Germans were teetering on the precipice of defeat.

It was viewed very differently at home. Monty's ill-judged comments on the first day had raised absurdly high expectations. The newspapers had taken their cue from his press statement: 'Second Army Breaks Through – Armoured Forces reach open country – General Montgomery well satisfied' had been the headline in *The Times* on the 19th. The phrases 'breaks through' and 'open country' were to say the least misleading. When Goodwood was eventually closed down, the same newspaper noted drily that the offensive had been 'too much boomed' in the first hours: 'It is always better to do the booming after complete success has been secured.' The press in the United States was even less kind – phrases like 'bogged down' and 'over-cautious' were regularly appearing in print. It was not good for Eisenhower's blood pressure. SHAEF's chief medical officer had prescribed 'slow down medication' for stress and plenty of rest. According to his friend and aide Harry Butcher, he was as 'blue as indigo': 'Ike is like a blind dog in a meat house – he can smell it, but he can't find it,' he wrote in his diary. 'The slowness of the battle, the desire to be more active in it himself, his inward but generally unspoken criticisms of Monty for being so cautious: all pump up his system.' After an advance of 11 kilometres (seven miles) with 7,000 tons of bombs dropped, Ike had moodily observed, 'Can we afford a thousand tons of bombs per mile?' There was much talk at SHAEF and in the press of the startling gains won by the Russians in the east that summer. Eisenhower was under pressure from Washington to put his stamp on the campaign and deliver a decisive 'American' advance in the west. Nor were all the voices raised against Monty American. On the 19th Eisenhower's deputy, Tedder, had phoned to complain about 'the Army's failure' and to promise his support if the time had come to sack Monty. There was precious little 'faith' in Monty's battle plan at SHAEF – even reluctance in some quarters to acknowledge that there was one. Bradley's decision to postpone Operation Cobra yet again did nothing to help Monty's case.

Goodwood had been launched in support of a break-out attempt that had not been made. Eisenhower visited TAC HQ on 20 July, the last day of the operation, to be briefed by Monty in person. It was a private exchange of views, but something of its tenor emerges from the letter Eisenhower sent Monty the following day: 'I feel that you should insist that Dempsey keep up the strength of his attack,' he wrote. As Butcher later interpreted it in his diary: 'military necessity dictates that Montgomery push on with every ounce of strength and zeal. In addition to the purely military need of elbow room for manoeuvre, there is the political situation to consider. The home fronts of both countries are naturally becoming impatient and querulous; they see the great successes in Russia . . .'

The Supreme Commander could speak on the 'political situation' with real authority. His visit was followed on the 21st by one from the Prime Minister. Monty had always had a stiff, uncomfortable relationship with Churchill, and there was a good deal of concern among the staff at TAC HQ about the visit.

'There was a little apprehension, a whisper that Winston was really coming out to sack Monty,' Monty's ADC, Captain Johnny Henderson recalled. But Monty was all brisk confidence as he took Churchill through the plans for Cobra. 'Set backs? What set backs?' was how Monty's first biographer later reported the scene. Churchill left greatly reassured and with a bottle of cognac to boot – 'a peace offering'. The great excitement of the visit was provided by the news from Germany. Monty had learned from Ultra that 'a sort of revolution' had taken place; could the Prime Minister confirm this? Churchill had handed Monty's intelligence chief the keys to his dispatch boxes, urging him to 'see what you can find'. Among the jumble of papers in the boxes were the first reports of the attempt on Hitler's life.

It had so very nearly succeeded. A dispatch case had been carefully placed under the long, heavy conference table, just a few metres from Hitler. The fuse had been set for a little before half past one on the afternoon of 20 July. Colonel Klaus von Stauffenberg made his excuses and left 'to use the telephone'. Minutes later a huge blast ripped through the room. The survivors stumbled through the acrid smoke into the sunlight outside – behind them lay a scene of utter devastation. Wounded men lay groaning in the debris, charred map fragments fluttered in the breeze.

The telephone rang in Rolf Munninger's office at the headquarters of Army Group B in France at about half past three:

It was from the OKW – there had been an assassination attempt on Hitler at the Wolf's Lair in Rastenberg [Hitler's headquarters in East Prussia] – he was dead. There were no other details. You cannot imagine the effect that news had on us. I instantly passed the news on to the 1A [staff operations officer] but he had listened to the call himself. His first words were something like 'Thank God he is gone'. I was also relieved, truly relieved. But two hours later there was another phone call telling us that Hitler was alive, just slightly injured.

If I could have crawled into some hole I would have done. It was one of the worst messages I could imagine.

When a dazed, blackened Hitler was led from the ruins of his conference room the last chance for an early end to the war was lost. The blast left his trousers in ragged tatters, his leg was scorched, his right arm temporarily paralysed and his eardrums damaged, but he was calm and determined. Those who had played any part in the assassination attempt would be found and ruthlessly dealt with. It was soon evident that the list of active conspirators included the names of generals and field marshals – many of Germany's most senior soldiers. The arrests began that night under the personal direction of the Reichsführer SS, Heinrich Himmler. Stauffenberg was fortunate to be shot that night. Those arrested would over the coming months be interrogated, tortured and then forced to appear before the 'People's Court' in Berlin. Hitler gave instructions that not only the conspirators but their families were to be exterminated. Many of the senior officers most closely implicated in the assassination attempt served in France. There were many more that had been approached and knew of the conspiracy but had refused to play an active part. They had kept their own counsel, nonetheless, and that in itself was enough to implicate them in the plot. Both Field Marshal von Rundstedt and his successor Kluge had discussed a Germany without Hitler with some of the conspirators – Rommel's chief of staff, General Speidel, was one of them.

Rommel had driven to the headquarters of I SS Panzer Corps on 17 July to discuss the attack the British were expected to make east of the Orne. He was greeted by its commander, the most famous 'Hackmeister' in the German army – Oberstgruppenführer Sepp Dietrich. A broad, balding, five foot seven inches, Dietrich was not a commanding presence. An Allied interrogator would later describe him as 'the antithesis' of an Aryan superman. He was despised by many senior staff officers, who thought him uncouth, garrulous and conceited. Dietrich had been one of Hitler's earliest followers – he had commanded the Führer's personal bodyguard in the 1930s, a post he retained when it became a division – the 1st SS Panzer (Leibstandarte Adolf Hitler). His loyalty to the Führer was beyond doubt. Yet on the morning of the 17th Rommel had asked him, 'Would you always execute my orders, even if they contradicted the Führer's?' Dietrich took Rommel's hand and warmly shook it: 'You're the boss, Herr Feldmarschall. I obey only you – whatever it is you're planning.' Both men had been among Hitler's most loyal supporters, but they were prepared to consider 'opening the gate' to the western Allies, who were in any case on the point of battering it down. The right time would probably come when the enemy finally managed to break out of the bridgehead. 'My father said: "the main thing is to finish in France; the war has to be stopped, no matter how. Then we might avoid the total destruction of Germany",' Rommel's son, Manfred, remembered. But when the bomb exploded in the Wolf's Lair it was too late for Rommel to influence events either way. On his way back to La Roche Guyon on the 17th the field marshal's car had been attacked by a British fighter plane. This time he had run out of luck. The car had been forced off the road into a ditch, the driver killed and Rommel severely injured. He would play no further part in the Battle of Normandy. In the coming weeks Rommel was to be one of those damned by association. Although it is unlikely he knew of the plot to kill Hitler, his name was mentioned to interrogators by a prominent conspirator, and it was enough to secure a death warrant.

Rommel was recovering at home in Herrlingen when on 14 October 1944 he was visited by two senior army officers he knew well. They had been directed by Hitler to present the field marshal with a choice. He could 'take the officer's way' and poison himself or accept arrest and trial for treason. If he chose suicide his family would be safe. For Rommel there was only 'the officer's way'. His son, Manfred, was at home on leave from his anti-aircraft battery: 'I kept relatively calm, he was also composed. I even followed General Meisel outside – he asked me in which unit I served and I told him: "Flak Battery 367." And then we were at the car and I said goodbye to my father and the car left. I knew that we'd receive a phone call in a few minutes to tell us that my father had died of a brain haemorrhage.' Rommel was given a hero's funeral – Rundstedt was there to represent the Führer.

Most German soldiers condemned the attempt on Hitler's life. Captain Ritgen of the Panzer Lehr was too busy to give much thought to it. By 20 July the division had been moved to the west of St-Lô to stiffen the line facing the American bridgehead. Ritgen had heard news of the bomb between American artillery barrages: 'My command post was in a farmhouse in a village and it was under attack. Normally we never wore steel helmets, but this time my adjutant told me to put mine on. It was much too small for me – it was perched on the very top of my head. Well, we had no idea what was happening in Berlin.' Later Ritgen had time to reflect: 'Although I loathed Hitler, his death would have been a disaster at that time and have caused such confusion that the enemy would have been confirmed in his goal – the destruction of Germany.' Captain Hans Bernhard of the 1st SS Panzer (Leibstandarte Adolf Hitler) was outraged: 'We felt it was treason and a great crime. We knew these people had to be enemies of the Reich. Legally this was high treason, which helped our enemies and not us. The generals were too short sighted. They were willing to lose the war in order to get rid of Hitler. Traitors normally get shot in most countries in the world.' Bernhard and his comrades were inundated with visits from neighbouring Wehrmacht generals – all anxious to prove their loyalty by visiting the SS division that bore the Führer's own name.

In the weeks following the assassination attempt Hitler was as interested in fighting his own senior officers as those of the enemy. Hundreds were rounded up, imprisoned or executed. All

General Staff officers were instructed to play their part in 'actively co-operating in the political indoctrination of younger commanders'. 'The worst thing for us was that we were no longer allowed to salute in a normal military fashion with our hand raised to our caps,' Otto Henning of the Panzer Lehr recalled. 'We had to have our arms raised in the Hitler salute. They turned us into "Nazi party soldiers". We could not get used to the fact that we had to salute with the raised arm, just like the SS. Well, we just stopped saluting.' In Manfred Rommel's opinion, 'Hitler's actions broke the back of the army – he knew how to completely disarm his own army.' There is no doubting the uncertainty and fear that gripped many of the army's most senior officers. 'Defeatist' talk was little short of treason. Hitler's influence on the conduct of the battle in Normandy had been wholly negative from the first, but after the attempt on his life he was even less willing to accept the advice of his professional soldiers.

It was at a little before eight o'clock on the morning of 25 July when the field telephone rang in the old farmhouse General Bayerlein had taken for his command post. The report was from one of the Panzer Lehr Division's outposts: 'the American infantry in front of our trenches is pulling back everywhere'. Nerves were on edge – what did this mean? The previous day an air raid by 300 Allied bombers had battered the division's positions along the St-Lô–Périers road. The US VII Corps had launched a half-hearted attack that had been easily beaten off. It was a defensive success, a temporary reprise. In the divisional order for 25 July Bayerlein warned his men to expect a 'continuation of the major enemy attack' and instructed reserve units to take up positions at a safe distance from the road 'to minimise the effects of carpet bombing'. The enemy bombers would use the road as a marker.

The Panzer Lehr had begun transferring to the St-Lô area on the evening of 7 July and had immediately found itself caught up in a grinding battle of attrition in the bocage with the best part of three fresh American divisions. Bayerlein estimated that his already battered division had lost 2,000 men in fourteen days – the Americans at least twice that number. But the Americans could count on replacements. By 25 July the Panzer Lehr's combat line was little more than a series of scattered strongpoints with Panzer grenadiers dug in around two or three well-camouflaged tanks. Captain Helmut Ritgen remembered one senior officer observing that 'those tanks are strung out like a pearl necklace. Every time a pearl is lost the enemy will come through the gap.' Behind the combat line was a mobile armoured reserve to be committed to the counter-attack wherever a break-through was threatened. Field commanders like Ritgen spent a good deal of time trying to fool the enemy into believing the line was defended more strongly than it was: 'We tried to mislead the Americans with all sorts of tricks – we put trees – "leaf blocks" – across the road with a sign on them, "Attention Mines", and they usually believed it. We had to play at being Indians.' The division had mustered 15,000 troops on D-Day and more than 150 Panther and Panzer IVs – that had been whittled down to just 2,200 men and forty-five tanks. The German line to the west of the Panzer Lehr was just as threadbare. 'It could start at any hour, Herr General. It is obvious the Americans are ready,' Bayerlein's intelligence officer had warned on 24 July. 'I believe only the weather is holding them up.' The morning of the 25th was a fine one.

The telephone rang again in the farmhouse at 9.40 a.m. – a wave of about fifty American fighter-bombers was attacking strongpoints and artillery positions along the front. The first wave was followed by another and then another. A total of 600 fighter-bombers attacked a strip of ground just 275 metres wide. Large numbers of a new type of incendiary bomb filled with jellied petrol or 'napalm' were dropped on the German line, setting the bocage alight and covering the ground with a pall of choking smoke. But through it the Panzer grenadiers could hear a new sound – the slow drone of four-engined aircraft. For an hour 1,500 heavy bombers saturated a rectangle of ground 5,500 metres wide and 2,000 deep on the St-Lô–Périers road. Then came a third and final attack by medium bombers. Almost three thousand aircraft had carpet-bombed a narrow, tortured strip of front, and the Panzer Lehr had borne the brunt of the attack.

'It was hell,' Bayerlein told his British interrogator after the war.

My flak had hardly opened its mouth when the batteries got a direct hit, knocking out half the guns and silencing the remainder. Everybody dived for cover. The planes kept coming overhead like a conveyor belt, and the bomb carpets came down, now ahead, now on the right, now on the left. I knew this was the opening of the big American attack, and that I must contact my forward positions.

By half past nine that morning all contact had been lost between divisional headquarters and the front-line units. Fritz Bayerlein set out on a motorcycle for one of the division's forward command posts:

Here, from a heavy stone pillbox, I watched the next wave of attack. The fields were burning and smouldering. The bomb carpets unrolled in great rectangles. At first I could see Amigny on the American side of the lines, but by noon nothing was visible but smoke and dust. I was still without communications, sending runners to my regiments. My front line looked like a landscape on the moon, and at least seventy per cent of my personnel were out of action – dead, wounded, crazed or numbed. All my front-line tanks were knocked out.

But there were infantry casualties on the other side of the line too. General Bradley had learned from bitter experience that 'the airmen' were not always as careful as they might be. He had ordered all front-line troops to draw back 1,100 metres immediately before the start of the bombardment. But as his aide, Chester Hansen, recalled, in spite of this precaution things did not go to plan: 'General Bradley had gone up to witness the bombing and I remember we were in a small village there in the bocage country and there were bombs breaking all over the place. So we knew instantly that the air force had missed the bomb line and some of them were dropping prematurely and hitting our people.'

Smoke from the first wave had obscured the target area and the follow-up aircraft had dropped short, killing one hundred men and wounding five hundred more. Among the dead was General Lesley McNair – the man sent by the War Office in Washington to observe the attack. 'Our troops were very, very angry about this and cursed the air people,' Hansen recalled. But as the last of the bombers drew away the lead units of VII Corps picked themselves up and began to push forward towards the strip blasted by the bombardment. The thrust was to have overwhelming force. The corps had been boosted to almost army strength with five divisions – three infantry and two armoured. The infantry were to push through the gap in the German line and hold it open for the armour. Once through, the corps commander, General 'Lightning Joe' Collins, had high hopes of a rapid advance. A sergeant with the 102nd Cavalry's Reconnaissance Squadron had come up with an ingenious solution to the bocage problem which promised to answer the prayers of tank commanders throughout the Allied bridgehead. Sergeant Curtis G. Culin Junior proposed welding a set of tusk-like prongs to the front of a tank. Moving at between 16 and 24 kilometres an hour, this was able to cut the roots of a hedge as it thrust forward but at no point did it expose its vulnerable, armour-less belly to the enemy. Bradley and Collins had been impressed and the US First Army's engineers had been given the task of secretly converting Rommel's beach obstacles into hedge-cutters.

The American infantry began to filter through the blasted strip, advancing from crater to crater beyond what had been the German outposts. No opposition was expected: 'they looked forward to the prospect of strolling through the bomb target area,' the official American history later recorded. But some Panzer grenadiers and a handful of tanks had survived. 'I had to organise my last reserves to meet them,' Bayerlein later recorded, 'not over fifteen tanks, most of them from repair shops.' To the west of the Panzer Lehr the 5th Parachute Division had escaped most of the bombing and it too began to resist the American advance. In spite of its overwhelming superiority VII Corps managed to make little more than two kilometres by nightfall. General Collins was not easily discouraged. On the morning of the 26th, the 2nd Armoured and the 'Big Red One' – the veteran 1st Division – joined the attack.

German resistance was confined to isolated pockets. Captain Helmut Ritgen's tanks had been ordered to occupy the ruined village of St-Gilles. Ritgen had just missed the carpet bombing of the previous day: 'I was incredibly lucky. The tank units were on a four-day rotation; four days on, four days off. We had just been relieved when the first carpet-bombing attack started.' On the morning of the 26th Ritgen's command Panzer found some cover in an orchard: 'The Americans launched their breakthrough attack, screened by the inevitable swarm of fighter-bombers.' By the afternoon Ritgen's orchard had ceased to exist:

Only a few naked tree trunks were still standing. Branches and over-turned vehicles formed a confused entanglement. Every road to my tanks was monitored by the murderous, circling Thunderbolts . . . it took an eternity to move along the road. The explosions continued unceasingly. All the Panzers were engaged in heavy fighting. Then even radio communications were lost. My command Panzer was found by a fighter-bomber and knocked out. Fortunately the crew was unharmed. Since there was nothing left to command, I gave the order to withdraw.

Ritgen and his tank crew began trudging back across country at some distance from the road: 'To my surprise American tanks and infantry began passing us. Totally carefree. They had broken through – the Panzer grenadiers just weren't there to stop them any more.'

At six o'clock that afternoon Bayerlein was visited by a special emissary from Field Marshal von Kluge – his son, Oberstleutnant (Lieutenant Colonel) von Kluge. The smart young staff officer stood before Bayerlein – grizzled, unshaven, dirty: 'Herr General, the Field Marshal demands that the line from St Lô–Périers be held.' At first there was a disbelieving silence in the command post. 'The line St Lô–Périers is to be held, with what?' Bayerlein asked. Kluge repeated his father's order: 'not a man may leave the position'. It was too much for Bayerlein; none of his men had left their positions, he told the Oberstleutnant – none were left alive to leave: 'They are lying in their holes still and mute, because they are dead. Dead, do you understand? The Panzer Lehr is destroyed.'

The division that had set out three months before to drive the Allies back into the sea had gone. Over the next four days the German line from St-Lô to the sea buckled and folded. The shattered remnants of the Panzer Lehr and the other German divisions were swept aside by the onward rush of American armour. Forward air observers travelled in tanks with the armoured columns and were able to call in fighter-bomber support whenever the advance was held up. Bayerlein had just established a new headquarters near the village of Pont Brocard when the American 82nd Reconnaissance Battalion pounced. 'I had called a staff meeting when a messenger rushed up and reported enemy tanks within 300 yards,' Bayerlein later recalled. 'My staff officers hid in a small house near the command post just as the tanks drove up. We hid about an hour while the tanks riddled the houses all about and then we slipped out and ran for it.' One of the division's radio operators witnessed his general's scramble to escape:

The division's radio echelon was located in an apple orchard on a hill. The command post was in a farmhouse below in the valley. Suddenly three men jumped out of the bottom windows and ran up the hill towards us. One of them lost his field cap, another still carried his map board and a small briefcase in his hand. It was General

Bayerlein and the Ia [staff operations officer] Major Kurt Kaufmann and a third man. The command bus caught fire next to the farmhouse. The general reached us, completely out of breath. He asked: 'Do you have something to drink?' We had a wicker bottle of cider in the radio station.

An exhausted and demoralised Bayerlein reported his division 'finally annihilated': 'The armour was almost completely wiped out, personnel either casualties or missing, all headquarters records lost. Its general had escaped with nothing but the clothes he stood up in, and those were in a bad state.'

It had almost become a rout. German divisions existed only as flags on the map at Army Group B headquarters. Field Marshal von Kluge pressed imaginary units to hold in the name of the Führer. He was an able strategist and respected soldier, but the finger of suspicion pointed at him in the days following the bomb plot and, to prove his loyalty, he was prepared to issue orders he knew were impossible to carry out. It was, he privately admitted, 'one hell of a mess'.

To the west of Collins's VII Corps, VIII Corps was pushing along the coast towards Avranches – the gateway to Brittany and southern Normandy. The town fell on 30 July to the 4th Armoured Division – it had driven 40 kilometres in just thirty-six hours. The American advance was relentless. When Bradley had lit the blue touch-paper five days earlier, he had hoped Cobra would break the deadlock by freeing the US First Army from the bocage, but it now promised to achieve much more. Enter centre stage General George C. Patton. After months on the shelf, Patton was like the cork in a well-shaken champagne bottle: 'I'm proud to be here to fight beside you,' he had told the handful of soldiers who had seen him arrive at Omaha three weeks before. 'Now let's cut the guts out of those Krauts and get the hell on to Berlin. And when we get to Berlin I am going to personally shoot that paper-hanging goddamned son of a bitch [Hitler] just like I would a snake.' On 1 August American forces in the field were split and the US Third Army was officially born with Patton as its commander. The battle would now be fought at a different pace – Patton's pace.

> So let us do real fighting, boring in and gouging, biting.
> Let's take a chance now that we have the ball.
> Let's forget those fine firm bases in the dreary shell raked
>   spaces,
> Let's shoot the works and win! Yes win it all.
>   (General George Patton, July 1944)

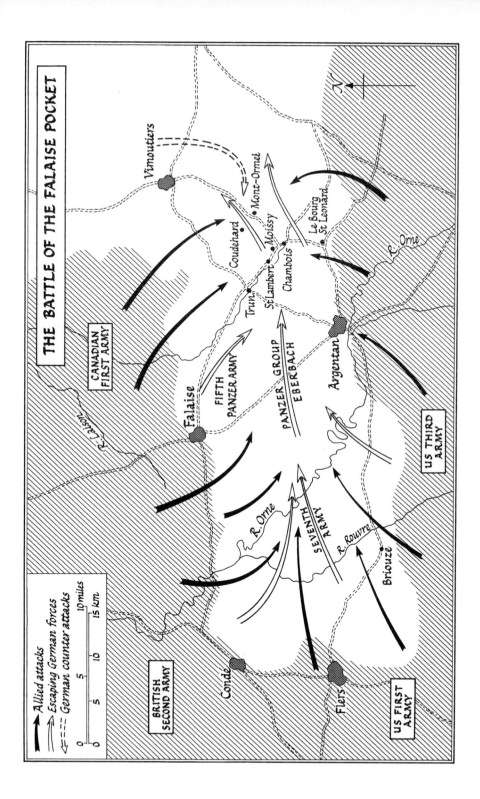

THE BATTLE OF THE FALAISE POCKET

CANADIAN
FIRST ARMY

BRITISH
SECOND ARMY

US THIRD
ARMY

US FIRST
ARMY

Allied attacks
Escaping German forces
German counter attacks

0   5   10miles
0   5   10   15 km.

Vimoutiers
Mont-Ormel
Coudehard
Moissy
Le Bourg
St Leonard
Chambois
St Lambert
Trun
R. Orne
Argentan

FIFTH
PANZER ARMY

PANZER GROUP
EBERBACH

SEVENTH
ARMY

R. Laison
Falaise
R. Orne
R. Rouvre
Briouze

Condé
Flers

CHAPTER SEVEN

THE CAULDRON

T
he stunning success of Cobra was to turn a battle that at times appeared dangerously close to stalemate into a spectacular victory. The gate was open and Patton's Third Army raced through it. In his personal memoir of the war, Patton observed that 'If the greatest study of mankind is man, surely the greatest study of war is the road net.' A great 'whoop' of joy would go up at Third Army headquarters when his divisions ran off one map and on to the next – there was no better commander to send in pursuit of a shattered enemy. Patton had feared he would 'die of old age' before he was given a chance to play a part, but now weeks of frustrating inactivity were at an end and he was determined to make his mark.

Patton loved war. 'Compared to war all [other] human activities are futile,' he wrote in his diary. Teasing, vulgar and arrogant, at fifty-eight he was the oldest of the Allied generals and also the most mercurial. He had risen to public prominence in the desert and in Sicily, where he had led the US Seventh Army with dash. Patton officially answered to Bradley, who had stepped up to command the new 12th Army Group with overall responsibility for both the American armies in Normandy. But Patton had next to no opinion of Bradley, or for that matter any senior field commander but himself: 'War is very simple, direct and ruthless. It takes a simple and ruthless man to wage war,' he confided to his diary; 'on reflection who is as good as I am? I know of no one.' 'Bradley and Hodges [US First Army

Commander from August] are such nothings', whilst 'Ike is bound hand and foot by the British and does not know it. Poor fool. We actually have no Supreme Commander.' He reserved particular disdain for that 'tired little fart' Montgomery. He disliked him intensely but was fascinated by him, and the two men were in some respects strangely alike. 'Monty is an actor but not a fool,' Patton wrote. Both men were 'actors'. Patton sported pistols with ivory handles, Monty a black tank beret with badges. Both men recognised the importance of being seen and of personality in leadership, and both had won unusually strong followings among the men they led. Bradley's aide, Major Chester Hansen, met Patton many times:

General Patton was a personality, a very distinctive one. General Patton was quite unlike everyone else, he wore rather flashy uniforms and he had kind of a Buck Rogers air that he wore when he was out in the field. People were scared to death of him. We met him for the first time down in the Mediterranean where General Bradley was his subordinate. He was a legendary soldier in the American army, even though he had really only fought in Sicily up until that time. Patton travelled in a command car – all the other generals seemed to prefer jeeps. In the command car, you sit way up high on the back seat and you look very magisterial. Patton had a big siren on his vehicle and he used to roar down the roads with this heavy command car with siren blaring and traffic would park on the road to allow him to get through. He was a very showy character, but a very good soldier, you could count on him. General Bradley counted heavily on him, because when Patton said he could do something, it got done. He was very aggressive. Kept his forces moving all the time.

Patton's military role models were Hitler's Panzer commanders, and over the coming weeks he would demonstrate their flare for the daring armoured dash. 'The British complex' was 'over-caution': stop, build up and start. 'War requires the taking of risks', and in Patton's judgement Monty would not take enough of them. Bradley showed worrying signs of 'the British complex' – it had taken him far too long to get going in Normandy. But now the Germans were reeling back in the west and this was the time to exploit their weakness.

Over the next three weeks Patton drove his army forward with remorseless energy. Against the better judgement of both Patton and Monty, Bradley ordered the bulk of the Third Army to execute a smart 'right' westward into Brittany. Patton nevertheless made the most of his orders, and within a week he had driven seven divisions down a narrow coastal road and then fanned out to seize the whole of Brittany – 'one of the loveliest battles you ever saw – it is a typical cavalry action,' he observed. Only the German garrisons in Brest and Lorient offered serious resistance. But on 3 August Bradley recognised that the real battle was still to be fought in the east. Patton was ordered to leave a single corps to secure Brittany while the rest of his army swung through the points of the compass and began its advance towards the Seine. The pace of this advance did not slacken for a moment. Patton led tirelessly by example, bullying and cajoling in turn: 'Of course, it is a little nerve-racking to send troops straight into the middle of the enemy with front, flanks, and rear open,' he confided to his diary. 'I had to keep repeating myself. "Do not take counsel of your fears."'

Major Edward Hamilton was serving with the 90th Division:

We were buoyed up. One of the first things that we heard was that Patton had said, 'Give me the 90th Division and two divisions of tanks and I'll be in Paris in a week.' Whether he said it or not, we heard it and, of course, that buoyed everybody's morale. We'd been fighting for every yard in the hedgerow country and suffering heavy casualties. So this was a new type of warfare, something that we readily adapted to.

The 90th had not covered itself in glory in the 'hedgerow country'. Its commander had been replaced and the division had been judged of poor quality, 'the men filthy, and the officers apathetic'. But this was a very different battle – one that suited it well. On 5 August the division covered almost 50 kilometres in less than half a day to reach the west bank of the Mayenne river. In the van were Major Hamilton's men from the 1st Battalion, the 357th Infantry Regiment. Hamilton was an Oregon boy who had followed his father into the National Guard and then on to the West Point Military Academy. He had been secretly posted to Iceland in 1941 to serve in the occupying force, and as such had become one of the first Americans to serve in the European theatre. Two weeks after landing in Normandy he had been given command of a battalion. On the afternoon of the 5th Hamilton was ordered to seize a bridge over the Mayenne:

We encountered resistance on the western outskirts of the town of Mayenne. I detrucked there and we advanced with one company into the town. We worked our way down to the river – it flows through the middle of town. There were three bridges there, two of these had been blown, the remaining bridge was mined with large aerial bombs. They were laid, four on either side of the street, on the sidewalks across the bridge. The Germans were occupying the eastern part of the town. The lead company worked its way along the wall that ran along the river. I had Turner tanks attached to my battalion and I lined these up about two corners from the bridge in a side street. And at six o'clock in the evening, I began a preparatory attack with artillery and the mortars, which was to lift after ten minutes. After about five minutes, one of these shells hit a German casement that was located on the eastern side of the river. A dense pile of smoke enveloped the street leading down to the bridge on the eastern side. It was an opportune moment. I called off the artillery and mortar fire and ordered the B Company commander on the radio to cross the bridge. At the same time I motioned to the tanks; they wheeled around the corner and charged across. The infantry were pushing across at the same time. It was a breathtaking moment because we didn't know whether or not those aerial bombs were going to be blown, whether the whole bridge would go down and everything on it. But they got across and severed the wires leading to the mines there and so we took the town and the only remaining bridge. That ensured the ready passage of the division.

Hamilton and his men had kept the 90th moving, but they had no time to rest on their laurels: 'Our objective was Le Mans, which was another forty miles. After taking Mayenne, they split the task force – we were in Task Force Bart and my battalion continued as the advance guard.' The Germans were repeatedly surprised by the speed of the American push. The 90th seemed, in the words of the historian Russell Weigley, 'to be picking up pep and ginger not only because of the new commander but because swift movement was what the American army was best designed for, including the infantry divisions'. The Americans had learned a good deal from their enemy. The German 'blitzkrieg' that had rolled through Europe between 1939 and 1941 demonstrated the importance of armour and aircraft working in concert, fast-moving tank forces supported by infantry in half-tracks or trucks. The German Panzer armies had been at their most efficient in the summer of 1941 when they had overwhelmed a tank force five times their number on the broad grasslands of the Soviet Union. But in the years since this extraordinary victory the American army had taken mobility one stage farther. By 1944 all the infantry in its armoured divisions was carried in half-tracks, all the artillery self-propelled. It was a fully mechanised and motorised army – the most modern in the world. While the Germans boasted the glory of the Tiger and Panther in France, they relied primarily on the horse for their mobility. There were only 14,500 trucks on the whole front, but more than 60,000 horses. The Americans had also moved one step farther in the development of air support for ground forces – 'the Anglo-American air force *is* the modern type of warfare,' Rommel's chief of staff observed. Above all, the Reich could not hope to meet the overwhelming material superiority, the extraordinary production capacity of the United States of

America. In 1944 it built some 600,000 army trucks – Germany managed just 88,000.

On the afternoon of the 6th Hamilton passed through St-Suzanne, then on to Viviers, where the battalion fought a night battle with a column of German infantry:

We moved right on that next day, without any real sleep, up very close to Le Mans, and we bivouacked overnight there and during the night a German vehicle ran into an outpost, I saw this the next morning – the driver of that vehicle had received so much automatic fire, his upper torso was absolutely severed from the lower portion of his body. That's the first time I'd seen that particular thing. I saw a German soldier back in Normandy who'd had his head run over by a truck and it was splattered out there like a pancake, the features were absolutely ground into batter. I mentioned this to the colonel and he said, 'You know, when I first saw those things in North Africa, that made me a little bit squeamish, but it doesn't bother me any more.' And that's what war does to one. That morning – the 7th – we resumed the advance on Le Mans. It took us along the main route that runs from west to east, from Rennes to Le Mans. As we got on this route, I saw a German column coming down the road towards us from the west. The lead vehicle was a command car with four officers and a driver in it. It swerved to the right of the tank and all the infantry around us opened fire. Several vehicles down the German column there was an ammunition truck and a 75mm shell from one of our tanks hit that and it went up in flames – a terrific explosion. We had an artillery liaison plane flying above and I had my liaison officer right there, and I said, 'Are you in contact with him?' He said, 'Yes.' I said, 'Walk the artillery fire up and down the column from that vehicle [the burning ammunition truck],' which he did. I also launched an attack against the left flank of that column with a company of infantry. We captured 230 Germans. It was on the radio across America that night.

The 90th's advance 'through enemy-infested country' had been extraordinary, but luck had certainly played its part, as its assistant commander, Brigadier General William G. Weaver, acknowledged:

We were too green at that time to know that we were supposed to have been preceded by an Armoured Division, so dumb, doughboy-like, we just went ahead and did the job by ourselves. The going had been so rugged and the speed so great that General George Patton came up to congratulate us right away. Enthusiastically he grabbed Ray McLain [divisional commander] in one big, powerful arm and me in his other, slammed us together and said, 'I knew you two so-and-so's would do it'.

On 8 August the city of Le Mans, the former headquarters of the German 7th Army, fell to the advance. 'This Army had a big day . . . I am quite tickled and not at all worried although I have been skating on the thin ice of self-confidence for nine days,' Patton noted in his diary. 'I am the only one who realises how little the enemy can do – he is finished. We may end this in ten days.' The pursuit had been unrelenting – nowhere had the Germans been allowed to settle and hold. It was a triumph, but one won against a shattered, defeated enemy.

So much was evident to the more discerning correspondents in the field, such as Andy Rooney of the US Army's newspaper, *Stars and Stripes*:

I thought Patton got more credit than he deserved. His Third Army was not committed until after we took St-Lô. They immediately went towards the west of France away from the main German forces, so naturally they made greater distances every day. They were able to. They weren't fighting anybody for quite a while, that was the thing. I was not a great admirer of George Patton. I mean, really ridiculous, he had his dog with him. Pearl-handled pistols. He was an ass, he was a pompous ass.

But Eisenhower was delighted. 'He was all smiles,' Butcher recorded on 2 August. '"If the intercepts are right, we are to hell and gone in Brittany and slicing 'em up in Normandy," he said.'

This was something the folks back home could understand – success measured in miles. But for all the headlines, the hard work was being done to the north by the US First Army, the British and Canadians. The British 2nd Army had kept up Monty's 'really hard fight' with the Panzer forces around Caen. It was a thankless task. Bradley and Patton were basking in the sunshine of a success won, not just on the battlefield, but in Monty's map caravan. The carping had continued at SHAEF – Eisenhower had personally 'run down' Monty to Churchill and 'described his stickiness and the reaction in the American papers'. Monty's great friend and supporter Field Marshal Sir Alan Brooke, the Chief of the Imperial General Staff, noted in his diary that 'national spectacles pervert the perspective of the strategic landscape'. It was galling, for Monty was the architect of an 'Allied' strategy, and it had been the British and Canadian soldiers' lot to plough the same selfless furrow. The blow on the western flank of the Allied bridgehead had always been 'the foundation of all our operations', Monty reminded his army commanders in a directive; 'the armies on the eastern flank must now keep up the pressure . . . so as to make easier the task of the American armies'. The long, grinding battles of June and July had made the break-out possible – they would now play a vital part in the final collapse. 'The general situation is now so good,' Monty wrote in his diary on 5 August, 'that I can issue my orders for the destruction of the Germans forces south of the Seine.'

But it was Hitler who was to play the decisive part in the destruction of the German armies in France. The crisis the Reich faced in the west and the east was a 'crisis of morale', he declared, one that could not be considered separately from the attempt on his own life. 'After all, what do you expect of an entire front,' he declared, 'if in the rear, as we see now, the most important positions in its supreme command are filled by absolute wreckers – not defeatists, but wreckers and traitors to their country.' In Hitler's muddled mind all Germany's ills could be traced to the door of the 20 July plotters and their friends in the army's officer corps. The army failed to recognise 'the historically decisive nature of this battle of destiny'; there could be no talk of negotiations or 'tactical skill'; it had become, Hitler told his senior commanders, 'a Hunnish sort of battle in which one must either stand or fall and die – one of the two'. In the febrile atmosphere of the Führer's headquarters no one was quite free from the finger of suspicion, and no one could be wholly trusted to act in the best interests of the Reich: 'I cannot leave the Western campaign to Kluge,' Hitler told the chief of operations at OKW. All Kluge needed to know was that withdrawal from Normandy would not be tolerated: 'Tell Field Marshal von Kluge that he should keep his eyes riveted to the front and on the enemy without looking backward.'

Hitler's new battle plans for Normandy reached Kluge at one o'clock on the morning of 3 August. The only sensible course was and had long been withdrawal to the Seine, but Hitler proposed to do entirely the opposite. Kluge was instructed to launch an armoured thrust towards Avranches with at least four divisions, to 'annihilate' the enemy and make contact with the west coast of the Cotentin. If successful the attack would drive a wedge between the US First and Third Armies. Kluge's corps and divisional commanders protested long and loud. The men were exhausted, they said, and it was impossible to concentrate armour without inviting attack from the air; if they pushed westward the 7th Army and the 5th Panzer Army risked being trapped in an Allied bag. To all these protests the field marshal answered only *'Es ist ein Führer Befehl'* – they are Hitler's orders. Kluge was powerless to alter the course of the battle.

The attack was launched at a little after midnight on 7 August – four Panzer divisions, all under strength, rolled westward from the Mortain area towards the sea. It began to peter out almost as soon as it began. The Allies had been expecting some sort of attack – although its timing and strength were a surprise. The first indication that Hitler planned a counter-offensive had surfaced in signals intercepted and decoded at Bletchley Park. It was enough to put the US First Army on its mettle. When the mist cleared on the morning of the 7th, Allied fighter-bombers began to swarm around the advancing Panzers, and by midday the Germans had ground to a halt. Hitler stepped in once again to order a second push by three more Panzer divisions – divisions that were already committed to holding the British and Canadians on the Caen front. Kluge fell into line: 'I foresee that the failure of this attack [at Mortain] can lead to the collapse of the entire Normandy front, but the order is so unequivocal it must be obeyed,' he told the commander of the 5th Panzer Army.

Such a collapse was now anticipated by the Allies. Bradley was visited on the second day of the Mortain offensive by the US Secretary of the Treasury, Henry Morgenthau. The British and Canadians were attacking south, Bradley explained, and would meet the American Third Army's advance north near Argentan – the Germans would be 'clamped' in the jaws of a great pincer movement. 'This is an opportunity that comes to a commander not more than once in a century,' Bradley told his guest. 'We're about to destroy an entire hostile army.' It would, he predicted, take just forty-eight hours to encircle the 7th Army and most of the 5th Panzer Army, and then 'we'll go all the way from here to the German border'.

But closing the neck of the bag around the German attack was an altogether tougher task than Bradley or Monty anticipated. The job of spearheading the northern thrust towards Falaise and Argentan had been given to the Canadians and the Polish 1st Armoured Division. It was a painfully slow advance in the teeth of stubborn resistance from the remnants of the 12th SS Panzer Divisions. What was left of the division had been relieved on 5 August and brought out of the line for a few days' rest. Their positions had been taken by the 272nd Infantry Division, but in order to convince the British and

Canadians that their old enemy was still in place the commander of the 12th SS, Brigadeführer Kurt Meyer, left a wireless set behind to transmit on the division's frequency. To ensure he was not surprised by an Allied push, the 12th SS liaison officers were left with the infantry formations that had moved into the line. On the night of the 7th/8th, the Canadian II Corps launched Operation Totalize with a lightning air bombardment followed by a night-time advance. The Allies had made good ground by the time news reached Meyer. He drove forward at once only to be caught up in the air bombardment:

I got out of my car and my knees were trembling, the sweat was pouring down my face, and my clothes were soaked with perspiration. It was not that I was particularly anxious for myself because my experiences of the last five years had inured me against fear of death, but I realised that if I failed now and if I did not deploy my division correctly, the Allies would be through to Falaise, and the German armies in the West completely trapped. I knew how weak my division was and the double task which confronted me gave me at that time some of the worst moments I had ever had in my life.

Groups of disheartened, exhausted infantry were trailing down the Caen–Falaise road away from the front. Meyer calmly lit a cigar and stood in the middle of the road, and in a clear voice asked the retreating men whether they were going to leave him to fight the Allied advance alone. 'One look at this young commander was enough and the men turned around and immediately started to take up defensive positions,' Meyer's British interrogator noted after the war. 'He must certainly have looked an impressive figure, this twenty-five-year-old divisional commander, wearing the highest decorations that the Germans could bestow on him, quietly and confidently facing this disorderly mob.' the 12th SS Panzer Division, supported by tanks from the 101st Heavy Tank Battalion and the remnants of the 89th Infantry Division, fought to hold a 14-kilometre front against the advancing Canadians. Among the casualties on 8 August was the tormentor of the British 7th Armoured Division – SS Obersturmführer (Lieutenant) Michael Wittmann. The German line buckled but did not break.

Monty had promised to rush his attack down the road to Falaise. On 11 August he told the commander of the new 1st Canadian Army, General Henry Crerar, to capture it within two days. But forty-eight hours later the Canadians were still 16 kilometres short of the town. Patton's XV Corps had advanced from the south without meeting any real resistance and had reached Argentan by the evening of the 12th. There he was ordered to stop and wait for Monty. 'We've got elements in Argentan,' Patton reported to Bradley. 'Let me go on to Falaise and we'll drive the British back into the sea for another Dunkirk.' That much he was prepared to say openly, but privately he was even more biting. The US XV Corps had been halted at Argentan by British 'jealousy', he complained. In fact the decision was Bradley's; he believed that, for all Patton's bravado, XV Corps might easily have been 'trampled' by a retreating enemy: 'Although Patton might have spun a line across that narrow neck, I doubted his ability to hold it.'

The Canadians were made to fight for every metre by a typically dogged German defence. Once again the Germans demonstrated great skill in shifting the little armour and artillery they possessed up and down the front to wherever a breakthrough was threatened. The Germans could muster only a handful of tanks on the Canadian front – less than fifty – against the Canadian II Corps' 700, and yet almost no progress was made in closing the gap on the 12th and 13th. A slow advance began again on the 15th, and Falaise was finally taken two days later. One building in the town held out. In a gesture of defiance a group of sixty grenadiers from the 12th SS Panzer Division had occupied the Ecole Supérieure in the town – they chose to fight to the last man rather than surrender. It had not been a distinguished chapter in the history of Canadian arms, and it is easy to understand the frustration of the Americans at Argentan. Monty had been exasperated too.

By the time the Canadians reached Falaise the shattered remnants of two German armies had begun pouring out of the bag. Less than 25 kilometres separated the Canadian and American forces at its neck. It was not until 16 August that Kluge issued orders for a general retreat. By then the British and Americans had squeezed what was left of fifteen German divisions into an area just 30 kilometres wide and fifteen deep. Hitler had kept up a steady stream of impossible orders for counter-attacks here, armoured thrusts there. It was clear to Kluge that he would finally have to act on his own initiative to save the men in 'the pocket'. 'It would be a disastrous mistake to entertain hopes which cannot be fulfilled,' he warned General Jodl, the chief of operations at OKW. 'No power in the world can realise them, nor will any orders which are issued.' Hitler suspected Kluge of secretly negotiating the surrender of the battered German armies – he confirmed the order to withdraw but relieved the field marshal of his post. His successor was a hard-bitten veteran of the Eastern Front – a specialist in 'fighting retreats' – Field Marshal Walter Model. Model's legendary toughness was immediately evident. He arrived at La Roche Guyon on the evening of the 17th to find the commander of the Panzer Lehr Division leaving the chateau. 'What are you doing here?' Model asked. 'I wish to inform Field Marshal von Kluge of my departure, for what's left of my division is to be withdrawn from the front to rest and refit,' Bayerlein replied. 'My dear Bayerlein, in the East divisions are rested at the front, and in future that will be the practice here. You and your units remain where they are.'

The Germans fought with great tenacity to hold the neck at Falaise open, and it was only in the last hours that order broke down and the retreat became a rout. Heavy casualties were inflicted by Allied fighter-bombers, flying up to three thousand sorties a day. The remnants of Otto Henning's reconnaissance battalion from the Panzer Lehr found themselves acting as an unofficial guide through the cauldron:

We had to rescue a large troop contingent because it had been surrounded. Their commanding officer wanted to break through in a westerly direction but this was impossible and we took them to the north. There were so many people on the roads, whole head-quarters units, medical staff, even ordinary cars with French civilians in them. During the day they didn't dare show themselves but chose instead to travel at night. The retreat moved towards Falaise and we also drove in that direction; the roads were very crowded and the attacks constant. Oberfeldwebel [Staff Sergeant] Keichel told me: 'We are pretty much surrounded, only one road is still open but under heavy fire, we will try tonight to break out along it.' We tried and came under heavy artillery fire but we pressed on and managed to get out at the last moment.

The commander of the 1st SS Panzer (Leibstandarte Adolf Hitler), General Teddy Wisch, was rescued by one of his staff officers – Hauptsturmführer (Captain) Hans Bernhard:

We were at the edge of a wood with the corps commander – a Wehrmacht general – Freiherr Hans von Funck. There was a big discussion – they were shouting at each other, everybody wanted to be right but nobody knew what was going on. Then the commander of the division and I set off across a field – eastwards – towards a village. There was an old stone bridge across the river there and I had an instinct that the enemy would fire on it. I told the commander, if I was in charge of the guns, I would fire in this direction. He didn't pay any attention and then suddenly there was an explosion. He was hit and his leg was gone. There I was – he was much bigger than me – he weighed 90 kilos or more. I was helpless. A Schützenpanzerwagen [armoured half-track] drove by – I knew the driver and ordered him to help us, 'the divisional commander is wounded and we have to get him out of here'. So we drove the SPW to the edge of the village where there was a big barn with a hayloft. I put him there and the staff doctor came to look at him and then we put him back in the SWP and set off towards the east.

It was a difficult journey down the crowded lanes, and the SWP came under fire: 'The driver was killed but the commander was OK. I went back on foot and found a unit from the 9th SS Panzer Division and they helped to get him out.'

One senior NCO from the 2nd Panzer Division remembered it like this:

The never-ending detonations, soldiers waving at us, begging for help – the dead, their faces still screwed up in agony, huddle everywhere in trenches and shelters, the officers and men who had lost their nerve, burning vehicles from which piercing screams could be heard and men driven crazy, crying, shouting, swearing, laughing hysterically – and horses, some still harnessed to the shafts, screaming terribly, trying to escape the slaughter.

After the capture of Le Mans, the US 90th had been one of the divisions Patton marched northward to Argentan. The division's artillery took up a position on the Bourg-St-Léonard overlooking the shrinking gap – as Major Hamilton recalled, it was an artilleryman's dream:

Frustratingly, my battalion had a defensive role at Falaise, we were on the right shoulder of the division to block any German attack from the direction of Paris, from the east. But I did get up on the high ground overlooking the gap, and to witness the destruction of an army is something that is beyond belief. It is awesome. The roads between Chambois and the Bourg-St-Léonard ridge were absolutely choked with armour, with vehicles, with horses, and the US 90th Infantry Division was given twelve additional battalions of artillery support on 18 August. Now, to give you some idea of this, one battalion of artillery has twelve guns in it, and the 19th Infantry Division had four battalions of artillery, that's forty-eight guns. You add sixteen more battalions and you have some 240 artillery pieces in the 90th alone, firing on those roads and the escaping German

7th Army. In addition to that firepower, of course, you had the infantry weapons, the tanks, the tank-destroyer guns, all pouring death and destruction on to those frantic columns, this German mess down there, this jumble. They were trying frantically to escape the noose that was being drawn around their necks.

On the 19th the Americans advancing from the south made contact with soldiers from the Polish 1st Armoured Division at the village of Chambois in the gap. But it was another two days before the cork was firmly in the bottle. In the last days between 20,000 and 40,000 German soldiers and most of their senior officers slipped through the Allied net. All but three of fifteen divisional commanders and four of the five corps commanders escaped to fight another day. The Reich would begin to rebuild its shattered armies in the west around them. It was to prove a costly error – the official Canadian history admits as much: 'Had our troops been more experienced, the Germans would hardly have been able to escape a worse disaster.' The two armoured divisions upon which the thrust southward had depended were fighting their first battle: 'less raw formations would probably have obtained larger and earlier results'. Nevertheless, the Germans had suffered a devastating defeat – that much was evident from the carnage on the battlefield they left behind.

'You couldn't walk without stepping on a dead horse or a dead man or some piece of flesh or an arm or a leg, it was the most hideous sight that one could imagine,' Major Hamilton recalled. 'I had mixed feelings about this. You can't be in combat for an extended period of time, and see comrades being killed and maimed, without developing an intense antipathy towards those that are doing it. In that respect this was a welcome sight, and on the other hand the sheer hideousness of it – it was something that touched one's feelings. So it hit you both ways.'

Major Martin of the 2nd Cheshires passed through the pocket with the 50th Division: 'I can remember the scenes of absolute carnage. The German army, apart from the Panzer divisions, relied on horse-drawn transport and so there were all these carts and dead horses in their shafts and the road was absolutely choked with dead and dying. And the stench – it was a really horrific sight and we were very glad to get past it and out on the road to the Seine.'

One of the British airmen who had contributed to the carnage visited the gap and wrote this account:

The roads were choked with wreckage and the swollen bodies of men and horses. Bits of uniform were plastered to shattered tanks and trucks and human remains hung in grotesque shapes on the blackened hedgerows. Corpses lay in pools of dried blood, staring into space and as if their eyes were being forced from their sockets. Two grey-clad bodies, both minus their legs, leaned against a clay bank as if in prayer . . . I stumbled over a typewriter. Paper was scattered around where several mailbags had exploded. I picked up a photograph of a smiling young German recruit standing between his parents, two solemn peasants who stared back at me in accusation. Suddenly I realised for the first time that each grey-clad body was a mother's son.

The Allies lost count of the number of prisoners they captured, but it is thought to have been close to 50,000 – another 10,000 bodies were found on the wreckage-choked roads of the pocket. Very few vehicles managed to escape through the gap – at least 220 tanks were counted, 1,000 artillery pieces, 130 half-tracks and 5,000 lorries and cars. An accurate estimate of the number of horses and carts was impossible because 'the stench of dead horses was so overpowering that where there was any number . . . that area had to be passed with all speed'.

The Battle of Normandy was over and the Germans had been decisively defeated. Hitler's hopes of holding France, of saving the Thousand Year Reich, died in the pocket. He had been the architect of the defeat. He bore sole responsibility for the impossible offensive at Mortain, and the stubborn refusal to withdraw when his two armies were threatened with annihilation. His personal involvement in the Battle of Normandy had been wholly damaging from the first. The decision to fight for every metre, to commit his divisions to the decisive battle so far forward, meant there were no significant German forces left between the Allies and the borders of the Reich. More than forty German divisions had been destroyed, 450,000 men lost – 240,000 of these were killed or wounded. The Allied victory in France had made the total, humiliating defeat of Germany inevitable. No longer could Hitler hope to defeat the 'Anglo-Saxons' in the west and then turn all his armies eastward. That summer the mighty German Wehrmacht had crumbled on both fronts. The Red Army had opened its offensive on 23 June and in two months rolled the Germans out of the Soviet Union – it was now knocking at the door of the Reich itself. 'The war was won,' Eisenhower later wrote, 'before the Rhine was crossed.'

On the eve of D-Day the Allied Supreme Commander had drafted a public statement: 'Our landings in the Cherbourg–Havre area have failed to gain a satisfactory foothold and I have withdrawn the troops . . . The troops, the air and the Navy did all their bravery and devotion to duty could do.' He had not needed to produce such a note. But as Professor Richard Overy has pointed out, it reflected the general anxiety about what was a highly risky operation. Churchill admitted to Eisenhower that he was haunted by a vision of the beaches 'choked with the flower of American and British youth'. Once ashore, the German divisions in Normandy proved tough and determined, and the Allies had good reason to thank the overwhelming air superiority they enjoyed from day one. It would have been a much closer-run affair in those first weeks if the German 15th Army had been committed to the battle – the Fortitude deception had been an unqualified success. Overlord had proved costly enough – with a daily casualty rate that often exceeded the grim trench struggle of nearly thirty years before. The Allies had suffered more than 200,000 casualties in seventy-seven days – 37,000 dead.

Field Marshal von Kluge did not witness the final collapse at Falaise. By then the poisoned chalice had passed to Model. Kluge was ordered to report to Berlin. He knew well enough that he faced disgrace, perhaps death – not for his failure in France but for treason – the latest on a long list of senior officers 'purged' in the wake of the July bomb plot. Kluge left La Roche Guyon at dawn on 19 August – his route to Germany took him through the First World War battlefields where he had served as a young officer. At noon he stopped for a picnic lunch in the shade of a small copse of trees and then, after writing one last letter to his brother, he broke open a cyanide capsule and held it to his face. Kluge was dead within seconds. In his last letter to Hitler, Kluge expressed his total loyalty, even in death, to 'my Führer', but he was blunt in his assessment of the defeat: 'Rommel and I, and probably all the leaders in the west who are familiar with the struggle against the materially superior Anglo-Americans, foresaw the development which has now taken place. We were not listened to.' Short of a miracle, only peace could now save Germany: 'my Führer, make up your mind to end this war. The German people have suffered so terribly it is time to put an end to this frightfulness.' After the madness of Mortain this was no more than a final expression of 'duty' – Kluge must surely have known that this appeal was not worth the paper it was written on.

Captain Helmut Ritgen had been ordered to Paris to supervise the refitting of the Panzer Lehr units and had missed the Falaise cauldron. It was a last 'goodbye' to Paris: 'We had a good time. We hadn't been able to spend any money for weeks. Now we paid the exorbitant prices for a menu and champagne. Later we danced. Under the circumstances, it was like dancing on a volcano.' There were drinks at the Hôtel Commodore, lunch in the sunshine of the Coq Hardi's garden, music and poetry with comrades, and some laughter. Ritgen remembered one joke in particular which brought secret, sad smiles: 'The Scene: The final days of the war in Hitler's command post in the mountains near

Berchtesgaden! A smoke-blackened figure emerges from a bunker and surrenders to the advancing Americans. Ripping his moustache from his upper lip he reports: "Agent 033 reports, mission accomplished – Germany destroyed!"'

General Patton had not waited for the last rites at Falaise. With Bradley's blessing he had sent the best part of three corps eastward to block the German flight across the Seine. The frantic pace of the pursuit did not slacken – Orléans fell to the advancing Americans, then Chartres and Dreux. On 19 August a combat team from the US 79th Division had crossed the Seine at Mantes-Gassicourt, and at dawn the following day the engineers started building a bridge across. The Third Army began establishing itself on the right bank just 48 kilometres from Paris. The chateau of La Roche Guyon was just a short distance down the river – Rolf Munninger was one of the last to leave Army Group B headquarters: 'I was in La Roche with the rearguard, the main body of the troops had left two days earlier. We realised that tanks were preparing to storm our HQ so we decided to leave during the night.' Munninger's last extraordinary mission in France was to the city of Reims:

I had orders to organise some champagne from the cellars there. I had a car with a driver. There was no organised defence, the troops just retreated from point to point – the officers had lost a good deal of their authority at this time. Everything was disintegrating, but my orders were to organise drinks. It had something to do with the general mood, but under Rommel I would certainly not have been sent to organise champagne.

The remnants of the Panzer Lehr's reconnaissance units did what they could to keep the ragtag army of infantry one step ahead of the Allied pursuit. Otto Henning remembered:

We had to reconnoitre carefully before driving through a village to make sure that the enemy had not yet been there and that we could get out if we entered it. The British and American advance was very fast and on a number of occasions we only just managed to escape. We drove through villages that had already been decorated with the Tricolour and the French civilians thought we were Americans. Our vehicles were so carefully camouflaged it was impossible to know whether we were friend or foe.

Henning's battalion had numbered twenty-five Puma tanks and eight other reconnaissance vehicles on D-Day – by the time it reached the German border there were just two vehicles left.

There were chaotic scenes on the banks of the Seine. Lieutenant Raimund Steiner of the 1711th Artillery Regiment had held the Merville battery at the mouth of the Orne until the night of 16 August. By then it was clear all further resistance was futile and the garrison had set out for the Seine and the road to Germany. Steiner crossed the river near Rouen: 'Horses were still harnessed to the guns and carts – they had not been fed for days. There were dead people lying around. There were no ferries left when we arrived there and we had to use rafts to row over.' Once across, Steiner was contacted by the garrison commander at Le Havre: 'He said, "We are going to defend Le Havre to the last man." I didn't want to and my sergeant, who was on the telephone, told him that he was stupid if he thought we would be his cannon fodder.' The band of eighty soldiers that left Merville had grown steadily as it crossed France – by the time it reached the Belgium border it numbered close to five hundred men. Steiner and his men were eventually caught by advancing Allied armour in Ypres and taken prisoner.

The British too had joined the gallop to the Seine. The Guards and the 11th Armoured Division were in the van under the new commander of XXX Corps – General Brian Horrocks. Major Martin of the 2nd Cheshires was summoned to a meeting to hear him speak:

He had all the officers together and he said, 'I congratulate you all on what you've done in Normandy. Thank God I wasn't there because

I'm a motoring general – not for me the attrition of Normandy. I'm going to get motoring and we're going to be up to Amiens in forty-eight hours and we're going to be in Brussels in four days.' And the effect on the morale of everybody after that awful period of stagnation in bocage was terrific, absolutely electric.

Trooper Austin Baker heard the same talk: 'Horrocks said that very soon we should be breaking out of the bridgehead and swanning off across France. That seemed absolutely incredible to us. We all thought that we should have to fight for every field all the way to Germany. But he was right.' The 'Great Swan' had begun – for eight days Baker and the 4th/7th Royal Dragoon Guards motored across France without firing a shot. The regiment reached the River Seine on 25 August – a heady 270 kilometres from Gold beach. On that day four Allied armies were established on the Seine. Free French and American forces, the best part of two more armies, were pushing up from the south. A task force of 150,000 men had landed on the French Riviera on 15 August – 'the other D-Day' – and were now preparing to join the battle proper. At his last major strategic briefing before D-Day, Monty had predicted the Seine by D + 90 – the Allied armies had managed it nine days ahead of schedule. Beyond D + 90 there were no detailed plans.

The great prize, Paris, fell on 25 August – the *Stars and Stripes* reporter Andy Rooney was with the 2nd French Armoured Division when it liberated the city:

There was no shooting really – the German soldiers were not attempting to defend Paris, but I have a clear memory of Germans being taken out of the buildings where they had worked or slept and they were all walking down the streets with their hands behind their heads, scared stiff, as well they might be, and there were a lot of French women hitting them with bottles and sticks and American soldiers were half-heartedly trying to protect them and load them on to trucks.

The following day the Free French leader, General Charles de Gaulle, led his officers on a triumphal, emotional march from the Arc de Triomphe to Notre Dame Cathedral for a service of thanksgiving. It was a Franco-American triumph – Monty had been invited by Eisenhower to take part in a victory parade but declined, a refusal that smacked a little of sour grapes. 'It is just as well,' Ike is reported to have said, 'the less I see of him the better it is for my blood pressure.' But there were representatives of the British army in Paris. As the Americans had approached, Lieutenant David Fraser and three friends from the 2nd Battalion (Armoured), the Grenadier Guards, decided to join them. Fraser managed to lay his hands on a car and the guardsmen set off on a 200-kilometre journey along roads packed with American armour – they reached the city in the evening. The tanks of the Free French armoured division were parked under trees in the Champs-Elysées. A wrecked German Panther was in the Place de la Concorde. 'Within our little group, although the junior, I had a certain "position", as it was known my family had lived in Paris before and at the start of the war,' Fraser recalled. 'The others gathered round. "Where do we go now?" "The Ritz," I suggested.' The hotel was full of American war correspondents – among them the writer Ernest Hemingway. Chic Parisiennes were perched on bar stools sipping champagne. Fraser was left with the impression that they had been there every evening since the war began. The contrast with the 'world of slit trenches, bivouacs and death we had left only hours before' could not have been greater, he recalled later.

Tentatively, we moved into the Ritz dining room and found it possible to order dinner, although the headwaiter apologised, in perfect English, for the limitations of the menu. Peter Carrington [Major Peter Carrington, who as Lord Carrington served as Britain's Foreign Secretary from 1979 to 1982] complimented him. 'Did you speak English when the Germans were here?' Face impassive, he simply said with a touch of reproof, 'I spoke German when the Germans were here.' They had left the hotel only hours before.

32. Monty visited Bradley's headquarters on 17 August 1944 to discuss the campaign beyond Normandy.

33. Liberation. Women applaud the Free French leader, General Charles de Gaulle, as he passes through Chartres in August 1944.

34. The other face of liberation. Old scores are settled in the city of Rennes. Armed bands of 'patriots' round up those accused of collaborating with the Germans. This man has already been beaten by the mob.

35. Locals cheer as American armour advances through Normandy.

36. The first tanks of General Patton's Third Army are cheered across the Seine to the north of Paris on 20 August 1944.

37. German soldiers watch the British air drops over Arnhem during Operation Market Garden in September 1944.

38. A Dakota drops supplies to the British 1st Airborne Division in Arnhem. The designated drop zones were overrun by the Germans and most of the supplies fell into their hands.

39. The north of the bridge over the Lower Rhine at Arnhem was held by the 2nd Parachute Battalion for four nights before they were overcome by German armour and infantry. The burnt and twisted remnants of German vehicles can be seen at the north end.

40. The nose of a heavy Horsa glider used to transport men and vehicles during Operation Market Garden. The British 1st Airborne Division was flown into Arnhem on 17 and 18 September 1944.

41. Sergeant Bill Higgs of the Glider Pilot Regiment – a D-Day veteran – took his Horsa into Arnhem on 18 September. He was seriously wounded in the fighting that followed.

42. A tired and frustrated Lieutenant Jack Reynolds is marched off into captivity at Arnhem. He demonstrates what he thinks of the German propaganda photographer with a traditional two-finger salute.

43. Dutch civilians are led from the burning ruins of their town. They welcomed the British as the liberators of Arnhem only to find themselves in German hands again a week later.

44. Panzergrenadiers were involved in house-to-house fighting as they tried to clear the British from the streets of Arnhem.

On 31 August Patton's Third Army crossed the River Meuse and its patrols were soon pushing on towards the Moselle near Metz. Three days later the British swept into Brussels and the following day seized the great prize – the port of Antwerp. Monty's 21st Army Group had advanced 400 kilometres in a week. Some of the headlines were at last being made by the British: 'We had regular newspapers and we heard the news on the radio and heard what it was saying about the speed of the American advance,' Major Peter Martin recalled. 'And I think the way it was reported stimulated a sense of rivalry.' Even Patton was impressed – at least he said so publicly: 'The perfectly phenomenal advance of the 21st Army Group under Field Marshal Montgomery has just completely buggered the whole [German] show,' he told war correspondents on 7 September. 'As a result of that, it would seem to me that the German plan of defence is completely dissipated. The advance of the Guards Division and the other divisions up there has been something magnificent.'

The 4th/7th Royal Dragoon Guards had pushed on at a less frantic pace, but the regiment enjoyed some of the glory when it led the 50th Division into the city of Lille. 'We were in the leading troop and as we belted along the road towards it I remember the squadron leader coming on the air to our troop leader and saying, "Splendid, you're going like a bomb – it would be nice if we got in first,"' Austin Baker recalled. 'Hundreds of thousands of people turned out and swarmed all over the tanks, beautiful girls kissing us, band playing the "Marseillaise", the lot.' It was impossible not to be moved by the joy of the liberated. 'There seemed to be no reason why we should stop,' Major Martin of the 2nd Cheshires recalled.

It was incredibly exhilarating and exciting. For the first time we were being greeted by civilians with open arms and flowers, it was marvellous. And of course, when things are like that, when you do get stopped it has an unpleasant effect on your morale. We got up into

Brussels and I can remember it was very difficult to move through the streets – someone put a baby on my map board in the front of my jeep and it marked it for me! But it was a tremendous welcome. We were told we were going to be there for four days, so I sent my platoons downtown to enjoy the fleshpots of the city. I went to bed at ten o'clock that evening, only to be woken an hour later by a dispatch rider saying we were to be off at first light to attack across the Albert Canal. First of all, how on earth do you find 150 soldiers dispersed all round Brussels – you knew the sort of places they would be making for but not where those places were. We left at first light the following morning with people running along behind the carriers, leaping on as if they were catching a train departing from the platform. We found ourselves twenty-four hours later doing an assault crossing over the Albert canal, back to the sudden reality of bullets and shells again.

Hidden among the cheering crowds, the flags and flowers were men and women who were sorry to see the Germans go. As British armour rolled on from village to town it frequently came across small groups of frightened and humiliated women – shaved, bruised and abused by their jeering neighbours. They were now on the losing side, traitors for money or love. Lieutenant David Fraser remembered passing through one village: 'the gutter in the long main street was actually running with the blood of French girls, some of whom were crouched pathetically on doorsteps, hiding their faces and their shame, beaten up, pouring out their grief'. The Guards passed on.

On 8 September the Guards Division established a bridgehead across the Albert Canal at Beeringhen – later that day the 50th Division pushed across at Gheel. Both assaults had met surprisingly stiff resistance. Major Peter Martin's machine-gun company had moved into the bridgehead that night:

As the mists began to clear in the morning, the enemy tanks started to take a toll of our tanks and transport. Our anti-tank guns were having no effect on the well concealed German armour, although a

German commander who stood up in the hatch of his tank, shouting in English, 'I want to die for Hitler,' had his wish fulfilled by one of my platoons. As the mist continued to lift, Du Pre, one of my platoon commanders, spotted a Tiger 100 yards away, facing in the opposite direction. He crawled to a Sherman nearby and directed its fire on to the Tiger, brewing it up. This seemed to mark the turn of the battle. The enemy may have sensed that they were in a very sticky position, and began to withdraw. As soon as their tanks came out of hiding, they were good targets for our anti-tank guns and Vickers. Du Pre's platoon engaged some German infantry withdrawing with a Mark IV tank. The tank turned, advancing in a menacing way. The platoon sergeant crawled on to a Sherman, directing the gun on to the Mark IV, brewing it up. The platoon, with their Vickers mounted on their carriers, drove in extended line straight for the enemy infantry, killing 15, wounding 20 and taking 60 prisoners.

By about 1400 hours, the enemy were all accounted for, hardly a man, gun or tank escaped. I found a young German hiding in a barn. I was very angry, one of my best soldiers, Private Price, had been killed during the night, just outside the barn. I thought this young man partly responsible. Price had been with me right through the war. I was hopping mad, pointing my finger at this young chap, shouting at him in fury. He was wounded. He said he was only seventeen, and had been in the army three months. His friends had stripped him of everything of value, including watch and money. I took him prisoner. It was one of those times, one was so angry that one was not in control − or hardly.

At the end of August a SHAEF intelligence assessment confidently predicted 'the enemy in the West has had it' and that 'two and a half months of bitter fighting have brought the end of the war in Europe within sight, almost within reach'. Eisenhower's chief of staff was prepared to publicly state, 'Militarily the war is won.' How could Germany fight on? Between June and September the Wehrmacht had lost more than a million men on its fronts east and west. Surely all it required was one last push over the Rhine and into the Reich. 'We must hurl ourselves on the enemy while he is still reeling,' Monty wrote in a directive to all commanders, 'let us finish off the business in record time.' But who was to finish it off and how?

CHAPTER EIGHT

ALLIES AT WAR

I t was Monty's finest hour. All the Allied commanders were scrambling for their share of the column inches, but no one deserved the credit, the public adulation, more than Monty. He was the architect of the victory in France. At no point had he allowed himself to be deflected by the anxious impatience of others. As land forces commander, he had acted in the best interests of the great Anglo-American coalition. He had allotted the less than glamorous role of hammer to the German anvil to the British at Caen. When Patton's Third Army succeeded, no one had been more pleased than Montgomery. There were many at SHAEF who were not prepared to concede anything to Monty, but Eisenhower's chief of staff, the fiery, abrasive General Walter Bedell Smith, was not one of them. He would write after the war that while 'no Montgomery lover' he had 'to give him his full due' – for certain types of operation 'he is without an equal' and Normandy was just such an operation. For his part Monty went out of his way to praise the American soldiers: 'We never want to fight alongside better soldiers,' he declared in his message to the troops on 21 August, and, in an oblique reference to the inter-Allied battle then brewing, he added, 'but surely it matters little who did this or that'. It did matter, it mattered a great deal.

Just six days earlier, the BBC had reported that the Supreme Commander, General Eisenhower, had taken personal charge of the land battle. 'A very curious incident,' Monty logged in his diary, 'this gave the impression that I had been deposed.' He dismissed it as a 'slip-up' but added, 'it will not do Ike any good; people will say that just as I am about to win a big victory, he tried to step in to scoop the reward'. Monty judged Ike 'far too decent' to do such a thing. He was quite wrong.

In the end it was not a question of decency, but of politics. Questions were being asked in Washington about Eisenhower's role. Why were the press talking about 'Monty's victories' when so many of the troops were American? Even President Roosevelt was concerned that 'Montgomery was hogging all the credit'. Eisenhower had resisted pressure to step in and take command until the victory in Normandy was won. But on 18 August he was prodded into action by a telegram from Roosevelt's chief of staff, General George C. Marshall: 'I and apparently all Americans are strongly of the opinion that the time has come for you to assume direct exercise of command.' Eisenhower was taken aback. 'It seems that so far as the press and the public are concerned,' he grumbled, 'a resounding victory is not sufficient; the question of "how" is equally important.' He declared himself indifferent to '*The New York Times* or any other newspaper', but he went out of his way to urge the War Department in Washington to emphasise his own 'supreme authority' in questions of strategy in the campaign to date. The following day he told Monty that it was his intention to take personal command of the Allied armies in the field from September. As two of Monty's most informed biographers noted: 'No one but a Monty, outstanding tactician though he had just proven himself to be, but isolated from political realities among his dogs, canaries and young men in that ivory tower of TAC HQ, so totally self-assured, could have been so blind to the writing on the wall.'

It was a bitter pill for Monty to swallow but it should not have been unexpected. By the end of August the balance of power in the alliance had shifted irrevocably. The United States was still pouring men and *matériel* into the European theatre –

by the end of the year it would have more than twice as many soldiers in the field as the British and Canadians. It had always been Eisenhower's intention to take over the direction of the campaign – the American administration and public would stand for nothing less. But as far as Monty was concerned a change of command was little short of disastrous. On the eve of D-Day Monty had written in his diary of Eisenhower that 'he is just the man for the job; he is a really "big" man and is in every way an allied commander'. During the course of the battle for Normandy his faith had been severely shaken. He had always had next to no respect for Eisenhower the strategist, so to hand over the day-to-day running of the campaign when the road to Berlin stretched before the Allies was in his judgement pure folly.

The two men were chalk and cheese. Monty conducted business in a crisp, efficient, soldierly manner – he was not impressed by the Supreme Commander's altogether more discursive style. After a meeting on 13 August he had complained to his friend Field Marshal Brooke that 'Ike is apt to get very excited and talk wildly – at the top of his voice!!! . . . His ignorance as to how to run a war is absolute and complete; he has all the popular cries, but nothing else.' Monty was supremely confident in his own fitness to command. He was rather a vain man; indeed, some judged him arrogant. In the last days of August he commissioned the distinguished artist James Gunn to paint him at TAC HQ. Gunn's brief was clear and he was instructed to be single minded in his task as Monty's ADC, Captain Johnny Henderson, recalled: 'Monty rang the bell he always had for us one day, and I didn't go straight away. "Where were you, Johnny?" he asked. I said: "Well, James Gunn was painting a portrait of me, because I have looked after him for the last fortnight." I had been sitting up in the mess having a drink at night with him. Monty said: "Well, send him here straight away, he came to paint me not you."' By contrast Eisenhower was the warm Kansas farm boy, open and generous to a fault – as Monty himself would have it, a thoroughly 'decent chap'. Bradley's ADC, Major Chester Hansen, met him many times:

There was no grandeur about him, he was very easy to talk to, not at all dictatorial or commanding in nature. He treated everyone as equal and he got along famously with his commanders. I remember going to Ike's headquarters once when he lived in the great red-brick mansion of a champagne king. I drove up in front of the house and rang the doorbell and Ike himself answered. He greeted me and then asked if I had any baggage with me, and I said, 'Yes, sir, in the jeep.' And he said, 'Well, let me help you.' So he came out to the jeep and helped me carry in my sack.

It was typical of the Supreme Commander's warm and charismatic informality. 'Eisenhower was highly respected by his staff, respected by Americans, and in all honesty we preferred an American as Commander to a Brit, because we thought an American might better understand the capabilities of our forces, what we were better at than the Brits,' Hansen recalled. 'We thought we were a little more aggressive. The Brits had taken so many beatings in so many places, we thought they're less likely to take risks than we are. We had built up the strength of our forces, we had a sector all of our own and it made sense to have Ike serve as the overall land commander.'

Monty and his staff viewed it rather differently: 'He liked Eisenhower, no one could fail to like him, he was an easy fellow,' Major Carol Mather of the TAC HQ staff recalled.

And Monty was quite happy to go along with him to begin with, but the trouble came, and we knew it would, when the American forces outnumbered the British. We knew Eisenhower might take over then, but we didn't believe it could happen really, because we had made such a success of the break-out and advance. We put it at the back of our minds. Monty viewed it with considerable misgiving because he didn't believe really that Eisenhower could do the job as well as he could, which was perfectly true.

Monty was an experienced, professional soldier who believed with absolute conviction that the war would be won more quickly and with fewer Allied casualties if the direction of the land campaign remained in his hands. In 'Notes on Future Operation' he argued that 'the great victory in NW Europe has been won by personal command. Only in this way will future victories be won . . . To change the system of command now, after having won a great victory, would be to prolong the war.' The change would 'prolong the war'. It was a blunt but heartfelt message. Monty gave his able and very diplomatic chief of staff, General Freddie de Guingand, the unenviable task of delivering it to Eisenhower. 'I knew I was arguing a lost cause,' de Guingand noted later.

At the root of Monty's frustration was the fundamental difference in strategy that had first begun to surface during the struggle for Caen. On 21 August Eisenhower met his staff at his advanced command post in Normandy to discuss plans for the campaign beyond the Seine. De Guingand was at the meeting and reported back to Monty later that day. It was unwelcome news. Eisenhower had decided to let the American 12th Army Group under Bradley continue its advance east towards Metz and the Saar. This was entirely contrary to Monty's plan for future operations, which called for a powerful Allied advance northward to clear the coast as far as Antwerp. The Allied armies would then strike towards the Rhine and the industrial heart of Germany, the Ruhr – a single, all-powerful thrust. 'We really did believe that if things went ahead according to plan,' Major Carol Mather recalled, 'the war could be over by Christmas.' Monty knew that as Britain entered its fifth year of war her soldiers and civilians were praying for just such a deliverance. Eisenhower's plan was quite familiar – the maximum amount of pressure at all points. He had come up with the same proposal in Normandy but then Monty had been able to fend him off. 'Bulling ahead' all along the line was how Monty described it, a push towards the Reich along the broadest of fronts. Eisenhower's strategy was in the mainstream of American military thinking, a doctrine, the historian Carlo D'Este has observed, that can best be described as 'the brute force method'. Bradley was schooled in the same doctrine – overwhelm your enemy by amassing a larger army and applying pressure until he breaks. Only a country with the men and *matériel* of the United States could place its faith in this brutally direct approach to war. The British, and Monty in particular, took a very different view. As D'Este points out, the British had buried nearly a million men on the battlefields of the First World War in the ruthless pursuit of this tactic. Neither Eisenhower nor Bradley had served in France twenty years earlier, they had seen nothing of the carnage caused by 'bulling ahead' regardless of cost, but Monty had, and he was haunted by the memory of it.

Eisenhower visited TAC HQ on 23 August at Monty's request. As soon as the pleasantries were over Monty announced, in typically high-handed fashion, that he wanted to see the Supreme Commander alone – 'the staff must not be present'. The two men retreated to the map caravan so Monty could lecture Ike on the strategic situation as he saw it. A Supreme Commander should 'sit on a lofty perch', Monty insisted, he should take a detached view of the overall campaign, not 'descend into the land battle and become a ground C-in-C'. If American public opinion demanded an American then Bradley should take the part – 'this suggestion produced an immediate denial', Monty later noted in his diary. Bradley was clearly not the man for such a role. Eisenhower refused to consider changing his mind on this point. Then Monty turned to the plans for future operations – fourteen divisions from the British 21st Army Group would be at the core of a northern thrust, but it would need the support of the Allied Airborne Army in England and at least twelve American divisions. Eisenhower could not agree. Bradley would be left with just one army and 'public opinion in the States would object'. 'I asked him why public opinion should make him want to take military decisions which are definitely unsound,' Monty recalled a few days later. 'He said that I must understand that it was election year in America; he could take no action which was calculated to sway public opinion against the President and possibly lose him the election.' As far as Monty was concerned this was 'the guts of the whole matter'.

By the time the two men emerged from the caravan they had managed to thrash out a messy compromise guaranteed to satisfy no one, least of all Bradley and Patton. Eisenhower refused to halt the American advance eastward to the Saar but was prepared to concede priority to Monty's northern thrust. His right flank would be supported by the left of the 12th Army Group – the best part of the US First Army. Monty would exercise 'authority to effect the necessary operational coordination'. It was agreed that the details of this arrangement would be spelled out in a directive to be drawn up by Eisenhower's staff in the days to come. Before it could be finalised the news was broken to Bradley and Patton. 'Bradley was madder than I have ever seen him and wondered aloud "what the Supreme Commander amounted to",' Patton logged in his diary. 'I told Bradley that if he, Hodges [commander, US First Army], and myself offered to resign unless we went east, Ike would have to yield.' Bradley chose instead to work on Eisenhower. He could count on the support of the same senior officers at SHAEF who had made life uncomfortable for Monty in Normandy. The directive that was finally drawn up did not give operational control of the US First Army to Monty, it merely 'authorised' him to effect 'necessary coordination' through Bradley. It was almost meaningless. 'That decision,' Eisenhower's biographer, Stephen Ambrose, noted, 'strengthened Montgomery's and Brooke's – and Bradley's and Patton's – conviction that Eisenhower always agreed with the last man he talked to.'

Bradley's own plan was for a thrust by the whole of the 12th Army Group – the US First and Third Armies – eastward across France and through the Frankfurt gap. It was a double thrust –

the British to the north, the Americans to the south and east. The British advance would be the poor relation. Eisenhower had rejected this plan, the northern advance was to be given priority, but Patton would be allowed to push on as far as luck and supplies would take him. The Allies would need a good deal of both. By the end of August it was clear that it would be impossible to maintain both the British and American thrusts. The SHAEF planners had not expected an advance across the Seine until D + 120 – by D + 90 sixteen American divisions were already more than 240 kilometres beyond it. Fuel, ammunition, food – everything nearly two million men needed to sustain them in the field was making its way from depots on or near the Normandy beaches, a journey of more than 600 kilometres. On 25 August the 'Red Ball Express' began rolling from Normandy to supply depots near Paris. Day and night hundreds of trucks – sometimes nose to bumper – ground along especially reserved roads. In their first eight days they delivered an indispensable 90,000 tons of supplies to the advancing armies. But it was not enough.

From a logistical point of view Monty's thrust northward seemed more promising than Patton's to the east. Eisenhower's own staff had reported that it was 'logistically practicable', but only if supply was concentrated in a single thrust. As the Channel ports began to open up to Allied traffic the supply line would shorten considerably. The route to the north and east offered the best hope of winning the war quickly. The Third Army's dash across the Seine to the Meuse was taking it farther and farther from the coast; a push into Germany by this route would be much harder to sustain. Patton had already begun to complain bitterly about his fuel allotment: 'I found that, for unknown reasons, we had not been given our share of gas – 140,000 gallons short,' he logged in his diary on 29 August; 'this may be an attempt to stop me in a backhanded manner.' The following day he met a sympathetic Bradley to complain that 'the British have put it over again. We got no gas because, to suit Monty, the [US] First Army must get most of it.' The Third Army commanders were instructed to push on until the 'engines stop and then go on, on foot'. Patton shared Montgomery's sense of urgency. 'We should cross the Rhine in the vicinity of Worms, and the faster we do it, the less lives and munitions it will take. No one realises the terrible value of the "unforgiving minute" except me.'

Eisenhower was assailed on all sides by bickering army commanders, all fighting for their share of fuel. Monty demanded priority for his advance while Bradley conspired with Patton to ensure that the US Third Army kept moving. 'The trouble with Ike,' Bedell Smith observed of his boss, 'instead of giving direct and clear orders [he] dresses them up in polite language and that is why our senior American commanders take advantage.' Monty was to make the same complaint after the war: Eisenhower's method was to talk to everyone and then seek a compromise: 'he had no plan of his own . . . Eisenhower held conferences to collect ideas; I held conferences to issue orders.' Eisenhower was the commander of a great coalition, his military judgement coloured by political necessity. As his biographer Stephen Ambrose noted: 'No matter how brilliant or logical Montgomery's plan for an advance to the Ruhr was (and a good case can be made that it was both) . . . under no circumstances would Eisenhower agree to give all the glory to the British, any more than he would agree to give it to the American forces.'

On 1 September Eisenhower took direct charge of Allied ground forces. In recognition of his service, and to soften the blow a little, it was announced that Monty had been promoted to field marshal, the highest rank in the British army. 'The Field Marshal thing made us sick, that is Bradley and me,' Patton wrote later that day. The Chief of the Imperial General Staff, Field Marshal Sir Alan Brooke, sent his congratulations, but also sounded a cautionary note: 'I should like at this moment of your triumph to offer you one more word of advice. Don't let success go to your head and remember the value of humility.' Wise words that were to be all too quickly forgotten.

The following day Eisenhower allowed himself to be persuaded by Bradley and Patton that with additional fuel the Third Army could 'push on to the German frontier' and be at the Rhine in a week. 'I hope to go through the Siegfried Line like shit through a goose,' Patton told the press corps. To help him on his way Eisenhower agreed to hold the US First Army in support. Monty was furious. There were just not enough supplies to support two offensives. Lieutenant Colonel Humphrey Prideaux was the quartermaster of the Guards Armoured Division, which was in the van of the British advance through the Low Countries: 'There were some very hairy moments, when we wondered whether we were going to be able to keep the division going. There was great competition for fuel, everybody was scrambling for it.' Prideaux was fortunate enough to have a brother on the Second Army's staff who was able to tip him off about supplies: 'I was occasionally able to find out from him about something that was on its way to another unit and we could divert it in our direction.' It was hand-to-mouth stuff – the Guards Armoured was reduced more than once to just a day's supply of fuel. Monty sent a signal to the new land commander on 4 September inviting him to choose: 'I consider we have now reached a stage where one really powerful and full-blooded thrust towards Berlin is likely to get there and thus end the German war . . . time is vital and the decision regarding the selected thrust must be made at once.'

Eisenhower had established a new 'forward' headquarters at Granville on the Cotentin peninsula. 'Forward' in this case meant 600 kilometres from the front. SHAEF staff had chosen a fine French villa with a wonderful view of Mont-St-Michel, but communication links were little short of a shambles. Monty was obliged to wait five days for the full text of Eisenhower's reply to reach him. It was a clear reaffirmation of Ike's decision to cross the Rhine on 'a wide front' and seize the Saar *and* Ruhr industrial areas. Monty was deeply disappointed: 'The command factor has broken down,' he complained to Brooke. 'He keeps saying that he has ordered that the northern thrust to the Ruhr is to have priority; but he has not ordered this.' At this most crucial of times Eisenhower seemed to have lost his 'grip' on the battle. The last time Monty had spoken to him in person was fifteen days earlier, and then only for ten minutes. 'Unless something can be done about it pretty quickly, I do not see this war ending as soon as one had hoped. It may well now go on into winter,' he warned Brooke. Monty had repeatedly asked Eisenhower to visit him and on 10 September he did. It was to be a tense, fateful encounter.

In keeping with Monty's custom that a senior officer should always visit his subordinate, Eisenhower flew to Brussels airport on the 10th for a midday conference. He had wrenched his knee and was in some pain, so Monty mounted the steps of the aircraft to join him. It began badly with Monty venting his frustration with Eisenhower's recent signals. He produced them from his pocket and waved them about the aircraft, and then in the language of the barrack room roundly condemned them as 'Balls, sheer balls, rubbish!' The angry stream-of-consciousness continued with a forthright denouncement of Eisenhower's plan – a dispersal of effort that would certainly end in failure. When Monty finally paused for breath, Eisenhower leaned forward and put his hand on the new field marshal's knee. 'Steady, Monty! You can't speak to me like that. I'm your boss.' Montgomery managed to mumble an apology: 'I'm sorry, Ike.' Eisenhower would not back down on his 'broad front' strategy and insisted that while the northern thrust had 'priority' this could not mean the 'absolute priority' Monty was demanding, and that scaling down Patton's drive towards the Saar was just out of the question. 'Monty's suggestion is simple, give him everything, which is crazy,' Eisenhower noted in his office diary later that day. Although no formal record of the meeting was kept it seems clear that one concrete decision was taken aboard Eisenhower's plane – final approval was given for an operation code-named 'Market Garden'.

The plans for a strike across Holland towards the Lower Rhine at Arnhem began to take shape in the first week of September. As Monty studied the maps in his caravan at TAC HQ it had become clear that to reach the Rhine the British 2nd Army would have to cross a number of formidable canals and rivers – the Germans were sure to make the most of them all. He had sent a signal to de Guingand on 3 September warning him that he was exploring plans for a 'considerable airborne drop to make certain of getting over MEUSE and RHINE. Order BROWNING to come to see me tomorrow and you come too.' The headlong dash across Belgium reached its climax the following day when the 11th Armoured Division seized the great port city of Antwerp. In the days since, the German line had begun to harden – it had taken XXX Corps four days to fight its way across the Albert canal at Beeringhen and then the Meuse-Escaut canal. The remnants of the German 15th Army were still holding the Dutch coast north of Antwerp. Until this substantial enemy force had been cleared from the Scheldt estuary the port would remain closed to Allied traffic. Eisenhower had made the capture of the Scheldt a priority, but when forced to choose between the port and Monty's ambitious plan to seize a Rhine crossing, he was unequivocal in his response: 'I not only approved Market Garden, I insisted upon it. What we needed was a bridgehead over the Rhine.' It was altogether more surprising that Monty pushed what was from the first a highly risky operation. But in those first days of September he could see time slipping away, and with it the chance to strike decisively at the Ruhr before winter. If the 21st Army Group could win the race to the Rhine it might just ensure the absolute priority Monty was seeking for his northern thrust. There was still the hope of Berlin by Christmas – just.

The idea seemed quite brilliant. A 'carpet' of airborne troops would be dropped along the road to Arnhem to seize the key river crossings over the Maas and Rhine. The Second Army would make a 'rapid and violent' thrust along the road, pressing through the airborne pockets to the final bridge. British armour would be required to crash through the enemy's line, and then push on for 100 kilometres along a single road that crossed six significant rivers and canals. This narrow corridor was hemmed in by small, open fields surrounded by drainage ditches – by no means ideal tank country. To meet the timetable imposed on the operation, the British would need to move 20,000 vehicles along the road in sixty hours. The Germans might choose to destroy one or all of the six bridges the British would have to cross. Everything depended on a crushing, lightning thrust and the tenacity of the airborne troops. These were drawn from the three divisions of I Airborne Corps under General Frederick 'Boy' Browning. The American 101st and 82nd Airborne Divisions were to secure the crossings in the Eindhoven and Nijmegen areas respectively, while the British 1st Airborne was 'to capture the Arnhem bridges, with sufficient bridgeheads to pass formations of Second Army through'. From the first it was clear it would require boldness and luck in equal measure. It was by necessity planned in haste. Problems that in other circumstances would have given a careful commander like Monty 'pause for thought' were brushed aside. The airborne operation would be the largest ever attempted – an armada of 2,000 planes and gliders was being assembled at airfields throughout the east of England. But this was still only large enough for half the airborne troops to be flown to the drop zones on day one – more flights would be required to bring the divisions up to strength. Good weather would be imperative for at least two days. It was quite evident too that the Allies were paying the price for the failure to capture senior German officers at Falaise. The staff at the US 82nd Airborne Division noted a new 'degree of control exercised over the regrouping and collecting of the apparently scattered remnants of a beaten army [that was] little short of remarkable. Futhermore, the fighting capacity of the new Battle Groups formed from the remnants of battered divisions seems unimpaired.'

The thrust of Market Garden would take the British away from the US First Army on its right, which was already on the point of crossing into the Reich near Aachen. But any question of an alternative 'full-blooded' Allied effort here was ruled out by a shocking, if not unexpected, attack on London.

Number one Staveley Road was all red brick and pebble-dash, with just a hint of mock Tudor – the typical 1930s house. There were hundreds like it in south-west London – three-bedroom, detached, prosperous and tidy. Mr Evelyn Clark was an accountant with an office on the nearby Chiswick High Road. 'E.J.' was working a little late on the evening of 7 September. His wife Edith was busy in the kitchen with supper, little Rosemary was already in her bed and five-year-old John was still up and playing in the bathroom with his boats. 'My sister was in the front bedroom – she was only three but a bit of a tomboy, fair hair, rather like my mother. I can remember I had been playing with wooden blocks, I thought of them as boats, and was having quite a good time,' John Clark recalled many years later. 'My mother called out and said, "John, it's time to go to bed." "Oh, Mum, please not yet." You know – how one does as a child. And because I hadn't been totally unreasonable that day she said: "Well, you can have another ten minutes before you've got to go and join Rosemary."' It was a little after seven o'clock in the evening. At the back of the house was a makeshift air-raid shelter, just a small iron lean-to. The family had not had much cause to use it; most of Hitler's V-1 flying bombs – 'doodle bugs' – were landing well to the east and south of Chiswick. John Clark recalled:

When the rocket hit us, the first thing I remember was when the airing cupboard in the bathroom crumpled. It was doing it silently, clearly I was deafened. The water ran out of the bath and I'd been leaning up against the wall between the bathroom and my parents' bedroom and it just disappeared. There was a heap of rubble underneath. I didn't quite understand what was happening. I called out to my mother – she had got as far as the dining room when a beam fell out of the ceiling. Fortunately it didn't crush her but it knocked her over and concussed her. It seemed like an age but it was probably five to ten minutes before the Home Guard came round. 'Come on, sonny. Jump down and we'll catch you,' they said. They were standing where my parents' bedroom had been. I wasn't going to jump for all the tea in China, I'm afraid. I had to be persuaded and in the end they did catch me.

The police took John to hospital to have his bleeding hand dressed – it was there he saw his sister, Rosemary, on a trolley. She was dead. Her lungs had collapsed in the blast and she had suffocated – the first victim of Hitler's new 'vengeance weapon', the V-2 rocket. A new, terrifying chapter had opened in the London Blitz. Number one Staveley Road had been all but demolished in the blast, Mrs Harrison at number three was also killed, and so too was a serviceman walking down the street. The V-2 rocket could carry a one-ton warhead 320 kilometres, before dropping towards the ground at a speed of 3,200 kilometres an hour. There was no warning, no defence.

The day before his meeting with Eisenhower in Brussels, Monty received a cable from Brooke's deputy informing him of the attack on London and asking him to report 'urgently' on his plans 'to rope off' the V-2 launch sites in Holland. A successful strike to Arnhem would help push the V-2 beyond range.

The 1st Allied Airborne Army had been ordered to prepare for action more than a dozen times since July, only to be told on the eve of each operation that it was no longer needed. There was widespread frustration throughout the Army – some of the best troops the Allies could call on were doing nothing. 'We were raring to go,' Sergeant Bill Higgs of the Glider Pilot Regiment recalled. 'I mean, we joined for that, you see, it's not a case of saying, "I hope we don't have to," we were ready to go.' Corporal David Salik of the Polish Parachute Brigade remembered the waiting as 'stressful, very exhausting and very frustrating'. No soldiers were keener to go into action than the Poles. That summer the Germans had suppressed the Warsaw Uprising with great brutality and then set about systematically destroying the city. The thirty-year-old Salik was a Pole and a Jew. He had been fortunate to escape the advancing German armies in 1939.

Although the 1st Allied Airborne Army was under the command of the American Air Force general Lewis Brereton, it was his smooth, well-polished deputy, General Sir Frederick 'Boy' Browning, who took ownership of the operation. There was a determination at 1st Airborne Corps to see this one through. As the commander of the 1st Airborne Division, General Roy Urquhart, observed later: 'By the time we went on Market Garden we couldn't have cared less . . . we became callous.' The troops were bored, and so were their commanders. 'We had approached the state of mind when we weren't thinking as hard about the risks as we possibly had done earlier.' There had long been talk in the messes of a Rhine operation, as Lieutenant Jack Reynolds of the 2nd battalion, the South Staffordshire Regiment recalled: 'We knew that sooner or later we were going to be in action and it didn't take a big brain to realise that crossing the Rhine was the next big obstacle which was suited for an airborne operation.'

The 'victory fever' that had gripped the advancing armies in France was just as strong on the other side of the Channel. It was unfortunate – to say the least – that none of the senior British commanders involved in the operation was prepared to listen to the reservations of their more experienced subordinates, Generals Ridgeway and Maxwell Taylor of the US 82nd and 101st Airborne Divisions to name but two. Of the mistakes made during the planning of Market Garden, one in particular stands out.

General Browning was fortunate to have on his staff at corps HQ a very bright young Oxford graduate with an eye for the detail of intelligence work. Major Brian Urquhart was the staff officer (GSO 2) with special responsibility for assembling all intelligence likely to be of use in airborne operations. He shared the same name and tartan 'set' as the commander of the 1st Airborne Division but was no relation. After the war Urquhart would serve as Under-Secretary-General of the United Nations. From the first Major Urquhart considered Market Garden strategically unsound; 'it seemed unlikely,' he later wrote, 'that they [the Germans] would fail to put up a strong resistance on the borders of the Fatherland.' Browning and his officers were in no mood to hear words of caution – they had begun to talk of Market Garden as 'the party'. 'I was increasingly unable to hide my own feelings and became obsessed with the fate of Market Garden,' Brian Urquhart wrote later. 'I was desperately anxious to go on the operation but I was even more anxious for it to be reconsidered carefully.' On 10 September, just seven days before the operation was to take place, Urquhart noticed a reference in a 21st Army Group intelligence summary to the 9th and 10th SS Panzer Divisions refitting in the Arnhem area. This report was confirmed by the Dutch Resistance.

Browning brushed aside his intelligence officer's evidence as 'probably wrong' and became annoyed when the point was pushed. But Urquhart was not prepared to let it drop – lightly armed airborne troops would be no match for two SS Panzer Divisions. He commissioned his own 'oblique' low-altitude photographs of the 1st Airborne's drop zones near Arnhem: 'The pictures when they arrived confirmed my worst fears. There were German tanks and armoured vehicles parked under the trees within easy range of the . . . dropping zone. I rushed to General Browning with the new evidence, only to be treated once again as a nervous child suffering from a nightmare.' Later that day Urquhart was visited by the 'chief doctor', who informed him that he was suffering from 'acute nervous strain and exhaustion' and ordered him to go on leave. The only alternative was a court martial for disobeying orders. On 15 September Major Urquhart left corps headquarters for home – the whole sorry episode left him 'deeply sceptical about the behaviour of leaders' and with the feeling that 'wisdom and principle' were no match for 'vanity and ambition'.

Urquhart's photographs were not the only piece of intelligence on the German Panzer divisions; there were indications aplenty from a very trusted source. The code-breakers at Bletchley Park provided a steady stream of decrypted signals which suggested a German armoured presence between Eindhoven and Arnhem. The Ultra material from Bletchley, Urquhart's photo reconnaissance and reports from the Dutch underground amounted to a substantial body of intelligence – important enough for Eisenhower's chief of staff, General Bedell Smith, to take the matter up in person with the new field marshal. But by then Monty had the bit firmly between his teeth. He 'waved my objections airily aside', Bedell Smith recalled.

The men who were to carry out the operation were encouraged to believe they would meet only light resistance. D-Day veterans such as twenty-four-year-old Bill Higgs of D Squadron, the Glider Pilot Regiment, were worried nonetheless:

We had a briefing. General 'Boy' Browning was there – immaculate, of course. I didn't like him. We had the 'spiel' about what we were going to do. 'Any questions?' he asked. I was acting squadron sergeant major and the boys were pushing me, saying, 'Bill, ask him why we are landing seven miles away when we landed next to the Orne bridges in the dark, and amongst Rommel's glider posts on D-Day.' So I opened my big mouth and I said: 'Excuse me, sir. Why are we landing seven or eight miles from the bridge in daylight when we landed . . .' And he stepped down half a step off the dais he was on and he put his finger out, upright, and he said, 'That is the plan.' And I never said another word. I was frightened to say any more than that. But what a plan it was.

When Higgs and the other glider pilots were dismissed there was a good deal of muttering about the distance from the drop zones to the bridge. General Roy Urquhart, the commander of the 1st Airborne Division, was an infantryman with very little experience of this type of operation, but he could see that the distance between the drop zones and the bridge all but ruled out a surprise attack by day. But his doubts were also brushed aside.

The morning of Sunday, 17 September 1944 was bright and clear, the conditions ideal for an airborne operation. The men of the 2nd South Staffordshire Regiment had arrived at Manston airfield in Kent the day before and spent a wet night under canvas. 'We had a rum ration issued before we went – which should have told us something,' Lieutenant Jack Reynolds recalled. 'We were not anxious as such but the adrenalin was flowing – there was certainly a flutter of excitement.' The 22-year-old Reynolds had won the Military Cross during the invasion of Sicily the year before when his glider had been one of the few to make the island – most had dropped short into the sea. Everyone was praying this operation would go more smoothly. The first wave was to take off from twenty-two airfields in the east of England and then pass along two corridors across the Channel to Holland.

'We whiled away time writing letters home, playing cards, joking, we cleaned our weapons until there was hardly anything left of them,' Thomas Smithson of the 1st Airborne's HQ Platoon recalled. Corporal Smithson had been just seventeen when he left his home in Birmingham for the army – in the three years since he had seen action with the Parachute Regiment in North Africa and Sicily:

We left our tents, which were just three fields away from the runway, for a drumhead service with the padre, then some sandwiches and tea. After that we lined up ready for the off. The planes were all marked off with big chalk marks and you were allocated your number. We'd got our parachutes fitted and kitted and were allocated our seats and we sat there and tried not to look frightened.

The air armada was to reach the landing zones at one o'clock in the afternoon and finish the drop by two o'clock. Half an hour later the heavy mortars of the 50th Division would begin opening up on enemy positions on either side of the road down which British armour was to force its passage to Arnhem. A barrage fired by seventeen artillery regiments would pick up the tempo of the assault, and as it crept forward the lead tanks of XXX Corps would break across the enemy's line and out along the road. The men of the Guards Armoured and 50th Divisions watched a sky thick with aircraft. 'We saw this incredible air armada go over us in an absolute unending stream,' Major Peter Martin of the 2nd Cheshires recalled. 'I don't think it occurred to us that anybody could possibly stop us. We might have delays such as roadblocks, but nothing serious.'

'We'd had a good take-off, the weather was good, and we had very little ack-ack [anti-aircraft] resistance on the way, it was copybook stuff,' Jack Reynolds of the South Staffords recalled. 'I shuffled towards the door, pulling my hook along with me,' Corporal Smithson recalled.

You stand together as close as you can – we were absolutely laden down with a big kitbag on our legs with all sorts of ammunition in it. All you can do is shuffle. My gun was strapped underneath my smock. We weren't frightened but we did have butterflies. We stood there watching for the light – the red one goes off and the green on and then it's everybody out the door as fast as you can possibly go. Cross your hands and out. You're hit by the slipstream, which knocks all the breath out of you, and then an almighty snatch as your parachute opens and then you start to float down. The sky was absolutely full of gliders and paras. A little bit of sporadic firing from round about but not a lot. By the time we looked down we were almost ready to hit the deck – in action you don't jump from a great height.

The first wave of British airborne troops was to land in the wooded country on the north bank of the Rhine near the village of Wolfheze. Corporal Smithson remembered:

We landed right up close to a mental asylum which had been bombed and was smoking. We had to make for that and make sure no Germans were left in it, because it overlooked the dropping zone. There were a few patients wandering around giggling – laughing at us. A young Dutch nurse had been wounded in the leg, just above the knee. She was bleeding heavily. We dressed her. I think she had about six field dressings on her by the time we'd all finished! Then we made off south to rendezvous with HQ in the village.

The main force on the first day numbered 5,700 men from the 1st Parachute and 1st Air Landing Brigade Groups. Urquhart had pushed for a larger drop but had been told no more aircraft were available that day. Inexplicably, priority had been given to General Browning's staff – thirty-eight gliders had been allocated to fly his headquarters into the Nijmegen area. The glider carrying Reynolds's mortar platoon landed smoothly enough: 'We took up defensive positions around the glider, and then, since the paratroopers had already secured the landing area for us, we reported to 1st Airlanding Brigade Headquarters.' Reynolds found the commander of the 2nd Staffords in conference with the brigadier: 'The brigadier summoned me and said: "Reynolds, you're my eyes, what's happening down the road?" So I looked slightly helpless. "Does he want me to walk?"' Reynolds managed to find a motorbike and set off towards Arnhem: 'There was a little bit of firing, obviously snipers, and we came across a burning tram. There was no point in going on under sniper fire, so I reported back that there was slight opposition.'

It was soon clear that opposition was anything but 'slight'. Not only were units from the SS Panzer divisions stationed in the area, but Field Marshal Model's Army Group B had established its headquarters in the western suburb of Oosterbeek. Model was sipping a pre-lunch aperitif when the British aircraft passed overhead. With the hard-bitten Prussian efficiency that was typical of the man, he directed a battle group of the 9th SS

Panzer to take up blocking positions in the west of the town. The British were soon caught up in fierce fighting along the roads to the bridge. Only the 2nd Battalion of the Parachute Regiment under Colonel John Frost managed to reach its objective. By dusk Frost's paras had established themselves at the northern end of the road bridge – the railway crossing had been destroyed by the Germans as they approached it. The divisional HQ was held up near the landing zone by stiff German resistance farther down the road. 'It's like a line of dominoes,' Smithson recalled. 'One down and they all stop all the way along the line.' Urquhart had gone forward in a jeep and found himself trapped in the western suburbs of Arnhem. Not until the 19th, two days later, was he able to resume command of the operation.

As the British and American airborne soldiers fought to establish themselves in the corridor, the vanguard of XXX Corps – the tanks of the Irish Guards – began to push on down the road to Eindhoven. Lieutenant David Fraser of the 2nd Battalion (Armoured), the Grenadier Guards, was waiting in the column: 'there was a delay, of a very familiar kind – we were at immediate notice to move, but "something" in front was holding things up. It was nearly dark by the time we moved across "Joe's Bridge" and it was already clear that the race to Arnhem via Nijmegen would be liable to delays. A significant number of Irish Guards tanks were burning beside the road.' By the evening of the 17th the Irish Guards were 10 kilometres short of Eindhoven, their objective for the day.

On the morning of the 18th the British people opened their newspapers to read that the commander of the 1st Airborne Army and his staff were 'highly elated' at the successful progress of the operation – 'successful beyond all expectation'. That was not how it appeared to the men on the ground at Arnhem. In the absence of Urquhart the CO of the 1st Airlanding Brigade had taken command of the division. 'Early next morning I was summoned to brigade HQ again and told to get the mortar platoon organised to march off down the road to the bridge,'

Lieutenant Jack Reynolds recalled. 'I heard the brigadier say, "I want all-round defence, three hundred and sixty-five degrees!" With that thought I went off down the road. I had no map – there were, I believe, just three maps in the battalion. I was told to go up the road and use my initiative. That's all I was told.' Reynolds's platoon set out for Arnhem with the mortars in hand carts: 'It was archaic, I felt quite embarrassed at times. But it was the only way you could transport them.' When he reached the main road running parallel with the Rhine, he tried to contact his company commander by radio. There was no reply; it was impossible to pick up a signal:

As we made our way along the road we were enfiladed from the opposite bank of the Rhine by the Germans who were using 75mm guns and 88s. You couldn't get off the road because the houses all had gardens with chain-link fencing. You couldn't get under cover, so you had to move along as fast as you could and spread out as much as you could. My platoon signaller had this terrible radio, an 18 set strapped to his back, and in the middle of quite a lot of stuff flying around he suddenly called out, 'Sir, message from brigade head-quarters.' 'What is it?' I said rather irritably. With a perfectly straight face he said, 'The men may shave.' That is Staffordshire humour. I told him to dump the radio and grab a Sten gun. The radio was useless, completely useless.

Radio communications between headquarters and the battalions was almost impossible – the sets had been prepared for flat coun-tryside, not for the wooded slopes of the Rhine.

Reynolds's platoon pressed on at a 'smart walk' through the leafy suburbs of Oosterbeek down the hill towards the northern bank of the Rhine until it reached what the British called 'the monastery' – the municipal museum on the western outskirts of Arnhem. 'I came up to D Company's [the 2nd South Staffords] position – they'd been ambushed and there were a lot of casu-alties lying about,' Reynolds recalled. The commander of D Company and his number two were wounded and one platoon commander had been killed. Most of the men had taken cover in houses near by. The situation appeared chaotic.

I left my platoon at the monastery, under cover, and I went forward to look for a way through to the bridge. I knew the Germans were ahead of me, but how far ahead I didn't know. To avoid sniper fire, we wore black boots and didn't carry map cases, because they were two things the snipers looked for – brown boots and a map case meant an officer. Not that we needed a map case – we didn't have a map. Unfortunately whichever way you turned there was firing, mortar fire put down by the Germans. And I found myself being driven farther and farther away from the river.

The 1st and 3rd Battalions of the Parachute Regiment managed to force their way to within a kilometre of the bridge, but attempts to push through were broken up by the enemy. Frost and his men – no more than 700 in total – were completely cut off from the rest of the division. The German forces in the town had been steadily strengthened overnight and at first light they began to press home the attack on the British with tanks and heavy mortar fire.

It was not until the afternoon of the 18th that the rest of the British airborne reached the dropping zones. Sergeant Bill Higgs's glider was in this second wave: 'We started to take a lot of flak. You could see all the puffs of smoke coming across the drop zone. Lots of gliders were hit. The skipper [on the towing aircraft] said, "Can you see the DZ?" "Yes, Skip, I can see it and I'm pulling off." I had a nice landing in a ploughed field.' But this time the Germans were expecting the landings, and as Higgs' glider bumped and slithered to a halt it came under small-arms fire: 'I'd landed as close as I could to the trees so we could get under cover, and we all ran out and under these. When we turned round there was a poor guy hanging out of my glider who'd been hit.' Higgs pressed on towards the town but was also held on the outskirts:

We went right down to Arnhem, near the music centre there, and my captain said, 'Higgs, come on, we'll have a look and see what's going on.' We got as far as the road looking up to the bridge, but we couldn't get any farther, they pinned us down with machine-gun fire. The guy up in the cupola of the music room – a Jerry sniper – was shooting at our men there. I remember they got the Vickers machine gun and turned it up and nearly blew the top off the cupola. Anyway, we realised we weren't going to get through there. There was armour coming up, and Jerry flame-throwers.

Corporal Smithson was amazed to find he was fighting a familiar and formidable enemy: 'I went upstairs in a house to see if there were any Germans there, and I'm sneaking upstairs with a Sten gun and this German officer comes across the landing at the top, so I shot him and he fell. He'd got the full SS Panzer regalia. Bloody hell. We're only supposed to meet sick, lame and lazy. Not these sorts of blokes.'

By the second day the battle for Arnhem and its outskirts had begun to take shape. The lightly armed British were already struggling to hold on in the streets and leafy suburbs of the town. Small isolated groups of airborne soldiers found themselves squeezed by the enemy's advance. The front line shifted continuously. 'Everywhere you turned, you came across a group of chaps wandering around just looking for orders,' Jack Reynolds recalled. 'The object was to get back to a coherent unit, where there was a reasonably senior officer who knew what was happening. At that stage it was perfectly obvious to me we were never going to get to the bridge.'

Repeated, bloody attempts were made by the paras and South Staffords to force a way through, but they were all broken by the enemy's armour. By the evening of 19 September the 1st Airborne had taken up positions on the western edge of Oosterbeek around Urquhart's HQ at the Hartenstein hotel. Over the coming days the men dug in on its perimeter were under continuous shell and mortar fire – beset on all sides by SS Panzer troops. Everything depended on XXX Corps.

The US 101st Airborne Division had some 20 kilometres of the main route to capture and hold. It had managed to take Eindhoven on the second day, but the British advance was held beyond the town on the Wilhelmina canal. The Germans had blown the main canal crossing at Zon and valuable time was wasted building a bailey bridge. At a little after six o'clock on the morning of the 19th the Guards armoured column began rolling forward again. They pushed on northward, and within three hours had managed to link up with the US 82nd Airborne Division near Grave. 'I remember the impressive silhouette of the long bridge across the Maas at Grave,' David Fraser of the Guards recalled. 'This had been captured by the American airborne troops and took us across the first main water obstacle at about ten o'clock in the morning of the 19th September. By then the operation had been running for over forty hours and was already well behind schedule.' General 'Boy' Browning was on the bridge to see the Guards across; by then he was already a worried man. Later that day the advance halted again in Nijmegen where the road and railway bridges across the Waal were heavily defended by the Germans. After three days of fighting the airborne divisions were still waiting for the final air drops that would bring their units up to strength. Thick fog over the Channel had bedevilled attempts to complete the airlift. David Fraser wrote later:

By nightfall on that first Nijmegen evening with our groups at various points in a town strongly held by the Germans it was evident that Nijmegen would have to be cleared methodically, and that that would take time. This was grim news – the operation had now been running about fifty-five hours. Our hopes of rushing a bridge across the enormous Waal had been frustrated. The bridge itself had not been blown, but to cross the river would need a battle.

Behind the vanguard of the advance, 20,000 British vehicles were crammed on to a road under constant threat from German counter-attacks. Field Marshal Montgomery had sent a couple of his liaison officers from TAC HQ to report on the progress of the advance – one of them was Major Carol Mather. His experience was to clearly demonstrate the difficulties the British were confronting on the single road:

The road was no wider than an average room, but there were side roads coming in, and when the Germans counter-attacked there was a major mêlée on the road. There were polders on either side and the land fell away to marshy fields. It was a scene of the utmost confusion, but everything was at such close quarters that no one really was able to use their weapons very much. I remember we were almost in touching range of Tiger tanks and I found myself to the north of this bottleneck, cut off from home. That was the only occasion when I failed to deliver my message to Monty at six o'clock in the evening. We spent the night sleeping in a kind of tavern of some sort, but the next day we managed to get through this blockage and report to Monty. And this did give him an absolute bird's-eye view of the situation and the difficulties. And he was obviously quite worried by this.

On the 20th the Guards and 82nd Airborne Divisions began clearing the town of Nijmegen, and during the afternoon an assault party of American paratroopers managed to cross the broad, fast-flowing Waal in canvas boats. In the teeth of heavy enemy fire they pushed on to capture the northern end of the railway bridge. At the same time the tanks of the Grenadier Guards made a lightning attack on the road bridge and crossed before it could be blown. Only 18 kilometres of road separated XXX Corps from the men fighting to hang on at Arnhem. Messages had been picked up that day from the 1st Airborne HQ, and they left no doubt about the parlous state of affairs there: 'Essential every effort is made to ensure earliest arrival Guards Division at Arnhem. Situation at bridge critical.' Another warned that 'earliest relief essential'. In spite of this the decision was taken to hold the Guards at Nijmegen for the night and continue the advance the following morning.

By then it was too late for the men holding the northern end of the Arnhem bridge. The 2nd Parachute Battalion had fought with grim determination to hold its small bridgehead against overwhelming odds. The Germans had systematically set about destroying resistance with close-quarters fire from tanks and mortars. The streets around the bridge were reduced to rubble as Colonel Frost's men were forced to retreat from one burning building to the next. Their heroic attempt to hold the position finally ended in the early hours of 21 September. By then all the PIAT anti-tank ammunition was spent and the exhausted, bloodied remnant of the British assault force was down to its last rounds. The Market Garden plan had given the task of holding the bridge to the division. It was to be relieved in forty-eight hours. It had been held by a force of only battalion strength for four nights. Half the airborne troops had been killed or wounded during the battle.

By the morning of the 21st the rump of the 1st Airborne Division was under very determined siege on the western outskirts of Oosterbeek. A few small, isolated groups of British soldiers that had been cut off by the German advance were still struggling to stay a step ahead of a ruthless street-by-street search. Lieutenant Jack Reynolds of the 2nd South Staffords had been on the run from street to street for the best part of three days:

The adrenalin was still flowing and that keeps you going for quite a long time. That and water. There were forty-eight-hour ration packs but water was in short supply after twenty-four hours. And sleep catches up with you eventually. I did have the odd catnap. The tanks stopped at night – they were too vulnerable to attack – but then at first light they were off again. You had a reasonable warning that a tank was going to attack and there was no point in being smoked out like that, better to keep moving.

Lieutenant Reynolds had a very narrow escape when he was spotted in the open by a German tank:

I liked to have a pipe and my paisley scarf around my neck. I always wore it. Good-luck symbols, you know, they make you bullet proof. You think. The pipe was empty usually, but in my mouth. We saw this tank below and I turned round to inspect it. It moved pretty smartly into action – fired, and a solid shell hit the bank in front of me. Debris shot up and hit my face, rammed the pipe halfway down my throat. So I had four or five broken teeth. A near-miss.

By the end Reynolds's group had shrunk to just three:

I eventually met up with the battalion intelligence officer. So I must have been somewhere near battalion headquarters, which was what I'd been trying to reach. We'd taken cover in this slit trench and just before dusk fell the tanks rolled in over the top and passed us, so we knew then we were surrounded. I got up in the middle of the night and there was something standing by the trench – it was a German tank. I put my hand on it. But there was no way we could break out, because the Germans had got men everywhere. So, in the morning, the battalion intelligence officer, who spoke German, got up and addressed a German officer. He marched us off.

Reynolds remembered feeling a sense of 'absolute fury at High Command' that the whole thing could have been so 'utterly incompetent': 'I was just thinking of all the people that I'd seen there, people I knew, who had been needlessly wounded or killed in an operation that was quite frankly ill conceived, ill planned and ill executed. There was nothing to commend it and I believe it was merely the megalomania of a certain field marshal.' Something of the anger and sheer bloody defiance he felt was caught in an iconic photograph taken a short time after his capture:

They were telling people to put their hands on their head. And I thought, to hell with that. Then I saw this German propaganda photographer, I can see his face now, and his forage cap. He pointed his camera at me, so I gave him the Agincourt sign – I felt that was only reasonable. I thought I might get a bullet for it, but the Germans obviously thought I was just giving the victory sign . . . but it was the universal English sign for derision.

Remarkably, on the day the men at Arnhem bridge were forced to capitulate the first of the Poles were finally dropped on the southern bank of the river. They were dropping into enemy territory with the Rhine between them and the 1st Airborne. No one had briefed them on the mess that greeted them on the ground. Corporal David Salik remembered the men in his aircraft singing during the flight across: 'We were just eager to jump out. We were young Poles and the Germans were a real enemy – they were murderers, and we all, Jew and non-Jew, felt very strongly that we should fight them. And we are all ready to fight.'

The Poles dropped under fire into the arms of the waiting Dutch Resistance. 'The Germans were shooting at us like ducks,' Salik recalled. 'We just immediately formed units and tried to get to the river. We had to cross it but there was no transport – there were only a few boats left and I was lucky enough to get one to the other side.' The Poles were soon drawn into the desperate street fighting. One incident above all others was to mark David Salik for life:

There was one chap, I told him, 'Wesolowicz, you jump now.' And he fell in front of me with a bullet, and we couldn't go out and save him because the sniper was there. Later I jumped and the rest jumped but we couldn't attend to that chap. I had for years later a guilty feeling that I sent him out; if I'd done the same I could have been killed myself. But I was the one who said, 'Jump now.' So, this was my personal sorrow. I knew him quite well, I go to his grave now.

A grim struggle for survival was being waged around the perimeter of the 1st Airborne box on the western outskirts of Oosterbeek. Corporal Smithson was dug in close to the divisional HQ in the Hartenstein hotel:

Towards the end of the battle their plan was to systematically destroy every house by putting a shell into it. They were moving forward wiping them out one at a time up the road. You can't fight tanks with rifle and bayonet. So you just moved back until there was nowhere to go back. Towards the end there was hardly anything that wasn't burning or smoking or collapsing or falling down. There were so many casualties they were wheeling them in all the time. They'd got nowhere to put them, so they were lying outside and getting wounded again by shellfire. It was always a question of: 'Any news of XXX Corps? No news.' During the night you'd hear the clanking and movement of armour and you'd think, oh, it's XXX Corps, but when it got light – no XXX Corps. It was German armour.

The dropping zones had been overrun by the enemy and almost all attempts to supply the hard-pressed defenders came to nothing. 'There was no way of saying "not there, we're down here",' Smithson recalled.

We did everything we could, like waving, but it didn't make any difference. I watched one afternoon – seven Dakotas came in slow and low. And the Germans had God knows how many 88mm guns and they shot the first five down – bang, bang, bang. Down they came. Missed the sixth one and shot the seventh one down. They were all dropping their stuff towards what is now the cemetery but you just couldn't get it. So we had no supplies whatsoever.

The *Daily Express*'s war correspondent, Alan Wood, was among those trapped in the shrinking perimeter:

It has been a nasty morning – cold and misty – and the Germans are plastering us plentifully with mortars, big guns and 88's. The 88's are worst because you do not hear them coming. Machine guns have just opened up on the right. In this patch of hell our men are holding a few houses that still stand. An old lady in black stumbled out of one of them a few minutes ago, and a British soldier ran out and put his arm round her. She collapsed and he carried her down to safety in a cellar. It is now just five days and five nights since we flew out from England. God knows from what secret source of strength these fighting men have drawn the guts which have kept them going.

In the last hours of the battle Sergeant Bill Higgs's luck finally ran out:

We were just fighting and running in the end because we were outnumbered, all our ammunition had gone. We were in a beer garden, I can remember having a bottle of Cherry Herring in my hand and the officer was looking at the map and he said: 'We'll get up there, Staff, and stay up there and try and hold that until we get news of what's going on.' But as we set off up the brow of the hill they could see us coming, and they let us have it from a house up there. The officer said, 'Let's get in,' and so we ran towards it. I fired a burst of my tommy gun and the next thing I knew I was down on the deck. I thought I'd lost my arm because the bullet went through it and into my chest, through my lung and out my back. I was lying on the ground there and I thought my arm's gone and then I felt the tommy gun and I thought, oh my God, I haven't lost my arm. Two guys turned me over on to my back and then dragged me down – I could still hear the bullets hitting the top of the road. They got me under the brow of the hill and into the yard of a house. There was a young Dutch couple in it, they'd got an old velvety armchair and they sat me in this. I could see how frightened this young couple was, so I said, 'Get me out of here, they'll mortar this place, let's get down to the main road, these people are frightened to death.'

Higgs was taken to an old farmer's hut and left there with another twenty wounded men:

The blood was running out of my mouth. It was filling up my lung, my breath was coming shorter and shorter, and I felt I was going to drown in my own blood, so I thought I've got to move, I was panicking. I thought if I don't move I'm going to die. Behind me was a rusty old rail they'd used to tie up the cattle and I got hold of this and I pulled myself over and as I did this I pulled off the patch the Red Cross blokes had put on my back where the bullet had come out. I could feel the hot blood running out of my lung down my back and within five minutes I was breathing again. And then the Germans came.

By the evening of the 23rd, units from the 43rd Wessex Division had pushed on from Nijmegen to the southern bank of the river near Driel. But attempts to reinforce the airborne bridgehead on the opposite bank came to nothing. On the night of 25 September the order was given to withdraw the remnants of the 1st Airborne: 'We thought we might get killed there, but we didn't think of getting out, running back,' David Salik, the Polish medic, remembered.

It was a terrible slap in the face for us to have to camouflage ourselves and make our way back to the river. I had a golden Star of David somebody had given me as a present. So on the way to the river, I took it off and buried it, because if there was any chance of being taken prisoner, I didn't want to demonstrate that I was Jewish. I felt that being Jewish, I hadn't got a chance at all. Most Poles, Jews or Christians, felt the same way.

'On the last day it was incessant shelling, mortar and machine-gun fire, just hell – it had been for a couple of days,' Corporal Thomas Smithson recalled.

We were wringing wet, starving hungry and very much depleted in men. There was nothing left to do but come out. You were supposed to withdraw a section or unit at a time. My little crowd was made up of all sorts of people – there was a glider pilot, a couple of artillery blokes, a couple of engineers, and the four of us from my section. We were to move back at fourteen minutes past ten on the Sunday night. We were still getting shelled. We checked ammunition, I had a few rounds left. We'd got two Bren guns and both had a magazine on them and I said, 'The drill is we're going down to the river and we're going to move when I shout go and we're not going to stop. If we run into any problem, both Bren guns open fire and we rush forward. We ain't stopping, don't get down. Keep moving and we'll get to the river with a bit of luck.' We started off and had travelled about 30 yards when mortar bombs landed in front and behind. And I looked round and there were four of us left standing. One of the lads on my right had taken a shrapnel wound under his ear, took a lump of jaw away and he was bleeding like mad. We stuck a field dressing on it, and got him on his feet and started off again.

When Smithson reached the Rhine he was bundled into a canvas boat manned by Canadian engineers:

There was a little outboard on the back and an enormous current running. We got the wounded man into the boat and off we started. There was incessant machine-gun fire. You could see the tracer bullets bouncing around everywhere. It was as much as the boat could do with the engine flat out to keep pace with the current. We'd got almost across the river when a load of machine-gun tracer bullets went into the front of the boat. The boat went down, and I made the last few yards up to my neck in water and finally scrambled up the river bank. We were met by a military policeman in a jeep and a very sorry state we were. The jeep went to get some more transport, but in the meantime we came across a German half-track that was knocked out, and there was a gallon of rum in it, so we had an enamel mug of that, which just about knocked us out – we didn't care what happened then.

Market Garden was over. Of the 10,000 men flown into Arnhem 1,400 had been killed and over 6,000 taken prisoner – half of them wounded. Just 2,183 men made it back across the Lower Rhine. Sergeant Bill Higgs of the Glider Pilot Regiment had been packed into an ambulance by the Germans and bumped along the road to hospital. On the ward he asked a medical orderly the name of the hospital: 'The orderly said, "I'm sorry, I can't tell you that." He wouldn't tell me anything. I'd thought, if I can get through the window, if XXX Corps are coming our way . . . but of course they never did come our way, did they? That was the tragedy.' Ten grim months as a prisoner of war were followed by two years of treatment in a sanatorium in 'Blighty'. Higgs had been a PT instructor with the regiment, a champion boxer, but the wounds he had picked up at Arnhem left him fit only for 'a light job in the open air'.

To the 1st Airborne's losses must be added 3,542 casualties in the American divisions and a further 3,716 in the Second Army. On the first day of the battle Allied aircraft had dropped hundreds of thousands of leaflets over the occupied Netherlands with a message from SHAEF promising 'the hour for which you have been waiting so long has struck'. The people of Arnhem had paid a terrible price for their brief 'liberation'. An elegant, once prosperous town of 100,000 people was devastated by the fighting and the fires that were left to rage unchecked. When the battle was over there was a further price to pay for 'collaboration' with the British. The Germans embarked on an orgy of looting in the town.

On 27 September a tired, demoralised General Urquhart arrived at Monty's TAC HQ to a warm welcome. A map was produced and he was asked to give the field marshal a blow-by-blow account of the battle. The following morning Monty emerged from his office caravan with the text of a message: 'I've written this,' he told Urquhart. 'I wrote it in my own handwriting, and I've had it typed since. And I'm giving it to my Public Relations Officer to issue to the Press. I want you to have this.' It was the handwritten original of the press release. 'There can be few episodes more glorious than the epic of Arnhem and those that follow after will find it hard to live up to the standards that you have set,' Monty had written. 'In years to come it will be a great thing for a man to be able to say: "I fought at Arnhem."' He was sure 'All Britain' would say, 'you did your best; you all did your duty; and we are proud of you'. It was heartfelt but also a first step in the creation of the glorious Arnhem 'myth' – an example of what the American historian Carlo D'Este calls 'that eccentric British practise of turning military disasters such as Dunkirk into glorious occasions'. 'We're wonderful at that, aren't we? Wonderful at that,' Jack Reynolds of the South Staffords observed. Reynolds had a good deal of time to consider the shortcomings of the operation – he spent the remainder of the war in Oflag 79 in the Reich: 'We were hammered, absolutely hammered. We'd done our best, the soldier on the ground right up to the battalion commanders, but higher command . . .'

Both Montgomery and Eisenhower worked hard during and after the war to dress up Market Garden as something short of the disaster it undoubtedly proved to be. The catalogue of mistakes in the planning and execution of the operation is long and well rehearsed. The single road through difficult country, the dependence on an extended period of fine weather, the choice of drop zones, command and control – a depressingly long list. Much has been made of the decision to hold the Guards at Nijmegen on the night of 20 September. Peter Martin of the 2nd Cheshires rose through the ranks of the post-war army to become Major General Martin – in his judgement more might have been done by the Guards Armoured:

The road ran along the top of embankments through flooded fields – you were very much a sitting target, but all the more reason why one should have gone on by night. I think if you ask the Guards, 'Why did you stop, why didn't you go on,' they tend to say, 'Yes, why didn't we?' Whether they would have had any decisive effect one can't know, but there was undoubtedly a possibility of their having done something.

Monty had urged XXX Corps to ensure that its thrust was 'rapid and violent, without regard to what is happening on the flanks'. It was Patton's oft-stated creed of leaving 'the flanks' to look after themselves, but one is left with the suspicion that a similar thrust by the Third Army would have been driven forward with a good deal more vigour.

Few of the senior commanders involved in the planning and execution of Market Garden emerge with much credit, but Montgomery and Eisenhower should shoulder the lion's share of the blame. General Sir David Fraser – the young Guards officer who played his part in the vanguard of XXX Corps' advance – asked, 'Why Arnhem?' Market Garden took the British 2nd Army away from the Ruhr and the most direct route into Germany. Monty had hoped to bypass the formidable German border defences known as the Siegfried Line, and then envelop Germany's industrial heartland from the north. But even if the bridge at Arnhem had been crossed, a good deal more would still have remained to be done before British armour broke through to the north German plain. With supplies still making the painfully long journey northward from Normandy, it would have been almost impossible to maintain an advance beyond Arnhem. The key to supply was Antwerp, but no effort had been made to wrest the approaches to the port from German hands. Priority had been given to Arnhem rather than Antwerp, although the ultimate success of Market Garden depended on the supplies that control of the port would ensure. 'Operation Market Garden was, in an exact sense, futile,' General Sir David Fraser wrote. 'It was a thoroughly bad idea, badly planned and only – tragically – redeemed by the outstanding courage of those who executed it.'

Market Garden had frankly amazed Bradley and Patton. 'Had the pious teetotaling Montgomery wobbled into SHAEF with a hangover, I could not have been more astonished by the daring adventure he proposed,' Bradley later wrote. But Bradley had 'never reconciled' himself to the venture. Why had a man with a reputation for careful preparation allowed himself to be blinded by the risks? Monty believed passionately in his single, all-powerful thrust into the Reich as the best, perhaps the only, path to a decisive victory. If Market Garden had succeeded his case would perhaps have been proven. But although pride would never allow Monty to admit it, without that last bridge across the Rhine the operation could only be counted a failure. No one had quite predicted 'the miracle of the west' – the extraordinary speed with which the defeated enemy had been able to collect himself, turn and hold the line. Victory at Arnhem gave renewed hope to the hard-pressed German armies in the west. There would be no First World War-style collapse at the borders of the Reich but rather a determined defence. Market Garden had left the British 2nd Army with a large salient in enemy-held Holland, and it was obliged to fight hard to keep it in the weeks following the collapse of the operation.

The Germans had also stolen a march on the Allies at Antwerp. They had recognised the vital importance of the approaches to the port, and whilst Allied eyes were turned towards the Rhine they had ferried more than 60,000 men to the north bank of the Scheldt. Clearing them from the estuary was to prove much more difficult than Monty had expected. Eisenhower had made the opening of Antwerp a priority, but had been coaxed and cajoled by Monty in turn into making Market Garden the immediate objective. 'Of all the factors that influenced Eisenhower's decisions,' his biographer Stephen Ambrose observed, 'the one that stands out is his desire to appease Montgomery. At no other point in the war did Eisenhower's tendency toward compromise and his desire to keep his subordinates happy exact a higher price.' The opening of Antwerp became inextricably caught up in sparring over strategy. After Market Garden, Eisenhower considered the debate about his 'broad front' strategy over. 'What this action proved was that the idea of "one full-blooded thrust" to Berlin was silly,' he wrote after the war. Monty did not agree. On 5 October he put in a rare appearance at one of the Supreme Commander's conferences. SHAEF had at last moved from Granville to the Trianon Palace hotel in Versailles, and it was here that the Allied commanders in the west met to thrash out priorities. There was forthright criticism of the failure to open Antwerp. The naval C-in-C, Admiral Sir Bertram Ramsay, pulled no punches: 'Monty made the startling announcement that we could take the Ruhr without Antwerp,' he recorded in his diary. 'This afforded me the cue I needed to lambast him for not having made the capture of Antwerp the immediate objective at highest priority and let fly at the faulty strategy we had allowed.' The Allied armies had practically ground to a halt for lack of supplies, Ramsay noted. There was widespread agreement around the table – even Monty's greatest champion, Field Marshal Sir Alan Brooke, was critical: 'I feel that Monty's strategy for once is at fault. Instead of carrying out the advance on Arnhem he ought to have made certain of Antwerp in the first place . . . Ike nobly took all blame on himself as he had approved Monty's suggestion . . .' In spite of this, 21st Army Group's priorities remained the same – plans for another push to the Rhine and then the Ruhr were given precedence over the operation to clear the Scheldt.

Monty could have been in no doubt as to Eisenhower's views for on 9 October the Supreme Commander restated them explicitly in a personal message. If Antwerp was not open by the middle of November 'all operations will come to a standstill', he warned. Monty was to give this, the most important of 'all our endeavours', his 'personal attention'.

Remarkably, the field marshal chose this moment to reopen the question of command – Eisenhower's fitness to direct the battle. A more sensitive man would have realised that after the bruising debates on strategy, after Arnhem and Antwerp, this was singularly poor timing. On 10 October Monty launched an intemperate broadside at the Supreme Commander: 'both British and American armies are involved in the capture of the Ruhr,' he noted, 'but the job is not handed over to one commander; two commanders are involved, i.e. the commanders of the two Army Groups [Montgomery and Bradley]'. Operations had become 'untidy and ragged'; the close control that had brought victory in Normandy had gone. Monty declared himself prepared to serve under Bradley – anyone who could get a grip on the battle; enough of compromise, this was 'suitable in polit-ical life . . . in battle very direct and quick action is required'. Eisenhower was furious. The real issue was not his own posi-tion as commander but Antwerp. Supply to the American armies in the field was in a 'woeful state', he pointed out in his tart reply; 'by comparison you are rich!' He went on to restate his position on command and warned that if Monty found it 'unsat-isfactory' the matter would have to be referred to 'higher authority for any action they may choose to take, however drastic'. There was no question of a single commander in the north for 21st Army Group was in no position to launch an attack on the Ruhr. The American armies, Eisenhower explained, would attack towards the Rhine under Bradley's direction when the time was right. Monty was in no position to take it farther and said so: 'You will hear no more on the subject of command from me,' he replied. 'I have given Antwerp top priority in all operations in 21 Army Group and all efforts will be now devoted towards opening up that place. Your very devoted and loyal subordinate, Monty.'

The Germans were finally rooted out of the Scheldt only on 8 November; it was another three weeks before the first Allied convoy entered the port. A battle that might have been won easily in the first week of September cost the 1st Canadian Army 12,873 dead, wounded and missing. It had taken sixty days to open. By then Dieppe, Boulogne, Calais and Ostend were also in Canadian hands, but none of these had the deep-water capacity of Antwerp.

It was a troubling time for Eisenhower. One by one the Allied armies had ground to a halt. Patton had pushed and pushed and wrung every gallon of fuel he could from Bradley and SHAEF, but the priority of supply Monty had won for Arnhem severely restricted the Third Army's operations. Eisenhower gave him the liberty to make what he could of his supplies and he had chosen to launch ill-advised assaults on the old French forts around Metz. Brilliant in pursuit, Patton was proving altogether less imaginative in his conduct of the set-piece battles the Third Army was waging against strongly held positions in Lorraine. Bradley's ADC, Chester Hansen, reported casualties in the Third Army to be running at more than a thousand a day. Patton pressed on through November and Metz finally fell on the 22nd of the month. During the three and a half months that lapsed from September to mid-December, the Third Army advanced less than 40 kilometres. The American First Army took Aachen in October – the first German city to fall. But the following month it became embroiled in a series of bloody encounters in the dense, unforgiving Hürtgen Forest to the south-west of the city. The battles to break through the Siegfried Line and close the Rhine cost the US First and Ninth Armies 57,000 casualties that autumn – a further 70,000 men fell victim to the rain, the mud and the first frosts of winter – trench foot, respiratory illnesses and combat fatigue were all commonplace. The grim struggle in the forest was 'basically fruitless', the official American historian recorded, and 'should have been avoided'.

It was an inglorious chapter, one Bradley wisely chose not to make much of in his memoirs. The warm optimism of summer was forgotten – it had become a bleak battle of attrition once again. Morale in the American armies had begun to suffer. Desertions were up, so too were incidents of rape, murder and looting. 'I visited Ninth US Army today,' Monty wrote to Brooke on 22 November. 'The general picture is one of tired, cold, and wet troops operating over country which is a sea of mud. There are no proper plans for giving hot food to the forward troops and some men have not had a hot meal for four days. 84 US Division tried to attack BEEK today and though the artillery fire came down according to plan the wet and tired infantry did not even attempt to start.' For Monty there were disturbing echoes of the First World War. The Allied armies were attacking everywhere but going nowhere. 'The handling of the battle,' he concluded, 'is I am afraid amateur.' Monty's own experience indicated clearly enough how little control Eisenhower was exercising on the campaign. A whole month passed in which he neither saw nor spoke on the telephone to his Supreme Commander. 'Our present strategy all seems so futile,' Monty grumbled to Brooke. 'Of course the Russians may do great things . . . but if we rely on getting deep into Germany on what we do on the western front, I am afraid we may prove a broken reed.'

Monty had agreed not to raise the issue of command and control again, but by the end of November he believed duty required him to break that promise. On 27 November he wrote to the War Office with a blunt assessment of the strategic situation. A new plan was needed but responsibility for it had to be wrested from the Supreme Commander: 'Eisenhower is useless.' The following day Eisenhower visited TAC HQ at Zonhoven in Belgium for what would inevitably be a difficult meeting. The two men retired to the map caravan, the scene of so many bruising encounters, so Monty could deliver his broadside in front of the great chart of the Western Front. The Allies had suffered 'a strategic reverse'; a new plan was needed, one that would 'get away from the doctrine of attacking in so many places that nowhere was the attack strong enough to achieve decisive results'. The Allies needed to concentrate strength on a 'main selected thrust-line'. The theatre divided naturally into two main fronts to the north and south of the Ardennes forests and a commander should be appointed to take 'full operational control' in each. Monty battered away for three hours and clearly felt he had won the day. Eisenhower seemed prepared to put him in 'operational command' of a powerful Anglo-American army group in the north for a thrust on the Ruhr. Bradley would retain responsibility for the 12th US Army Group but would answer to a British field marshal. The 6th US Army Group would hold the line in the south, but the great weight of the Allied effort would be concentrated in the north against the Ruhr.

Could the Supreme Commander wriggle out of it? All of it had been agreed without reference to Bradley and the staff at SHAEF. Experience suggested that Eisenhower could be swayed by the last commander to put his case. So it was to prove again. Eisenhower spent the evening of 1 December with Bradley, the following night at SHAEF headquarters with his chief of staff, Bedell Smith. Four days later he was back with Bradley and on 7 December the two men drove together to Maastricht to meet Monty. By then everything had changed again. Monty found himself confronted by the old SHAEF-American plan for offensives north and south, to the Ruhr and Frankfurt. His own plan for a full-blooded thrust on the Ruhr with fifty Allied divisions was dismissed by Bradley as nothing more than an attempt 'to command the whole show'. He had already warned Eisenhower that he would not serve under Field Marshal Montgomery. Bradley was cock-a-hoop. Maastricht was the most significant victory he had won in months. 'He is now in the position to exploit a gain in either sector,' his ADC, Chester Hansen, observed in his diary. 'General Bradley believes the best approach to the German heartland may be made through the southern approach on the Frankfurt axis.' It had been agreed in September that the main thrust across the Rhine would be in the north, but all options appeared open again.

'The whole thing is really rather a tragedy,' Monty wrote after the Maastricht meeting, 'we shall split our resources, and our strength and we shall fail.' The War Office in London, Field Marshal Brooke, the Prime Minister – all shared many of his misgivings, but British voices were drowned by the all-American roar. 'Ours is now the main effort,' Hansen recorded in his diary. 'Monty has arrested himself in the abortive Holland push . . . his forces are now relegated to a very minor and virtually unimportant role in this campaign where they are used simply to protect the left flank of our giant steamroller.'

'The experience of war is that you pay dearly for mistakes; no one knows that better than we British,' Monty wrote on 7 December. The enemy would demonstrate how 'dearly' just nine days later.

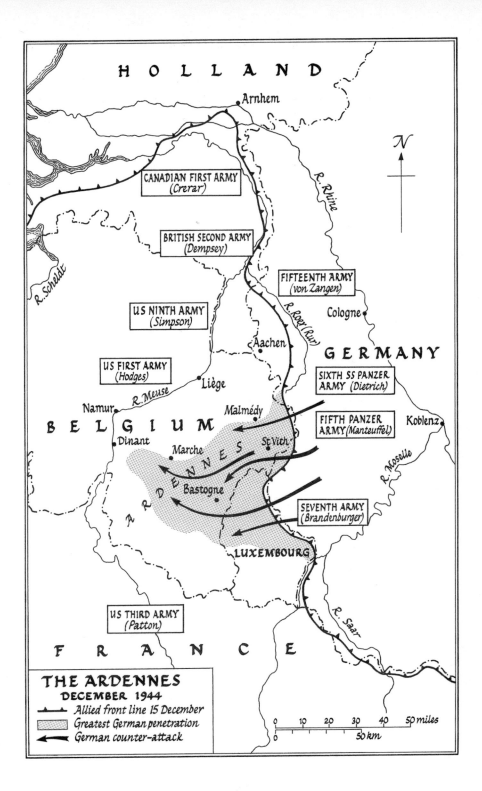

THE ARDENNES
DECEMBER 1944
⊢▲⊣ Allied front line 15 December
░░░ Greatest German penetration
◄━━ German counter-attack

CHAPTER NINE

THE BULGE

I t was a day for celebration. First there was the wedding of Eisenhower's valet in the chapel of the French kings at Versailles – 'a sweet ceremony, but everyone shivered,' Harry Butcher noted in his diary. Eisenhower hosted a jolly reception in his own quarters at Versailles and presented the newlyweds with a hundred-dollar war bond. Then to cap it all there was the news that the President had nominated 'General Ike' for a fifth star. If approved by the Senate, and who could doubt that it would be, Eisenhower would become General of the Army. In his diary for the day – 16 December 1944 – his aide, Harry Butcher, observed that 'the man who always cautioned his family not to expect him to be promoted has risen from lieutenant colonel to a five-star general in three years, three months, and sixteen days – six promotions, one about every six months'. The fifth star made 'General Ike' equal in rank at least to Field Marshal Montgomery. Even on this happiest of days it was impossible to entirely forget Monty. A letter had arrived from him that morning reminding Eisenhower that he had wagered five pounds that the war would be over by 31 December 1944. Monty had scribbled in his own hand, 'For payment, I think, at Christmas.' If the war was not won in the next nine days, Eisenhower replied, Monty could look forward to the money in his Christmas stocking.

Later that day Bradley arrived to discuss the manpower situation at the front. All but one American division was committed, SHAEF had no reserves to speak of, athough by December some front-line units were seriously under strength. The broad-front strategy required more men, more of everything, and the casualties of autumn had not been replaced. It was a cause for concern, but not one that would be allowed to overshadow Eisenhower's fifth star. 'We had a glass of Champagne or two to celebrate the event – Ike felt pretty good about that fifth star,' Bradley's ADC, Chester Hansen, recalled. 'General Bradley joshed him on all of that rank, and wondered how they could get along now with all that rank in the house. The whole thing was treated with a great deal of levity.'

The new General of the Army had just joined SHAEF staff in the war room when the meeting was interrupted by his intelligence chief. A number of German attacks had been launched in the Ardennes that morning against positions held by the US First Army. This was, Bradley later admitted, 'the most vulnerable point in our entire Allied line' – 100 kilometres of front held by just four divisions, one of them the rookie 106th. Bradley had dismissed the possibility of an attack through the Ardennes in winter – enemy armour would surely struggle in its densely forested slopes, its frozen lanes. The first reports of the German attack did nothing to shake his confidence. It was merely a local action, he declared, designed to draw men away from Patton's offensive to the south. 'That's no spoiling attack,' Eisenhower observed, the Ardennes was of no value in itself, the Germans must be in pursuit of something altogether more important. Bradley was to send help at once – both the 7th and 10th Armoured Divisions. The only reserves available to SHAEF were the veteran 82nd and 101st Airborne Divisions. They had taken a battering in Holland and were being rested out of the line near Reims, but Eisenhower decided to put them on immediate stand-by for deployment. Little more could be done that night so both men settled down to a bottle of whisky and a few hands of bridge. It was a worrying end to a happy day.

By the morning of 17 December the situation was clearer. Eisenhower was right. The latest intelligence suggested the

Germans had launched an all-out armoured thrust through the Ardennes. It was certainly no 'localised attack'. The Allies had been caught completely off guard.

'We didn't think the German had that much left in him,' Hansen recalled.

We thought we were on the road to the end of the war, and suddenly he turned around and had the initiative, and yes, we were surprised by the strength of the German attack. We learned of this at Ike's headquarters and General Bradley immediately sped back by car to his quarters in Luxembourg. We had his Packard and his very good driver, Sergeant Stowe. We drove about ninety miles an hour all the way back across France to Luxembourg. And I remember when we got to Luxembourg – we were in the railroad building there – General Bradley ran up the stairs and into the war room to look at the wall maps and saw all these red arrows indicating the German advance. And General Bradley, who almost never used profanity of any kind, said, 'Where in the world did that son-of-a-bitch get all of that stuff?' He was surprised by the strength of the attack in so many, many places.

Bradley would devote a number of pages in his memoirs to an explanation of why he was caught unawares. He was anxious to emphasise that his 'embarrassment was not unique' and that on the very day of the attack Monty had produced his own appraisal concluding that 'the enemy is at present fighting a defensive campaign on all fronts' and was quite unable to turn to the offensive. But Bradley had been warned by SHAEF's intelligence chief only days before that the Germans might be preparing for an attack through the Ardennes. He had dismissed the risk as insignificant and had made no attempt to prepare for it. By the time Bradley reached his headquarters the enemy had been pressing forward for thirty-six hours. 'Our lines have not been built in depth with the offensive mindedness of our command,' Hansen confided in his diary on the evening of the 17th, 'it is difficult to estimate how much of a drive they might be able to contain.' Eisenhower's broad front was being cruelly exposed.

The Germans had managed to assemble three armies to the east of the Ardennes – a total of twenty divisions – without giving away their intention. The blow had fallen at 5.30 a.m. on 16 December. From his observation post atop a water tower near the village of Hosingen, a soldier with the American 110th Infantry Regiment could see the strange flicker of countless tiny lights through the morning mist. He telephoned his report through to his company commander. Within seconds the source of the lights became all too clear as the darkness was rent by the whine and crunch of shellfire, the prelude to the heaviest bombardment the Germans had launched in the west. The seriousness of the assault was not at first appreciated by either the corps commanders or the staff at US First Army. A stubborn defence held the attack at Monschau in the north of the Ardennes but a powerful thrust by five SS Panzer divisions was able to force a gap in the line between the US V and VIII Corps. To the south of this the 5th Panzer Army attacked on a 50-kilometre front held by just five regiments from the US VIII Corps. Bradley's thin line fought desperately to hold its position but it was an impossible task and by the morning of the 17th the Germans had broken through.

As the Germans poured more men and armour into the hole they had punched in the front it became clear they were intent on splitting the British and American army groups. The Panzer divisions were racing for the River Meuse and beyond that the port of Antwerp. How had an enemy that had seemed beaten in September – hard pressed in the west and east – managed to rebuild and launch an attack that threatened to inflict a serious reversal on the Allies?

The idea of a 'rebound offensive' had been born three months earlier as the crushed remnants of the German divisions in France retreated towards the borders of the Reich. It came from a man used to thinking the unthinkable – Adolf Hitler. It would be a last desperate gamble upon which the fate of Germany would turn, a winter offensive where the Allies would least expect it, one that defied military logic – a thrust through the tightly forested hills of the Ardennes. If his armies could force their way across the Meuse and push on to Antwerp, the Western Allies might yet be persuaded to talk peace. It was an impossible dream and Hitler's senior commanders knew it. Both Field Marshal von Rundstedt, who had been reinstated as commander-in-chief in the west, and Field Marshal Model, the commander of Army Group B, attempted to shake their Führer's faith in the offensive, but to no avail. Rommel's old 'desert hands' at Army Group B considered Model to be a 'Hitler general', 'but even he objected', *Gefechtsschreiber* (battle writer) Rolf Munninger recalled; 'of course he couldn't make himself heard'. Munninger was to become part of the small team at Army Group B headquarters charged with drawing up plans for the new offensive: 'We were housed in a barracks-like building near Krefeld which was easy to guard. We were specifically told not to say a word to anyone. The secrecy was kept one hundred per cent because the plans were held in such a tight group – only five or six people at Army Group B were involved in the complete Ardennes planning: Field Marshal Model, his chief of staff, the ordnance and operations officers and "little me" – Munninger.'

There was no more enthusiasm for the offensive among the army and divisional commanders. Even Hitler's most dedicated followers – SS Oberstgruppenführer [Colonel General] Sepp Dietrich for one – were dismayed at what appeared to be another suicidal *Führerbefehl*. Dietrich had spent two and a half months rebuilding the SS Panzer divisions mauled in France – the 1st SS (Leibstandarte Adolf Hitler), 2nd SS, 9th and 10th SS and the 12th SS or Hitler-Jugend. It seemed to Dietrich that the new 6th SS Panzer Army was being asked to perform nothing short of a miracle. 'I grew so big with these plans,' he observed sarcastically after the war.

I had merely to cross a river, capture Brussels and then go on and take the port of Antwerp, and all this in the worst months of the year, through the Ardennes where snow was waist deep and there wasn't room to deploy four tanks abreast, let alone six armoured divisions; when it didn't get light until eight in the morning and was dark again at four in the afternoon. The divisions had just been reformed and contained chiefly raw, untried recruits; and at Christmas time.

'I can't do this, it's impossible,' Dietrich told the operations chief at OKW. General Jodl just shrugged his shoulders – it was a *Führerbefehl*.

The Panzer Lehr Division had also been rebuilt for the Ardennes offensive and was to spearhead the attack of the 5th Panzer Army. It had been able to salvage only a handful of vehicles from the fighting in France, but a core of experienced officers and *Unteroffiziere* had returned to the Reich, among them the desert veteran, twenty-year-old Sergeant Otto Henning:

We had wondered what would happen when the fighting reached Germany. The civilians asked us soldiers what to do, 'Should we flee, should we stay?' We told them what we had seen in France, that if the enemy troops moved quickly through a region nothing would happen but if the front stabilised in a region everything would be destroyed. We knew well enough that German towns had already been destroyed. We saw the bomber formations crossing the skies over us in Normandy on their way to Germany. I had sleepless nights at the thought that a German officer might be forced to give the order to German guns to open fire on a German village full of women and children. I saw such things in France. We went to war to protect the homeland and now to see our own artillery fire into our own villages, I could not understand it. I wondered for days, what will happen?

A grim determination to keep the enemy out of the Reich had been at the heart of the 'miracle of the west' – the remarkable stiffening of the German line that autumn. The Red Army had already reached the borders of eastern Germany and contact with family and friends there had become difficult. Rolf

Munninger witnessed the distress of one staff officer at Army Group B headquarters: 'He was a very good pianist, and I can still see him today, playing Beethoven's Moonlight Sonata and crying like a child. This may sound ridiculous but it describes the mood perfectly. He was an East Prussian and he had lost contact with his whole family.' It had been a struggle to re-equip the armies in the west for the Ardennes offensive; fuel in particular was in short supply. The Reich's Minister of Armaments and War Production, Albert Speer, had visited Army Group B during the planning of the offensive to explain the difficulties he faced. 'I had to record his orders and ideas,' Munninger remembered.

He came quite frequently to lend his support and to buck us up. He was constantly on the move to see how the best weapons, in this case the latest tank we had, could reach the front. There was a tank factory in the east, about 150 to 200 kilometres from the front, but there was no fuel to transport them overland, the railway no longer functioned because of constant bombings. I remember Speer saying, 'I could give you the best tanks built, but there is no way I can get them to you.'

The Panzer Lehr Division had refitted at Paderborn under its resilient commander, General Fritz Bayerlein: 'I received sixty new tanks, and I demanded more flak guns, in view of my experience with air attack. In training I stressed anti-air discipline. We practised on the basis of an air attack every day. By this time the fuel shortage was such that much of our actual manoeuvre was theoretical. I got no fuel at all for training – legally. To get my division ready, I wangled fuel by personal connections.' Just four days before the start of the Ardennes offensive Bayerlein was summoned to Field Marshal von Rundstedt's headquarters at Ziegenberg Castle. He was ordered to 'come alone':

There I found all army, corps and divisional commanders assembled. After dinner, it was announced we would attend a special briefing. We were required to leave pistols and briefcases in the cloakroom, and then we entered a bus. It was dark and raining. We drove around for half an hour, then we stopped and we were taken between a double row of SS troops into a heavy bunker and were seated at a table with a line of SS men at our backs. Hitler came in with Generals Keitel and Jodl.

Bayerlein was surprised by the 'old and broken' man before him. His hands shook as he read from a prepared manuscript. For an hour his army commanders listened motionless to a rambling, self-pitying harangue on their Führer's 'gifts to Germany'. 'We dared not fidget or so much as draw a handkerchief,' Bayerlein recalled, 'the SS men glowered at our slightest movement.' Hitler then turned to his plans for the Ardennes offensive:

He said he had scraped together everything for this effort. If it failed, the war was lost. But it could not fail. General von Manteuffel [commander of the 5th Panzer Army] would take Antwerp. General Dietrich would take Liège. We would neatly bag Montgomery's 21st Army Group. The shock of losing a whole army group would so discourage the United States that America would become a negligible factor in the war.

No one argued – who would have dared?

The offensive remained a closely guarded secret until the day before it was to be launched. On 15 December Field Marshal von Rundstedt's daily order was read to the troops: 'We gamble everything! You carry with you the holy obligation to give everything to achieve beyond human possibilities for your Fatherland and our Führer.' 'The mood was not euphoric – quite the opposite, we were desperate,' Gerda Ehrhardt recalled. The twenty-three-year-old Ehrhardt was a vivacious, popular Stabshelferin [staff aide] at 53rd Army Corps, where she typed orders and helped with operational matters. A veteran of the Eastern Front, she had volunteered to follow her commanding officer, General Graf von Rothkirch und Trach, westward earlier in the year. Ehrhardt was a familiar, trusted comrade, and Rothkirch made no attempt to hide his feelings from her: 'He said, "Hitler is crazy! I think that the Führer Headquarters issued this order in pure desperation. It is the Desperation Offensive." I asked the general: "Why do you play along when you know that every-thing has become pointless?" He told me, and this is verbatim: "I don't want to be put up against a wall."'

The Panzer Lehr Division had begun moving up on the night of the 15th – Otto Henning's reconnaissance battalion was, as always, in the van.

I was in Oberfeldwebel [Staff Sergeant] Keichel's unit and he told us that we would function as *Schweinerei-spähtrupp* [a dirty tricks patrol]. We were supposed to penetrate deep into enemy territory and create as many diversions as possible to confuse the enemy. This was unpleasant news. It was a very depressing thought that we were on the point of going out to face the enemy again in this the sixth year of the war. We thought the war was behind us, we were back in the homeland.

During the first two days the Panzer Lehr Division pressed across the River Our and on towards its first major objective – the key road junction at Bastogne. 'My unit provided constant recon-naissance during the advance towards Bastogne,' Henning recalled. 'The advance began to slow down as we encountered more American opposition on our march through the various towns and villages, but we were pushed forwards without regard for any losses.' 'I had to decide to proceed straight towards Bastogne by a bad road or make a rectangular detour by a good one,' Bayerlein later recalled. 'Surprise was important, so I struck straight ahead.' It was a poor decision. On the 18th the divi-sion's Panzers attempted to push forward along tracks flooded by rain and the ground was soon churned into an impossible quagmire. Wheeled and horse-drawn vehicles stuck fast. Bayerlein decided to postpone the attack. A golden opportunity to snatch the town was missed. 'Bayerlein absolutely failed,' General von Manteuffel, the commander of the 5th Panzer

Army, observed later. 'He was six kilometres northeast of Bastogne. These cases happened in Russia daily or monthly. He should have ordered his Panzer grenadiers to dismount and go on foot. He would have made it in two hours. The attack on the town did not begin until a little before six o'clock on the morning of the 19th; by then the American 101st Airborne Division was firmly established in the town.

The 101st had won the race for Bastogne – just. Orders to move reached the division on the 18th. 'We heard from the radio in the barracks about the big German offensive in the Ardennes,' Lieutenant Richard Bowen of the 3rd Battalion, the 327th Glider Infantry, recalled. 'Most people didn't know where the Ardennes was. As a platoon leader I was called to the company command post and told to get my platoon ready to move.' Many of the platoons were at half strength. The division had fought hard and with distinction in Holland and had been moved to a camp thirty kilometres to the west of Reims for rest and reinforcements. The men had expected to spend Christmas away from the front. But on the 18th the division began the 190-kilometre drive to Bastogne. The soldiers of the 101st had struggled to find the town on their maps. It was a modest market town of just 4,000 souls, surrounded by rolling hills of pasture and coniferous woodland. But its importance was instantly obvious to the military mind. Five major roads cut through the Ardennes forest to converge on the town. All roads led to Bastogne, and that made it worth fighting for.

The thirty-year-old Bowen was a veteran of both the D-Day and Market Garden operations and had twice been wounded in action with his battalion. 'No one that I knew wanted to go through more of it,' Bowen recalled. 'We were looking forward to being relieved and sent to the Far East.' It was a tough journey north, a grim taste of the battle to come:

We rode in open-bodied trucks and it was very cold and windy. We nearly froze because many of the men did not have winter clothing.

They had no overcoats, overshoes or gloves. So we were very cold and we huddled together, fifty to sixty men in one of these trucks. When we got into Belgium all the civilians were waving to us with the victory sign, the V for victory, but you could tell by their manner that they were very scared, they thought the Germans were coming back.

By the time the 327th Glider Infantry reached the town the first German probes had begun in strength. Bowen's company was ordered to take up positions to the south of Bastogne:

The battalion command post was set up in a copse of trees to our rear and our company command post in a little house near a secondary road. We only had three officers: the company commander, one platoon leader and an executive officer – his experiences in Holland had really cracked him up, so he wasn't much good for commanding platoons. I was instructed to set up a road-block to the east of our main position. While we were there, I could see in the distance figures coming from the north. One of my squad leaders thought they were Germans. I said, 'No, I don't think they are because I see their uniforms are khaki,' – they were refugees from the 28th Infantry Division, one of the divisions holding the main line in the Ardennes at the time of the breakthrough. Most of them did not have any weapons or packs, in other words they'd panicked. We had never seen American troops flee before the enemy. They just took off. They left their weapons and everything else behind. This squad of mine brought in at least fifteen or twenty and we sent them back to Bastogne and they were used as replacements. But there were also some civilian refugees coming down the road from the west, men, women and children – about twenty or thirty on bicycles, and the Germans came up behind them and started to fire. So they dropped the bicycles and ran into a big house near by which we used later as an aid station. They were screaming and crying and it was really upsetting everyone because we had to put the wounded in among these people, and it took a lot to quieten them down.

By 20 December the 101st was dug in around the town – 10,000 lightly armed airborne troops, short of helmets, winter clothing, weapons and ammunition. The division was supported by only a small tank force from the 10th Armoured but could call on eleven battalions of artillery – 130 pieces. Formations from three divisions of the 5th Panzer Army – including Bayerlein's Panzer Lehr – were taking up positions around the town. On the afternoon of the 20th General Anthony C. McAuliffe of the 101st left Bastogne to confer with the commander of VIII Corps at Neufchâteau. 'Don't get yourself surrounded,' he was told. Within half an hour of his return the last road was cut. The town was under siege. The battle for Bastogne was to be an epic, week-long struggle; during the course of it Hitler's last great offensive would begin to crumble.

Field Marshal Montgomery had spent the first day of the German offensive on the golf course, and it was there that he heard of the breakthrough in the Ardennes. The Germans had done exactly what Monty himself had been advocating for so many weeks – they had concentrated their armies in a single mighty punch, and in doing so had succeeded in ripping a hole 80 kilometres wide in the Allied line. Monty's liaison officer at the headquarters of the 12th Army Group in Luxembourg reported General Bradley to be not unduly worried by the situation. The great German 'bulge' in the Allied line had separated Bradley from the beleaguered US First and Ninth Armies to the north, but perversely he had decided not to relocate his headquarters. Nor did he visit General Hodges at the headquarters of the US First Army in Spa. 'The situation is rapidly deteriorating,' Hodges's ADC noted on 18 December. 'It is not yet known whether 12th Army Group fully appreciates the seriousness of the situation though both General Hodges and General Kean [chief of staff] talked with General Bradley half a dozen times during the day.' During the course of the 18th the German advance drove Hodges and his staff from Spa to his rear headquarters at

Chaudfontaine. No one at First Army saw fit to inform Bradley or the other Allied commanders that their headquarters was in retreat. The following morning Bradley was under the impression that Hodges was still at Spa, although his ADC admitted in his diary that 'the situation remains obscure'. The silence was deafening at TAC HQ. No one had been able to reassure Field Marshal Montgomery that the US First Army had a grip on the battle, and Hodges he considered a weak commander. He decided to send liaison officers to the US First Army – Major Carol Mather was one of them:

We'd heard these rumours about things going wrong in the American sector, no one knew, and Monty wanted to find out what was happening so he sent three of us down to Spa. It was a difficult journey, the weather was bad, snow and ice on the roads and there were lots of checkpoints. The Americans had learned that the Germans had dropped people dressed in American uniform behind the lines, so they were jumpy. The First Army headquarters was in a hotel at a kind of crossroads in Spa. We walked in and all the tables were laid for Christmas lunch. The offices were still full of classified papers, the telephones were still in place, but there was not a soul about. There were no Americans there and we couldn't gather from the local people what had happened. They just said they'd left in a hurry.

Mather pressed on to US First Army's rear headquarters at Chaudfontaine, where, he recorded in his report later, he found Hodges 'considerably shaken'. He could give 'no coherent account of what has happened. Nor is he in touch with General Bradley's 12th Army Group under whose command he comes. Communications seemed to have completely broken down.'

Mather returned at best speed to Monty's TAC HQ with his troubling news. The situation seemed to be much more serious than Monty had been led to believe. 'He felt that the southern flank of the 21st Army Group was threatened and that the route to Antwerp was wide open,' Mather later recalled. Monty decided to send Mather back to Chaudfontaine that night:

He said, 'I want you to go and see General Hodges, wake him up if he's asleep and tell him that these are my orders.' So I said to him, 'Sir, I can't give him orders because he's not under your command.' 'Oh, don't worry about that,' said Monty, 'just tell him.' I was to tell him that he had to defend the Meuse bridges at all costs, with every means at his disposal. He said, 'Officers should be put in charge of every bridge, he is to use any obstacle he can find, vehicles, including farm carts, and make them into roadblocks, including farm carts.' Finally, I was to tell General Hodges that British XXX Corps would sidestep into the area north of the River Meuse to block the route to Antwerp. So off I set, and I arrived at Chaudfontaine at two o'clock in the morning. The First Army's chief of staff was sitting on his bed with a blanket over his shoulders. The army commander was next door and had to be woken up. I gave my message, much to their disbelief. There was a lot of muttering about proving my identity, although they had seen me a short time before. They said, well, tell the field marshal not to worry about the bridges, there's no problem about that at all. But they really didn't know what was happening. I arrived back at Monty's headquarters at six o'clock in the morning and he was already sitting up in bed with a cup of tea. I told him there was a pretty chaotic situation down there and the commanders didn't really know what the position was and he said, 'Right, I want you and four other liaison officers to leave immediately for the American front to find out exactly what is happening.'

Monty had taken it upon himself to impose the necessary order. 'He was on a high, he liked the immediate challenge,' Monty's ADC, Johnny Henderson, recalled, 'there was no doubt he was extremely pleased.' He would soon have very good reason to be. Eisenhower was on the point of stepping in too.

On the morning of the 19th, while Mather was hacking down the road to Spa, the Supreme Commander and senior SHAEF staff were making their way to Verdun to meet Bradley and Patton. It was a bleak place to choose for a crisis conference, for it conjured memories of the ghastly battles of 1916. The meeting was held in a cold, bare barracks room with just one small pot-bellied stove to take the edge off winter. 'There will be only cheerful faces at this conference table,' Eisenhower told those gathered in the room that morning. Patton managed to lighten the general gloom by quipping, 'Hell, let's have the guts to let the sons of bitches go all the way to Paris, then we'll really cut 'em up and chew 'em up.' Patton was to be given the chief responsibility for rescuing the situation: 'George, I want you to command this move – under Brad's supervision of course – making a strong counterattack,' Eisenhower told him. 'When can you start?' Patton said he could do it in forty-eight hours. 'When I said I could attack on the 22nd, it created quite a commotion,' he logged in his diary later that day; 'some people seemed surprised and others pleased – however I believe it can be done.' It was a dangerously ambitious timetable. The Third Army would need to swing northward, three divisions would have to be ferried to the battle area along icy roads, and then the men and armour would be supplied from dumps well to the south.

But Patton had anticipated Eisenhower's request and had already begun planning for the operation. As the battle for Normandy had demonstrated, no Allied general was better qualified by temperament or experience to meet this challenge. Patton briefed those assembled – cigar in hand – on his intentions: 'the Kraut's stuck his head in a meatgrinder,' he told them, 'and this time I've got hold of the handle.' Bradley had said little during the conference – it had been Patton's show. Within hours he would be relegated to the role of a spectator.

Reports of the uncertainty in command that Mather had encountered at US First Army headquarters had also begun to reach staff at SHAEF. At first Eisenhower's chief of staff, Walter Bedell Smith, was inclined to dismiss any suggestion that Bradley was not on top of the situation. But by the morning of the 20th it was clear that the crisis called for firmer leadership. Monty's headquarters was north of the Bulge – it was surely 'logical' to put the direction of the US First and Ninth Armies temporarily in his hands. Eisenhower agreed and telephoned Bradley to tell him. It was a difficult call to make – the spiky, troublesome Monty had argued the case for a single command north of the Ardennes at Maastricht just three weeks earlier, but Bradley had carried the day. That Eisenhower recognised the need for the change at this critical point, and was prepared to tame Bradley's anger to bring it about, demonstrated his unique suitability for the role he had been charged with carrying out – that of 'Allied' Supreme Commander. It would have been easier to have done nothing, but he was convinced of the case and told Bradley so. The British field marshal Patton liked to dismiss as 'a little fart' was to play a significant part in what was in all other respects an American battle. Bradley could not have been more shocked if Eisenhower had slapped him in the face. He was left with just the Third Army, and that needed no direction. He would later write that if Monty had been American he would have supported the move: 'it could be interpreted as a loss of confidence by Eisenhower in me – or more significantly in the American command'. That was certainly how many on his staff viewed it. 'It was a smart military move, a necessary one,' Bradley's ADC, Major Hansen, acknowledged. 'But General Bradley's staff had some reservations about the need for it. I wouldn't say there was animosity between the British and the American forces at that time, but a sense of competitiveness between the two certainly. And the thought of putting American forces under British command did not particularly appeal to us, and we thought it slighted General Bradley.' But Bradley had only himself to blame – he had shown bad judgement in refusing to move his headquarters. He had left the First Army to flounder.

At half past one on the afternoon of the 20th, Monty's staff car, sporting the largest Union Jack that could be mounted on it, and preceded by eight motorcycle outriders, swept into the forecourt at US First Army headquarters. It was, one American officer noted, 'like Christ come to cleanse the Temple'. Generals Hodges and Simpson (Ninth Army) had seen nothing of Bradley. Monty had stepped into the vacuum and was intent on providing leadership – 'they seemed delighted to have someone to give them firm orders,' he observed later that day. British divisions were moved into reserve, hopeless positions abandoned, the line consolidated and a force assembled under Hodges's 'most aggressive fighting corps commander', General 'Lightning Joe' Collins – all in preparation for a counter-attack. American front-line units that had seen little of their own army commanders were visited by a British field marshal who wanted to give them his thoughts on the battle. 'To the American soldiers he was like a man from Mars really,' Mather recalled, 'they couldn't quite make him out.' After the war a number of senior American commanders were critical of Monty's high-handed manner, his imperious tone, but at the time he impressed those who served under him with his 'professionalism'. 'The staff spoke of Montgomery with amusement and respect,' General James Gavin of the 82nd Airborne Division later observed.

In the first four days of the battle the 6th SS Panzer Army had been held in the north of the Bulge, well short of the River Meuse. A battle group from the 1st SS Panzer Division – Kampfgruppe Peiper – had narrowly missed capturing two vital American fuel dumps near Stavelot. One of the dumps was set alight to create a blazing roadblock, whilst American engineers blew the bridges before the advancing German Panzers. A vital opportunity had been missed, for the fuel was desperately needed to sustain the German advance.

The 5th Panzer Army had made better progress. More than 7,000 American prisoners had been captured in the first days, but the vanguard of General von Manteuffel's push was still 48 kilometres short of the Meuse. The Germans had achieved much less than surprise and superior numbers had initially suggested they might. A number of American units had fought with tenacity and great distinction to slow the onward rush of German armour. Allied aircraft had been grounded for the most part by the weather – a window of opportunity that was on the point of shutting. An offensive that had little chance of succeeding in the first place was grinding to a halt. None of the senior commanders charged with its conduct were surprised. Manteuffel had concluded after just three days that even the Meuse was beyond reach and told the commander-in-chief in the west, Field Marshal von Rundstedt, so. But Hitler dismissed such talk as defeatist – the attack was to be pressed home without delay.

The failure to take Bastogne had played a significant part in slowing the 5th Panzer Army's thrust to the Meuse. It had become a sore in the southern flank of the German bulge. Repeated attempts to burst through American positions on the perimeter of the town were beaten back by a skilful and determined defence. On 21 December the main body of the Panzer Lehr Division was ordered to bypass the town and press on towards the Meuse near Dinant. But a combat command – Kampfgruppe 901 – remained with the 26th Volksgrenadier Division to continue the attack. It began to snow on the 21st and a cold, bleak battlefield became significantly worse for the soldiers on both sides. 'It was typical farmland where we were,' Lieutenant Richard Bowen of the 327th Glider Infantry recalled.

Big open, rolling fields and the wind blew across them – very chilling. Trying to dig foxholes after the weather dropped below freezing was terrible. It would take hours just to get three or four feet deep. I tried to get my men in a barn every five hours or so – I would bring a squad in at a time, let them stay around the stove for ten minutes, and then they had to go back out on the line. They suffered terribly because of the cold weather.

The artillery was down to little more than ten rounds per gun per day. Makeshift hospitals had been established in the church and cellars of the town to deal with an ever lengthening casualty list. The wounded could not be evacuated – the 101st were what a member of the divisional staff dubbed 'the hole in the doughnut'. At noon on 22 December two German officers crunched through the snow to an American outpost on the Remoifosse–Bastogne road. They had come under a flag of truce. 'We want to talk to your commanding general,' Lieutenant Hellmuth Henke of the Panzer Lehr's operations staff announced in English. The officers were blindfolded and led to the command post of F Company, the 327th Glider Infantry. There Henke delivered an ultimatum addressed 'to the USA Commander of the encircled town of Bastogne'. The American airborne forces faced 'total annihilation' if their commander did not agree to surrender. An attack on the town would result in serious civilian losses, the ultimatum added, and that 'would not correspond with the well-known American humanity'. The message was delivered to the division's acting commander, General Anthony C. McAuliffe. His famous one-word reply was: 'Nuts'.

The following day the Germans tried to make good their promise. The heaviest blows fell on the south and west of the 25-kilometre perimeter. A battalion of the 327th Glider Infantry was defending the Bastogne–Marche road. 'On 23 December we had a roadblock a mile west of our company command post, manned by our Second Platoon with two tank destroyers, a tank and an anti-tank gun,' Lieutenant Richard Bowen recalled.

It had snowed heavily, and it was about eight or ten inches deep on the ground, and so foggy it reminded me of an English morning in winter, but as soon as it lifted the battle began. We had been expecting Patton's 4th Armoured Division to come down the road and relieve us. We had gotten word of that. And so the 2nd Platoon allowed these tanks to get real close before they realised they were German and opened fire on them. The fight went on all morning. The company commander called me and asked me to take two squads of men and reinforce the 2nd Platoon. One of their tank destroyers had been knocked out, the anti-tank gun had frozen in the ground and they couldn't traverse it to fire at the Geman tanks on the road. So I started up with two squads. We had to cross this open field several hundred yards wide. The only way I knew how to do it was to put my head down and run like the devil, which I did. When I got to where the 2nd Platoon had dug in, I had three men left with me. The rest of them never got across the field. There was an officer from the tank destroyer who had been commissioned that very day, a lieutenant from our 1st Platoon and I was an acting platoon leader. We fought all morning – the tanks were getting closer and I tried to knock one out by crawling out in the snow and firing at it and I hit the thing but the rocket glanced off. We had no artillery support. We held the Germans mostly with mortars and the rifle fire from our 2nd Platoon, but our men were being blown out of their foxholes. The tanks were so close they could see the foxholes and they were just shooting them out. I was having a conference with the other two officers at about four o'clock when a shell came over the tank destroyer and landed near by. It wounded all three of us. I was hit in the stomach and in the right arm. They put me in the basement of a house near by that was being used as an aid station – there were a lot of our wounded in there and they gave me morphine and it sort of knocked me out. We had a medic who was Jewish and who spoke good German and at about six o'clock he left the aid station to go outside and I heard him talking in German to someone else. The Germans had cut the road behind us and they captured all the medics, the wounded and some observers for our mortar section. We were taken out into the snow and examined and the Germans stole everything they could off of us and then we were taken to their command post.

The 3rd Battalion had withdrawn when it became clear it was in danger of being outflanked but the wounded had been left for the enemy. Bowen spent the rest of the war in a German hospital and then a prison camp.

The 101st did have something to cheer on the 23rd – the weather had lifted and by late morning the hum of C-47 transport planes had been heard over Bastogne. The sky was soon thick with brightly coloured parachutes – food, ammunition and medical supplies, a lifeline for the division. But during the day the Germans had fought their way into the village of Marvie and established themselves on the road into the town. 'Prisoners were taken, enemy defensive nests assaulted, the hills south of Marvie captured,' the commander of the 26th Volksgrenadier Division recalled later. 'The enemy fought bitterly, even when he was outflanked and cut off. He was strong and inflicted heavy casualties on the attackers during night combat. In spite of this, he could not hold.' The attack petered out only at ten o'clock that night, when it became clear that no more progress could be made without significant tank and infantry reinforcements. It was now a race against time. General Patton's divisions were driving up from the south – if Bastogne were to be taken it would have to be soon. Preparations began for an all-out attack on Christmas Day.

There was little Christmas cheer in the frozen foxholes, cellars and command posts on the perimeter of the town. McAuliffe did his best to lift the spirits of the 101st with a Christmas message: 'What's merry about all this, you ask? We're fighting – it's cold – we aren't home.' The Germans had thrown everything against them, he wrote, but they had been 'stopped cold'. The world was watching – the defenders were 'giving our country and our loved ones at home a worthy Christmas present'. The same day McAuliffe received a message card from Patton: 'Xmas Eve present coming up. Hold on.'

The German attack began at three o'clock on Christmas morning. Panzer grenadiers in white camouflage capes began to infiltrate the American line to the west of Bastogne in two places. In confused night fighting they managed to force a break in the airborne perimeter near the village of Champs. A determined armoured thrust took the Germans to within a kilometre of Bastogne, but the attack was broken by a wall of anti-tank fire. An assault group of just thirty grenadiers from the Panzer

Lehr Division fought through to the fork in the road at the southern entrance to Bastogne, where it was reported to have been 'cut off and destroyed'. By nightfall it was apparent that the Germans had failed and that without substantial reinforcements there was no prospect of dislodging the American airborne troops. At a little before five o'clock the following day the first of the Third Army's tanks trundled into Bastogne – the siege was over. 'The speed of our movements is amazing, even to me, and must be a constant source of surprise to the Germans,' Patton logged in his diary that day. 'The German has shot his wad.' The 101st Airborne had taken 1,641 casualties and the combat units from the 9th and 10th Armoured Divisions at least a thousand more.

The relief of Bastogne was to mark a symbolic turning point in the great Ardennes battle. 'We must face facts squarely and openly,' the chief of operations at OKW, General Jodl, bluntly told his Führer. 'We cannot force the Meuse river.' The formations at the spearhead of the 5th Panzer Army's attack had fared no better than those encircling Bastogne. The main body of the Panzer Lehr Division had advanced rapidly westward from Bastogne in support of the 2nd Panzer and was within striking distance of the Meuse. But by 23 December both divisions had spluttered to a halt – the armour was down to its last drop of fuel. The tanks had been promised enough fuel to carry them 500 kilometres – that proved to be hopelessly optimistic. Helmut Ritgen of the 130th Panzer Lehr Regiment had left his hospital bed to join the Ardennes offensive. He had been recovering from wounds received during a night air attack on his car; 'the shell only burned my pants and split my eardrums,' he recalled. The newly promoted 'Major' Ritgen had reached the division in time to lead his battalion into St-Hubert:

We were singing our soldier songs, 'When we take the town, ta ta ta . . .' We played dice and drank wine. And then the next day we tried to find fuel, but we only found empty jerry cans. We could go no farther. The armoured cars had to give us their fuel, so at least the division's tanks could move. As long as there was rain, fog, snow, we were all right. But as soon as it cleared up, the fighter-bombers came and that was very unpleasant.

On December 23 the cloud lifted and it was a bright, clear winter day – perfect flying conditions. Allied aircraft returned to the skies above the battlefield to harass the long, dark columns of German supply vehicles that moved conspicuously through the snow. A battle group from the 2nd Panzer Division at the vanguard of the advance found itself isolated and without fuel. The situation was also viewed as critical at the Panzer Lehr Division's headquarters. 'My rear columns were taking severe losses from air attack,' Bayerlein later recalled.

A flak battery was caught on the march and badly cut up. And worse, both my tank recovery vehicles were destroyed from the air. The replacements I had ordered lay back at the railhead without gasoline. My tank repair shops were badly bombed. Gasoline was scarce and had to be brought up by truck and I had lost thirty tanks in the drive – bogged down, in need of repair or out of gas – in addition to those knocked out by enemy fire. But without tank recovery vehicles they were lost.

On Christmas Eve Bayerlein was instructed to do all he could to save the beleaguered forward units of the 2nd Panzer Division near Celles. Unteroffizier [Sergeant] Otto Henning of the 130th Panzer Lehr Reconnaissance Battalion 130 was preparing to celebrate Christmas under a roof when he was ordered back into the field:

We had received a lot of American provisions as loot and had decided to keep one parcel per head and to open these on Christmas Eve. They had quartered us with some Belgian civilians, although I am fairly sure they were unwilling hosts. But these Belgians allowed us into their kitchen and we put up a Christmas tree. Later that evening our unit leader, Oberfeldwebel Keichel, came and told us that some officers were going out on reconnaissance and we had to accompany them. We had to move out towards the Meuse. I have to admit that I really did not want to be part of this reconnaissance mission, I even tried a bit of passive resistance but it didn't work. We had prepared our Christmas party and now we were on the march again. The officers disappeared and we were left to ourselves again. Unit leader Keichel found the bridge we were to secure for the division's advance. We stood on that bridge at about midnight, it was extremely cold, about minus 10°C, and we opened our food parcels and devoured the contents. Then we noticed shadows coming towards us – we thought that an enemy reconnaissance unit was approaching our position. They approached, stood still then approached again. When they'd almost reached the bridge I thought I had better run to my tank but Keichel told me to stay put. I crouched down and heard Keichel order 'Fire' in a loud voice, but the approaching group started to shout: 'Don't shoot. Don't shoot.' When the order 'Open fire' was given during reconnaissance missions we always opened up. It wasn't important to hit anything – the shooting was useful because it forced an enemy to take shelter. Our motto was 'He who shoots first lives longer.' But this time we didn't shoot. I was sent instead to check these men – they were German soldiers from the 2nd Panzer Division. They were older than us and completely exhausted. Some of them just fell to the ground, shaking all over. I think they believed their end had come. We sent them back to our lines and advised our troops by radio that they were on the way – a group of fifteen or so men. We continued our march the next day but received new orders by radio ordering us to return. Our unit was supposed to reinforce the 2nd Panzer Division but the enemy's artillery fire was so intense we didn't dare move out of the forest. All of this happened on Christmas Day and, of course, we knew that the Ardennes offensive had failed.

On Christmas Day a battle group from the American VII Corps had attacked the 2nd Panzer and destroyed its forward units. The Panzer Lehr's attempts to break through and relieve them were repulsed with heavy losses. More than 1,200 prisoners were taken, 82 tanks and 440 other vehicles destroyed. Some 600 men managed to trudge back through the snow to the German line. Hitler's great armoured thrust was over.

The Allied armies were prepared to turn once again to the offensive. Bradley had visited Monty on Christmas Day to discuss plans to pinch the Germans in the Bulge from the north and south. A subtler, more diplomatic man would have recognised that with the battle at Bastogne still in the balance, with 600,000 Americans struggling in atrocious winter conditions to hold the German tide, it was not the time for recriminations and 'I told you so' lectures. But Monty was not the man to let the opportunity pass. The unfortunate Bradley was told in no uncertain terms that the Allies had suffered a 'bloody nose', that they had better admit 'a proper defeat'. In Monty's opinion it could all have been avoided but for Eisenhower and Bradley's 'two thrust' strategy – the broad front. The enemy had seen his chance and taken it. It was humiliating stuff. Bradley had not visited Monty to rake over old ashes, or to discuss the campaign beyond the Ardennes. 'Poor chap,' Monty noted in his diary later, 'he is such a decent fellow and the whole thing is a bitter pill for him.' Monty had scored his points, but Bradley never forgave him. Nor was the tension between the army group commanders north and south of the Bulge helped by Monty's refusal to consider a prompt counter-attack. The Third Army had already begun thrusting into the German Bulge from the south – a full-blooded attack was planned for 28 December. But Monty was not prepared to commit himself to an attack from the north before 3 January – almost a week later. He would move to the offensive, he declared, only when he was sure the Germans had shot their last bolt.

No one had heard much from the Allied Supreme Commander since the meeting at Verdun. The news that a German commando brigade had infiltrated Allied lines and was intent on assassinating Eisenhower had sent staff at SHAEF into a flat spin. Eisenhower had become the prisoner of his own 'security boys'. Monty – the commander of four Allied armies – had spoken only briefly to him in eight days. But on 28 December Eisenhower was allowed to venture out again. The two men met aboard Ike's heavily guarded train at Hasselt railway station in Belgium for what was, at Monty's insistence, a private discussion. It was to follow the confused pattern set by previous encounters. The immediate business was settled amicably enough when Eisenhower agreed, if a little reluctantly, to accept Monty's cautious timetable for a counter-attack in the new year. But then, like a terrier with an old bone, the field marshal turned to Ike's plans for the conquest of the Reich and the question of command. The German offensive had surely demonstrated the need for a single land commander – Monty, of course – and a single, all-powerful northern thrust towards the Ruhr. Eisenhower was, Monty later reported, 'in a somewhat humble frame of mind and clearly realises that the present trouble would not have occurred if he had accepted British advice and not that of American generals'. It is possible to detect the curl of the field marshal's lip in the slighting reference to 'American generals'. Monty clearly felt he had carried the day. Eisenhower believed he had conceded nothing. Monty's intelligence chief remembered Ike stepping into the frozen corridor of the train after the meeting to observe 'Monty as usual'.

The following day Monty wrote an arrogant, ill-judged letter to Ike pressing his case; 'one commander must have powers to direct and control the operations; you cannot possibly do it your-self,' he noted. 'I put this matter up to you again only because I am so anxious not to have another failure.' As his foremost supporter, Field Marshal Brooke observed, this was the height of tactlessness, 'too much of "I told you so" to assist in producing the required friendly relations'. Monty's case was perhaps a good one – Brooke certainly thought so – but he had put it intemperately and once too often. To make matters worse, Eisenhower had been needled by reports in the British press suggesting that it was Monty who had dragged the American fat from the fire in the Ardennes.

The field marshal was most fortunate in his chief of staff. Freddie de Guingand sensed the trouble brewing at SHAEF and on 30 December he flew through a blizzard to Paris intent on doing all he could to paper over the cracks in the alliance. Things had reached a critical pass. 'The Supreme Commander looked really tired and worried,' de Guingand later recalled. 'Eisenhower went on to say that he was tired of the whole business, and had come to the conclusion that it was now a matter for the Combined Chiefs of Staff to make a decision . . . With Montgomery still pressing for a Land Forces Commander it was impossible for the two of them to carry on working in harness together.' It was clear to de Guingand that Eisenhower was intent on forcing the issue and that if he did there could only be one outcome – 'Monty would be the one to go'. It was 'a crisis of the first magnitude'. De Guingand was able to persuade Eisenhower to hold his hand for twenty-four hours; 'I virtually went down on my bended knees,' he later recalled. It was not until the afternoon of the following day that de Guingand reached TAC HQ, and by then time was short. 'I've just come from SHAEF and seen Ike, and it's on the cards that you might have to go,' he told 'the Chief'. Monty was completely nonplussed. 'I don't think I had ever seen him so deflated. It was as if a cloak of loneliness had descended upon him. His reply was, "What shall I do, Freddie?"' De Guingand had already drafted a signal:

Have seen Freddie and understand you are greatly worried by many considerations in these very difficult days. I have given you my frank views because I have felt you like this . . . whatever your decision may be you can rely on me one hundred per cent to make it work, and I know Brad will do the same. Very distressed that my letter may have upset you and I would ask you to tear it up. Your very devoted subordinate, Monty.

It was enough. Eisenhower took the matter no farther. The relationship between the two commanders and the alliance itself had been strained to breaking point. Only at the eleventh hour had Monty understood that the last battle of the Second World War had to be commanded by an American; as Carlo D'Este has observed in his study of Eisenhower, the Supreme Commander knew that President Roosevelt and public opinion back home would stand for nothing less. But Monty would continue to ruffle American feathers. At an ill-judged press conference on 7 January he gave the impression that it was he and the British army who had ridden to the rescue of a helpless ally. Ironically he had summoned the press to praise the fighting qualities of the American soldier and his tribute was a handsome one. But Bradley in particular felt slighted again. The sniping would continue through the last days of the war and beyond it, but for better or worse the issue of command had been settled once and for all.

The Battle of the Bulge ground on into January as the Allies slowly squeezed the Germans from the salient they had won at such great cost. They fought with characteristic tenacity for every town and village – the battle to wrestle Bastogne from the US Third Army was joined with renewed ferocity, but it was, as it had always been, an impossible struggle. Otto Henning had taken command of one of the Panzer Lehr's reconnaissance units:

It was my duty to visit the various German positions and on one occasion I had a run-in with a battalion commander who just lost his composure and shouted at me: 'I do not need spies [reconnaissance], I need soldiers, I need weapons and I need ammunition.' He had lost almost all his men; only 150 remained from his battalion. These heavy losses, particularly among the infantry, affected the morale of the troops.

Hitler bowed to the inevitable and gave the order to withdraw from the nose of the Bulge on 8 January, before the Allies were able to cut the neck and trap his hard-pressed armies. Bradley and Patton had been impatient for Monty to begin his push from the north. His decision to delay until 3 January had prompted Patton to observe in his diary that even Ike was a 'lion' compared to Montgomery.

The Panzer Lehr Division began its withdrawal from the tip of the salient during the night of 11/12 January. 'An almost unbroken snake of vehicles of all types, panzers and guns, wound its way through the hilly icy roads to the east,' Major Ritgen recalled. 'Details of soldiers were busy spreading sand and all available officers directed traffic and were charged with clearing the road when vehicles slipped or otherwise broke down. Only occasionally were damaged panzers towed away.' Bayerlein later reported that he was forced to leave fifty-three tanks by the roadside in the course of the retreat for lack of fuel, spare parts or recovery vehicles. It was not until 16 January that the US First Army, pressing southward, met the Third Army advancing north at Houffalize. Atrocious weather conditions had grounded Allied aircraft again and slowed the counter-attack, as tanks and trucks stalled and skated on hillside roads. An opportunity had been missed. A combat group from the Panzer Lehr was among the last German units to escape before the trap snapped shut on an empty salient.

The German armies had fielded half a million men for the offensive – at least 81,000 of these became casualties; 12,500 were killed. The Allies took over 50,000 prisoners. But the Americans had also paid a heavy price – 81,000 of the 600,000 involved in the fighting were listed as casualties. Of these more than 10,000 were killed. The British recorded 1,400 casualties – the Bulge was an American battle.

One young American private faced the grim reality of the statistics every day. 'All I saw was death,' Maury Laws remembered. The twenty-one-year-old Laws was serving with the 328th Infantry Regiment – part of the 26th Division. He had arrived in France three months earlier and had joined the Graves Registration Unit: 'We didn't register anything, we picked up dead people.' Laws's division had driven northward into the Bulge with Patton's Third Army:

We began to do our job – picking up people. I remember walking in front of this little truck in this dense fog at night, moving step by step along this icy road. When the bodies fell they would be warm and would melt the snow, then they would freeze and we had to chip them out of the ice with something like a log. Americans and Germans. We had been rather taught through our training that the Germans were different, that they were 'Godless'. I think our training was based on the most severe SS person you could find and I remember being surprised when I found pictures of wives and sweethearts and children and little Bibles in the pockets of dead Germans. The Germans would have these little things, same as Americans. They were the same as me, they were human.

As a child Laws had been haunted by pictures of Germans killed during the First World War: 'I remember thinking, this is like those pictures. I had always had dreams about walking through bodies as a kid, I had been afraid that this would happen to me and here it was, I was living it out, and it was terrible.' Laws was later transferred to a reconnaissance unit.

'The victory in the Ardennes,' Russell Weigley wrote, 'belonged pre-eminently to the American soldier.' The stubborn resistance at Bastogne, and on the northern shoulder of the Bulge, had 'wrestled the momentum of the battle away from the enemy and in time restoring it to the Allied Command'. The final outcome was never really in doubt, for the German offensive had been doomed to failure from the first. 'This plan hasn't got a damned leg to stand on,' Field Marshal Model had observed. His 'battle writer' at Army Group B, Rolf Munninger, put it like this: 'All in all the Ardennes offensive was a catastrophe really. What insanity to start an offensive without the necessary resources. I would say it was the *coup de grâce* for our army in the west. This catastrophe took our best divisions.' The exhausted SS divisions had been withdrawn from the battle in the second week of January and were making their way eastward to another front. They were to be thrown into the desperate struggle to hold the relentless Soviet advance. But Germany's last strategic reserve had gone; the losses in men and equipment were irreplaceable.

Hitler had warned his divisional commanders on the eve of the Ardennes offensive that if it failed the war was lost. 'Hitler had spoken the truth that night,' General Bayerlein reflected later.

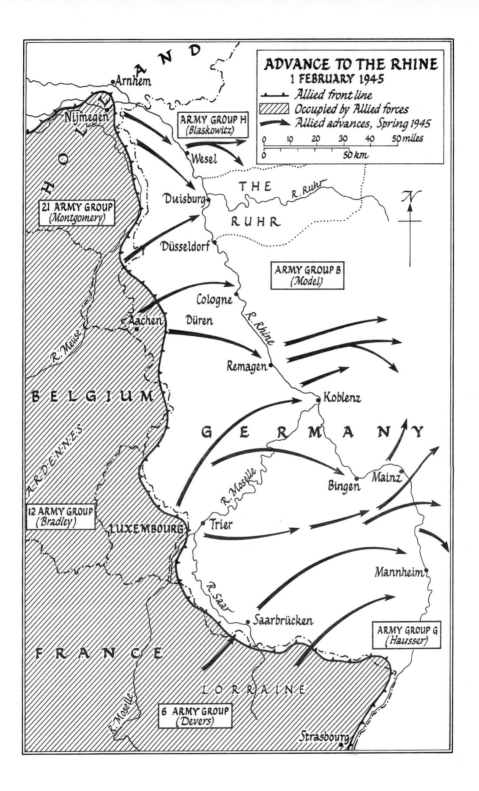

ADVANCE TO THE RHINE
1 FEBRUARY 1945

Allied front line
Occupied by Allied forces
Allied advances, Spring 1945

0 10 20 30 40 50 miles
0   50 km

HOLLAND

Arnhem

Nijmegen

ARMY GROUP H
(Blaskowitz)

Wesel

THE

R. Ruhr

RUHR

Duisburg

21 ARMY GROUP
(Montgomery)

Düsseldorf

ARMY GROUP B
(Model)

R. Meuse

Cologne

Düren

Aachen

R. Rhine

BELGIUM

Remagen

A·R·D·E·N·N·E·S

Koblenz

GERMANY

R. Moselle

12 ARMY GROUP
(Bradley)

Bingen   Mainz

LUXEMBOURG

Trier

Mannheim

R. Saar

Saarbrücken

ARMY GROUP G
(Hausser)

FRANCE

LORRAINE

R. Moselle

6 ARMY GROUP
(Devers)

Strasbourg

N

CHAPTER TEN

BERLIN

For the briefest of moments Hitler had been warmed by a wild hope that winning in the west would save his Reich from crushing defeat in the east. That he was able to plan and execute his 'desperation offensive' in the Ardennes was in no small part thanks to the great Soviet enemy. Few would have predicted in the summer of 1944, when the Red Army advanced through Poland to the banks of the Vistula, that it would still be camped there three months later. But by the end of December it was clear to staff at Army Command (OKH) that the Soviet armies were ready to launch a new offensive. The chief of staff at OKH, General Heinz Guderian, had visited Hitler's field headquarters near Frankfurt on Christmas Eve to warn of impending disaster in the east. For every German dug in along the Vistula there were eleven Soviet soldiers, Guderian told his Führer, and the Red Army enjoyed an overwhelming superiority in tanks, artillery and aircraft. This was too uncomfortable to accept, and Hitler chose instead to dismiss the intelligence on which it was based. But Guderian's estimates were by no means exaggerated. More than 4 million Soviet soldiers were massed in Poland for a winter offensive that within weeks would take them from the Vistula to the Oder and beyond – just 60 kilometres from Berlin.

The Red Army attacked on 12 January through heavy snow and fog. Prisoners were herded through the German minefields to create a channel for the infantry and tanks of the 1st Ukrainian Front. Resistance collapsed before the Soviet 'blitzkrieg'. The following day the Soviet armies attacked East Prussia and on the 14th Marshal Georgy Zhukov's 1st Belorussian Front broke through the German line before Warsaw. Within a week the Red Army had advanced 160 kilometres along a front more than 480 kilometres wide. The shattered remains of Warsaw fell on the 17th, and two days later the Soviet war machine reached the borders of Silesia. The city of Warsaw had been designated a 'fortress' to be defended to the last; its surrender was, Hitler railed, another betrayal by the army. The ranting paranoia that had characterised his dealings with senior officers since the bomb plot was proving as destructive in the east as it had already been in the west. Within hours of Warsaw's capture members of Guderian's staff at OKH were rounded up and taken for interrogation by the Gestapo. Even the unfortunate Guderian was obliged to submit to questioning. His chief 'offence' was his willingness to present the unvarnished truth to a man who had little interest in hearing it. His Führer's orders were unflinchingly brutal – stand, fight and die for the Reich no matter how senseless the battle. Nor did they make any sort of military sense. Hitler stubbornly refused against all reason to consider the evacuation of Army Group North from the Courland peninsula on the Baltic. Some 200,000 soldiers had been trapped by the Soviet advance. At home old men and boys were being pressed into the Reich's citizen militia – the Volkssturm. The remnants of Army Group North were sorely needed for the defence of Germany itself – so too the soldiers committed to Hitler's 'fortress' towns. The desperate defence of these did nothing to slow the enemy's advance; only Königsberg and Breslau held out for long. Fear motivated most who fought – fear of the unforgiving enemy, and fear too of the Nazi civil and military authorities, who threatened those who talked of surrender or flight with summary execution. The battle was fought with the same disregard for humanity that had characterised the German invasion of the Soviet Union in the summer of 1941. The German people had been encouraged by the Nazis to think of 'Slavs' as little more than beasts, and their soldiers had treated them accordingly. Only the very young and the simple were naive enough to expect anything less than equal measure from the Russians.

Propaganda Minister Joseph Goebbels spared Germans nothing. Newsreel footage had been shown a few months before of the bodies of sixty-two women and girls raped and murdered in East Prussia by the soldiers of the Red Army. The propaganda message was clear – fight to drive the barbarians back from the gate. At the vanguard of the Soviet advance were the elite Guards divisions, tank and artillery soldiers, professional and well disciplined. But a great army of peasants followed in their wake, riflemen intent on punishment and pleasure. Towns were looted and torched, prisoners shot, women and girls gang-raped – most of the victims were German, but by no means all. Drunken Soviet soldiers cared little for the nationality of their victims. Senior officers made only half-hearted efforts to rein in their troops – one 'Comrade Marshal' observed that 'it is now time for our soldiers to issue their own justice'. Millions of frightened German refugees trailed westward – those caught in the path of the Soviet advance were ruthlessly swept from the roads, sometimes by automatic fire. On 30 January the first Soviet troops crossed the frozen River Oder under the cover of night to form a small bridgehead near the town of Küstrin. Another crossing was established to the south the following day. Here the headlong advance halted, while pockets of resistance in East Prussia and the Baltic states were systematically crushed. The Red Army had advanced nearly 500 kilometres in two weeks to stand before the capital of the crumbling Reich.

It was richly ironic and fitting that the Soviet tide should reach the Oder on 30 January, for this was an auspicious day in the history of the Reich – the twelfth anniversary of Hitler's rise to power. To mark it he made what would be his last broadcast to the nation: 'We are going to force a turn of the tide,' he promised; Germany would never surrender. Events would, he declared to incredulous Berliners, be decided by 'our unalterable will, by our readiness for sacrifice'. Just a few hours earlier, police in the district of Neukölln had fired into a desperate crowd intent on looting food. That same day the Reich's armaments minister, Hitler's erstwhile architect and friend, Albert Speer, had bluntly informed him that the war was over: 'After the loss of Upper Silesia, the German armaments industry will no longer be able even approximately to cover the requirements of the front for ammunition, ordnance, and tanks . . . From now on the material preponderance of the enemy can no longer be compensated for by the bravery of our soldiers.' The 'unalterable will' of the German people counted for nothing without ammunition. Those who demonstrated this sort of 'defeatism' on the streets of Berlin were threatened with imprisonment or death. The Berlin newspapers carried an official warning that 'any person who attempts to avoid fulfilling his obligations towards the community' would be punished with 'appropriate severity'. The interests of the state must not be threatened by the 'failure of the individual citizen'. The Reich's armaments minister was beyond the drumhead justice of the street, but Hitler did take him aside and warn him, with a quiet chill that Speer found much more menacing than the rages he had witnessed many times before, that he could not question his Führer's 'conclusions'.

Hitler had driven through the ruins of Berlin on his return from the west with the blinds of his car pulled down – he had no wish to be reminded of the misery he had brought upon the city. His own personal quarters at the Reich Chancellery had been destroyed and he chose instead to move into the barely finished bunker beneath the garden. It was in this strange, subterranean world – members of his personal staff called it 'the concrete submarine' – that Hitler would spend his last days. Whilst he was obliged to meet his generals to discuss the war – he insisted on being consulted on every detail – it was the comfort of old Nazi Party comrades like Goebbels and his Private Secretary Reichsleiter Martin Bormann that he sought whenever possible. 'No one was admitted to these gatherings,' Speer later recalled. 'No one knew what they were talking about, whether they were reminiscing about their beginnings or talking about the end and what would come after it.' Speer heard not 'a single feeling remark about the future of the defeated nation'; there was talk instead of leaving no more than 'a desert to the Americans, English and Russians'. Those who cared something for the German people clung to the forlorn hope that a separate peace could still be negotiated with the Americans and British. Guderian had broached the subject with Hitler's Foreign Minister, Joachim von Ribbentrop, on 24 January. The war was lost, he bluntly declared; surely an armistice could be reached in the west so Germany could concentrate her forces against the Soviet advance in the east. Ribbentrop, who had neither the power nor the courage to act on his own initiative, chose instead to dutifully inform his Führer. In a blind rage, Hitler warned his generals that 'anyone who tells anyone that the war is lost will be treated as a traitor, with all the consequences for him and his family'.

The end could only be weeks away, but rather than spare the German people more suffering, Hitler was intent on dragging them even farther into the pit. The Allies would accept nothing less than unconditional surrender and the total destruction of the Nazi state. For Hitler and his inner circle, there could be no Germany without the Nazis. His evil genius was his ability to convince many Germans to believe the same. In the last days National Socialist guidance officers visited the front to urge soldiers to do their 'duty'. One Nazi guidance officer later recalled asking a company of men what they would say to their Führer 'when the war is over and he comes and says, "Well, you've thrown away your weapons! I wanted to find a good ending!" We do not want to expose ourselves to this reproach.'

Nazi propaganda was able to make great play of the Allied demand for 'unconditional surrender' in particular. It was, Goebbels claimed, nothing short of a plan for the elimination of the German 'Volk', and there were many who believed him. A British intelligence report concluded before D-Day that the policy of 'unconditional surrender' was stiffening the morale of German soldiers and citizens alike. But the Allies made only half-hearted efforts to reassure Germans that this was not an attempt to enslave them, merely a policy for the complete eradication of Nazi militarism. Goebbels had been presented with a propaganda gift in the autumn of 1944 when President Roosevelt threw his weight behind a plan for the dismemberment of a post-war Germany and the destruction of its industry. The Morgenthau Plan had been discussed at the Quebec Conference in September, and Churchill had been persuaded against his better judgement to sign a paper agreeing in principle to the conversion of Germany 'into a country primarily agricultural and pastoral in its character'. The Nazis had carried out the selfsame policy in their occupied territories in the east. Fortunately wiser counsels in Britain and America prevailed. As Roosevelt's Secretary of War observed in his diary, the plan 'would lead to starvation for 30 million Germans'. Morgenthau was shelved, but it had damaged the Allied cause. The plan was clear evidence of Allied intentions to 'exterminate forty-three million Germans', Goebbels argued. The relentless bombing of German cities and towns, some of no industrial or military importance, seemed to add weight to his case.

Above all Germans were persuaded to fight to the bitter end because the Allies had made common cause. 'Our motivation was simple,' Hans Bernhard of the 1st SS Panzer staff recalled; 'we had to keep fighting in the east, we had to keep the Russians out of the country.' As one member of the general staff, Johann-Adolf, Graf von Kielmansegg, put it: 'For me this is the decisive reason: all those who had been in Russia at least knew what Germany could expect if Bolshevism came to Germany . . . If it had only been England and France, we would have stopped earlier in a simplified manner. Not against Russia.' Otto Henning of the 130th Panzer Lehr Reconnaissance Battalion was struck by how determined many civilians were to fight on to the end – and by their naivety:

I did not know anything about the Volkssturm when I started my leave. Anyway, while I was in Lübeck I saw a military band marching one Sunday – a group of soldiers with civilians behind. Some of the civilians had steel helmets, some had guns. I didn't know what to make of it and asked someone standing next to me: 'Why are they marching?' He said: 'That is the Volkssturm, the people's defence of the fatherland.' I went home and asked my father about the Volkssturm and he told me what it was all about and that he was in it too – in the second line. My father had lost a foot during the First World War and yet he was in the Volkssturm. But he maintained that 'the second line' was the most important in the Volkssturm because men like him couldn't run away.

Henning found the visit home depressing and was relieved to return to his unit: 'The newspapers were full of death notices, there was not much to eat, and everything seemed grey and cheer-less. The papers full of the names of men who had fallen for "Führer and Fatherland", and to meet former classmates who had already been widowed, that was very depressing.' 'Many of the women in Germany had lost their sons or their brothers and they couldn't imagine that all this was in vain, that they were killed for the wrong reason, they couldn't believe it,' a former diplomat, Hans von Herwarth, recalled.

Just three days after the Russian breakthrough on the Oder 'the Big Three' gathered at Yalta on the Black Sea to discuss the division of Germany and the post-war settlement of Europe. President Roosevelt had come to secure agreement for his 'World Instrument of Peace' – the future United Nations; Stalin sought a Soviet zone of influence in eastern Europe. Nothing brought the different moral outlooks of the participants into sharper focus than the issue of Poland. Britain had gone to war in 1939 to ensure a free Poland and Churchill was intent on securing nothing less than her independence when it finally came to an end. Stalin appeared reasonable – 'this was a matter of life and death for the Soviet State,' he declared, for the Soviet Union's security required a strong and powerful Polish neighbour. 'That was the whole basis of the Soviet attitude,' Churchill later recalled, 'they wanted to see Poland independent, free and strong.'

So much for the rhetoric. The strong, free and democratic Poland was to be on Stalin's terms. Churchill was forced to agree to withdraw his support for the Polish government-in-exile in London after securing a promise of free and fair elections. There was final agreement too on post-war boundaries, and this was Stalin's map. Germany east of the Oder would cease to exist. It would mean moving 6 million Germans into the borders of a new, much smaller Germany. Churchill observed: 'it might be managed, subject to the moral question, which I would have to settle with my own people'. Stalin replied that there were no more Germans in these areas for 'they had all run away' – run before the advancing Soviet armies. Stalin also signalled his intention to implement his own Morgenthau Plan by stripping Germany of her industry as a first payment of war reparations. The communiqué issued at the end of the conference called for 'the peoples liberated from the domination of Nazi Germany' to create their own 'democratic institutions'. It affirmed the 'right of all peoples to choose the form of government under which they will live' and called for the establishment of Roosevelt's new 'International Organisation', which would 'provide the greatest opportunity in all history to create in the years to come the essential conditions of such a peace'. Rarely has rhetoric fallen so short of reality. It is hard to believe that Churchill had confidence in Stalin's assurances, but Poland was already in Soviet hands.

The Germans had concluded the Nazi–Soviet pact for the dismemberment of Poland in 1939 – they understood and shared Stalin's totalitarian disregard for the truth. Hitler's propaganda minister was in no doubt that a new order was being created in Europe, and it would not be based on 'democratic institutions'. Writing in *Das Reich*, Goebbels warned that: 'If the German people lay down their weapons, the Soviets according to the agreement between Roosevelt, Churchill, and Stalin would occupy all of East and Southeast Europe along with the greater part of the Reich. An iron curtain would fall over this enormous territory controlled by the Soviet Union, behind which nations would be slaughtered.'

The British and Americans had agreed at Yalta to do all they could to help Stalin's armies by launching bombing raids on cities that stood in its path. Four cities were selected for special attention – Berlin, Leipzig, Chemnitz and Dresden. RAF Bomber Command had been considering launching a blow of 'catastrophic force' on a town hitherto untouched. The beautiful baroque capital of Saxony seemed an ideal choice. On the night of 13 February – two days after the Yalta Conference ended – more than eight hundred aircraft from Bomber Command attacked Dresden. The following day four hundred bombers from the American Eighth Air Force renewed the aerial assault on the city. A population of over 600,000 was swollen by nearly 300,000 refugees who were fleeing the approaching Soviet armies. There were terrible scenes as the Allied firestorm swept through the centre of the city. So many bodies were incinerated in the intense heat, it was difficult to estimate the number of dead, but it is thought to have been no less than 30,000. The American writer Kurt Vonnegut was a witness to the terrible aftermath. The twenty-two-year-old Vonnegut had been taken prisoner in the Ardennes on almost his first day in combat. He had sheltered from the firestorm in a slaughterhouse, but was put to work collecting the dead in the days after the bombing. 'Our guards pointed out here and there what appeared to be charred logs, and these were people, who had been caught out in the open,' he recalled.

There were no real air raid shelters. People could only go down into ordinary cellars, we were brought in to dig down to these. We would get into a cellar and people would be sitting there, as if on a streetcar waiting for the next stop. It was the carbon monoxide that had killed them. They gave us stretchers, so we were able to bring these bodies out and we made these big piles of corpses and kerosene or something was thrown on them. But there were so many cellars to be cleaned out, of course the town began to smell. Not that anybody was living there any more.

While Dresden was selected for special attention it was only one of the cities to suffer from a bombing campaign that grew in intensity in the final months. More bombs were dropped on Germany in March 1945 than in any other month of the war. German economic effort had finally begun to collapse under the weight of this massive air assault. For most ordinary Germans the war had become a desperate daily battle for survival, a struggle for food and shelter in the smoking ruins of their towns and cities. The intensity of the Allied air assault in the last year of the war was turning Germany into the industrial wasteland the American Treasury Secretary Henry Morgenthau had proposed in his plan.

In the dark December days of the Ardennes offensive the Western Allies had been desperate for the Red Army to attack in the east. Stalin had obligingly brought the great Soviet offensive on the Vistula forward by a few days. It was a small sacrifice, for the campaign had been months in the preparation. By the time Soviet tanks began to roll westward the tide had already turned in the Ardennes – Eisenhower was grateful nonetheless. The emerging crisis in Poland was of such magnitude every German division that could be spared, and many that could not be, was transferred from the Western Front to the east. But after the 'bloody nose' in the Ardennes the Allies were slow to exploit their overwhelming superiority in men and *matériel*. Progress in the west was painfully slow in January and in marked contrast to the bold Soviet advance to the Oder.

The wrangling over strategy that had bedevilled inter-Allied planning in the autumn was, if anything, even sharper in the last months of the war. British confidence in Eisenhower was at rock bottom. It was the fixed view of both Churchill and Brooke that Ike's 'broad front' had been discredited by the German break-through in the Ardennes, and yet he appeared to be proposing the same strategy for the final campaign of the war. This was no longer purely a military question. If Allied forces were obliged to struggle towards the Rhine on a broad front, precious time would be lost in the race for Berlin. It was still a race – just. Eisenhower's enthusiasm for an assault on the capital of the Reich seemed to have cooled markedly. In September he had been quite clear that it was 'the main prize' and the ultimate object of the Anglo-American campaign. British eyes were still firmly fixed on this prize. Whilst Eisenhower had reaffirmed his inten-tion to give priority to Monty's northern thrust he showed no inclination to make it the only one. In truth Eisenhower was once again caught between a rock and a hard place. The burden of the battle in the west was being shouldered by the Americans and yet the main thrust into Germany was to be commanded by a troublesome Brit. Bradley was incandescent with rage when Eisenhower informed him on 31 January that the US Ninth Army would remain under Monty's operational control for the crossing of the Rhine. He acknowledged the logic of Eisenhower's deci-sion – the 21st Army Group was simply not strong enough to punch through on its own – but he was not prepared to accept that Monty should command the main thrust. It was a bitter pill to swallow for a man who was still smarting from the humil-iation of losing the Ninth and First Armies during the Ardennes campaign. The British had won pride of place for the final assault on the Rhine, but there would be a secondary southern thrust by Bradley's 12th Army Group (First and Third Armies).

Monty launched his push towards the Rhine on 7 February with a massive air and artillery bombardment of German defen-sive positions around the towns of Cleve and Goch. With what the historian Russell Weigley describes as 'an un-American devo-tion to concentrating', five infantry divisions supported by three armoured brigades were thrown at a twelve kilometre front between the Rhine and the Maas. The month-long battle to clear the west bank of the Rhine was to see some the hardest fighting of the campaign. The chief obstacle for the British and Canadians was the Reichswald forest at the western end of the Siegfried Line. Twelve kilometres long and some five kilometres wide, the forest contained rides that were little more than the width of a tank. On 9 February the tanks of the 4th/7th Royal Dragoon Guards advanced towards the forest with the 43rd Division: 'We set off along the road to Cleve, a town which had been thoroughly plastered by Lancasters and was now being assaulted,' Trooper Austin Baker recalled.

Before we moved, the infantry of 214 Brigade piled on to the backs of the tanks to be ferried up the line. I suppose each tank carried about ten – we even had two inside, squatting on the turret floor. It was a nightmare journey. The Cleve road was absolutely jammed with vehicles, moving forward at a snail's pace. If Jerry had had anything like equality in the air there would have been slaughter on that road. The column moved in fits and starts, all night. It was horribly cold and I was frozen stiff, even in a zoot suit and a jerkin. I was sorry for the infantry clinging miserably to the outsides of the tanks. As a matter of fact I was sorry for myself, because the trip was made especially unpleasant for me by a bad attack of diarrhoea. You can imagine how awkward it was. Every time we stopped I had to crawl over the two infantrymen on the turret floor, squeeze past Le Maitre [the tank commander] and get out of the hatch, and climb down into a field by the roadside. Having got there, I had to divest myself of a leather jerkin, a zoot suit, a suit of denims and a battle-dress – with the column likely to move on at any moment.

The following day Baker's tank, 'Shaggy Dog', pushed on into the forest itself. It had barely gone a few hundred metres when the ride beneath its tracks crumbled away: 'We slid sideways into the ditch to lie there hopelessly bogged down,' Baker recalled. 'The trouble was the path was so narrow that the tank completely blocked it, and all the huge column of vehicles which was following behind us was held up. The forest on either side was too thick for them to make a detour.'

Farther up the road the regiment's A Squadron had reached 'Tiger Corner' near the village of Hau, and one of its tanks had been hit. 'An ambulance came bumping slowly down the path towards us and pulled up in front of "Shaggy Dog". It was carrying two of the crew of the knocked-out A Squadron tank. One of them was the commander, and he was able to walk in spite of being shaken up, but the other chap had one leg off and, as far as I could see, an arm as well.' The drip, drip of casualties continued even though victory appeared to be within reach. Baker recalled:

Third Troop [of A Squadron] had got forward to a little spinney, where they were stuck, holding a precarious position with a small force of infantry and a self-propelled 17-pounder. Under cover of a smokescreen, Thorniley, then 3rd Troop leader, tried to move his tank forward, but a Jerry tank or SP (Self-Propelled Gun) had also taken advantage of the screen to get into a good firing position and it brewed up both Thorniley and the 17-pounder. Thorniley's tank blew up instantly – nobody had time to bale out. Thorniley himself was ejected from the turret with such force that his webbing belt was ripped in two on some projection, but he wasn't very badly wounded. The rest of the crew was killed – Corporal Sam Weaver, Ryan, Robinson and Barrs. Sam Weaver had just returned to the squadron after being wounded in Normandy. I remember him telling me that he believed that there was only one shot with your name on it, and if you had a very narrow escape then the one with your name on it had missed and you would be safe in future. Evidently there were two with Sam's name on.

The British and Canadians suffered 15,000 casualties in the battles to close the Rhine, the US Ninth Army more than 7,000. Field Marshal Model had orchestrated another of the stubborn retreats with which he had made his name in the east. Discipline was enforced with a characteristically iron hand. Stabshelferin (Staff Assistant) Gerda Ehrhardt had transferred to Army Group B in January: 'I remember seeing a good number of soldiers hanging from trees – they'd been executed because they had tried to desert.' Model refused to tolerate any sign of 'defeatism', especially from his own staff at Army Group B Headquarters: 'I have to tell you honestly how I thought of him, our "Bierkutcher" [a common wagon driver], he behaved just like one,' Ehrhardt recalled. 'He used to give pep talks to his officers, although deep down none of them believed it was worth fighting any longer.' For the most part the ordinary soldier had fought with his usual determination, this time in the knowledge that every village surrendered to the enemy was German. But it had cost Army Groups B and H a further 90,000 men – most had been taken prisoner. The last great obstacle remained, and the Reich had precious few soldiers left to defend it.

To the south Bradley's armies began their advance on 23 February when the US First Army jumped the River Roer and pressed rapidly on towards the Rhine just south of Düsseldorf. 'Resistance is on the point of crumbling,' the staff at First Army reported three days later; 'the Boche although not in any sense getting up and surrendering in mass, are fighting a disorganised defensive battle. Stiff resistance where it has been encountered has been centred in the small towns and usually after an hour or so of fighting, the soldiers have come out with their hands up.' On 6 March Patton's Third Army burst through the weak German defences in the Eifel, and without pausing to clear the surrounding hills dashed on towards the Rhine north of Koblenz. 'We are in a horse race with Courtney [Hodges, US First Army commander],' Patton wrote to his wife that day. 'If he beats me [across the Rhine] I shall be ashamed.' The Third Army raced 40 kilometres in three days and on 9 March Patton's men were able to spit in the Rhine. But by then it was too late to trump Courtney Hodges. On 7 March soldiers of the US First Army had advanced towards the Ludendorff railway bridge at Remagen, one of the last remaining crossings of the Rhine. Tanks and infantry fought their way through Remagen towards the twin stone towers at the western end of the bridge. Frantic activity on the other bank of the river suggested the Germans were preparing to blow the bridge as soon as the Americans set foot on it. A company of men from the 9th Armoured Division's reconnaissance force pressed forward nevertheless. As they began to edge their way across under fire the Germans detonated the explosive charges. The bridge rose from its supports, amid a cloud of dust and falling wooden planks, before settling back into place. Large holes had been blown in the planking but it was still very much intact. The Americans pressed on, cutting anything they passed that resembled a detonation wire, and were soon in possession of all 325 metres of the bridge. That evening Hodges telephoned Bradley with the news:

'Brad, we've gotten a bridge.'

'A bridge? You mean you've got one intact on the Rhine?'

'Yep,' Hodges replied, 'Leonard nabbed the one at Remagen before they blew it up . . .'

'Hot dog, Courtney,' Bradley said, 'this will bust him wide open. Are you getting your stuff across?'

'Just as fast as we can push it over.'

Bradley was cock-a-hoop, but his joy was tempered somewhat by the reaction of Eisenhower's staff at SHAEF, who asked, not unreasonably, 'Where are you going to go from Remagen?' Beyond the bridge, the steep wooded hills of the Westerwald presented a serious obstacle to an advancing army – the going was incomparably better to the north, where Monty was preparing to cross the Rhine. 'What in hell do you want us to do,' Bradley asked, 'pull back and blow it up?' He blamed the general reluctance at SHAEF to exploit a remarkable opportunity on Eisenhower's 'British-dominated staff', who were wedded to their 'neatly ordered plan'. There was also that man Monty

45. A fragile-looking Hitler with Grand Admiral Karl Dönitz [right], Field Marshal
Wilhelm Keitel and Foreign Minister Joachim von Ribbentrop [left] at the
Wolfsschanze, his field headquarters in East Prussia. This was taken on 18 September –
two days before he had announced his intention to launch a new offensive through the
Ardennes.

46. Soldiers of the US First Army push on up to the front during the Battle of the Bulge in December 1944.

47. German prisoners shoulder the body of a GI killed during the Ardennes offensive. No stretcher is needed because the body has frozen solid.

48. American soldiers try to dig slit trenches in the frozen ground to take cover from the German artillery fire near Berismenil. It has already claimed the life of the soldier in the foreground.

49. The last bridge over the Rhine at Remagen was seized by the US First Army on 7 March 1945 before demolition charges could be detonated. An army observer keeps watch from 'Flak Hill' on the east bank.

50. British carriers bowl over one of the Allied bridges built across the Rhine. The east bank was forced by 21st Army Group during the night of 23–24 March after a massive bombardment by 3,000 guns.

51. The grim aftermath of the Allied bombing of Dresden on 13 and 14 February 1945. The city was swollen with refugees from the Soviet advance in the east.

52. The Big Three, Churchill, Roosevelt and Stalin, at Yalta in February 1945, where the finishing touches were applied to the new European order. Stalin got what he wanted, the borders in the east were redrawn and Poland fell into the Soviet sphere of influence.

53. The bomb-ravaged centre of Munich in the last days of the Reich. The Allied air assault on Germany's cities killed an estimated 650,000 people – most of them women, children and old men.

54. Hitler considers plans for the rebuilding of the city of Linz while Berlin is reduced to rubble about him, March 1945.

55. American medics consider the Nazis' legacy of inhumanity at Dachau concentration camp, which was captured on 30 April 1945.

56. General Alfred Jodl arrives in Reims for the signing of the surrender document on 7 May 1945.

57. The ruins of the Reichstag in Berlin, the symbolic end of Hitler's Reich.

again – Bradley was determined to see his hand in every personal disappointment. But Eisenhower was no more convinced of the wisdom of exploiting the Remagen crossing than his staff. He was insistent that the Allied armies should close the Rhine along the entire front before a bridgehead was exploited, and the northern route would then offer the best hope of a rapid advance. It was a painfully cautious approach – there was evidence aplenty that German resistance was crumbling – but Eisenhower was committed to a deliberate build-up.

Monty was in full accord. He had already prevented General Simpson from pushing elements of the US Ninth Army across the Rhine. The field marshal would cross the Rhine in his own good time, and only after much careful preparation. A quarter of a million men would be massed along a 30-kilometre front for Operation Plunder. In the two weeks before the final assault more than seven thousand Allied sorties were flown against road and rail networks between the Rhine and the Ruhr. At first Monty had endeavoured to make it a British affair. Simpson had been tactlessly informed that a corps from his Ninth Army would be needed, but it would be commanded by General Dempsey of the British 2nd Army. This plan was only dropped when Dempsey joined Simpson in objecting to the arrangement. Monty had insisted on the need for the Ninth Army, and was indeed pressing for ten more American divisions to join the operation beyond the Rhine. The eyes of the world would be watching the main assault crossing of the Rhine, and Simpson quite rightly wanted it to be an Allied operation.

'Who' would claim the lion's share of the credit for the final victory in the west was becoming as important as 'how' it would be achieved. The last battles of the campaign were to be dominated by questions of national prestige, and an unseemly jostling for newspaper headlines. Bradley and Patton were convinced that Monty was intent on hogging the limelight for himself and the British. Just hours before the start of Operation Plunder, Patton managed to 'sneak a division' across the Rhine. There had been no preliminary bombardment and the Germans were taken completely by surprise. Patton telephoned Bradley with the news: 'Brad, for God's sake tell the world we're across . . . I want the world to know Third Army made it before Monty starts across.' The Americans were capable of crossing the Rhine, Bradley told correspondents, without a massive air and artillery bombardment.

The great northern assault on the Rhine near Wesel was launched on the night of 23 March under a protective barrage fired by 3,500 guns. At nine o'clock the first of the assault battalions from the famous 51st (Highland) Division, supported by amphibious DD tanks, set out for the east bank. They were met by only light opposition and were soon pressing inland towards the town of Rees. An hour later a second crossing was made three kilometres downstream by the 1st Commando Brigade. The artillery bombardment grew in intensity as the Allied air forces pounded enemy positions inland. By the following morning the Allies had established five separate bridgeheads across the river and were moving forward to link up with the airborne armada that had begun dropping behind enemy lines along the east bank. By 28 March the Allies were firmly established in a bridgehead 50 kilometres wide and some 30 kilometres deep. Preparations were already under way for a drive eastward to the Elbe and the plains of north Germany, where Monty had promised his soldiers, 'we will crack about . . . chasing the enemy from pillar to post'. Beyond the Elbe there was the great prize – Berlin.

The time had come to throw caution aside. German forces in the west had steadily dwindled to a nominal sixty-five divisions. Many of these were little more than small battle groups – short on armour, ammunition and morale. By contrast Eisenhower commanded the equivalent of ninety-four full-strength Allied divisions. The Rhine had been breached and British, Canadian and American troops were flooding across it. Monty was for pushing on with all speed to the Elbe, merely 'masking centres of resistance' as his armies passed. He sent a signal on the 27th to Eisenhower, informing him that he had issued orders to the Second and Ninth Armies to move their armour forward at once and to 'get through to the Elbe with the utmost speed and drive'. He added as a postscript the details of the axis of his thrust: 'Wesel–Munster–Wiedenbruck–Herford–Hannover–thence via the autobahn to Berlin I hope'.

Monty's armour had already begun to roll forward when, the following day, he received a reply from Eisenhower. It was a crushing blow and the first indication that the Supreme Commander had performed a complete volte-face. 'My present plans . . . are now being co-ordinated with Stalin,' Eisenhower revealed, with more than a touch of self-importance. Monty was to make contact with the advancing 12th Army Group to the east of the Ruhr, whereupon the Ninth Army would fall once again under Bradley's command. Precious time would then be spent 'mopping up' the Ruhr before advancing through central Germany on the axis Erfurt–Leipzig–Dresden. It was to be Bradley's operation and the 21st Army Group would act in support. Only three days earlier Eisenhower had met Monty, Churchill and Brooke on the Rhine. No mention had been made of this sudden change of plan or of his intention to 'co-ordinate' with Stalin. Eisenhower had repeatedly approved the decision to make the main thrust in the north because it offered the most direct route to Berlin, and the capital had been acknowl-edged as the ultimate objective of the Allied effort. On 15 September he had written, 'clearly, Berlin is the main prize . . . there is no doubt whatsoever, in my mind, that we should concen-trate all our energies and resources on a rapid thrust to Berlin'. Now Berlin was to be surrendered to the Russians. Eisenhower made no reference to the capital in his reply, but by signalling his intention to shift the Allied thrust to a new axis he had all but ruled out a drive to capture it. 'Dirty work' was Monty's verdict.

Stalin, on the other hand, was delighted. The crossing of the Rhine had not been welcome news in Moscow. Stalin had called

Marshal Zhukov to the Kremlin to discuss the assault on Berlin. 'The German front in the west has collapsed for good,' he informed him, 'and it seems that Hitler's men do not want to do anything to halt the advance of the Allied forces. In the meantime they are reinforcing all their army groups facing us.' The Germans might choose to give them a free run to Berlin, Stalin warned, so Soviet forces would need to begin their offensive at the earliest possible opportunity. Eisenhower's cable outlining his plans to attack the Ruhr and then drive towards Dresden was as pleasant as it was surprising. The Soviet leader sent a typically disingenuous reply back. Perhaps with tongue firmly in cheek he assured Ike that he would make his main thrust in this direction too, for 'Berlin has lost its former strategic importance . . . only secondary forces will therefore be allotted in the direction of Berlin.'

When asked by Monty to clarify his new position, Eisenhower dismissed the capital: 'that place has become nothing but a geographical location; I have never been interested in those'. But the war would be finally won only when Berlin fell. 'The National Socialists,' Goebbels had declared, 'will either win together in Berlin or die together in Berlin.' As Anthony Beevor pointed out in his study of the city's fall, Stalin would have been familiar with Karl Marx's maxim that Berlin was the key to Germany and 'whoever controls Germany, controls Europe'.

Whilst it was astonishing that Eisenhower had changed his mind so markedly and in such a short time, perhaps the most remarkable aspect of all was his decision to communicate his intentions to Stalin before he had discussed them with America's principal ally or even the Combined Allied Chiefs of Staff. Churchill was as amazed and disappointed as Monty. Neither a rapidly fading Roosevelt nor his chiefs of staff were prepared to intervene. All Churchill's direct pleas to Eisenhower to reconsider his new strategy also foundered. 'I could at this stage only warn and plead,' Churchill was to write later. 'I moved amid cheering crowds, or sat at a table adorned with congratulations and blessings from every part of the Grand Alliance, with an aching heart and a mind oppressed by forebodings.' What would be born in the ashes of Germany? Churchill felt sure he knew. The Soviet Union had become 'a mortal danger to the free world'. The Anglo-American armies should, he argued, establish a new front 'against her onward sweep' as far east as possible. The 'prime and true objective' of the Allied armies was Berlin. 'The United States stood on the scene of victory,' Churchill wrote, 'master of world fortunes, but without a true and coherent design.'

What was the point of winning the battles, Monty would later ask, if the war was to be lost politically? Nor was he the only one of Ike's senior commanders to question the wisdom of halting the Allied armies short of Berlin. On the evening of 12 April Patton entertained Eisenhower and Bradley at his head-quarters near Ohrdruf. The Third Army had swept out of its bridgehead across the Rhine at Oppenheim and along Hitler's admirable autobahns to the city of Erfurt and beyond. Eisenhower was in expansive mood, and the three generals had talked into the early hours. Patton learned for the first time of SHAEF's new strategy. It was highly inadvisable tactically for the American army to take Berlin, Eisenhower told those present, and he hoped political influence would not force him to try, for it had 'no tactical or strategical value'. 'Ike, I don't see how you figure that one,' an incredulous Patton replied. 'We had better take Berlin and quick, and [then go eastward] on to the Oder.' Later that evening Eisenhower returned to the Berlin question. Who would want it? he asked. Patton turned to him and, placing both hands on his shoulders, replied: 'I think history will answer that question for you.'

The key decisions on the post-war settlement of Germany had been taken long before the Allies crossed the Rhine. The most important battles had been lost at the conference tables, first at Quebec in September 1944 and then again in Yalta. Germany had been divided into occupation zones and Berlin was in the

Soviet sector. An assault on the capital might cost the Allies another 100,000 casualties. The Red Army was only 65 kilometres from the capital and had been preparing for the final siege for many weeks. If the Allies pushed on beyond the Elbe they would run the very real risk of a clash with advancing Soviet forces. There was also talk at SHAEF of a last stand by fanatical SS units in the south of Germany. It was empty talk, but it may have influenced Eisenhower's decision to 'mop up' in the west – the course of least resistance. The decision on Berlin was taken by a soldier whose only real objective was the defeat of Germany's armed forces. 'As soldiers we looked naively on this British inclination to complicate the war with political foresight and non-military objectives,' Bradley admitted later. President Roosevelt had declared, 'I can handle Stalin,' and was of the view that the Soviet leader should be given a chance to uphold the agreements reached by the Big Three. Stalin felt no compunction about breaking these before his signature was even dry on the final page of the joint declaration. As the Red Army marched westward, Moscow-friendly governments sprang up in the countries left in its wake. The United States had bent over backwards to win Stalin's trust. Not enough thought had been given in Washington to the new post-war order in Europe – hardly surprising then, that the question of Berlin, which should have been thrashed out in Whitehall and at the White House, was left to the senior soldier in the field. Roosevelt had dropped a bombshell at Yalta when in Stalin's presence he had announced his intention to withdraw the American armies from Europe within two years of the final surrender. Who would fill the vacuum? 'Above all,' Churchill wrote later, 'a settlement must be reached on all major issues between the West and the East in Europe *before the armies of democracy melted.*' It was important to grab as much of Germany as possible and then negotiate.

It is very unlikely that a British and American advance would have met with the same degree of stubborn resistance that the Red Army was soon to encounter around Berlin. General

Simpson's Ninth Army reached the Elbe on 12 April and immediately seized a crossing. The Americans were only 100 kilometres from Berlin: 'My plan was to have the 2nd Armoured
Division accompanied by an infantry division in trucks take off
at night and push down the autobahn rapidly towards Berlin,'
Simpson wrote after the war. He anticipated little resistance: 'My
mistake was in not doing this promptly, immediately after we
got across the Elbe. I was completely surprised and chagrined
when Bradley ordered me to stop and withdraw back across the
Elbe. I really believe that the Ninth Army could have captured
Berlin with little loss well before the Russians reached the city.'
Montgomery, the commander Eisenhower and Bradley had often
accused of excessive caution, was of the same mind. It is not
clear what Stalin would have done if the Allies had pressed on,
but Beevor is firmly of the view that he would have resisted any
attempt to seize 'the Red Army's prize from under its nose'.

Germany was defeated, further resistance was futile, and yet even
in the west there were many who stubbornly refused to acknowledge it. Germans soldiers were still prepared to die for Führer,
Volk and Fatherland. Robert Vogt had been wounded in the leg
in Normandy, and after a spell at military school had returned
to active service as an Unteroffizier with the 396th Infantry
Regiment: 'We were soldiers and we had taken the oath [to the
Führer]. I didn't believe that our Panzerfausts could win the war
but to desert, well, that never crossed my mind. Besides, a fanatical officer might have shot us. We'd fight as long as we had
weapons and some kind of command.'

Vogt's anti-tank unit joined two from a Waffen SS division in
an effort to hold the autobahn near Limburg:

We dug in on both sides of the autobahn and waited for the
Americans. As usual the fighter-bombers came first, shooting at
anything and everything, and we took casualties. There were far too
few of us to hold it and we were left with no choice but to retreat

into the forest. We stayed there for five or six days, and like parti-
sans, we tried to harass the enemy by shooting at passing American
vehicles. It was pointless. We were gambling with our lives for a lost
cause. It became clear, even to us, that the war was lost, so we threw
our weapons in a stream and, waving a white pocket handkerchief,
moved towards the autobahn. The Americans collected us and took
us to Idstein. It was over.

The newly promoted Feldwebel (Sergeant Major), Otto Henning
of the 130th Panzer Lehr Reconnaissance was one of more than
300,000 German soldiers trapped between the pincers of the
advancing US First and Ninth Armies in the Ruhr: 'Survival was
what mattered to us. To lose a war was terrible. We all felt that.
We spent a good deal of time speculating about what we might
have to face, imprisonment, that sort of thing. How can life go
on, what will happen. Our towns were in ruins.'

It was particularly galling for Allied units to take casualties
from an enemy too stubborn to acknowledge that the war was
lost. At Wunstorf airfield near Celle in northern Germany the
13th Battalion of the Parachute Regiment found itself engaged
by a group of teenagers from the Hitler Youth. The battalion's
medical officer was twenty-four-year-old D-Day veteran David
Tibbs: 'They were manning multiple-barrelled 40mm rapid-fire
anti-aircraft guns, and every time we appeared they fired at us,
in spite of our efforts to get them to surrender. They wounded
several of our men.' A member of Captain Tibbs's medical team,
Sergeant Scott, went out on a motorcycle to try to help the
wounded lying out in the open. 'In spite of his red cross the
Hitler Youth turned their gun on him and he fell to the ground
dead beside this wounded man,' Tibbs recalled.

When I reached him I found his head was completely shattered. The
wounded man he had gone to help was lying close by with a severe
leg wound. He looked at me with a strange intensity and said in a
low, urgent voice, 'Doc, please remove Sergeant Scott's brains from
my tunic.' Aghast, with great care I cupped my hands and lifted the

still-warm tissue across to Sergeant Scott's body. It seemed as though I was holding the very essence of this man in my hands. A man admired and respected by all, who had been awarded the Military Medal and the Croix de Guerre for his courage in repeatedly retrieving so many wounded from dangerous positions, whether they were British or Germans, and always an inspiration by his cheerful acceptance of arduous conditions. We had been comrades through many formidable times together and his loss left a huge void.

The 40mm cannon was silenced by a tank. A young British officer walked towards the Germans with his gun pointed down to demonstrate he was not going to fire. The youths surrendered and several were later taken to Tibbs' regimental aid post to have their wounds dressed. 'There was no hint of recrimination against them but I fear this generous attitude was wasted because when I tried to treat one Hitler Youth who was slightly wounded, he hurled abuse at me,' Tibbs recalled. Many Allied soldiers were altogether less patient, and those foolish enough to offer even token resistance were met by heavy shellfire or an air strike. Makeshift barricades were swept aside as impatient Allied armour swept through villages and towns, leaving a trail of German corpses in its wake.

The American trap around the ruins of Germany's industrial heartland had snapped shut at Lippstadt on Easter Sunday – 1 April. Hitler had issued his customary 'stand fast' order, and as so often in the past it proved to be nothing short of disastrous. The remnants of the 5th Panzer, 1st Parachute and 15th Armies were squeezed into a pocket measuring 50 by 120 kilometres. So too was Field Marshal Model's Army Group B headquarters. American divisions that were well placed to strike at Berlin would spend the next two weeks battering away at the beaten forces in the pocket. Resistance was patchy and was often dependent on the presence of Waffen SS troops. Civilians had begun to hang white bed sheets from the windows of flats and houses. Desperate to save their homes from destruction, some risked pleading with their 'defenders' to choose another battlefield. Model's head-quarters moved from village to village in an effort to avoid the ever present Allied fighter-bombers. He was followed by a stream of impossible Führer orders, including one for the destruction of bridges, rail installations and industry – Germany's future. 'We can no longer afford to concern ourselves with the popula-tion,' Hitler had told his inner circle. He was intent on orches-trating a mad Wagnerian end to the Reich.

On 13 April Model's headquarters at Wuppertal-Sonnenborn was bombed. The staff assistant, Gerda Ehrhardt, was buried alive in a cellar when the building she was in took a direct hit: 'After I crawled out from underneath the rubble I made my way to the headquarters building and Model was there. He was striding up and down like a tiger in a cage. He did not know what to do. I still see him today in my mind's eye. It was just over for him.' The following day Model's headquarters moved on, but without Ehrhardt. 'I didn't care any more. I lay flat out in an apple orchard and the American shells screamed over me, one after the other. Then I saw Model's cartographer. "I'm walking to Munich," he said, "come with me." I'd had enough – it was high time to get home.' That same day, 14 April, Model rejected a call to surrender on the grounds that his oath to the Führer required him to fight to the bitter end.

Rolf Munninger was still serving at Army Group B:

After Wuppertal we were hunted, really hunted. There was no longer a proper HQ, we just parked our vehicles where we could and always in a wood, then at least we had some cover. It was raining. The mood was zero. I was the duty officer on the 16th when at around four in the morning we received a 'Führerbefehl' – a personal order from Hitler. It stated that all army units in the Ruhr area with vehicles were expected to fight their way through the front and on to Berlin to join the defence of the city. We were supposed to grab our supplies from the civilian population – oh, and to start reprisal actions. These might include setting fire to homes. I thought, well, this idiotic order isn't urgent at all. It was four in the morning and I thought, as it was ridiculous anyway, I would send it to Model at six o'clock – that would be early enough. I sent it to Model at six and within five minutes a row had begun. Where are those two idiots who are responsible for this? Bring them to me this instant. Dr Dimmler was my superior but it had been my decision. Model stood there and screamed: 'Who received this telex?' I said, 'Field Marshal, that was me.' 'Are you completely insane? The telex came at 4 a.m. and I get it at 6 a.m.?' Fortunately for me, I had not made any notes in the margins, something like 'complete rubbish', so I pretended to be repentant and said nothing. Model continued screaming and told us, 'I ought to have you both executed on the spot for this.' He had obviously lost his nerve. The whole thing didn't bother me too much. It would have been difficult to have shot us anyway – we didn't have any guns or ammunition left.

By 18 April resistance to the Allied advance had melted away. The Allies had bagged twenty-five generals, an admiral and 317,000 other prisoners. Rolf Munninger had been given official release papers just before the end:

Model said to us, 'Gentlemen, it's over, there is nothing more we can do. It is up to you what you do from here.' He said his goodbyes and left with a handful of officers. That was it – the end. There were no more orders. Six of us left, still in uniform. I can remember hiding in a stream with British tanks on the road above us. We could have brought them down with a bazooka, they were too busy enjoying the euphoria of the victory and had thrown all caution to the wind. We'd done the same once.

Model was not to be found among the prisoners. 'A Field Marshal,' he had said, 'does not become a prisoner. Such a thing is not possible.' On 21 April he walked into a wood near Duisburg and shot himself.

Allied soldiers were shocked by the utter devastation that greeted their advance through Germany. It was only on 16 April that the air assault on 'military, industrial and economic systems' officially ceased. By then most of Germany's cities and major towns lay in ruins. 'I do loathe all this destruction and suffering,' Captain David Fraser of the Grenadier Guards wrote in March. 'I loathe the sufferings of the old and the children, of whatever nationality. It is only possible to hate from a distance. You know how people chuckle and say "1,000 more bombers over some-where last night" with glee, but when one sees the results one feels nothing but pain.' Fraser did not underestimate the part played by the Allied air forces in the defeat of Germany, but it was impossible not to be moved by the sea of rubble that greeted those who visited cities such as Cologne. The bombing of Berlin was to continue well into April as the Allies prepared the city for the ground assault.

Sympathy for the plight of civilians was tempered by the grim legacy of hate the Allied armies discovered as they advanced through Hitler's Reich. On 12 April the British reached the town of Celle, and at the request of a local delegation a small detach-ment was sent forward to take possession of a camp near by – Belsen. One of the first to reach the camp was Sergeant William Wood, who had landed in Normandy on D + 1 and was still serving with the 32nd Casualty Clearing Station: 'Shortly after we left Celle we ran across this horrible smell. We couldn't make this out, I'd never smelled anything like it and it got worse and worse. When we reached the camp we could see the perimeter wire and the guards in brown uniform – Hungarians – but we didn't go in that day.' The medical team pitched its tents in nearby fields for the night. The following morning the senior medical officer addressed the rest of his unit:

He said that we were going to be the first medical unit to go into the camp and that he'd been in the night before and it was terrible. He couldn't explain to us and we'd have to see it for ourselves. So then we were all absolutely coated with DDT powder and issued with a rum ration. We trucked down to the camp and past the guards and it was a terrible sight. There were dead bodies, people dying, people trying to move from one place to another. The stench there was terrible, and the huts themselves, the beds were very close together – three-tiered wooden beds and they were absolutely full of people – the dead and the living.

The Germans had crammed 40,000 men, women and children into a camp designed for just 8,000. Many were Jews who had been brought to Belsen from camps that were on the point of falling to the Soviet advance. The scale of the task was daunting. Where to start? 'They looked at us but didn't see us,' Wood recalled. 'They were starving, but with typhus on top of that. . . . We couldn't take them out of the camp because of the typhus. There was no food in the camp. No toilet facilities, no washing facilities – there was nothing. The Germans had just walked out and left them.' For more than a month the inmates had been given no more than a bowl of swede soup a day. The only water available was from filthy tanks, many contaminated by corpses. A few of the desperate inmates had begun to eat the dead.

The officer commanding the 11th Light Field Ambulance, Lieutenant Colonel Mervyn Gonin, remembered a camp littered with 10,000 unburied bodies:

Corpses lay everywhere, some in huge piles, sometimes singly or in pairs where they had fallen as they shuffled along the dirt tracks. Those who died of disease usually died in the huts. When starvation was the chief cause of death, they died in the open. It is an odd characteristic of starvation that its victims seem compelled to wander till they fall and die. Piles of corpses naked and obscene, with a woman too weak to stand propping herself up against them as she cooked the food we had given her over an open fire. Men and women crouching down just anywhere in the open relieving themselves of the dysentery which was scouring their bowels. A woman standing naked washing herself with some issue soap in water from a tank in which the remnants of a child floated.

Captain David Tibbs of the 13th Parachute Battalion was ordered to take his team on an instructional visit to the camp. Many of the medics who were serving with great distinction alongside him were pacifists:

The colonel came to me and said, 'David, I want you to take some of your conscientious objectors over to an extraordinary place which has just been discovered a few miles away, so they can see why we needed to stop the Nazis.' So the padre, myself and three of the conscientious objectors went over to Belsen. Strictly we weren't supposed to because we were literally going to have a look, but I felt it was important. The huts were indescribable, nearly all the inmates were in late stages of starvation. All absolutely seething with lice – numerous cases of tuberculosis and typhus were spreading among them.

At the far end of the camp the SS guards had left huge open pits full of decomposing bodies. More mass graves were dug and the SS put to work clearing the corpses. The survivors were washed, shaved and deloused and then sent out of the camp to the nearby German barracks. Sergeant Wood was in charge of two wards with eighty-five women patients:

I had two Hungarians who worked continuously for me, and some camp internees who'd been cleaned and powdered and were fit to help. The biggest problem was feeding them, it took almost all day. I couldn't speak to any of them, I had one interpreter who was not very good, and all sorts of patients, Russian, Danish, some who spoke German, quite a few Jewish people, but there was nobody who spoke English funnily enough, and I was very much alone there. At first I went there in the morning to find an average of twenty-three to twenty-four deaths overnight, and then the beds were filled again with people waiting. My death rate went down over the days and I think by the time we left the camp I was down to about eight a day still dying.

The citizens of Celle were brought to see the camp on their doorstep. Sergeant Wood was not impressed by the catalogue of denials he heard; no one would admit to knowing about the conditions in the camp.

On 12 April Eisenhower, Patton and Bradley visited the Ohrdruf concentration camp near Gotha. The SS guards had murdered all the inmates here to ensure no one would bear witness against them. The smell of half-burned and decomposing corpses was appalling. Patton was sick. Bradley was speechless. This was, Eisenhower told those assembled, 'beyond the American mind to comprehend.' 'Still have trouble hating them?' Eisenhower asked a GI who was standing near by. The following day Patton told the press that he had sent as many of his men to see the camp as he could, 'so as to know the kind of people they are fighting'.

The chief architect of this misery was still bullying the German people to further pointless sacrifice. Even in the last days he clung to desperate hope. Its flame burned most brightly on 13 April – the day after Eisenhower's visit to the Ohrdruf concentration camp. That evening Albert Speer was summoned to the Führer bunker to be greeted by an unusually animated Hitler: 'He held a newspaper clipping in his hand. "Here, read it! Here! You never wanted to believe it. Here it is!" His words came in a great rush. "Here we have the miracle I always predicted. Who was right? The war isn't lost. Read it! Roosevelt is dead!"' History was repeating itself, Goebbels observed – Germany had been saved at the eleventh hour by the death of a single great leader. The death of the Tsarina Catherine of Russia had saved Frederick the Great of Prussia; now with Roosevelt gone peace might yet be possible. Speer looked on in disbelief, and he sensed later, in spite of all the deceitful optimism of those around him, that Hitler too had given up hope.

The final battle for Berlin began three days later. The Red Army had massed two and a half million men along the length of the Oder, supported by more than forty thousand field guns and mortars, and six thousand tanks. The weight of two army groups – the 1st Belorussian and 1st Ukranian Fronts – would fall on the German line before the city. It would be a race – the winner would be given the honour of the final assault on the heart of Berlin. The final offensive of the war began on 16 April with a blistering Soviet bombardment. More than one and a quarter million shells were fired by Zhukov's 1st Belorussian Front on the first day alone. The German defenders resisted with desperate courage but by the 19th Soviet tanks had broken through their main line on the Seelöw Heights to the west of the Oder. Two days later, on Hitler's birthday, the first Russian troops began approaching the outskirts of Berlin itself.

As the news became ever bleaker Hitler began to rant more and more of betrayal, and for the first time admitted to his inner circle that the war was lost. The Führer was broken. Visitors to the bunker met a man seemingly twenty years older than his fifty-six years, stooped and grey, with a trembling hand and quavering voice. He had made up his mind to stay in Berlin and in time take his own life. The city would not be allowed to surrender. 'If the war is lost, the nation will perish,' he had told Speer a few weeks before, for 'those who will remain after the battle are only the inferior ones, for the good ones have been killed.'

The encirclement of the city was completed on 25 April, and on the same day American and Soviet forces met at Torgau on the banks of the Elbe. There were only the last rites to perform. Berliners sought what shelter they could find from the torrent of Soviet shellfire falling incessantly upon the ruined streets of their city. All but a few Nazi fanatics were desperate for the agony to end. On 30 April Marshal Zukhov's forces fought their way into target number 105, the chosen symbol of victory over the 'fascist beast' – the Reichstag. On the same day Hitler shot himself. In the last hours he had married his mistress Eva Braun, and she had dutifully taken her own life too. Even those closest to him were relieved. Within hours of his death negotiations had begun for a ceasefire in the city. By May Day, Red Victory banners had been unfurled above all the important buildings in the city.

When Soviet soldiers captured the Reich Chancellery they found only the charred remains of Hitler's corpse. Close by in the garden was the body of his most loyal supporter and friend, Joseph Goebbels. The mouthpiece of the Reich had taken not only his own life but those of his six children too. Stalin was at his dacha on the outskirts of Moscow when Marshal Zhukov called with news of Hitler's death. 'So that's the end of the bastard,' the Soviet leader replied, 'too bad it was impossible to take him alive.'

The meeting of East and West at Torgau on the Elbe had been filmed, photographed, and celebrated around the world. American GIs drank vodka and danced with Soviet women soldiers. General Bradley was entertained in some style by Marshal Konev, the commander of the 1st Ukranian Front, a soldier with a well-deserved reputation for ruthlessness. 'A great Russian chorus got up and sang the "Star Spangled Banner",' Bradley's ADC, Major Chester Hansen, recalled. 'It was quite a moving spectacle. We were getting along very well with the Russians. They were tweaking us about the British, the Russians didn't care for the Brits.' Gifts were exchanged. Bradley gave Konev an American jeep, and received in return a horse. 'General Bradley had never liked horses. He said to me, "See that Patton gets the animal,"' Hansen recalled.

But the official smiles and toasts masked a chill of suspicion and mutual distrust. In the north British forces had crossed the Elbe on 28 April, intent on securing the Danish frontier from a Soviet advance. As they pushed eastward they were met by a steady stream of German refugees and soldiers seeking refuge in the west. 'We came face to face with a full regiment of Waffen SS troops,' David Tibbs of the 13th Parachute Regiment recalled.

At that time we were way ahead of any support but Colonel Luard stood on a lorry, fired a shot into the air and shouted in German, 'Lay down your weapons and march to the west or I shall call up British artillery and Typhoon rocket planes to destroy you.' This was a complete bluff but after a few minutes a ripple ran down their long, well-armed column and they all started to drop their weapons and walk westward! They came through us laughing and shouting, obviously happy to surrender to us rather than stay for the Russians. For them the war was over. Many thought it was a huge joke to throw their side arms into my ambulance, which visibly sank down on its springs with the weight of them.

Beyond the Elbe, Tibbs was comfortably billeted in a schloss belonging to an elderly Prussian count: 'When we told him that we were moving on because we were in fact now in the area allocated to the Russians he asked for one of his guns to be returned. This was so that he could shoot himself and his wife rather than endure the raping of his wife and a cruel death at the hands of the Russians. Colonel Luard told him instead to load up a horse and cart and flee the area together with his wife and staff.'

Berliners were less fortunate. The Red Army embarked on an orgy of looting and raping. At least 100,000 women were raped in the city, many of them more than once. Soviet soldiers are thought to have raped more than 2 million German women in the final stages of the war. Life remained a grim struggle for survival, for food and shelter. The old Nazi slogans and flags were replaced with pictures of Comrade Stalin and the hammer and sickle. Perversely, Hitler might have considered it just. In the last days he had observed to Speer that if the war were lost, 'this nation will have proved to be the weaker one and the future will belong solely to the stronger eastern nation' – the Soviet Union. Speer had often noted more than a hint of admiration for Stalin in his Führer.

Field Marshal Montgomery accepted the unconditional surrender of all German forces in the north-west of the country, Holland and Denmark at his tactical HQ on Lüneburg Heath on 4 May 1945. The reluctant German delegation had at first offered to surrender to the Western Allies only, but Monty had refused to agree. The formal surrender of all German forces was signed three days later at Eisenhower's headquarters in Reims. Hitler's chosen successor, Admiral Karl Dönitz, had attempted to stall to allow time for the largest possible number of German soldiers and civilians to escape from the east. Only Eisenhower's threat to seal the Western Front at the Elbe persuaded him that further prevarication was hopeless. General Alfred Jodl signed on behalf of the German High Command (OKW) – Eisenhower made a point of absenting himself from the ceremony as a mark of his contempt for the defeated enemy. But in a terse, businesslike signal he was able to report to the Combined Chiefs of Staff: 'The Mission of this Allied Force was fulfilled at 0241, local time, May 7th 1945.'

There was wild rejoicing in London and Washington, quiet relief at the front. Trooper Austin Baker's squadron was near Bremerhaven:

It all seemed a bit of a come-down really, nobody celebrated very much. I mean, it's not as if they were sorry it was over, but they somehow weren't thrilled either. I remember our commander got drunk and that was about the limit of the celebrations. And in a funny way you did seem at a bit of a loss because it had been going on so long and it was so full of incident and excitement and you did at least feel it was part of a 'crusade', and the thought that it had all gone somehow left you a bit flat.

Peter Martin of the 2nd Cheshires had been reluctantly posted back to England in December 1944 when the 50th Division was broken up. He had been forced to say goodbye to his company, the men he had served with in North Africa, Sicily and Normandy:

I listened in on the radio to the sounds of exuberance and so on from Trafalgar Square and I wept bitterly. It was an awful feeling, the people I should have been celebrating with had all gone and there were just a few of us left out of the original battalion and I didn't feel like celebrating anything at all. There was this feeling of anticlimax too, that since the age of just over nineteen, the war had been my life and suddenly here was the end of the war.

Not quite over, there was still the war against Japan to be won. Martin would be one of those ordered east.

In Warsaw, Prague, Budapest and Berlin there was precious little to celebrate. In the last days of the war the young Guards officer David Fraser had written home to warn of the shadow of the new post-war world that was emerging: 'I cannot see that this war has or will have accomplished anything except a military decision as unimportant as a victory in one of the dynastic wars. The root of evil still flourishes, and everybody knows and daren't say. Wretched Europe!' Over the coming months the British and Americans would sit alongside a Soviet representative at Nuremberg to judge the Reich's war criminals in an empty pretence of shared values. The guilt of Hitler's chief henchmen was not in doubt – only the part played by Stalin's representative in judging them.

The eleven months' hard fighting from the D-Day beaches to the heart of Hitler's Reich cost the Western Allies three-quarters of a million casualties. The great burden of the campaign had been shouldered by the United States. More than two-thirds of the casualties were American, of whom 109,824 were killed. The British and Canadians suffered nearly 200,000 casualties and 41,000 of these soldiers lost their lives. At times it had been a troubled alliance, fractured by debates over strategy and the personal jealousies of those charged with directing the campaign. But the alliance had been united in its shared values and purpose and in a vision of a better future for the world. As Churchill had observed to Roosevelt just ten days before the president's death: '*Amantium irae amoris integratio est*' – 'Lovers' quarrels are part of love.' To defeat a great evil they had been obliged to make common cause with a dictator whose hands were no less stained than those of their Nazi enemy. But without the extraordinary sacrifices of the Soviet people the war would not have been won. Their suffering was immeasurable. The battle in the east was fought on a scale and with a ferocity beyond anything experienced in the west. A staggering 27 million Soviet citizens lost their lives in this great struggle, although by no means all of these in the face of the enemy. Three million Soviet prisoners died in German labour camps and remarkably another million in Stalin's Gulags at the end of the war. More than one and a half million soldiers who had fought for their country and endured inhuman treatment in Nazi captivity were sent to Siberia. In Stalin's eyes they had been tainted by time spent with 'fascists' and were now 'potential enemies of the state'. These rough hands now held the peoples of eastern Europe in their grip. The Iron Curtain that Goebbels had been the first to warn of had fallen across Europe, and the American soldiers Roosevelt had promised to bring home in two years were still there forty years later.

For all the uncertainty and pain it was a great victory. The Western Allies had triumphed over an evil enemy and system. In his victory broadcast Churchill warned the British people that 'on the continent of Europe we have yet to make sure that the simple and honourable purposes for which we entered the war are not brushed aside or overlooked in the months following our success, and that the words "freedom", "democracy" and "liberation" are not distorted from their true meaning as we have understood them'. It was in the name of these that the Allies waged war in the west. The bonds forged in victory remained strong in the post-war years, and in the fullness of time they have brought freedom and democracy to the whole of Europe.

Bibliography

PUBLISHED

Ambrose, Stephen, *Eisenhower 1890–1952*, London, Allen & Unwin, 1984

Ambrose, Stephen E., *Pegasus Bridge*, London, Simon & Schuster, 2003

Balkoski, Joseph, *Beyond the Beachhead: the 29th Infantry Division in Normandy*, Harrisburg, Stackpole, 1989

Beevor, Anthony, *Berlin: The Downfall*, London, Penguin, 2003

Bennett, R., *Ultra in the West*, London, Hutchinson & Co., 1979

ed. Blumenson, Martin, *Patton Papers 1940–5*, New York, Da Capo Press, 1974, p.472

Bradley, Omar, *Soldiers' Story*, London, Eye & Spottiswoode, 1951

Bryant, Arthur, *Triumph in the West*, London, Collins, 1959

Butcher, Harry, *My Three Years with Eisenhower*, New York, Simon & Schuster, 1946

Carell, Paul, *Invasion They're Coming!* New York, Schiffer Publishing, 1995

Carrington, Peter, *Reflecting On Things Past*, London, Collins, 1988

Churchill, Winston, *The Second World War Vol. 5*, London, Cassell & Co, 1954

Churchill, Winston, *The Second World War Vol. 6*, London, Cassell & Co, 1954

Churchill, Winston, *Triumph and Tragedy Volume VI*, London, Cassell & Co., 1954

Collins, J. Lawton, *Lightning Joe*, Louisiana, Louisiana State University Press, 1979

Ehrman, John, *Grand Strategy Vol. V*, London, HMSO, 1956

Ellis, L.F., *Victory in the West Vol. 1 the Battle of Normandy*, London, HMSO, 1962 and *Vol. 2*, 1968

D'Este, Carlo, *Decision in Normandy*, London, HarperCollins, 1983

D'Este, Carlo, *Eisenhower: A Soldier's Life*, New York, Henry Holt, 2002

Fisher, David and Read, Anthony, *The Fall of Berlin*, London, Pimlico, 1993

Fraser, David, *Knight's Cross: A Life of Field Marshal Erwin Rommel*, London, HarperCollins, 1993

Fraser, David, *Wars and Shadows*, London, Allen Lane, 2002

Galante, Pierre, *Hitler Lives and the Generals Die*, London, Sidgwick & Jackson, 1982

Gavin, James M., *On to Berlin*, New York, Bantam, 1978

Guderian, Heinz Günther, *From Normandy to the Ruhr*, Pennsylvania, Aberjona Press, 2001

De Guignand, F.W., *Generals at War*, London, Hodder & Stoughton, 1964

Hamilton, Nigel, *Master of the Battlefield*, New York, McGraw Hill, 1983

Hastings, Max, *Overlord*, London, Pan Macmillan, 1993

Hastings, Max, *Victory in Europe*, London, Weidenfeld & Nicholson, 1985

Holmes, Richard, *War Walks*, London, BBC Books, 1996

Horne, Alistair and Montgomery, David, *The Lonely Leader*, London, Macmillan, 1994

Howard, Michael, *Strategic Deception in the Second World War*, London, Pimlico, 1968

ed. Howarth, T.E.B., *Monty at Close Quarters*, London, Secker & Warburg, 1985

Irving, David, *Hitler's War*, New York, Viking, 1977

Irving, David, *The War Between the Generals*, London, Penguin, 1981

Irving, David, *The Trail of the Fox*, London, Weidenfeld & Nicholson, 1977

Keegan, John, *Six Armies in Normandy*, New York, Penguin, 1983

ed. Keegan, John, *The Times Atlas of the Second World War*, London, Times Books, 1989

Lamb, Richard, *Montgomery in Europe 1943–45*, London, Buchan & Enright, 1983

Lewin, Ronald, *Ultra Goes to War*, New York, McGraw Hill, 1978

von Luck, Hans, *Panzer Commander*, New York, Random House, 1989

Luther, Craig W.H., *Blood and Honor – The History of the 12th SS Panzer Division*, California, Bender Publishing, 1987

MacDonald, B.J.S., *The Trial of Kurt Meyer*, Carke, Irwin & Co., 1954

MacDonald, Charles B., *The Battle of the Huertgen Forest*, New York, Jove, 1963

MacDonald, Charles B., *The Last Offensive*, Washington, US Government Printing Office, 1973

Mather, Carol, *When the Grass Stops Growing*, Barnsley, Pen & Sword Books, 1998

Miller, Russell, *Nothing Less Than Victory*, London, Michael Joseph, 1993

Mitcham, Samuel W. Jnr, *Hitler's Field Marshals and their Battles*, London, Guild Publishing, 1988

Montgomery, B.L., *Memoirs*, London, Collins, 1958

Moorehead, Alan, *Montgomery*, New York, Coward McCann Inc., 1946

Morgan, Kay Summersby, *Past Forgetting*, New York, Simon & Schuster, 1977

Neillands, Robin, *The Battle of Normandy 1944*, London, Cassell, 2002

Neufeld, Michael, *The Rocket and the Reich*, Cambridge, MA, Harvard University Press, 1987

Overy, Richard, *Why the Allies Won*, London, Jonathan Cape, 1995

Patton, George S., *War As I Knew It*, Boston, Houghton Mifflin, 1947

Rees, Laurence, *The Nazis*, London, BBC Books, 1997

Reynolds, Michael, *Sons of the Reich – II SS Panzer Corps*, UK, Spellmount, 2002

Ritgen, Helmut, trans. Welsh, Joseph, *The Western Front 1944: Memoirs of a Panzer Lehr Officer*, Canada, J. J. Fedorowicz, 1955

Roberts, Andrew, *Hitler and Churchill: Secrets of Leadership*, London, Weidenfeld & Nicholson, 2003

Rommel, E., *The Rommel Papers*, ed. Liddell-Hart, B.D., New York, Da Capo Press, 1953

Ryan, Cornelius, *A Bridge Too Far*, London, Simon & Schuster, 1974

Scott, Desmond, *Typhoon Pilot*, London, Leo Cooper, 1982

ed. Selwyn, Victor, *Poems of the Second World War*, London, Michael Joseph, 1995

Sixsmith, E.K.G., *Eisenhower*, New York, Da Capo, 1973

Speer, Albert, *Inside the Reich*, London, Macmillan, 1970

Stacey, C.P., *The Victory Campaign: The Operations in North West Europe 1944–5*, Ottawa, QPCS, 1960

Taylor, Daniel, *Villers Bocage Through the Lens – After the Battle*, London, Buckram, 1999

Thompson, Julian, IWM *Book of Victory in Europe*, London, Sidgwick & Jackson, 1995

Toland, John, *The Last 100 Days*, New York, Random House, 1967

Urquart, Brian, *A Life in Peace and War*, London, Weidenfeld & Nicholson, 1987

War Report, *A Record of Dispatches Broadcast by the BBC's War Correspondents*, Oxford, OUP, 1946

Warlimont, Walter, *Inside Hitler's Headquarters 1939–45*, London, Weidenfeld & Nicholson, 1964

Weaver, William G., *Yankee Doodle Went to Town*, Michigan, Edwards Brothers, 1959

Weigley, Robert F., *Eisenhower's Lieutenants*, London, Sidgwick & Jackson, 1981

Wilmot, Chester, *The Struggle for Europe*, London, Collins, 1952

Wilson, Andrew, *Flamethrower*, London, Kimber & Co., 1984

Woollcombe, Robert, *Lion Rampant*, Edinburgh, B & W Publishing, 1994

LIDDELL-HART MILITARY ARCHIVE, KING'S COLLEGE, LONDON

Wilmot, Chester, *Notes on Conversation with General Dempsey*
LH PSG 9/8/12B
LH 6/2/26
LH 6/2/27
LH 9/24/91
LH 6/2/07
LH 9/24/98

PUBLIC RECORD OFFICE, KEW
PRO WO 171/258
PRO WO 205/1021
PRO 10/6 WO 2055C
PRO 219/1905
PRO WO 205/2
PRO WO 205/1020
PRO WO 205/5C
PRO CAB 106/1060
PRO WO 205/58

IMPERIAL WAR MUSEUM
IWM, *Book of Victory in Europe*
IWM Sound Archive 11061/2
IWM Documents 78/68/1
IWM 11061/2
IWM Sound Archive 12778/20

BIBLIOGRAPHY

ROYAL ARMOURED CORPS JOURNAL
1D (2): 58–64 (1956)
XIII (6) April 1959
II (I): 25–29

OTHER
BBC interviews for *Turning the Tide*, 5 June 1994 and *The Battle for Normandy*, 6 June 1994
Daily Express 23 September 1944
Hansen, Chester B., diary, Military History Institute, Carlisle
Adams, Kingston, diary manuscript
Ministry of Information, *By Air to Battle*
No Better Soldier pamphlet by Brigadier Harry Illing
Cornelius Ryan Archives, Vernon R. Alden Library, Ohio University
Baker, Austin, manuscript account
Henderson, Johnny, Manuscript diary

I am especially grateful to all those who were prepared to help in the production of this book and the series it accompanies, by sharing their memories or their own written accounts. They have been my chief source and I am full of admiration for their courage and for their extraordinary recollection of what they endured sixty years ago.

Notes on Sources

CHAPTER ONE

p.1 'his two-year-old son Terry' Ambrose, Stephen E., *Pegasus Bridge*, London, Simon & Schuster, 2003, p.7

p.2 'I was a bit emotional as we took off' BBC interview with Charles Wheeler 5 June 1994 and IWM Sound Archive 11061/2

p.2 'there is nothing you can do about it' Denis Edwards, IWM Documents 78/68/1

p.3 'The first thing I remember' BBC interview 5 June 1994

p.4 'up this slope towards the bridge' ibid.

p.6 'The garrison numbered some 130 men' Carell, Paul, *Invasion They're Coming!*, Schiffer Publishing, 1995, pp.52–7

p.7 'The Führer himself had stated' Warlimont, Walter, *Inside Hitler's Headquarters 1939–45* London, Weidenfeld & Nicholson, 1964, p.403

p.8 'placed under his command in the Normandy sector' Fraser, David, *Knight's Cross: A Life of Field Marshal Erwin Rommel*, London, HarperCollins, 1993, p.479

p.8 'No one at headquarters was sure what this meant' Author interview with Manfred Rommel, ibid., pp.478–9, ibid., p.485 and Irving, David, *The Trail of the Fox*, London, Weidenfeld & Nicholson, 1977, p.336

p.10 'The storm broke upon an 80-kilometre stretch of coast' Ellis, L.F., *Victory in the West Vol. 1 the Battle of Normandy*, HMSO, 1962, p.161

p.11 'Wound my heart with a monotonous languor' Carell, p.28

p.12 'while the 15th Army could mobilise seventeen' Carell, p.15 and Fraser, *Knight's Cross*, p.458

p.12 'I know *nothing* for certain about the enemy' ibid., p.461

p.12 'strung out along a 3,200-kilometre front' Ellis, Vol. 1, p.117

p.14 'We used to tell each other it wouldn't happen here' BBC interview with Charles Wheeler 5 June 1994

p.14 'On the eve of D-Day it was considered likely' Howard, Michael, *Strategic Deception in the Second World War*, London, Pimlico, 1968, p.131

p.15 'Rommel ordered 50 million mines for the Atlantic Wall' Ellis, Vol. 1, p.119

p.17 'General Alfred Jodl recorded in his notes in April' ibid., p.120

p.17 'by this time Rundsted's arteries were hardening' Hastings, Max, *Overlord*, London, Pan Macmillan, 1993, p.76

p.17 'He was tired, disillusioned and altogether pessimistic' Irving, *The Trail of the Fox*, p.287

p.17 'The Allies would certainly be able to fight their way ashore' Liddell-Hart Military Archive, King's College, London

p.18 'I refuse to work with you any more' Irving, *The Trail of the Fox*, p.307

p.18 'General Hans Speidel later observed' Ellis, Vol. 1, p.177

p.19 'I'm convinced that the enemy will have a rough time of it when he attacks' ed. Rommel, *The Rommel Papers*, ed. Liddell-Hart, B.D., New York, Da Capo Press, 1953, p.461 and p.464

p.19 'But to old comrades from the desert he painted' von Luck, Hans, *Panzer Commander*, New York, Random House 1989, p.166 and Fraser, *Knight's Cross*, p.478

p.20 'those joining the field marshal were warned to be on their guard' ibid., p.476

p.20 'It was only at 6 a.m.' Hastings, p.92

p.21 'hold their fire until the enemy was almost on the beach' Carell, p.84

p.21 'Yet we're all here, we're all going, as ordered' Bannerman, Alastair, manuscript

p.22 'one of the greatest expeditions ever known in history' Colonel Adams, diary p.23 'Prime Minister Winston Churchill wrote to President Roosevelt' Ehrman, John, *Grand Strategy Vol. V*, London, 1956, p.108

p.23 'drive off the German reserves rather than the initial breaking of the coastal crust' PRO WO 205/2 and Hastings, p.33

p.23 'Say, Broadie, that's the first time I've seen a dead body!' Horne, Alistair and Montgomery, David, *The Lonely Leader*, London, Macmillan, 1994, pp.62–3

p.24 'he had first met Eisenhower in North Africa' Horne, p.63

p.24 'He had spent the night studying them' Churchill, Winston, *The Second World War Vol. 5*, London, Cassell, 1954, p.393

p.24 'he told Allied commanders in May' Hamilton, Nigel, *Master of the Battlefield*, New York, McGraw Hill, 1983, pp.587–8

p.28 'From there they were funnelled into ten lanes' Ellis, p.67 and pp.146–7

p.28 'Hitherto we had studied maps' from letter quoted in *No Better Soldier* pamphlet by Brigadier Harry Illing

p.31 'It was very novel and unpleasant' Austin Baker, manuscript

p.32 'My radio operator and policeman were both killed' Miller, Russell, *Nothing Less Than Victory*, London, Michael Joseph, 1993

p.32 'he was dead without even getting ashore' Miller, p.343

p.34 'We turned round in a field' Austin Baker, manuscript

p.35 'ninety were lost or damaged that morning' Ellis, p.179

p.37 'the battalion would be moving up there and would join me' Bannerman, manuscript

p.37 'our first experience of an angry missive' Illing, *No Better Soldier*

p.38 'Luckily we managed it' Adams, diary

p.39 'At last I knew they were English' Ministry of Information, *By Air to Battle*, pp.5–7

p.39 'this was the time to celebrate' Howard, interview, IWM 11061/2

CHAPTER TWO

p.40 'an hour earlier than on the British beaches' Butcher, Harry, *My Three Years with Eisenhower*, New York, Simon & Schuster, 1946, pp.566–7

p.40 'The morning papers' Johnny Henderson, diary manuscript

p.42 'By now Overlord had run beyond the reach of its admirals' Bradley, Omar, *Soldiers' Story*, London, Eye & Spottiswoode, 1951, p.268

p.43 'They're going to sail right under our guns' Carell, pp.82–4

p.50 'the Pointe du Hoc was in Allied hands' Ambrose, *D-Day*, p.414

p.51 'I know you won't let me down' ibid., p.430

p.52 'the concussion from the bursts of these guns' Balkoski, Joseph, *Beyond the Beachhead: the 29th Infantry Division in Normandy*, Harrisburg, Stackpole, 1989, p.158

p.52 'At last a young, red-headed soldier volunteered' Hastings, p.118 and Ambrose, *D-Day*, p.423

p.53 'all he had left to fire were night tracer bullets' Carell, p.92

p.55 'Now we have them where we can destroy them' Irving, David, *Hitler's War*, New York, Viking, 1977

p.55 'So, we're off' Warlimont, p.427

p.56 'If this isn't the invasion, what are they going to come with?' Carell, p.100

p.57 'Luck's regiment was within striking distance of the bridges' Luck, pp.172–5

p.58 'small attachments in woods and villages' Interrogation of Bayerlein – LH 9/24/91 Liddell-Hart Papers, King's College, London

p.58 '200 tanks and 600 tracked vehicles' Ritgen, Helmut, trans. Welsh, Joseph, *The Western Front 1944: Memoirs of a Panzer Lehr Officer*, Canada, J. J. Fedorowicz, 1955, p.20

p.59 'the 21st Panzer Division, at least, should press on' Irving, *Trail*, p.338

p.60 'this was defended by thirteen battalions of infantry with 260 field guns' Ellis Volume 1, p.197

p.61 'a Sherman could blow up in this way' BBC interview, 1994

p.64 'It was typical "Monty"' Horne and Montgomery, p.118

p.64 'more than 156,000 Allied soldiers had landed in France' Ellis Volume 1, p.223

p.65 'Rommel's staff car finally swept up to the steps of the ancient chateau' Irving, *Trail*, p.338

p.65 'I should have had the Panzer Lehr' interview, Cornelius Ryan Archives, Vernon R. Alden Library, Ohio University

CHAPTER THREE

p.69 'The battalion had left one rifle company' Illing, *No Better Soldier*, p.20

p.69 'regulars numbered less than fifty' Illing, interview

p.69 'I would have given anything for a good wash and shave' Adams, diary

p.76 'described it as "vital" to future operations' Neillands, Robin, *The Battle of Normandy 1944*, London, Cassell, 2002, p.51

p.76 'like a windlass in the direction of Paris' Bradley, *Soldiers' Story*, p.239

p.76 'so the Americans could swing towards Paris and the Seine' Hamilton, *Master of the Battlefield*, p.588

p.76 'to knock about a bit down there' Bradley, *Soldiers' Story*, p.241

p.76 'heavy air raids reduced the city to rubble' Neillands, p.51

p.77 'I had to ring up and tell you myself' BBC interview, 1994

p.77 'thank God I wasn't captured by them' ibid.

p.78 'good at Utah but very bad at Omaha' Horne and Montgomery, p.119

p.78 'he is best at the spoiling attack; his forte is disruption' Hamilton, *Master of the Battlefield*, p.586

p.79 'Meyer at least was confident his division would do just that' Interrogation of Feuchtinger, PRO WO 205/1021

p.79 'The 12 SS Division had been created' Luther, Craig W.H., *Blood and Honor – The History of the 12th SS Panzer Division*, California, Bender Publishing, 1987, p.59

p.79 'the enemies of Germany are the enemies of Europe' ibid., p.71

p.79 'His mind, paralysed by propaganda' Interrogation of Meyer, PRO WO 205/1021

p.81 'the Allied bridgehead would be much more constricted' Stacey, C.P., *The Victory Campaign: The Operations in North West Europe 1944-5*, Ottawa, QPCS, 1960, p.133

p.82 'The attacks were pressed with courage and determination' Stacey, p.137

p.82 'They only eat our rations' Luther, pp.181-2

p.83 'an occasional scream could be clearly heard' MacDonald, B.J.S., *The Trial of Kurt Meyer*, Carke, Irwin & Co., 1954, p.110

p.83 'the fist was unclenched just as it was ready to strike' Irving, *Trail*, p.342

p.83 'General Jodl to argue against the transfer of divisions' ibid., p.343

p.84 'enforced camouflage discipline with a will' Interrogation of Bayerlein, Military Archive, King's College, London, LH 9/24/91

p.86 'The British 50th, Bayerlein, our special friends' Carell, p.141

p.88 'The promises did not last all that long' IWM Sound Archive 12778/20

p.88 'The Prinz had lost his usual composure' Ritgen, *The Western Front 1944*, p.59

p.88 'It was the final attempt by the enemy, before pulling out' IWM Sound Archive 12778/20

p.89 'The material equipment of the Americans, with numerous new weapons' ed. Liddell-Hart, *The Rommel Papers*, pp.474-8

p.90 'I often think of you at home, with heartfelt wishes' ibid., p.491

p.90 'He judged the ground to be totally unsuitable for armour' Ritgen, *The Western Front 1944*, p.60

CHAPTER FOUR

p.92 'Tired and weary faces lighted up, soldiers waved from all directions' Henderson, diary manuscript, 8 June 1944

p.93 'a plan that promised to squeeze the German Panzer divisions into an Allied pocket' Butcher, diary, 11 June 1944

p.93 'The General was in the highest spirits' Churchill, Winston, *Triumph and Tragedy Volume VI*, London, Cassell & Co., 1954, p.11

p.94 'I selected each personally, and my standard was high' Horne and Montgomery, p.100

p.94 'Send him over at once' PRO 10/6 WO 2055C

p.95 'a battle of about a million a side, lasting through June and July' Churchill, *Triumph and Tragedy Volume VI*, p.13

p.95 '7th Armoured would need to make good speed' Bennett, R., *Ultra in the West*, London, Hutchinson & Co., 1979

p.96 'before the front congeals' Hamilton, *Master of the Battlefield*, p.643

p.96 'the tactics to be employed while fighting through bocage country' Hastings, p.43

p.98 'there were graves by all the others' Royal Armoured Corps Journal XIII (6) April 1959

p.99 'Nobody ever found any sign of Wally' Austin Baker, manuscript

p.100 'that night we leagured several miles farther inland' Royal Armoured Corps Journal 1D (2) 58–64 (1956)

p.100 'to the west there appeared to be open country' Taylor, Daniel, *Villers Bocage Through the Lens – After the Battle*, London, Buckram, 1999

p.100 'Lieutenant Cloudsley-Thompson's headquarters troop was near the head of the column' Royal Armoured Corps Journal 1D (2): 58–64 (1956)

p.103 'The enemy was thrown into total confusion' Taylor, p.38

p.105 'it mounted a 95mm howitzer, of little use' ibid., p.59

p.106 'to be held at all cost' Ellis Vol. 1, p.255

p.108 'here the long gun came into its own' Liddell-Hart Military Archive, King's College, London, LH9/24/91

p.108 'His final remarkable tally is thought to have been twelve tanks' Taylor, p.76

p.109 'by this time the 7th Armoured Division was living on its reputation' Wilmot, Chester, *Notes on Conversation with General Dempsey*, Liddell-Hart Military Archive, King's College, London

p.109 'to prove one of the costliest Allied mistakes' D'Este, Carlo, *Decision in Normandy*, London, HarperCollins, 1983, p.198

p.110 'They cannot be alert while in this condition' PRO CAB 106/1060

p.112 'when every tank becomes one of these types' PRO WO 205/58

p.112 'we were to make our break on the long roundabout road towards Paris' Bradley, p.241

p.112 'Ike also said that yesterday we had made no gains, which he didn't like' Butcher, p.581

p.113 'The only thing necessary to move forward is sufficient guts on the part of the ground commanders' Irving, David, *The War Between the Generals*, London, Penguin, 1981, p.167

p.114 'its broken contours and abundance of cover' Ellis Vol. 1, p.276

p.114 'in its wake the build-up was cut by more than half' ibid., p.274

p.118 'But not standing up in the open, so we could identify their officers' BBC interview, 1994

p.119 'Tears run down my face and I begin to hate this war' Luther, p.213

p.120 'I know him! He was in my ward in hospital' Woollcombe, Robert, *Lion Rampant*, Edinburgh, B & W Publishing, 1994, p.69

p.120 'And mud and dust are much the same' Herbert, A.P. as quoted in Thompson, Julian, IWM *Book of Victory in Europe*, London, Sidgwick & Jackson, 1995 p.124 'continue the battle on the eastern flank till one of us cracks' PRO WO 205/5C

p.124 'There were no Panzer divisions in the Cotentin Peninsula' Overy, Richard, *Why the Allies Won*, London, Jonathan Cape, 1995, p.167

p.124 'it is your duty to defend the last bunker' Collins, J. Lawton, *Lightning Joe*, Louisiana, Louisiana State University Press, 1979, p.219

p.126 'the maximum number of enemy divisions in our eastern flank' Hamilton, *Master of the Battlefield*, p.700

p.127 'He said he preferred staying in his room rather than shuttling back and forth' Butcher, p.584

p.127 'Most of the people I know are semi-dazed from loss of sleep' ibid., p.585

p.127 'It struck me as curious that he should express such slighting comparisons' Irving, *The War Between the Generals*, p.183

p.127 'Eisenhower, Montgomery and I had agreed to the plan' Bradley, p.317

p.127 'advance was not going to take place as originally planned' Irving, *The War Between the Generals*, p.176

p.128 'the Allied newspaper readers clamoured for a place name called Caen' Bradley, pp.325–6

p.129 'an elastic conduct of operations is the better course' Ellis Vol. 1, p.321

p.129 'I still would not have been able to budge a division if Hitler disagreed' PRO WO 205/1020

p.130 'we could hear the ringing of bells mingled with the thunder of cannon' Hansen, Chester B., diary, Military History Institute, Carlisle

p.130 'fed up with Monty's lack of drive' ed. Blumenson, Martin, *Patton Papers 1940–5*, New York, Da Capo Press, 1974, p.472

p.131 'the British would never dare destroy the grave of one of their kings' BBC interview, 1994

p.131 'this great air weapon which could in the last resort be used' ibid.

p.131 'Not a word of reproach; not a word of self-pity' BBC War Report 10 July 1944

p.131 'a major full-dress attack on the left' Liddell-Hart Military Archive, King's College, London 6/2/26

CHAPTER FIVE

p.135 'To replace the division is practically impossible' Butcher, p.622

p.136 'Waste all the ammunition you like, but not lives' Hastings, *Overlord*, p.180

p.136 'I consider the Divisional Commander is to blame' Liddell-Hart Military Archive, King's College, London 6/2/27

p.136 'if we've got to can every senior officer in it' Bradley, p.298

p.136 'Infantry divisions seem to have been less well prepared for bocage fighting' Neillands, p.177

p.137 'Untrained or semi-skilled three-inch mortar men would fire their mortars from underneath trees' Thompson, IWM, *Book of Victory in Europe*, p.94

p.138 'some rifle companies turning over 100 per cent of their total strength' Neillands, p.176

p.138 'well beyond Villers-Bocage and Caen' Hamilton, *Master of the Battlefield*, p.585

p.140 'Whenever the enemy infantry is energetically engaged' PRO WO 171/258

p.141 'it received no new tanks and only half the new recruits it needed' Ritgen, p.86

p.146 'their German enemy was often obliged to make do' Hastings, *Overlord*, p.234

p.148 'the fire rose in one fierce, red wall' Wilson, Andrew, *Flamethrower*, London, Kimber & Co., 1984, p.67

p.149 'Only their helmets and boots remained' Wilson, p.123

p.149 'everything more thoroughly and conscientiously than ever before' ibid., p.125

p.149 'In most wars one is closer in spirit to the enemy' Fraser, David, *Wars and Shadows*, London, Allen Lane, 2002, p.211

p.150 'the Allies are waging war regardless of expense' PRO WO 219/1905

p.151 'the will and tenacity of the German army to resist' Neillands, p.184

p.151 'I Corps was attacking with twelve battalions and three tank regiments' PRO WO 171/258

p.152 'They allowed the junior commanders too little initiative' Ritgen, p.76

p.152 'only an energetic commander will get his men to go forward' PRO WO 219/1905

p.154 '6DWR is not fit to take its place in the line' Liddell-Hart Military Archive, King's College, London PSG 9/8/12B

CHAPTER SIX

p.161 'Monty hoped that the three armoured divisions of VIII Corps' Ellis Vol. 1, p.329

p.162 'Cloudsley-Thompson had taken over a troop in B Squadron' Royal Armoured Corps Journal II (I): 25–29

p.162 'to muck up and write off enemy troops' Ellis Vol. 1, p.329

p.163 'At the same time all is ready to take advantage' Ellis Vol. 1, p.330

p.163 'take all the time you need' Hamilton, *Master of the Battlefield*, p.723

p.164 'to overstate the aims of the operation' ibid., p.733

p.164 'who would succeed Monty if sacked' Ambrose, Stephen, *Eisenhower 1890–1952*, London, Allen & Unwin, 1984, p.319

p.165 'in the American sector it was eight to one' Hastings, p.272

p.165 'one can't beat the *matériel* of the enemy with courage alone' Fraser, *Rommel*, p.506

p.167 'It was a terrible sight, you know' BBC interview, 1994

p.167 'the insane howling of men who had been driven mad' Holmes, Richard, *War Walks*, London, BBC Books, 1996, p.209

p.167 'The whole area was dotted with British tanks' Luck, pp.192–3 p.168 'Within minutes they had killed sixteen tanks' BBC interview, 1994

p.169 'The effect of the air bombing was decisive' Liddell-Hart Military Archive, King's College, London 6/2/07

p.170 'We were held up all day by the Guards Armoured Division' Royal Armoured Corps Journal II (I): 25–29

p.170 'We advanced across an open stretch of corn' ibid.

p.171 'The shelling continued and several tanks were hit' ibid.

p.172 'I had an uneasy feeling as we left the wood' ibid.

p.172 'We sat in holes under our tanks, shivering' ibid.

p.172 'We thought it was a dismal failure' ibid.

p.172 'I picked up the torn fragments' ibid.

p.173 'It is always better to do the booming after complete success' Ellis Vol. 1, p.353

p.173 'It was not good for Eisenhower's blood pressure' D'Este, Carlo, *Eisenhower: A Soldier's Life*, New York, Henry Holt, 2002, p.556

p.174 'The slowness of the battle, the desire to be more active' Butcher, diary, 19 July 1944

p.175 'Set backs? What set backs?' Horne and Montgomery, p.222

p.175 'a peace offering' ibid., p.223

p.179 'actively co-operating in the political indoctrination of younger commanders' Ellis Vol. 1, p.374

p.180 'I believe only the weather is holding them up' Carell, p.241

p.181 'All my front-line tanks were knocked out' Liddell-Hart Military Archive, King's College, London LH 9/24/91

p.182 'they looked forward to the prospect of strolling through the bomb target area' Neillands, p.282

p.183 'Since there was nothing left to command, I gave the order to withdraw' Ritgen, p.114

p.185 'We had a wicker bottle of cider in the radio station' ibid., p.110

p.185 'I am going to personally shoot that paper-hanging

goddamned son of a bitch' ed. Blumenson, Martin, *Patton Papers 1940–5*, p.477

p.186 'Let's shoot the works and win! Yes win it all' ibid., p.492

CHAPTER SEVEN

p.188 'If the greatest study of mankind is man' ed. Blumenson, Martin, *Patton Papers 1940–5*, p.92

p.188 'Compared to war all [other] human activities are futile' ibid., p.496

p.190 'the men filthy, and the officers apathetic' ibid., p.497

p.192 'to be picking up pep and ginger not only because of the new commander' Weigley, Robert F., *Eisenhower's Lieutenants*, London, Sidgwick & Jackson, 1981, p.192

p.192 'There were only 14,500 trucks on the whole front' Overy, p.227

p.192 'the Anglo-American air force *is* the modern type of warfare' ibid., p.277

p.193 'In 1944 it built some 600,000 army trucks' ibid., p.225

p.194 'I knew you two so-and-so's would do it' Weaver, William G., *Yankee Doodle Went to Town*, Michigan, Edwards Brothers, 1959, pp.122–3

p.194 'We may end this in ten days' ed. Blumenson, Martin, *Patton Papers 1940–5*, p.304

p.194 'If the intercepts are right, we are to hell and gone in Brittany' Butcher, p.630

p.195 'described his stickiness and the reaction in the American papers' Hamilton, *Master of the Battlefield*, p.756

p.195 'so as to make easier the task of the American armies' ibid., p.758

p.195 'The general situation is now so good' Horne and Montgomery, p.232

p.196 'a Hunnish sort of battle in which one must either stand' Ellis Vol. 1, pp.396–7

p.197 'We're about to destroy an entire hostile army' Bradley, p.375

p.198 'some of the worst moments I had ever had in my life'
Liddell-Hart Papers LH 9/24/127

p.198 'quietly and confidently facing this disorderly mob' ibid.

p.199 'Let me go on to Falaise and we'll drive the British back
into the sea' Bradley, p.376

p.199 'Although Patton might have spun a line' ibid., p.377

p.200 'You and your units remain where they are' Carell, p.267

p.202 'and horses, some still harnessed to the shafts, screaming
terribly' Reynolds, Michael, *Sons of the Reich – II SS Panzer
Corps*, UK, Spellmount, 2002, p.84

p.203 'The Reich would begin to rebuild its shattered armies'
Weigley, p.214

p.203 'less raw formations would probably have obtained larger
and earlier results' Stacey, p.276

p.204 'Suddenly I realised for the first time that each grey-clad
body' Scott, Desmond, *Typhoon Pilot*, London, Leo Cooper,
1982, p.129

p.204 '130 half-tracks and 5,000 lorries and cars' Weigley, p.214

p.204 'that area had to be passed with all speed' Ellis Vol. 1,
p.448

p.205 'The war was won' Overy, p.179

p.205 'choked with the flower of American and British youth'
ibid., p.178

p.210 'the less I see of him the better it is for my blood pressure' Morgan, Kay Summersby, *Past Forgetting*, New York,
Simon & Schuster, 1977

p.210 'Within our little group, although the junior' Fraser, *Wars
and Shadows*, p.216

p.210 'I spoke German when the Germans were here' ibid., p.217

p.212 'the gutter in the long main street was actually running
with blood' ibid., p.225

p.213 'It was one of those times, one was so angry' Thompson,
IWM *Book of Victory*, p.145

p.213 'two and a half months of bitter fighting have brought
the end of the war' D'Este, *Eisenhower*, p.587

CHAPTER EIGHT

p.215 'he is without an equal' D'Este, *Eisenhower*, p.58

p.216 'it will not do Ike any good' Horne and Montgomery, p.257

p.216 'Montgomery was hogging all the credit' D'Este, *Eisenhower*, p.555

p.216 'No one but a Monty, outstanding tactician though he had just proven himself to be' Horne and Montgomery, p.258

p.220 'the brute force method' D'Este, *Eisenhower*, p.553

p.220 'descend into the land battle and become a ground C-in-C' Ambrose, *Eisenhower*, p.341

p.221 'He said that I must understand that it was election year' Hamilton, *Master of the Battlefield*, p.815

p.221 'I told Bradley that if he, Hodges [commander US First Army], and myself offered to resign' ed. Blumenson, Martin, *Patton Papers 1940–5*, pp.526–7

p.221 'Eisenhower always agreed with the last man he talked to' Ambrose, *Eisenhower*, p.342

p.222 'The SHAEF planners had not expected an advance across the Seine' Weigley, p.268

p.223 'We should cross the Rhine in the vicinity of Worms, and the faster we do it' ed. Blumenson, Martin, *Patton Papers 1940–5*, p.531

p.223 'instead of giving direct and clear orders [he] dresses them up in polite language' D'Este, *Eisenhower*, p.602

p.223 'Eisenhower held conferences to collect ideas; I held conferences to issue orders' Liddell-Hart Military Archive, King's College, London, Chester Wilmot collection

p.223 'under no circumstances would Eisenhower agree to give all the glory to the British' D'Este, *Eisenhower*, p.603

p.224 'time is vital and the decision regarding the selected thrust must be made at once' Ellis, *Victory in the West* Vol. 2, p.16

p.225 'It may well now go on into winter' Hamilton, *Monty: The Field Marshal 1944–76*, p.45

p.225 'Balls, sheer balls, rubbish!' D'Este, *Eisenhower*, p.606

p.225 'Steady, Monty! You can't speak to me like that' Ambrose, *Eisenhower*, p.348

p.225 'Monty's suggestion is simple, give him everything' ibid., p.348

p.226 'Order BROWNING to come to see me tomorrow' Hamilton, *Monty: The Field Marshal 1944–76*, p.22

p.226 'I not only approved Market Garden, I insisted upon it' Hamilton, *Monty: The Field Marshal 1944–76*, p.30

p.227 'Furthermore, the fighting capacity of the new Battle Groups formed' Weigley, p.296

p.230 'We had approached the state of mind when we weren't thinking as hard' Hamilton, *Monty: The Field Marshal 1944–76*, pp.66

p.231 'would fail to put up a strong resistance on the borders of the Fatherland' Urquart, Brian, *A Life in Peace and War*, London, Weidenfeld, 1987, p.70

p.231 'I was desperately anxious to go on the operation' Urquart, p.71

p.231 'I rushed to General Browning with the new evidence' ibid., p.73

p.232 'a German armoured presence between Eindhoven and Arnhem' Bennett, *Ultra in the West*, pp.147–8

p.236 'A significant number of Irish Guards tanks were burning beside the road' Fraser, *Wars and Shadows*, p.234

p.236 'successful beyond all expectation' *Daily Mail*, 18 September 1944

p.240 'By then the operation had been running for over forty hours' Fraser, *Wars and Shadows*, p.234

p.240 'The bridge itself had not been blown' ibid., p.236

p.245 'God knows from what secret source of strength' *Daily Express*, 23 September 1944

p.248 'Just 2,183 men made it back across the Lower Rhine' Thompson, IWM *Book of Victory in Europe*, p.176

p.249 'And I'm giving it to my Public Relations Officer to issue' Hamilton, *Monty: The Field Marshal 1944–76*, p.94

p.250 'that eccentric British practise of turning military disasters such as Dunkirk' D'Este, *Eisenhower*, p.617

p.251 'It was a thoroughly bad idea, badly planned' Fraser, *Wars and Shadows*, p.242

p.251 'Has the pious teetotaling Montgomery wobbled into SHAEF with a hangover' Bradley, *Soldier's Story*, p.416

p.252 'the one that stands out is his desire to appease Montgomery' Ambrose, *Eisenhower*, p.350

p.253 'This afforded me the cue I needed to lambast him' Hamilton, *Monty: The Field Marshal 1944–76*, p.104

p.253 'Ike nobly took all blame on himself' Bryant, Arthur, *Triumph in the West*, London, Collins, 1959, p.291

p.254 'Your very devoted and loyal subordinate, Monty' Ellis Vol. 2, p.91

p.255 'trench foot, respiratory illnesses and combat fatigue were all commonplace' MacDonald, Charles B., *The Battle of the Huertgen Forest*, New York, Jove, 1963, pp.195–6, 200

p.255 'incidents of rape, murder and looting' D'Este, *Eisenhower*, p.628

p.256 'I am afraid we may prove a broken reed' Hamilton, *Monty: The Field Marshal 1944–76*, p.142

p.257 'His own plan for a full-bodied thrust on the Ruhr with fifty Allied divisions' Hamilton, *Monty: The Field Marshal 1944–76*, p.163

CHAPTER NINE

p.261 'the most vulnerable point in our entire Allied line' Bradley, p.449

p.263 'the prelude to the heaviest bombardment the Germans had launched in the west' MacDonald, *The Battle of the Bulge*, pp.102–3

p.263 'To the south of this the 5th Panzer Army attacked on a 50-kilometre front' Ellis, *Victory in the West* Vol. 2, p.180

p.265 'The divisions had just been reformed and contained

chiefly raw, untried recruits' Liddell-Hart Military Archive, King's College, London LH 9/24/98

p.266 'I wangled fuel by personal connections' ibid., LH 9/24/91

p.267 'America would become a negligible factor in the war' ibid., LH 9/24/91

p.271 'The division was supported by only a small tank force from the 10th Armoured' MacDonald, *The Battle of the Bulge*, p.503

p.271 'It is not yet known whether 12th Army Group' Hamilton, *Monty: The Field Marshal*, p.190

p.272 'Communications seemed to have completely broken down' Mather, Carol, *When the Grass Stops Growing*, Barnsley, Pen & Sword Books, 1998, p.285

p.274 'some people seemed surprised and others pleased' ed. Blumenson, Martin, *Patton Papers 1940–5*, p.600

p.275 'it could be interpreted as a loss of confidence by Eisenhower in me' Bradley, *Soldier's Story*, p.477

p.278 'would not correspond with the well-known American humanity' MacDonald, p.512

p.280 'He was strong and inflicted heavy casualties on the attackers' Ritgen, p.276

p.281 'The tanks had been promised enough fuel to carry them 500 kilometres' ibid., p.256

p.285 'if he had accepted British advice and not that of American generals' Hamilton, *Monty: The Field Marshal*, p.265

p.285 'Monty as usual' D'Este, *Eisenhower*, p.655

p.285 'I am so anxious not to have another failure' Montgomery, *Memoirs*, pp.137–9

p.286 'impossible for the two of them to carry on working in harness together' De Guignand, F.J., *Generals at War*, London, Hodder & Stoughton, 1964, pp.106–112

p.287 'Your very devoted subordinate, Monty' D'Este, *Eisenhower*, p.657

p.287 'public opinion back home would stand for nothing less' ibid., p.656

p.288 'Of these more than 10,000 were killed' Weigley, p.574

p.289 'in time restoring it to the Allied Command' ibid.

CHAPTER TEN

p.292 'the Red Army enjoyed an overwhelming superiority in tanks' Beevor, Anthony, *Berlin: The Downfall*, London, Penguin, 2003, p.6

p.294 'Newsreel footage had been shown a few months before of the bodies' ibid., p.28

p.294 'it is now time for our soldiers to issue their own justice' ibid., p.33

p.295 'a desperate crowd intent on looting food' Fisher, David and Read, Anthony, *The Fall of Berlin*, London, Pimlico, 1993, p.226

p.295 'From now on the material preponderance of the enemy' Speer, Albert, *Inside the Reich*, London, Macmillan, 1970, p.424

p.295 'No one knew what they were talking about' ibid., p.426

p.296 'anyone who tells anyone that the war is lost' ibid., p.423

p.296 'We do not want to expose ourselves to this reproach' Rees, Laurence, *The Nazis*, London, BBC Books, 1997, p.231

p.297 'If it had only been England and France, we would have stopped' ibid., p.224

p.298 'Many of the women in Germany had lost their sons or their brothers' ibid., p.231

p.299 'they wanted to see Poland independent, free and strong' Churchill, Winston, *The Second World War Vol. VI*, London, Cassell & Co., 1954, pp.322–3

p.299 'they had all run away' ibid., p.327

p.299 'provide the greatest opportunity in all history to create in the years to come' Ellis Vol. 2, p.217

p.300 'figures range from 35,000 to 135,000' Fisher and Read, p.243

p.302 'an un-American devotion to concentrating' Weigley, p.606

p.303 'Having got there, I had to divest myself of a leather jerkin'
Baker, diary manuscript

p.305 'the soldiers have come out with their hands up' Weigley,
p.617

p.305 'We are in a horse race with Courtney' ed. Blumenson,
Martin, *Patton Papers 1940–5*, p.652

p.306 'Just as fast as we can push it over' Bradley, p.511

p.306 'Where are you going to go from Remagen?' ibid.

p.307 'Brad, for God's sake tell the world we're across' ibid.,
p.522

p.309 'clearly, Berlin is the main prize . . . there is no doubt
whatsoever' Ellis Vol. 2, p.300

p.310 'only secondary forces will therefore be allotted in the
direction of Berlin' Fisher and Read, pp.274–5

p.310 'that place has become nothing but a geographical location' Ellis Vol. 2, p.300

p.310 'will either win together in Berlin or die together in Berlin'
Beevor, p.139

p.310 'whoever controls Germany, controls Europe' ibid.

p.310 'a mind oppressed by forebodings' Churchill Vol. VI,
p.400

p.311 'master of world fortunes, but without a true and coherent
design' ibid., p.399

p.311 'We had better take Berlin, and quick' ed. Blumenson,
Martin, *Patton Papers 1940–5*, p.658

p.312 'I think history will answer that question for you' D'Este,
Eisenhower, p.689

p.312 'As soldiers we looked naively on this British inclination'
Bradley, p.536

p.312 'a settlement must be reached on all major issues between
the West and the East' Churchill Vol. VI, p.400

p.313 'I really believe that the Ninth Army could have captured
Berlin with little loss' Weigley, p.699

p.313 'the Red Army's prize from under its nose' Beevor,
p.144

p.315 'We had been comrades through many formidable times together' Tibbs, David, *The Doctor's Story*, manuscript

p.315 'squeezed into a pocket measuring 50 by 120 kilometres' Weigley, p.677

p.316 'We can no longer afford to concern ourselves with the population' Speer, p.439

p.317 'A Field Marshal . . . does not become a prisoner' Macdonald, Charles B., *The Last Offensive*, Washington, US Government Printing Office, 1973, p.372

p.317 'military, industrial and economic systems' Ellis Vol. 2, p.317

p.318 '1,000 more bombers over somewhere last night' Fraser, *Wars and Shadows*, p.250

p.319 'A woman standing naked washing herself' Thompson, IWM *Book of Victory*, p.253

p.321 'beyond the American mind to comprehend' ed. Blumenson, Martin, *Patton Papers 1940–5*, p.684

p.321 'Still have trouble hating them?' Toland, John, *The Last 100 Days*, New York, Random House, 1967, p.371

p.321 'Read it! Roosevelt is dead!' Speer, p.463

p.321 'forty thousand field guns and mortars, and six thousand tanks' Beevor, p.206

p.321 'The final offensive of the war began on 16 April with a blistering Soviet bombardment' ibid., p.217

p.322 'those who will remain after the battle are only the inferior ones' Hastings, Max, *Victory in Europe*, London, Weidenfeld & Nicholson, 1985, p.151

p.323 'too bad it was impossible to take him alive' Fisher and Read, p.458

p.324 'Many thought it was a huge joke to throw their side arms into my ambulance' Tibbs, manuscript

p.324 'Colonel Luard told him instead to load up a horse and cart' ibid.

p.324 'Berliners were less fortunate' Beevor, p.410

p.324 'this nation will have proved to be the weaker one' Hastings, *Victory in Europe*, p.151

p.324 'more than a hint of admiration for Stalin' Speer, p.306

p.325 The Mission of this Allied Force was fulfilled at 0241' Ellis Vol. 2, p.344

p.326 'The root of evil still flourishes, and everybody knows' Fraser, *Wars and Shadows*, p.249

p.326 'More than two-thirds of the casualties were American' Ellis Vol. 2, Appendix

p.326 'Lovers' quarrels are part of love' Churchill Vol. VI, p.409

p.327 'soldiers who had fought for their country and endured inhuman treatment in Nazi captivity were sent to Siberia' Beevor, p.423

p.327 'on the continent of Europe we have yet to make sure that the simple and honourable purposes' Churchill, *Triumph and Tragedy Vol. VI*, p.478

Glossary

Army Group – a collection of armies under a single commander-in-chief, varying in size from 300,000 to a million men. In the Red Army known as Front

Army – made up of two or three corps. Anything from between 40,000 and 100,000 men

ARV - Armoured Recovery Vehicle

Battalion – Infantry unit of between 700 and a thousand men. Made up of four rifle companies of between 100 and 150 men; headquarters and support companies. A company was divided into three or four platoons of between 30 and 40 men and each platoon into three sections. Battalions were rarely at full strength in the field

Bazooka – American shoulder launched anti tank weapon

Bren – British .303 light machine gun

Brigade – British organisational unit made up of three infantry or tank battalions

Carrier – a lightly armoured, tracked vehicle used by infantry battalions

CCS – Casualty Clearing Station

CIGS – Chief of the Imperial General Staff

Cobra – American break-out operation 25th July 1944

Corps – An organisational unit consisting of at least two divisions

DD – Duplex Drive amphibious Sherman tank, fitted with a propeller and inflatable canvas sides

Division – In the British and American armies a division numbered some 15,000 men, most German divisions were smaller. British armoured divisions were usually made up of three brigades – two tank and one infantry

88mm – German anti-aircraft gun, by 1944 it was widely used as an anti-tank weapon. Its high velocity and flat trajectory made if a very effective weapon. Mounted in the Tiger tank

Epsom – British offensive operation, June 26th

Flail – Sherman tank fitted with a roller and chains. The flail was used to clear mines

Flak – German anti-aircraft fire

Fortitude – Allied deception plan for OVERLORD

Goodwood – British operation to the south east of Caen, 18th July 1944

LCI – Landing Craft Infantry

LCT – Landing Craft Tank

Market Garden – Market Garden was the code name for the operation to seize river crossings in Holland including the bridges over the Rhine at Arnhem. Began 17 September 1944

MG 34 – German machine gun with a rate of fire of up to 800 rounds a minute

MG 42 – A tripod mounted German machine gun capable of 1,300 rounds a minute. Known to the Allies as a Spandau

Nebelwerfer – German multi-barrelled mortar, known by to allied soldiers as the 'moaning minnie'

OKH – Oberkommando des Herres. German Army High Command

OKW – Oberkommando der Wehrmacht. German Armed Forces High Command, it controlled army, air and naval forces

Panzer – tank or unit of tanks or armoured fighting vehicles

Panzerfaust – German hand-held, single shot anti-tank weapon

Panzer Grenadier –infantry in armoured unit, often motorised

PIAT – British hand-held anti tank weapon

Regiment – made up of two or three battalions. Equivalent in size to a brigade in the American and German armies

SHAEF – Supreme Headquarters Allied Expeditionary Force

Sten gun – British 9mm machine gun

Ultra – the name given to decrypts of German Enigma cipher signals

Vickers – British belt-fed, tripod mounted .303 machine-gun

Photographic Acknowledgements

Bundesarchiv, Koblenz: 37, 38, 40–44. Walter Frentz: 1–5, 10, 11, 18, 19, 20, 45, 53, 54. Imperial War Museum, London: 6 (BN1184), 7 (SC320894), 8 (SC190682), 9 (SC190268), 12 (189943), 13 (TR1838), 23 (PIC27552), 24 (B5667), 25 (B6119), 26 (HN62152), 27 (CL347), 28 (CL383), 29 (B7525), 30 (B8188), 31 (HN3021), 32 (SC192764), 33 (BU8), 34 (AP33307), 35 (BU382), 36 (PL34607), 39 (MH2061), 46 (HU81502), 47 (KY51704), 48 (EA50367), 49 (EA58196), 50 (HU3644, 51 (HN44935), 52 (NAM237), 55 (KY65491),56 (EA65734). Private Collections: 14–17, 21, 22. US National Archives: 7, 8, 9, 12, 57.

Index

INDEX

INDEX